W9-ASL-532

The New History of England

General Editors
A. G. Dickens and Norman Gash

DA332
E497

Reform
and Reformation

England, 1509–1558

Geoffrey Rudolph

G. R. Elton

Harvard University Press
Cambridge, Massachusetts
1977

FEB 2 8 1979

205818

Copyright © 1977 by G. R. Elton

All rights reserved

Printed in the United States of America

Library of Congress Cataloging in Publication Data

Elton, Geoffrey Rudolph.
  Reform and Reformation—England, 1509-1558.

  Bibliography: p.
  Includes index.
  1. Great Britain—History—Henry VIII, 1509-1547.
2. Great Britain—History—Edward VI and Mary, 1547-1558
3. Reformation—England. I. Title.
DA332.E497   941.05'092'2   77-6464
ISBN 0-674-75245-7

Preface

This book owes its existence to two ambitions. In the first place, it seemed that the time had come to pull together the varied and massive labours which the last quarter century has seen devoted to the earlier sixteenth century, in recent years one of the most active areas of English historical writing. Much of the best work done is still hidden in unpublished doctoral dissertations, and this book has provided a welcome opportunity to bring it to light and allow it to affect general interpretation and understanding. Secondly, I felt I owed it to self-respect to prove, if I could, that the advice I have so freely offered touching the writing of narrative makes sense nowadays when historians rightly insist on answering questions and treating issues which it seems only particular analysis can resolve. I have therefore used the passage of time to shape this book, but I hope that the choice of main theme and the attention paid to all sorts of problems have nevertheless saved me from resting content with the surface of things and from confusing the reader. I am very conscious of having left many things insufficiently explored: the book could without difficulty have been half as long again. It is, in all conscience, quite long enough.

One result of these twin ambitions has been to produce rather a different air and approach from those I adopted, in younger and more reckless days, in *England under the Tudors*. I should think it distressing if twenty-five years of constant activity (by myself as well as so many others) had not made me alter many parts of the story, but for myself I incline to the view that in essentials the forecast written in 1953 differs little from the retrospect concluded in 1976. While others, of course, may come to less complacent conclusions, I should like to make it plain that this book neither recants nor denounces, though it often (and I hope humbly) reconsiders.

My debts to fellow scholars are great and pervasive, and are acknowledged in footnotes and bibliography. But I should particularly like to thank those friends whose dissertations (as it happens, all either supervised or examined by myself) have so heavily contributed especially at points where I have been made to change my mind: Brendan Bradshaw, Michael Bush, Philip Edwards, Steven Ellis, Rodney Fisher, John Guy, Felicity Heal, Michael Kelly, Charles Knighton, Tony Knox, Stephen Lander, Glenn Lemasters, Jim Miklovich, Rex Pogson, David Potter, Peter Roberts, Jack Scarisbrick, Roger Schofield, David Starkey. The names of Claire Cross, Dermot Fenlon, Christopher Haigh, Rudy Heinze, Dale Hoak, Stan Lehmberg, David Loades and Bill Wilkie would also be in that list if their dissertations had not already found consummation of print; and those of Susan Brigden, Christopher Coleman, Noela Corfield, Gregor Duncan, Norman Jones and Graham Nicholson should be added ahead of their reaching the first apotheosis of the doctoral typescript. Other such friends, whose studies lay outside the period treated, have taught me much in debate and conversation: Maria Cioni, Leslie Croxford, DeLloyd Guth, Peter Holmes, Erkki Kouri, John McKenna, Joel Samaha, Tom Scott and Fred Youngs. I am grateful to the general editor, Geoff Dickens, for much kindness and tolerance; we have long been well agreed on the age of Henry VIII and Thomas Cromwell, a fact I have always found highly reassuring. Since the demands of historical interpretation compel me to express some disagreements with Professor Scarisbrick's magisterial account of the reign of Henry VIII, I wish to make plain my respect and affection for my first doctoral student and his work. Lastly thanks are due to the publishers for their long-suffering willingness to permit a repeated expansion of the work which I thought and think necessary.

G.R.E.

Contents

1 The Call for Reform

In 1510, lying in the Tower under sentence of death, Edmund
Dudley reflected upon the needs of the realm and the prospects open
to the new monarch who had decided to kill him for serving the old
one too well.[1] The public weal of England, he felt, had for a long
time 'been in sore decay', but Henry VIII was 'the prince that shall
revive it'. He therefore proposed to offer advice. Henry, he knew,
was determined to amend all that was amiss: was he not generally
the best intentioned of kings, and did he not owe as much to his
father's last will and testament? After so vigorous a start, the rest of
Dudley's pamphlet comes as something of a disappointment. He
confessed his own misdoing and hinted at some excessive rapacity in
Henry VII, but in general he offered neither a description nor an
analysis of what supposedly was wrong with England. The
insufficiencies he found in the commonwealth were essentially moral:
people did not behave as God would have them do. His answers, too,
were therefore moral ones: let everyone, from the King down to the
last peasant, properly fulfil his duty to God and his place in society.
A few particular points did emerge. The Church, he felt, should
have its old freedom of electing prelates and abbots without interference from the secular power. Usury, plain or disguised, must be
prevented. Peace is necessary for the well-being of trade. The
education of noblemen's children—worse in England than anywhere
else—must be improved. But through it all runs a total inability to
think to the roots of problems or offer advice beyond the most
commonplace exhortations to a better living and a better discharge
of duties. As his highly charged language showed, Dudley felt deeply
about the deficiencies he saw in society, but he had no real concept
of reform. He never even contemplated changes in structure or
management, and while he deplored abuses of power he also objected to attempts to stamp them out by novel instruments of justice.
His 'tree of commonwealth' was barely even a metaphor for the
social entity of the realm; he saw it only as a static picture—a mild
fancy—with its roots formed by moral imperatives and its branches

[1] Edmund Dudley, *The Tree of Commonwealth*, edited by D. M. Brodie (1948).

signifying the estates of the body politic. There is here no sense of organic relationship, no notion of change. Go back, he cries, to God's good law, behave yourselves as you should, subordinate everything to the fear of God (the 'necessary sauce' of the fruits of decent living), and all will be well. All very worthy and, in a man on the threshold of death, commendable, but as analysis merely woolly and as advice quite empty.

Henry VIII never saw this curious, and curiously barren, treatise, but if he had he would have derived no practical benefit from it. And yet Dudley, a man of great practical experience, was right in thinking that too many things were wrong in England. Even in so personal a monarchy as that of the Tudors—in any case well restrained by law, custom and necessity—the accession of a new king left the kingdom at heart unaltered, but it could produce a new atmosphere. The fundamental problems of the realm were of long standing and had received attention before, but it is apparent that as Henry VIII ascended the throne a good many people expected to see real changes. The country was passing through a period of economic upheaval, drastic enough for an agrarian society in which change is always bound to be slow, and rendered more drastic still by the inability of contemporaries to understand what was happening. For some two generations the population had been rising. We have no reliable figures, but since the disputed calculations range around a mean of about two and a half millions it will be clear that even ten thousand more mouths to feed, twenty thousand more hands to employ, would cause some real convulsions in that economy. The pressure was heaviest on the peasantry, the men who had benefited from the shortage of labour created in the demographic disasters of the fourteenth century and who now found the terms of life turn against them. Prices were also rising, not yet dramatically but with a certain ominousness, and it increasingly became inadvisable to live on fixed incomes. All men with assets to develop saw reason why they should do so. In particular this meant pressure on rents and efforts to increase the premiums charged to incoming tenants (entry fines). It is often alleged that the early sixteenth century was an exceptionally materialist and unspiritual age, but this is to take contemporary laments at face value and to forget that business letters have a better chance of surviving than less 'materialist' effusions. Agrarian troubles and unrest did not spring from the greed of landlords and the harshness of bailiffs whose activities represented an often necessary and usually understandable reaction to the impact of change.

The most obvious manifestation of that change was enclosure against which a comprehensive but unenforceable act had been passed in 1489. It was widely believed that for the sake of profit from wool production landlords were converting arable to pasture, destroying units of agriculture, and ejecting tenants. The true situation was much too complex to be subsumed under so ready a generalization. Quite apart from the often effective limitations that the peasant's legal and customary rights placed upon the landlord's freedom of action (as a result of which agrarian changes differed greatly from region to region, even when economic circumstances were very similar), enclosure meant several practices, some laudable, some disastrous. It could signify the amalgamation of dispersed strips in the open field into efficient arable farms, as well as the enclosing of wastes and commons for the grazing of an entrepreneur's sheep or cattle; and the first was as advantageous to the commonweal as the second was likely to lead to depopulation and the disappearance of villages which could not survive without their commons. Most of this enclosure, good or bad, had taken place before 1489, so that the act caught relatively few enclosers. The most insidious rural problem of Henry VIII's reign, which the age had not yet diagnosed, was not touched on in the statute—the practice of buying up leaseholds and taking them out of husbandry. In this game the entrepreneurs were as often graziers (cattlemen) as sheepfarmers, and clergy as well as laity; by allowing a derelict building to survive on the converted property, they could evade the legislation directed at the 'decay of houses'.[2]

Unquestionably all this drove some men off the land, though no one could then, or can now, tell the numbers affected. Some of these products of rural unemployment joined bands of vagrants, mostly young people seeking work, though contemporaries were far from wrong in supposing that the freedom of the roads and the attractions of crime helped to create those bands of wandering beggars which by giving means of physical violence to people disconnected from the normal forms of social control soon threatened the peace of mind and even the stability of this society. Population growth played its part; even without the agrarian changes many men would have found difficulties in getting work. This unsettled state was aggravated by changes in industry, too, especially in England's premier manufacture, that of woollen cloth. In the course of the fifteenth century, the clothing industry had shifted location, so that old centres of manufacture like Bristol and Gloucester declined while new areas of prosperity opened up in the Yorkshire dales and the villages of Suffolk. The measures taken by Henry VII to encourage the trade in cloth assisted a major shift both in manufacturing regions and the types of cloth produced. His commercial treaties

[2]See below, p. 67.

with the Netherlands promoted the specialist trade between London and Antwerp monopolized by the uncharteched association of the London Merchant Adventurers who rose to wealth and eminence by supplying the Antwerp market with what it wanted—white (unfinished) cloth for the finishing trades that flourished in that great entrepôt of the first half of the sixteenth century. In consequence the English finishing trades declined, unable to compete in quality and in the cost of materials; in London, for instance, the Mercers' Company, engaged in selling white cloth, took over the primacy hitherto occupied by the drapers who coordinated the production of finished cloth. Another consequence was seen in the gradual decline of the so-called outports—Hull, Bristol, Southampton—as more and more of England's export trade flowed through London, with its easy access to the main continental inlet.

Thanks above all to its export of woollen products, but also because it supplied such other materials as grain, leather and tin to foreign countries, the English economy was very definitely tied to a European complex which itself was being affected by changes in population and wealth, and by an inflation of prices. Englishmen, however, for the most part did not look beyond the boundaries of the realm, shire or even village; and they naturally sought the causes of distress close to home. The agitation against enclosers and engrossers always revived in times of corn shortage and harvest failure, as did (more rationally) the attempts to prevent unlicensed exports of grain. As it happened, the beginning of the reign was blessed with good weather, and it was only in 1515 that the argument rose high again. Exports of cloth, too, remained buoyant from early in Henry VIII's reign until the end of the second decade of the sixteenth century.[3] Thus few outward signs of the underlying causes of unrest made themselves felt in about 1510: while people could not but sense that uncomfortable changes were coming over the commonwealth, relative prosperity cushioned shocks and confined really ill effects for the moment to the truly powerless and necessarily silent. However, though the reign opened in an atmosphere of economic euphoria, it must be remembered that changes in population, shifts of wealth, transformations of manufacture and trade, and the insidious beginnings of price inflation were all present. At the foundations of society, stability was under attack, not necessarily to the disadvantage of society as a whole (for profit and prosperity lurked in the cracks opening in the traditional structure) but certainly to the detriment of a social philosophy which saw security and hope solely in maintaining what had always been. Men's daily lives passed

[3] J. D. Gould, *The Great Debasement: Currency and the Economy in mid-Tudor England* (1971), p. 129.

against a background of increasingly rapid change, but apart from at intervals lamenting the fact they had no thought to offer.

Above all, nothing so far suggested that anybody was really attempting to analyse the inwardness of the changes or thought of prescribing remedies designed to control them constructively, beyond forbidding whatever seemed contrary to past practice—a practice identified with the natural order of the universe. Even the complaints testify to a striking absence of radical thinking, being marked by an undeviating belief in a past good order that these recent and degenerate days had managed to lose. Dudley's sterile faith in reiterating moral platitudes corresponded to a common enough attitude, one hallowed by tradition. Men, it was held, could not so much alter the terms of their lives as manage themselves within them by obeying God's injunctions against envy, covetousness and anger. Certainly it was thought possible to apply positive controls to such anarchic and selfish instincts when self-control failed to suffice, and society had a duty to take the necessary action. That was what the Church preached, diligently though ineffectually, in sermons that made no impact even on ecclesiastical possessors, as pressed in their growingly insufficient income as their lay brethren and on the whole more competent at taking the allegedly antisocial steps required to meet the crisis. And that, too, was what the law supposedly stood for—the maintenance of an existing order, not the creation of a new one. Society existed in and by a known system of law which supposedly regulated each man's rights and duties and which provided remedies and punishments when men ruptured concord by innovatory abuses. The prevalent attitude treated law as the guarantee of continuity and not as a fruitful instrument of change.

This is not to say that people could not conceive of the idea of making laws: they did, and they had settled that it was properly one of the tasks of the king's High Court of Parliament. The view was once current among historians that 'the middle ages' treated the making of law as impossible because all human laws merely embodied the discovery (in revelation and conscience) of the eternal law divine; but this view was both insufficient and misleading. It ignored inconvenient philosophies of the law: the 'realist' concept—according to which the force of human laws lay exclusively in their consonance with God's will—had long been rivalled by a 'nominalist' voluntarism which treated law as the emanation of a human lawgiver's will and judged its validity by the nature of the legislator's authority. This will-centred interpretation, which was gaining ground steadily in the first quarter of the century, opened the door to self-help and the use of law as an instrument of social transformation, though the full effects of all this lay as yet in the future. As the medieval statute book testifies, grievances and deficiencies had in practice always called for some new law, regardless of the search for eternal values; medieval governments legislated, and medieval judges, under the guise of interpreting the law, innovated. Yet it remains true that no one saw new laws and new interpretations in the light of novelty (which remained a term of abuse for most of the century); new laws were expressly designed to elucidate or amend the existing law. They formed rather a comment upon that which alone carried authority, namely the customary law of the courts, than a command to those courts from a sovereign social will. The common law of England was conventionally described as the custom of the realm, equal in principle to the custom of any manor though, of course, more weighty; and nothing could more strikingly express the refusal to treat the instruments that ordered the life of society as dynamic or creative. In an uncertain world, a world full of death and disorder and misery, a precarious stability could, it seemed, be preserved only by prohibiting all change; and if change could not be avoided it must at least appear to be the restoration of a better past rather than the institution of a better future.

In fact the law and its area of operation—enforcement as well as litigation—had by 1510 entered upon a career of great expansion. The number of lawyers increased; the profession flourished. Men sought the decisions of the law the more eagerly because the restoration of royal power seemed to offer a chance for right to assert itself over might or mere patronage. Henry VII's greatest achievement had been to resume that control of the machinery of justice and government which kings had created and factions had lately usurped. However, in two ways he had allowed this work to go somewhat astray. He had made it appear that his major purpose was not to bring justice and suppress violence, but to raise money: he had acquired a reputation for rapacity and oppression (though it is worth noting that in 1536 the northern rebels looked back with nostalgia to the good days of his rule). And he had freely multiplied instruments outside the traditional machinery of the common law in order to bring his power (and possibly his extortion) to bear on evaders of justice to whom the technicalities and delays of the law offered undoubted protection. Thus the one area in which he had consistently applied the methods of reform was also the one area on which discontent centred at his death, and therefore the one area in which his successor in turn promoted counter-reform.

Dudley (with Richard Empson) was in the Tower because Henry VIII looked for sacrificial victims whose execution could demonstrate his care for his subjects and exploit the popularity which a new and young King naturally enjoyed. The fallen minister might spend his unhappy leisure writing a meritorious treatise equating social virtue with obedience, moral elevation and humility before God, but it was not this writing of his that served the new regime. It got more benefit from another paper listing over eighty cases in which the late King had allegedly oppressed his unfortunate subjects by taking excessive bonds for minor or non-existent offences.[4] Dudley knew, as he said, that Henry VII had not so much intended to extract money as to put potentially dangerous men under threats which would keep them in order, but in drawing up this list he was both discharging his own conscience and offering a sop to powerful interests determined to escape the fetters which strong policy had put upon them. The reaction against Henry VII greatly exaggerated both his rapacity and the alleged illegality of his deeds, but its demonstrable unfairness did not, of course, weaken its immediate impact—or indeed its long-term success with historians.

Henry VIII and his Council encouraged the reaction, partly because they believed it to be justified. The late King's executors, obeying his seemingly remorseful will, set about sorting justified from unjust bonds, a task which occupied them for some ten years of diminishing activity and relieved some genuine sufferers as well as some rather more lucky offenders, though in the end by no means all bonds were cancelled. The Council appointed nationwide commissions of enquiry designed to discover the many alleged offences by officers administering the late King's stringent policies. The first Parliament of the reign, which met in January–February 1510, was encouraged to pass acts prohibiting supposed breaches of the laws committed in the fiscal exactions of the previous reign. The Council committees instituted by Henry VII lapsed, the judicial activity of the Council in Star Chamber declined drastically, and steps were taken against the promoters (professional informers) who had been active in initiating cases before both these 'bye-courts' and the Exchequer. On the face of it, a whole policy was officially condemned and disavowed. But all this turned out to be not so much a sham as a misguided piece of propaganda. The general commissions found hardly any of the sort of cases expected, and the Council grew tired of hearing nothing but the private quarrels of men trying to get the most out of the new circumstances. The pressure of suitors was enough to revive the Council's more formal judicial activities as well as the use of arbitrating committees, all of which continued to take suits away from the common-law courts. No promoter, despite rumours to the contrary, is known to have suffered physically, and

[4] C. J. Harrison, 'The Petition of Edmund Dudley', *English Historical Review* LXXXVII (1972), pp. 82 ff.

informations laid by their like did not cease. The acts of the 1510 Parliament provided no remedies because in fact, reports to the contrary notwithstanding, the alleged evasions of the law had not been practised. Nothing so well justifies the policy of Henry VII as the pitiful outcome of these attempts to reverse and disavow it. He had been too tough at times and usually, in his last years, too dour; some improper gains had been made. Nevertheless, so long as real and fundamental reform was out of the question, England had to be governed by the methods he had used, and before long Henry VIII's government resumed them.

Thus the reign opened with neither genuine reforms nor even any recognition that reforms were required. By and large, Dudley exemplified a general attitude of mind when he spoke vaguely of the ills of the commonwealth, specified none, and sought the remedy in prayer. Relative economic prosperity made it for the moment less pressing to tackle the major ills of the body politic; and the machinery of a law-governed monarchy, revived in Henry VII's Chamber and Council system, was perfectly adequate for the needs of the state. Or so it seemed—though even at that point some very real problems (the state of Ireland, for instance) could be denied only by being ignored. But in general Henry VIII could suppose that he had come to a safe inheritance, to a crown rendered respected in England by the energetic enforcement of its just claims and abroad by dynastic alliance and some successful assertions of England's presence in the world. He could think of himself as a monarch of means and spirit whose only immediate problem lay in finding the way in which he could best employ both means and youthful energy. In the choice he was to make he immediately demonstrated how well he fitted the conventions of sixteenth-century kingship, and how far short he fell of constructive statesmanship or even positive vision.

No doubt it was true that the nation at large (that not inconsiderable part of it which shared in some way in the conduct of affairs) expected from their new King only a release from the pressures exerted by his predecessor, and also perhaps some display of power and glory which would cheer a new generation bored with the devious caution of old men. But there were some people who looked for very different things, men as depressed as Dudley by the problems of the commonweal but more able and willing than he was to do some positive thinking. They came to offer a very different diagnosis and much more solid remedies. There were those who despaired of the spiritual state of the nation and more particularly of its Church. The English people had a reputation for formal piety. They offered freely to saints and went on pilgrimages; Our Lady of Walsingham and Becket's shrine at Canterbury continued to prosper. Masses for souls in purgatory remained a very popular item in testaments. Though the monastic ideal was ceasing to attract recruits—with the exception of the stricter orders like the Carthusians or the Observant Franciscans—chantries were still being founded in large numbers, despite the increasingly heavy payments demanded by the Crown for the necessary licences. This pattern stretched right across the nation, with the monarchs giving a strong lead: Henry VII endowed thousands of masses in his will, and Henry VIII performed a well-publicized pilgrimage to Walsingham in 1514. No country in Europe enjoyed better relations with the papacy. The disputes of the fourteenth century, which had produced parliamentary statutes defending the rights of the King and his courts from invasion by Rome (the Acts of Provisors and Praemunire), lay in the forgotten past, though private persons occasionally exploited those statutes in wriggling their way between royal and spiritual courts. King and pope worked happily together in the rule of the Church in England, though it is worth noting that the pope's ability to trench upon the King's general control over episcopal appointments was greater than historians have of late been willing to admit. At Henry's accession, the English Church was a long way from national independence. Indeed, the English Crown was virtually the only European power still to take seriously the claims to spiritual headship and pious devotion put forth by the Italian politicians who in succession occupied the Holy See. Conventional English Christianity may have been, without much spiritual ardour even among the clergy, but it was none the less real for that and deeply entrenched in the minds and manners of the people.

Yet all was not well with the Church in England. For one thing, while its ministrations and its services, designed to offer reasonable assurance of salvation to men almost as constantly troubled by the horrors of the after-life as by those of this vale of tears, were readily accepted, the clergy themselves attracted more dislike than love. The state of the Church was widely believed to be rotten. Popular anticlericalism thrived on tales of gluttonous monks, lecherous friars, ignorant and dishonest parish priests. The oppressive and omnipresent network of the ecclesiastical courts excited much hatred. Church lawyers were accused of corruption even more often than their lay counterparts: did they not promote false suits for their own financial profit and offer protection to clerical misdeeds? The archdeacon, the disciplinary officer closest to the villagers whose failure to pay the tithe or avoid fornication he was ever happy to punish, had not without reason become a hated stereotype in the later middle ages. Modern research has demonstrated the falseness of many of the conventional charges against the clergy: neither simony nor sodomy were as prevalent as the legend supposed, and the quality of the parish clergy, measured by the number who held university degrees, was in fact improving from the later fifteenth century onwards.[5] But, for one thing, though popular beliefs may have been mistaken they nevertheless created a general climate of anticlerical feeling quite strong enough to make the apparent security of the clergy's claims to wealth, obedience and influence very problematic indeed. For another, there was enough truth in the accusations to keep anticlericalism alive.

The Church did enjoy enormous wealth, even though this was mainly concentrated in the hands of monastic institutions, episcopal sees and cathedral chapters, leaving the mass of rural incumbents, and even more the greater mass of unbeneficed clergy, often in a state near to destitution. The contrast between a bishop of Winchester with an annual income of over £4,000 (better than any earl's) and the condition of a chantry priest subsisting on a few pounds a year, did not encourage respect for the clergy as a whole. There was much absenteeism, from the bishop-councillors like Richard Foxe whom service to Henry VII prevented from ever visiting the three extremely wealthy sees (Bath and Wells, Durham, Winchester) with which a grateful monarch kept him in affluence, through the university dons who subsisted on livings held in plurality and failed to serve the cure in any of them, to the rectory left vacant except for the occasional visit from a brother of the religious house which had bought the living for the financial benefits it carried. Satirists unquestionably exaggerated the evils in the Church, but they had enough reality to draw on to carry widespread conviction. The Church was showing all the signs of an institution in danger but unaware of its peril. Seemingly powerful, immovable, eternal, commanding the apparent obedience of high and low, firmly established in vast possessions and entrenched in its exclusive power to save the anxious souls of men, it was in fact corrupted with the service of Mammon and the service of the king on earth. Few seemed to respect it.

Indeed, signs were not lacking that the surface piety of the nation could not be trusted to support the claims and behaviour of the spiritualty for ever; and anticlericalism, so readily combined with formal devotion, was not perhaps even the most serious of them. Genuine piety was in any case inclined to forms of mystic devotion quite unconcerned with hierarchies and powers; the sizable output of old and new writings of this kind in the first four decades of the century testifies to the surviving strength, among the middling sort of

[5] P. Heath, *The English Parish Clergy on the Eve of the Reformation* (1969); M. Bowker, *The Secular Clergy in the Diocese of Lincoln, 1495–1520* (1968).

laity who eagerly bought and read them, of the late medieval search for a direct relationship with God through the love of Christ. Furthermore, the English so emphasized their orthodoxy because a hundred years earlier they had for the first time produced, and suppressed, a native heresy, the heresy called Lollardy. By now the Lollards formed a barely surviving underground movement among some artisans and labourers, maintaining a debased tradition of Wycliffe's attacks on the official Church in secret gatherings where the Bible was read in Wycliffe's translation and forbidden tracts were devoutly absorbed and discussed. Lollardy embraced tenets ranging from rationalist ribaldry to a simplistic faith full of personal spirituality, but its chief characteristics were two: it denied the need for a special category of beings to intercede for man with God, and it had no chance at all of gaining the means of worldly power. Thus it formed a ready target for attack; the Church feared it because it undermined its whole position, the secular authorities feared it because it attracted the despair of the poor and threatened the established order, and both enjoyed working off their apprehensions on the helpless. It is therefore of importance that in the early years of the century this heresy showed signs of reviving. Some of the secret tracts, hitherto transmitted in manuscript, found printers, and the hierarchy took fright sufficiently to seek out and destroy what Lollards it could find. There was, especially, a wave of persecutions and burnings—in London, Kent and Coventry—around the years 1510–12, but surviving Lollardy has been found throughout the country, including the north. Behind the established and respectable orthodoxy, a much more devout though exceedingly simple heterodoxy maintained itself, precariously but persistently.[6] The bishops were aware of it and always alert for any signs of opinions which attacked the ascendancy of the Church. The church courts, in fact, were quite used to having to deal with heretics; if Lollardy managed to survive, so did a tradition of persecution and intolerance.

The Lollards, however, could exercise no influence on policy; another line of attack on the unsatisfactory state of the Church had a better chance of doing so. Among the weaknesses of this Church was the fact that its leadership contained very few—hardly any—men of spiritual excellence and theological distinction. Not that the bishops were fools: far from it—the average quality was high. But for a generation or more advancement in the Church had come mainly to men useful to the King's government; Henry VII in particular liked to use bishops as councillors and administrators (partly because they could be paid out of the revenues of the Church), and it was thus the men of practical skills, worldly wisdom and legal training who most

[6] J. A. F. Thomson, *The Later Lollards* (1965).

readily rose to the top. Often, indeed usually, they were perfectly good men—upright, respectable, competent, hardworking. But they were neither spiritual leaders nor intellectually distinguished. In 1509, the only bishop to fit the part of a Christian mentor was John Fisher of Rochester, and he owed his promotion to the fact that even Henry VII needed a theologian of spiritual distinction for his confessor. Much more typical were Foxe of Winchester, lord privy seal, William Warham of Canterbury, lord chancellor, and Thomas Ruthal of Durham, the King's secretary. Every country in Europe used bishops in government, but none used government office so regularly to fill the bench of bishops as did England, a country which at this point, despite its powerful monarchy and ancient nobility, could well be considered as priest-ridden. One consequence of this was that those members of the Church who found their vocation in faith or theology were readily convinced that the official leadership lacked both. A breach had opened in the clergy itself between the intellectuals and the hierarchy.

Uusually we sum up this phenomenon as the emergence of humanism—the new learning reacting against conventionalized education and thought—and humanism did play its part in undermining the security of the established order, even though many of the administrators, bishops and deans and lesser men, were touched by it. England played an important part in the north European development of this innovating intellectual fashion, in part because for a time it became the second home of Desiderius Erasmus, the Dutchman around whom the movement gathered to such an extent that some would speak of Erasmianism rather than humanism. On his first visit, in 1499, he fell under the influence of John Colet, dean of St Paul's, who showed him a liberating way out of the moribund tradition of Bible study, and he formed a life-long friendship with the young Thomas More. He also met a precocious boy, the King's second son, Henry. When Erasmus returned in 1506, the boy was heir to the throne and still full of bright promise. The new reign had barely opened before Erasmus answered an invitation from William, Lord Mountjoy, patron of scholars, and arrived for his longest stay (1511–15). Though he abominated the climate, food and beer of Cambridge, he enjoyed its scholars as well as his many contacts elsewhere in the realm; and this time he stayed long enough to consolidate an intellectual revolution whose tentacles spread through the court, the universities, the episcopate, and other clergy (including some surprising abbots).[7]

Humanist thought—an interest in the ancients (especially the Greeks) and in philological soundness, a concern to study the sources

[7] J. K. McConica, *English Humanists and Reformation Politics* (1965), chapters 2 and 3.

of the faith in a human fashion, a revulsion against the methods and views of the prevalent thinkers of the schools (Scotists and Occamists)—had come to England with William Grocyn and Thomas Lineacre in the 1480s and 1490s. In Colet it acquired a practitioner of force, deep seriousness, and ineffable puritanism. Thomas More contributed a very necessary touch of frivolity and ease, his interests at this time centring upon the Platonic revival promoted at Florence by Marcello Ficino and Pico della Mirandola. But until Erasmus's third and last visit to England humanism had not been a movement, merely the practice of a small circle of friends uninterested in giving the consequences of their thought effect in the world at large. The important change which came over these scholars and their place in affairs owed something to Erasmus and something to circumstances.

Erasmus's chief contribution at this stage needs defining. The Erasmus of 1511, though already well known, was not yet the prince of scholars he later became, and especially not yet the editor of patristic texts and of his immeasurably influential New Testament (1516). His fame rested on two works, his *Adagia* (a collection of morally improving tales and proverbs, a commonplace book to end all commonplace books), and on his *Enchiridion Militis Christiani*, a handbook of Christian piety. On arrival in England he added to these his most enduring work, *The Praise of Folly*, with its savage satire on abuses in lay and clerical society. At this point, therefore, Erasmus stood forth as a teacher, preacher and satirist. His message was pellucidly simple. The Christian faith, hopelessly encumbered with pernickety scholarship of the most arid kind and popular superstition of a devastating impurity, needed to be brought back to its essentials, and these consisted in a conscious re-identification with the life, precepts and inner being of the Founder. Erasmus's faith altogether lacked mystical quality: the *Enchiridion*, a huge success at the time and rather a bore to read now, has an air of homespun practicality. Follow in Christ's footsteps, adjured Erasmus, and by the same token attack the absurdities, abuses and abominations with which human greed and folly have encrusted the living truth of the gospel's message. The edification of the *Enchiridion* and the savagely funny indignation of *The Praise of Folly* were two strands in the same programme.

The programme was so effective because it met with a well prepared reception. Not only Erasmus had been influenced by the simple piety of the late medieval *devotio moderna* of his teachers at Deventer and of Thomas à Kempis's *Imitation of Christ*. As usual in such cases of a pious revival, women, especially of the upper sort, carried the message most effectively. In England, the Lady Margaret

Beaufort, Henry VIII's grandmother, sponsored a translation of this last work to which she contributed a part herself. Henry's queen, Catherine of Aragon, shared this state of mind; and she collected like-minded people around her, especially the Spaniard Juan Vives, second only to Erasmus in his influence on English humanists. In fact, Erasmianism now penetrated the court. The King himself, very well educated and glad to play the part of a patron of scholars, encouraged the proliferation of earnest piety; Mountjoy, impresario to the humanists, was among the more favoured courtiers of the early part of the reign; around the Queen and her women a devout circle developed whose spiritual counsellor was Fisher, bishop of Rochester. All looked to Erasmus and swallowed his teaching, if not his scholarship. Thus active piety in high places came to be identified with a widespread reform of manners and morals. These people were not revolutionaries and may not fully have grasped how drastic Erasmus's real demands were—what implications they had for a hierarchic Church possessed of great wealth and power in this world. They continued to practise all the forms of the faith, to respect the monastic ideal even while they denounced so many of its practitioners, to adhere to the Church universal and its head at Rome even while they protested against the existence of warlike popes and worldly prelates. In all simple seriousness they were playing with ideas too strong for them, and in due course the fire was to burn most of them. But for the present they gave ready support to views which called for active reform in Church and state.

For the Erasmian programme, though it sprang from a Christian source, did not confine itself to religion. Christian humanism, with its attachment to the true faith of the gospel and its imitation of Christ, was also practical and social humanism, concerned with the improvement of life in this world. Its leaders were usually born teachers—writers of textbooks and reformers of education. They had a profound faith in the effects of good education and well worked out theories about it. This was particularly true of Erasmus and Vives; and, once again, they met in England with a readier comprehension because their writings marched in step with what other people had been thinking and doing. Thomas More translated educational theory into the practice of his family life. Colet had demonstrated his belief in education when he founded St Paul's School, and he had had Erasmus's assistance in the drafting of its regulations. Leading churchmen were active in setting up new colleges at the universities,[8] and both the new schools and the new colleges were intended to

---

[8] For example, John Fisher (Christ's College, Cambridge, 1505, and St John's College, Cambridge, 1511); John Alcock (Jesus College, Cambridge, 1496); Richard Foxe (Corpus Christi College, Oxford, 1517).

provide a sounder and more purposeful education under the double banner of classicism and biblical Christianity. In particular, Erasmus and his kind wished to educate the rulers of this world: they addressed themselves to princes. In Henry VIII they fancied they had found one such ruler ready made, and they welcomed his arrival with songs of extravagant praise—praise for his beauty, his zeal, his intelligence, his near angelic perfection—which owed less than one might suppose to the conventions of poetry and the chase for place and favour. Erasmus, and More too, thought that the new King could be made to bring the light of learning and faith to bear on the doings of the powers.

Thus through the active part of public life, both in politics and the Church, the ideas of reformist thinkers began to spread quite rapidly in the early days of the reign. Humanism, even in its Erasmian form, did not mean the same thing to all its followers. Colet and Fisher, for instance, shared a severe moral stance and headmasterly insistence on upright behaviour, but little else; Colet could, not without reason, be thought touched with heresy, while Fisher from first to last remained the most orthodox of theologians. Erasmus and More, close friends, shared both a belief in true piety and a liking for lively literature, as their collaboration in translating Lucian shows. But More, professionally busy as a lawyer, was always more the *littérateur* and Erasmus very definitely the scholar; while by a possibly strange reversal of the implications of this More always had a greater apprehension of the mystery of God and a greater fear of the darkness of the faith lost. More, in fact, had more imagination as well as greater involvement in public life, and the ultimate effects of all this were to be devastating. The devout piety of Catherine of Aragon (who really remained incurably Spanish even though she did learn to speak English well) had little to do with the pragmatism and rather empty rhetoric of Erasmus's *Enchiridion*. What united all these people was dissatisfaction with the state of society and a consciousness that change was needed, together with a so far somewhat nebulous sense that human deficiencies could be remedied by human action. Erasmus provided a programme, and for the present it proved possible to ignore the dividing differences by concentrating on discovering and denouncing all things wrong.

Those years saw the high-water mark of Christian humanism as a conscious movement, unrivalled by any other reform movement, in Spain, in the Netherlands, in France, and now also in England. It was not yet clear that the reasonableness and the intellectual flaccidity which marked especially its views on religion condemned it from the first to ultimate failure. The Christian humanists did not really understand the forces—especially in men's souls where true devotion so readily mingles with envy, ire and covetousness—or the passions which they might help to unleash; and probably only Thomas More came quickly to see how far from reality they were moving. But with all their deficiencies they did two things: they assisted in undermining unsatisfactory certainties which more formidable enemies were soon to destroy, and immediately they brought into a world sadly in need of a general spiritual rehabilitation a conscious demand for reform. The things they wanted were often entirely inadequate or off the point, or unrealistic; some quite crucial problems of the public weal had not yet reached their consciousness; but unlike everybody else they perceived that changes were required and suggested some understanding of how to go about them. The determination with which they turned away from helpless resignation, from that leaving it all to God with which earlier generations had viewed the human condition, deserves every respect, and they offered to the leaders of the nation a new and unwonted ethos of intellectual and practical innovation.

But they made one demand which embraced everything else. The crown of their programme of reform—the purpose to which all education especially of princes, all moral regeneration, all elimination of the old corruption, tended—was a universal Christian peace. For twenty years they had watched Europe tear Italy to pieces, with willing assistance from Italy herself, and they had conceived a furious hatred of war which, especially in Erasmus, comes out as the one deeply felt sincerity of all those writings. They looked to Henry VIII as a prince of peace.

2 The King in his Youth

When Henry VIII ascended the throne, on 22 April 1509, he was still some months short of his eighteenth birthday. Thus he was technically still a minor, though this seems to have bothered nobody.[1] It helped that he looked the part. Though new reigns usually called forth cries of delight and transports of hope, nothing has ever equalled the chorus of praise and expectation that welcomed Henry VIII. And much of it was sincere. The new King was a paragon of physical splendour allied to bright intelligence, cheerful charm, and unrelenting activity. Poets and humanists could welcome one who spoke several languages, read books, and especially excelled as a musician and composer. The younger generation of aristocratic sprigs gathered eagerly round England's most tireless horseman, foremost wrestler, a first-class archer and hawker and jouster. The nation at large could look forward to a change after the old King's stern and demanding government. A new age was obviously dawning.

To those able to keep their heads in the general rejoicing, some things should have given pause. Henry had absolutely no experience of government or affairs; he had been brought up in severe seclusion, under the eyes of a prematurely aged father and a notoriously pious and precise grandmother; he had discharged no official functions, and outside the court no one had ever seen him. On top of this comprehensive inexperience he soon proved himself to be exceptionally impetuous; inexperience was no bar to imperious wilfulness in this very large and very vigorous young man. The reign was only two days old when, listening to the complaints released by Henry VII's death, he ordered the immediate arrest of Empson and Dudley, the most hated men in England. And immediately also he decided to marry, choosing, after all, Catherine of Aragon, his

[1] Under the feudal law of inheritance, the age of majority was twenty-one. Kings seem usually to have been thought out of their minority at eighteen. The accession of minors had troubled the English monarchy intermittently since 1216 and especially in the fifteenth century; no one wanted another such occasion. Thus, presumably, Henry's actual age was simply ignored, though it is worth noting that he was not crowned until 29 June 1509, the day after his eighteenth birthday.

brother's widow, some seven years his senior, once allocated to him
by his father and then withdrawn. The marriage was celebrated on
11 June 1509, as soon as (or rather sooner than) the obligatory
mourning for the old King could be thought over. Both these
precipitate actions led to complications. The first did so immediately
because it soon proved impossible to convict the fallen ministers by
legal means; once committed, Henry could not draw back, and his
councillors were forced to manufacture false charges of treason
against his victims who had been guilty of no genuine capital
offence. The second caused trouble in the short run because it
severely limited England's freedom of action on the European stage,
and in the long run because marrying an older wife is not a good
idea for an adolescent king. (At the same time, some of his councillors clearly felt that so physically lavish an adolescent was better
married.) Much of the reign could have been predicted from the
rashnesses of its first few months—its tone at least, if not its events.

The English monarchy, limited by its duty to observe the laws and
its inability to make new laws or levy taxes without consent in
Parliament, was nevertheless just then an exceptionally personal
one. Henry VII had seen to this, by his methods of government;
Henry VIII, so formidable and immediate a personality, could
not help but put his own stamp on it. A change of kings meant
many things, all of them real. It affected the fortunes of
individuals—councillors, courtiers, companions—and of the nation,
for the policy of the state was very definitely that of its head. Henry
had to discover a role for himself, and his choice would determine
the events of the day even though the working out of it, and possibly
also the exact definition of the action to be taken, would very likely
fall to others, as throughout his reign it often did. Erasmus had
reason to preach the duties of the Christian prince—peace, order,
learning and piety. Henry, as it happened, was both learned and
pious, being at heart a rather simple man whose natural (and
youthful) inclination to see things in terms of right and wrong took
courage from the position of a monarch who could, it seemed,
translate will into action. He was not, however, even at first glance,
exactly a peaceful man. What would he decide to do with his
kingship and power?

The King's personality drove towards action and public glory: he
was a sportsman, and war was recognized as the greatest sport of
kings. The setting within which he lived and worked encouraged the
same ambitions and also suggested that they be fulfilled by war. The
political nation of England—that part of the people who shared in
rule and commanded power—though it ranged through variations
of wealth and gradations of rank, nevertheless composed a cohesive

body of men, identifiable by rank, manners, taste and ethos. Henry's world was aristocratic. Immediately beneath him stood the nobility, defined in England as the families whose heads made up the parliamentary peerage. At the beginning of Henry's reign, these were quite few in number and, despite the alleged bloodletting of the civil wars, mostly fairly ancient in ancestry. England had only one duke (Edward Stafford, duke of Buckingham, aged thirty-one in 1509) and one marquess (Thomas Grey, marquess of Dorset, a year older). Neither was the first holder of his title. Of the nine earls,[2] one (Ralph Nevill, earl of Westmorland) was a minor, nine years old, but the fourth earl of that line. John de Vere, the thirteenth earl of Oxford, was also the oldest at sixty-seven; the second oldest, a year younger, was one of the two upstarts among them, Thomas Howard, earl of Surrey, whose father had forfeited the dukedom of Norfolk by supporting Richard III at the wrong moment. The other new man was Thomas Stanley, second earl of Derby, too young to carry much weight. The power of the Staffords was demonstrated when in the King's first year Edward's brother Henry was elevated to the vacant earldom of Wiltshire. The Percy earl of Northumberland was the fifth of his line, the Talbot earl of Shrewsbury the fourth, the Fitzalan earl of Arundel the tenth. The highest in the land owed little or nothing to the Tudors and possessed a sufficiency of pride of birth, Derby and Surrey excepted (in both respects). The baronage, too, was at this point dominated by established families and represented mostly by men in their late thirties and forties.

A solid body of men, settled upon their lands, active in their counties which they ruled sometimes in conflict with one another but more commonly by agreement—most of the nobility answered to this simple enough description, though their ranks included a few with intellectual tastes (William Blount, Lord Mountjoy, the patron of scholars; John Bourchier, Lord Berners, poet and translator of Froissart) and the occasional professional soldier like Surrey or Thomas, Lord Darcy, preoccupied with the defence of the northern border against Scotland. Few of the nobility were courtiers because Henry VII had promoted very few courtiers to noble title; their individual centres of gravity lay in the shires. But at the same time all were committed to the Tudor King. Not one of them displayed personal political ambitions, not even, at this time, the duke of Buckingham, and certainly not those once great northern magnates, Northumberland (much enfeebled) and Westmorland (too young in any case). The aristocratic top layer lived contentedly and somewhat

[2]The Courtenay earldom of Devon was in abeyance until revived for William Courtenay in May 1512.

demurely beneath their King, no rivals to power but a steady source of stability.

Much the same was true of the lesser nobility, the landowning gentry, less magnificent in display, less immediately powerful in local politics, but on a reduced scale identical with the aristocracy proper. No one can tell the number of gentle families, especially because even at the time there was much uncertainty concerning what entitled a man to inclusion. Those distinguished by the titles and dignities of knight or esquire belonged without question, but many asserted the right to be called gentlemen whose wealth and influence gave them only a modest standing in society. Yet all could be identified, like the nobility, by two basic characteristics: they possessed landed estates, and they pursued policies of family improvement—by marriage, by deals in land, by the intensive exploitation of their properties, and by legal chicanery. Their lives revolved around the realities of land and family, and their behaviour was governed by the ambitions enshrined in both. The greatest landowner of the day was the Church, the second the King. But between them, gentry and nobility already held more land in England than King and Church combined, and on this wealth as much as on pride of ancestry rested their claim to be heard.

Loyalty notwithstanding, this diffused aristocratic power laid down particular rules of political conduct for the King. England was a more united and uniform country than most contemporary European structures, but this still left room for a powerful localism. From the Crown's point of view, the major problems were the less obvious ones. True, the King of England owned possessions overseas which were calling for his attention. In Ireland, English rule had retreated into the narrow strip of land around Dublin, called the Pale, and into the small towns of Cork and Waterford; beyond lay the region dominated by the half-English magnates (Kildare, Desmond and Ormond) who behaved as semi-independent powers; the main, Gaelic, areas were ruled by Irish lords who had long abandoned the law of England which did not recognize them and had no authority over them.[3] Henry VII, after a short and abortive attempt at direct rule, had remitted the island to the rule of the Fitzgeralds whose leader, the eighth earl of Kildare, remained its uncrowned king until his death in 1513. Unless Henry VIII's title of lord of Ireland was to lose all practical meaning, that dominion needed urgent attention, but for the present it received none at all. Next, the Pale of Calais, England's bridgehead on the continent, needed new defences if it

---

[3] The history of early Tudor Ireland has been restudied and recast by B. Bradshaw, 'The Irish Constitutional Revolution, 1515–1557' (unpublished dissertation, Cambridge, 1975). For the tripartite division of the island (Pale, 'colony', Gaelic regions) see his chapter 1.

was to be retained in the face of French desire for its reconquest; in an age of siege warfare, as fortifications were being modernized in Italy and France, the old walls and forts stood no chance of surviving a serious attack. Calais, like Ireland supposedly capable of covering all its needs out of local revenues, was in fact (like Ireland) always a drain on the English Exchequer; but at least its government was at this time safely in royal control. The third of the King's overseas dominions, the Channel Islands, seem practically never in this reign to have entered into the English government's consciousness.

Though on a rational assessment of the situation these outliers should have engaged an active reforming government's concern, and though the condition of Calais was vital if Henry VIII really meant to involve himself again in continental war, their shaky position at least did not affect the power of the crown in England itself. There the more patently independent parts of the realm had had the attention required and by 1509 can hardly be said to have been distracting from the King's sovereign rule. In the later middle ages some quasi-independent territorial complexes had been built up from bases in the northern and western marches; but the greatest of these—the duchy of Lancaster, covering the county palatine and great possessions in Yorkshire and elsewhere, and the earldom of March which incorporated the Mortimer inheritance in the Welsh marches—had fallen back to the crown in 1399 and 1461 respectively. The independence of the Welsh border in particular was a thing of the past; most marcher lordships were by now in crown hands, and by promoting the loyal interest of the Herberts in Pembrokeshire Henry VII had pretty thoroughly acclimatized those regions to ordinary rule, at least on the political level. There remained the task of introducing English law and any sort of public order along the Severn border and in Wales.

Things were less clear-cut in the north where some liberties (such as Tynedale and Redesdale, notorious refuges for fugitive criminals) remained a thorn in the side of good government, and where the continued danger from Scotland forced the Crown to equip the local nobility with delegated powers as wardens of the three marches. Earlier experiments to govern the north through a special council (inherited by Henry VII from the Yorkists, but found to be expensive and hazardous) had lapsed, and the whole region north of Yorkshire had never returned to the settled condition that vanished when Richard, duke of Gloucester, accepted ruler of the north, went south to usurp the crown. However, at this juncture the King could rely on a reasonable amount of support. The Percies proved loyal, and the Nevills had not recovered from the beating they had taken

in the civil wars; and both great families had troubles with slightly
lesser barons whom Tudor policy had promoted as some sort of
counterweight. Nevertheless, in the border counties and north of the
Tyne it remained the case that Percy and Nevill, Clifford and Dacre,
counted for more than Tudor, and tentacles of these aristocratic
spheres of influence extended well into Yorkshire; peace and obedience depended not on direct royal control but on a species of
alliance between the King and the great families.

On a smaller scale, this relationship was repeated elsewhere. In
the southwest the Courtenays, sadly reduced from their great (and
lawless) days, still carried more weight than was comfortable; this
encouraged support for gentry families like the Grenvilles and
Denyses, capable of transmitting the authority of the crown to their
locality. In Norfolk, the Howards were building up their power in
succession to the Mowbrays; the Fitzalans in Sussex, the Greys in
Kent, the Stanleys in Cheshire and south Lancashire, the Talbots in
Derbyshire and south Yorkshire, all exercised a species of local rule
under the King which unquestionably limited the monarch's ability
to translate claims to power into the reality of government. And even
in regions lacking the presence of a true magnate, powerful men of
gentle status commanded both loyalties and physical force enough to
give them a political power which kings could not ignore. Bulkeleys
in north Wales, Herberts in the south, Breretons in Cheshire, Stonors
in Oxfordshire, Savilles and Tempests and Constables in Yorkshire,
these and their like combined family ambition with the means to
fulfil it. They played their politics locally, on the stage defined by the
shire, but any monarch really wanting to govern needed these men if
his orders and authority were to penetrate into the shires so ruled.
Below their ranks, others anxious to move upwards struggled to
emulate and displace their betters, and everywhere political alliances and groupings were formed which endured so long as their
heads could produce the goods, that is provide the favours and
advantages sought by those who followed. Shire politics were real,
continuous, and often savage, expressing themselves visibly in elections to Parliament, in contests over the membership of the commission of the peace, in unending litigation, and too often still in
physical clashes. They also, of course, expressed themselves in
marriages, dinners, festivities and regular cooperation. The enforcement of the King's law—the nation's law—still took a deal of
achieving, and the policies of government had to take constant
account of the local realities.

What prevented this centrifugal aristocratic dominance from
breaking up the commonwealth (as it had broken it up only forty
years before) was, in the first place, the re-establishment of

monarchy—its mystique and its means of rule. Henry VIII inherited a realm in which the worst aspects of the localized and hierarchic power structure had been subdued by his predecessors; in the main they had recovered the ascendancy which the great medieval kings had created. By 1509 there was really no danger that local rivalries would engulf the throne, the more so as the Yorkist interest had been virtually destroyed by Henry VII. Politics, and the factions which conducted it, had returned where they belonged, to the King's court. Henry VIII continued the work, especially when on the outbreak of war in 1512 he decided to guard his rear by carrying out the sentence of death pronounced in 1499 upon that poor prisoner the earl of Warwick.[4] But while it may be plain to us that the aristocratic ambitions of the age would not again spill over into subversion of the throne, the point was less manifest to contemporaries, very well aware of the thin line which divided one effect from the other; and Henry VIII, not entirely without reason, became increasingly suspicious of overweening individuals or potentially dangerous rivals. No more than his father did he wish to destroy or even undermine the aristocracy; his rule, his mode of life, and his policy depended entirely on cooperation with an order of society to which he himself belonged. All he needed to do was to stand forth as its leader, set apart by the divine grace which had chosen him King—an image of rulership, dominant, unrivalled, glorious—and to keep watch that no man's aspirations should drift from the legitimate ambition proper to men of power under the throne into illegitimate designs upon the highest place of all. Here Henry's outwardly formidable and impressive personality helped from the first, despite his youth. This was a King that men could look up to—indeed, had to look up to because none could match his physical size. The feelings he inspired always mingled some fear with the awe, and it would be hard to say that any of his subjects—even his close companions at court, even his wives—came to love him; but for a man so manifestly King to every eye, so quick at judging men and situations, and so capable of exercising both easy charm and unchallenged authority, awe and devotion and apprehension did more than affection could have done.

Henry established this palpable hold over his people's imagination and obedience as soon as he ascended the throne, and he retained it largely unimpaired to the day of his death. By itself, however, it was not enough to give force to his kingship, nor should we be bemused by the carefully cultivated monarchism of this egocentric monstrosity (a classical monster in his mixture of the remarkable and the totally

[4]Richard, the last Yorkist claimant of the de la Pole family, lived in exile and died in 1525 at the battle of Pavia.

intolerable) into believing that he could really do as he pleased. He was neither despot nor dictator, and despite some tyrant's instincts never a tyrant. The political nation's consensus under the King depended rather on a mutual nexus of need. The King, as has been said, needed the nobility and gentry to transmit his authority into the shires; in the virtual absence of a paid crown service in the localities, government depended upon executive action demanded on behalf of the centre from locally ascendant men and readily discharged by them. The making of laws, the creation of machinery (especially that of justice), the devising of taxes, the planning of armies and war, all these belonged to the central institutions of government; without the policing of the realm by justices and magnates, without sessions of the peace and letters of information, without the collecting of tax money and the mustering of men locally by local worthies commissioned from above, royal policy had no existence. The central bureaucracy (in need of reform, but nevertheless quite well established and in sufficient working order) did reach out directly into the shires: customs officers and receivers of land revenue, for instance, were necessarily men of their locality and exposed to its influences, but they took the King's pay and worked as his servants. That bureaucracy also included the judges whose two annual visits on the assize circuits brought additional force to the central presence in the provinces. Yet, in spite of all this, the King's government worked upon the nation only because the naturally dominant elements in the localities thought it their duty and proper place to act as its agents. Much the same was true of that much smaller part of the political nation which inhabited and ruled the towns—those bodies of merchants and traders who, fundamentally self-governing in their narrower localities and equipped to be so with powers and privileges, in effect operated the King's government at their own free will. Yet free will is again too strong a term for these subtle relationships, for however powerful the local rulers might be the language in which their unpaid and relatively voluntary services were sought was always that of authority. The King's government worked by instruction and command, not negotiation and request; but it was clear to those in charge of it that the reality presupposed a good deal of social diplomacy.

In return for services rendered, these lesser and non-bureaucratic authorities expected their reward. To the King they were loyal and useful (and often competent) servants; he was to them the fountain of honours and patronage. In the last resort the power of the crown depended quite as much on its possession of valuables that the aristocracy wanted as it did on a mystique of kingship, the legal prerogatives of the crown, and the machinery of government.

Offices, manors, wardships, distinctions, titles, church livings, special favours, help in lawsuits, not to mention plain money—such things were the coin in which kings paid for what enabled them to rule. The oldest and most important archive of their Chancery, the patent roll, was no more than a register of the purposeful distribution and articulation of their necessary bounty. The history of the times could be written around its record of keeperships of parks and castles, of places in the royal guards or the garrison of Calais, of offices in Household and Exchequer, of sinecures and grants of land, with the addition of the Chamber accounts and their entries of 'rewards', plus a batch of letters advocating to the departments responsible for settling them this man's cause or that man's claims. Men sought these products of royal bounty not only for themselves but for their families, dependants, servants and associates; and influence under the King belonged to him—minister of state or gentleman within the Household—who could most regularly determine the direction in which the stream should flow. This network of patronage and service extended through the whole of society, the situation between King and suitor being repeated at every level down the scale; but the ultimate source of the currency in which the system worked was the patronage of the Crown. He who could tap it carried influence wherever it happened to matter to him; he who wished to advance himself needed to show that he knew the way to the source of all good things. It was a system which could readily succumb to corruption and was almost bound to create a measure of sycophancy, but vigilance on the part of those who guarded the immediate access to the King could keep it in sound working order, while the simple fact that there was never enough to satisfy all demands prevented it from stagnating and preserved the authoritative ascendancy of the giver. Kings had to show themselves generous, open-handed and grateful. They also had to display good stewardship of their patronage and political skill in distributing it: common sense and experience underlined this. A King too careful lost face (Henry VII came near to doing so), but one who (like James I) proved too undiscriminating lost even more. In Tudor practice, the relatively tight fists of Henry VII and Elizabeth no more prevented loyalties from being cemented by the search for patronage than did Henry VIII's lavish but often capricious bestowal (and withdrawal) of his bounty.

Sentiment, local ambition, and the desire for the benefits available from the Crown—enlightened self-interest, in fact—thus prevented the centrifugal and locally disruptive potential of this competitive aristocratic society from undermining the very real rule that Henry could expect to exercise. Per contra, the existence of this chain of lesser hierarchies and authorities, jostling for favour but apt to resent its withholding, prevented even the visibly powerful rule of Tudor kings from tipping over into despotism. Rulers so dependent on relatively independent men, so often forced to adjust policy to the wishes of demanding subjects and the accidents of local rivalries, simply could not afford to rule by mere will or dictate. This situation resolved itself into a polity organized by law, and it did this the more readily because the common law of England was ancient, well established, served by an entrenched profession, and yet flexible enough to meet changing circumstances. In theory the law defined each man's position with respect to his fellows—his rights and his duties—and it did so for everyone, king and peasant; in practice it offered a way of discovering those rights (and perhaps of evading those duties) by the hazards of litigation rather than the use of force. Force was very much present in Tudor society, but law did in the end rule all, if only because the monarchy deliberately, consistently (except now and again in high political matters), and instinctively obeyed the need to work inside it. One of the very real achievements of the Tudors, to which Henry's reign (thanks to his ministers) contributed much, was the realization to a degree really quite extraordinary in so hierarchical a society of the principle that before the law men were equal;[5] and that equality comprehended the Crown itself whose prerogatives existed only under the law—that is, could be tested and controlled in the courts. Thus the inner realities of the social structure and the formal realities of law observance made out of those volatile, dynamic and self-assertive subjects as well ordered and manageable a kingdom as any in Europe, and out of those wilful, quick-tempered and flamboyant Tudors a race of constitutional monarchs.

The ethos (to say it once more) of this acquisitive and law-centred society was firmly aristocratic. The aristocracy of England felt less violently hostile to the non-aristocratic pursuits of merchants and lawyers than was usual among medieval aristocracies, even as it was on the whole more mobile internally and more open to fresh recruitment from outside than its counterparts elsewhere. Nevertheless it was still an aristocracy which rested its assurance of importance on the possession of land, not on wealth in any other form, and which fondly thought of itself as a warrior class. William Caxton, in 1485, could lament the decay of knightly virtues in England (knightly virtues being among the things that are never as good as they used to be), and it is true that few of her many knights resembled the Lancelots and Guys of Warwick of the chivalric tales, or even the

[5]The conviction for murder of young Lord Dacre of the South (1541) shocked opinion, but he was executed none the less.

Black Prince and John Talbot of fairly recent reality. But the nation had a strong martial tradition: in the fourteenth century, English armies had been the most formidable in Europe, and the reputation then built up still sufficed to command unmerited respect from the French in Henry VIII's wars. And if most noble landowners of the early sixteenth century looked more at home on the justices' bench or in the company of their stewards or surveyors than on the field of battle, their education and their amusements still gave some substance to the martial image they liked to present. Humanist reformers like Erasmus and Vives might dream of a ruling caste led by princes who read the ancients for advice on government; the reality embraced hawking and hunting, wrestling and the quarter staff, and the simulated combat of the tourney. In particular was this true of the young men in those aristocratic circles, the young men overjoyed to find themselves serving a young King of like tastes. Henry VII in his counting house, checking his accounts and assessing fines for breaches of the law, may well command more respect among historians themselves unlikely to break a lance in a joust; to his nation he had increasingly become an incubus devoid of that passion of honour and zeal of chivalry which passed for virtue among young men brought up in the necessary occupations of landed idlers.

From Henry VIII's point of view, what mattered was the company he kept. It was not the aristocracy of the shires that set the immediate tone of his life, but the aristocracy of his court which, of course, included younger sons on the make and others who, as distant fathers died, departed to the country. And while the court comprised some solid men of business, episcopal administrators, and serious-minded survivors from the previous reign, the people among whom he immediately had his being were the young men of his Privy Chamber, friends and companions of a like age (all a little older) and a similar disposition. In that circle the prize went to physical prowess, a species of elegance and dalliance, the amusements of the dance, the masque, the chase and the tilting-yard, and ultimately—despite the pleasure taken in poetry, music and occasional learned discourse—the prospect of glory in the greater world of aristocratic tastes. Given that atmosphere, given his lack of serious training in the business of government, given his exceptional excellence in all the exercises of a courtly paragon, and given his superabundant energies, there was never any chance that Henry VIII might turn out a prince of peace. The wonder was that he took so long before he went to war; but even young kings bursting with a thirst for glory cannot simply manufacture war out of nothing.

Henry did want to prove himself in war, but to do him some sort of justice it must be added that his ultimate purpose was to display

general prowess, not necessarily military, on the European stage. He
wished to impress fellow monarchs as well as his subjects with his
greatness and splendour, actually a very proper ambition in the eyes
of contemporaries. What he could hope to do depended on the
situation in Europe, a situation in turn dictated (as it had been since
1494) by events in Italy and the rivalry there between France and
Spain. In 1509, these two temporarily cooperated, together with the
Emperor and most of Italy, in Pope Julius II's League of Cambrai
against Venice, and when Henry had had time to take stock he
found the great republic in a bad way and desperate for allies.
England was the only uncommitted power left, and by the summer
of 1509 Venetian ambassadors were pressing for her intervention.
Even the old King had in his last years involved himself in the
European scene; his eager young son, anxious for glory, seemed a
safe bet. By his marriage, Henry had in effect committed himself to
the Spanish interest, a point of significance as the unusual amity
between Ferdinand of Aragon and Louis XII of France began to
break up in the course of 1509. It was also easy to revive English
hostility to France, temporarily settled by Henry VII at the cost, to
France, of an annual tribute of about £5,000. Quite apart from
English memories of Crécy and Agincourt and from ambitions to
reassert Henry's claim to the crown of France which remained
fossilized in the English king's title until 1803, France was patently
at this time an aggressive power, with undisguised designs upon,
among other things, Calais. Sentiment and logic aligned Henry with
any anti-French coalition that might be going, and Venice laboured
to bring this about.

However impetuous the King might be, things could not move at
a fast pace, especially so long as the League of Cambrai was in
being. Characteristically, Henry sought to walk in the wake of the
papacy. His first significant step on the international scene was the
despatch in November 1509 of Archbishop Bainbridge of York as a
kind of resident ambassador to Rome, charged with the task of
weaning Julius away from France. The Pope recognized the young
King's personal devotion to the Holy See, an attitude compounded
of piety and ill-informed innocence; one of the pillars of English
policy for the next twenty years—support of Rome—was firmly
erected among exchanges of mutual esteem and honorific gifts in
these early negotiations. However, despite these high-minded senti-
ments and Venetian pressure, England did not immediately join the
League called Holy, formed by the Pope in August 1510 for the
expulsion of the French from Italy; the decision to take part did not
come until November 1511 by which time the League's fortunes had
reached so low a point that the Pope's continued participation

seemed very doubtful. However eager Henry was to display himself before the eyes of Europe, and also to assist the holy father at Rome, he found it far from easy to start a war. The immediate cause of delay was probably the influence of his wife, ever her father's best ambassador: until late in 1511 Ferdinand himself held off from the renewal of the Italian wars and did not want his son-in-law involved. In any case, Henry's desire, even determination, to join in meant the mounting of a major expedition into Europe, the first such since the English had been driven from France sixty years before. Such a step could not be taken overnight.

War was not only the finest sport of kings; it was also far and away their most expensive amusement. Could Henry afford it? Despite the exaggerations of contemporary rumour, the resources of his Crown were far from lavish. The recovery of the royal finances from the 1460s onwards had depended on the exploitation of the 'king's own', that is the regular income belonging to the prerogative which was held to be designed to cover 'ordinary' (peace-time) expenditure; for war purposes, this could be augmented, but only by means of special grants voted in Parliament. By energetic exploitation, Henry VII had raised the ordinary revenue to approximately £110,000 a year, a sum which, though it included such windfalls as the French pension and the dowry of Catherine of Aragon, was mainly derived from the crown lands (up to £50,000) and the customs revenue (tunnage and poundage) granted for life in every king's first Parliament (c. £40,000). Both these sources showed a decline in the early years of Henry VIII. The crown lands yielded barely £34,000 in 1512 and only £25,000 in 1515, in the main because some lands improperly seized (or so it was claimed) before 1509 had been restored to their rightful owners and because more had been granted away in the new reign.[6] The customs, naturally affected by the outbreak of war, were not to reach the level of 1509 again until they exceeded it in 1519, but they did remain more satisfactory.[7] At the same time, the ordinary expenditure of a court and regime as lavish as that of Henry VIII soon proved itself to be rose sharply; allocations to Household and Wardrobe, for instance, more than doubled. Thus the ordinary revenue of the crown, far from yielding a surplus for reserves as it had done under Henry VII, could now barely satisfy the normal annual expenditure.

The problems of the ordinary revenue were increased by administrative complications. Henry VII had developed further the Yorkist reliance on a Chamber treasurer and special auditors, particularly

---

[6] For the crown lands cf. B. P. Wolffe, *The Crown Lands, 1461–1536* (1970), especially pp. 84–5, 179–82.

[7] G. Schanz, *Englische Handelspolitik gegen Ende des Mittelalters* (1881) ii, p. 59.

for the land revenue, at the expense of the cumbersome Exchequer machinery, but the reaction against his methods affected also this system. The efficiency of land revenue collection had depended on the general surveyors of crown lands, officials set up, with a staff, in the Prince's Council Chamber at Westminster, equipped with powers to summon defaulters, and responsible solely and directly to the King. Though in the new reign John Heron, Henry VII's treasurer of the Chamber, was at once confirmed as collector and paymaster of crown monies, the general surveyors were subjected to audit as the Exchequer (as it usually did at the death of a king when Household government was at its weakest) sought to re-establish its lost control. An act of 1512 restored the earlier machinery and, by giving the general surveyors statutory authority, protected them against the sort of fate that had struck in 1509, but it was only in 1515–16 that further legislation restored the degree of independence that the office had enjoyed under Henry VII. The time taken to eradicate the consequences of conservative reaction speeded the decline of the vital land revenue which never again reached the level or played the part characteristic of the pre-1509 system. The beginnings of the general inflation also, naturally, reduced the value of a distinctly inelastic income.

There were thus only two ways of financing an active foreign policy and especially war—previously accumulated reserves, or special taxation. It has for long been held that Henry VIII's early wars used up the magnificent treasure left by his father, a sum elevated by rumour to nearly £2 million. Recent investigations would appear to have diminished this legendary treasure to almost nothing: it has been shown that at Henry VII's death his chief treasury, the Chamber, was mildly in the red, and that the accounts for the war of 1512–13 seem to include only about £10,000 from reserves.[8] Even the author of this revision agrees that there is a possibility of reserves to the tune of £30,000 having been put by in jewels and plate, though it cannot be shown that much conversion into cash took place at the crucial time. However, until recently no one was aware that Henry VII initiated a practice of diverting surpluses to a more intimate treasury still than the Chamber, called vaguely the king's coffers, which was administered by the executive officer of the Privy Chamber, the groom of the Stool.[9] We have no means of knowing the totals accumulated there, but the possibility

[8] B. P. Wolffe, 'Henry VII's Land Revenues and Chamber Finance', *English Historical Review* LXXIX (1964), especially pp. 253–4, and *Crown Lands*, p. 186. Dr Wolffe is certainly right in writing off the *c.* £226,000 which Henry VII had lent to the Emperor Maximilian. None of this was ever repaid.

[9] D. R. Starkey, 'The King's Privy Chamber, 1485–1547' (unpublished dissertation, Cambridge, 1973), pp. 393 ff.

remains that Henry VIII inherited a useful sum of money which helped to pay both for the heavy costs incurred in getting the new reign under way and in the preparations for war. On balance, however, it does look as though Henry VIII acceded to no more than a position of comfortable solvency with modest surpluses (itself a rare thing for sixteenth-century kings), maintained and maintainable only by those methods of rigorous exploitation and close supervision which he immediately abandoned.

That left direct taxation, obtainable only with parliamentary consent; on the other hand, the established principle that the King could properly justify the call for taxes by the fact or expectation of war made it easy to get something.[10] Unfortunately, what was to be got neither sufficed in the conditions of the early sixteenth century nor fairly tapped the wealth of the country. The recognized tax was the fifteenth and tenth, originally a levy on movable wealth assessed on every occasion. However, as early as 1334 this tax had been converted into fixed sums imposed on every tax district (vills and urban wards) which the local authorities were left to raise from the inhabitants by whatever arrangements they pleased. This system produced an assured yield of about £30,000 and made collection relatively easy. On the other hand, it made it impossible to adjust yield to need except by the unpopular device of asking for more than one fifteenth and tenth at one time, while the fixed levy of 1334 in no sense any longer represented the country's ability to pay. The geographical distribution of wealth had shifted markedly even at county level, let alone at the level of the small administrative units used for this tax. Thus by 1510 Lincolnshire and Norfolk were relatively overcharged, while London and Devon got off pretty lightly.[11] All attempts to remedy these deficiencies by newly designed forms of taxation had so far failed before Parliament's suspicion of open-yield taxes and realistic records of assessed wealth, and before taxpayers' ability to evade their commitments.

The financial resources of the crown, therefore, even allowing for clerical taxation,[12] were very far from lavish and hardly justified the supposition, held at the time and often repeated since, that at least Henry VIII could afford to engage in continental war, whether or not he was wise to do so. The ordinary revenue barely sufficed for the ordinary expenditure, while the inadequate parliamentary taxes

[10] The discussion of parliamentary grants rests throughout on R. S. Schofield, 'Parliamentary Lay Taxation, 1485–1547' (unpublished dissertation, Cambridge, 1963).

[11] R. S. Schofield, 'The Geographical Distribution of Wealth in England, 1334–1649', *Economic History Review*, 2nd series, xviii (1965), pp. 483 ff.

[12] J. J. Scarisbrick, 'Clerical Taxation in England, 1485–1547', *Journal of Ecclesiastical History* xi (1960), pp. 41 ff., calculates that the sum raised over those sixty-two years averages out at £9,000 p.a., but no one has yet worked out the actual yield of any grants made.

were in addition slow to come in even when granted. Something
could be done by borrowing in anticipation of supply grants, though
of this there is no evidence in the early years, and something by
soliciting ostensibly free gifts (benevolences) from those best able to
pay—courtiers, wealthy merchants, greater landowners. As a substitute for general taxation by consent, benevolences had been
declared illegal in 1484, but nothing in the law stopped appeals to
the generosity of individuals (moved in addition by hopes of favour
and fear of displeasure), and such methods—never very
productive—seem to have been employed in 1513. The situation
described, and the figures cited, indicate why the £5,000 obtained
annually from France played such a part in government planning
and was pursued with such vigour; the pension was in fact paid right
to the eve of war in November 1511.

Given that he could raise the cash (a dubious proposition), could
Henry raise an army? This turned out to be a less serious problem
than might have been thought. Henry had very little in the way of a
standing force—a foot guard (the yeomen) approximately 200 strong
(increased for the war to 600), to which in 1510 he added a cavalry
corps du garde of a more distinguished kind, the gentlemen pensioners
or 'spears'.[13] In addition there were permanent garrisons at Berwick,
Carlisle and Calais and the other Calais forts, but these barely
sufficed for their particular duties and could not be used for a field
army. Although all adult males from sixteen to sixty stood liable for
militia duty, organized by county musters and raised by commissions
of array, this system at the time lay in virtual ruin, quite apart from
the fact that these forces could not be compelled to serve overseas.
Henry therefore had to rely on traditional methods—the hiring of
foreign mercenaries and the companies raised and contributed by
individual noblemen and gentlemen. In this method of retinues lay
hidden the dangers of private armies which legislation against
retaining and the giving of livery had tried to suppress; since,
however, the Crown needed noblemen's retainers to fight its wars it is
no wonder that the codifying statute of 1504, which lapsed at Henry
VII's death, was never renewed. In any case, the notorious evils of
the system had vanished with the ending of dynastic disputes and the
restoration of royal government; the armies so raised were King's
armies supplied and paid by the Crown. The method had the
advantage of producing an army of competent fighting men, eager
for glory and loot, rather than useless conscripts.

The more specialized aspects of the military problem were also in
fairly good order. Henry possessed an impressive train of the new

---

[13]There were fifty gentlemen pensioners, but each 'spear' consisted of a gentleman, an
archer, a light cavalry man, and a mounted attendant, making 200 men in all.

weapon, artillery, both siege and field guns, and before war broke out he added to it. He was particularly devoted to his 'twelve apostles'—siege guns named after the Lord's disciples—as well he might be since each cost him over £1,300 (with another £12 for the gun-carriage). For individual weapons English armies still relied on the longbow and bill (a long-handled axe) rather than the hand-guns and pikes which were taking over on the continent; but in 1511 such backwardness was not yet serious and had the advantage that existing stores could be used effectively. The army which invaded France in 1513 was in fact equipped with new weapons, clothing and armour from head to foot, an expensive but impressive achievement. And the King from the first showed some appreciation of the place that the navy was bound to occupy in the military needs of an island kingdom. Henry's interest in building and equipping warships partook of the play-acting pretence that marked so many of his activities: we need not take very seriously the golden bosun's whistle he blew and the sailor's shirt of fine lawn he wore at the launching of the *Great Harry* in 1514. Nevertheless, the praise he has received for his attention to the royal navy is not undeserved.

One way or another, therefore, especially if the mounting expense was ignored, England was in 1511 capable of making war. In addition Henry disposed of a good institutional machinery capable at need of organizing war. His father had consolidated government around two interlocking administrative centres—the royal Household and the King's Council, both used flexibly and ubiquitously as need arose. The Household was not only the traditional instrument for overseeing a war but also the obvious one, including as it did the only organization in England used to managing the supply and maintenance of a sizable establishment. Even King Henry's Household and court came nowhere near the 30,000 men he took to France in 1513, but Household officers knew all about victualling, field bakeries, the purchase of cloth and leather, and so forth. They could very readily be transferred to war duty. The Household also included men used to handling and accounting for large sums of money, and treasurers at war were appointed from its ranks.

However, while the Household could be used to do the intensive donkey work direction had to come from somewhere else, and with a King who neither knew about nor cared for the daily grind of administration that duty fell in the first place to his Council.[14] This was not, however, initially well equipped to manage a war. The King's Council was a large and undifferentiated body of usually about forty or fifty members, though most of its sittings were

[14] Traditional accounts of Henry VIII's Council (e.g. that it was appointed for him by the Lady Margaret Beaufort) are legendary.

attended by some eight or ten persons. It comprised representatives of five types—peers, bishops, ecclesiastical lawyers ('doctors'), common lawyers ('learned men'), and courtier-administrators mostly of knightly rank. In its sessions it dealt indiscriminately with advice to the King, administrative business, and the adjudication of suits brought before it by bill of complaint. This last activity could take the form of private arbitration or, increasingly, of public sittings in the manner of a court in the public room at Westminster called the Star Chamber; from this last the Court of Star Chamber was to develop, but in 1509 no valid distinction existed between it and the Council in its other capacities. Henry VII had employed individual councillors, informal groups of them, and regular committees to discharge specialized tasks, but in the reaction against his government the last in particular went under for a time. The regular and only recorded meetings of the full Council took place in term time, usually at Westminster; some councillors—a fluctuating selection from all the types represented—accompanied the King in and out of term, carrying on much the same functions as the formally complete body and also keeping a register. The Council was *par excellence* an extension of the King's power of government; it had no power of its own, and though it possessed a small clerical staff mainly required for the judicial work, it lacked institutional definition.

Henry VIII's first Council simply continued his father's, in function and membership; there is no sign that he introduced any men of his own. Its leader and most regular attender was the chancellor, William Warham, archbishop of Canterbury, but the most influential councillor, to whom Warham deferred, remained that experienced official and administrator Richard Foxe, bishop of Winchester, lord privy seal. The episcopal element received reinforcement from Thomas Ruthal of Durham (principal secretary), Richard Nixe of Norwich, and (more rarely in attendance) John Fisher of Rochester. The most important of the lesser clergy at first were John Young, master of the Rolls, and William Atwater, dean of the Chapel Royal. Among the peers the lead unquestionably belonged to the earl of Surrey, experienced in affairs and in personal survival, but Buckingham and Shrewsbury rivalled his influence. The common lawyers included the judges, the King's serjeants, and the attorney and solicitor general; though in theory their chief function was to superintend the Council's judicial work and protect the King's interests in the courts, they attended most assiduously for all sorts of business and were regular members of the ordinary Council. Among the administrators we may note the chancellor of the Duchy of Lancaster (Sir Henry Marney) and the undertreasurer of the Exchequer (Sir John Cutt), leading civil servants rather than

knights of tourney and battlefield. Sir Edward Belknap and Sir John
Dauncy, two men bred up in Henry VII's Chamber system which
they were to help revive from 1513 onwards, may have been
councillors from the start though they are vouched for as attendant
only from about 1514. The most significant name to make its
appearance early in the reign first turns up in June 1510—Thomas
Wolsey, King's almoner, a protégé of the bishop of Winchester. The
Council was reported to be divided between a war party led by
Surrey and a peace group led by the bishops, but there is no good
evidence for this. What is clear is that until the emergence of Wolsey
it lacked energetic leadership; more important, it lacked the man
who could organize the King's war for him. We do not know
whether he promoted it on the Council; the chances are that, when
it finally came, Henry alone, with the aid perhaps of Surrey and
certainly of Catherine, was responsible for the decision.

But war was some way off yet in late 1509 when the planning first
began. Married in June, crowned soon after, anxious to make his
mark in the great concourse of princes, Henry still needed to get the
reign under way. Empson and Dudley had been dealt with: convicted of non-existent treasons, they lay in the Tower awaiting
death, the first victims of Henry's recognition that by means of false
charges he could best unload the odium attendant upon strong
government on to loyal servants and available scapegoats. He waited
till August 1510 before ordering the sentences to be carried out, for
no obvious reason; perhaps he thought to get more of their alleged
haul of wealth out of them, perhaps amidst the round of pleasures
that engaged his time he simply forgot about them.

In October 1509 the writs went forth for a Parliament which met
on 21 January 1510. Once more the opportunity was taken for a
marvellous display of splendour, to such good effect that upon his
return from high mass in Westminster Abbey the King had great
difficulty in getting through the press of people to the Parliament
chamber. The Parliament sat for less than five weeks, but its meeting
was very necessary, not only for purposes of public ceremony and to
advertise the new reign. From the King's point of view, the chief
reason for calling it lay in the act granting him the customs duties for
life. This was one matter in which the Council refused to concede
anything to the many dubious charges of extortion spread about in
the reaction against Henry VII; when the London merchants tried
to get the duties reduced and to make out that none had been
payable in the months between Henry VII's death and the passage
of the act, they got very short shrift. Statutory allocations were made
for the King's Household and Wardrobe—customary acts whose
provisions, as was also usual, proved insufficient. For the rest, both

Houses, spurred on by petitions from various lobbies, passed acts
against the alleged misdoings of Henry VII's government, acts of
little consequence because they professed to remedy wrongs never
actually committed. No one attempted to consider the larger needs
of the realm or of social policy; no member of Henry's inner circle at
this point favoured reform, and in the euphoria accompanying the
new reign no one pressed for it from outside. At least the spurious
reforms of this Parliament helped to assuage discontent. So did the
activities of the Council in reviewing the bonds taken by the late
King, but most of all was achieved by the well advertised display of
exuberant rejoicing which filled the lives of King, Queen and court
(and the pages of Edward Hall's *Chronicle*)—and put money in the
pockets of court contractors. From the first, Henry was nothing if not
extravagant about his pleasures.

Meanwhile, and despite the warlike growls uttered as early as
mid-1509, the problem of intervention in Europe hung fire. Chiefly
this was because now there really was no war to join. The Pope came
to terms with Venice early in 1510, which eased Venetian pressure
on Henry VIII, and though from September that year Julius was
fighting with poor success against the French in the Romagna, the
rest of Europe remained uninvolved until the enlargement of the
Holy League in October 1511. At this point Ferdinand, having
himself come off the fence, gave the signal, and England joined in
November. The alliance planned an encircling attack upon the
common enemy, France, and Henry's accession to the League
completed that circle. The first preparation for war consisted,
inevitably, in the calling of a Parliament to raise the necessary
money. Parliament met on 4 February 1512 and, twice prorogued,
did not finally go home until twenty-five months later; in that time,
an entirely new tax was first tried and essentially perfected.

This tax was the Tudor subsidy,[15] effectively an income tax raised
on either lands or movables (depending on whether a man had more
of one or the other) and, where applicable, on wages. Each levy was
newly assessed, and this together with a skilful varying of the terms
(rate per pound, extension or contraction of the taxed population)
gave the subsidy the reality and flexibility lacking in its predecessor.
Of course, it called for more sophisticated administrative techniques,
and it says much for early Tudor government that these were rapidly
produced. Administrative costs, though higher than the fantastically
low one per cent of the fifteenth and tenth, still ran at only three and

---

[15]The subsidies raised in the two sessions of the 1515 Parliament completed the evolution of
the tax. The early subsidies yielded far less than had been forecast, but this was the result not
of taxpayers' revolts but of faulty budgeting. The figures offered to Parliament rested on
neither knowledge or investigation.

a half per cent; and in the reign of Henry VIII at least both assessment and collection remained efficient. The subsidy hit hardest those best able to pay: though as a rule about sixty per cent of the adult male population were taxed, the bulk of the yield came from the top tenth. In the four years 1513–16 the crown collected about £170,000 from this source, as well as £90,000 from three fifteenths and tenths; to this should be added possibly £40,000 from the taxation of the clergy. Since the war cost at least £600,000 (and quite possibly a million) vast sums remain unaccounted for. There is no evidence of extensive borrowing, while the French pension, of course, ceased as soon as war broke out. Obviously, despite the doubts cast on Henry VII's leavings, the difference must have been made up from reserves, but at present this remains an unsolved mystery. The subsidy, a highly successful innovation, should almost certainly be credited to Wolsey, though the actual work of drafting the acts was done by John Hales, a lawyer and tax expert who by way of reward was soon promoted to a career on the Exchequer bench.

To begin with, the war went abominably. To assist his father-in-law, Henry in 1512 despatched 10,000 men under the marquess of Dorset to the western end of the Pyrenees. Kept inactive by Ferdinand who used them to distract the enemy while he conquered Navarre, this force became quickly demoralized by drink and ruined by disease; in October the survivors struggled ignominiously back to England. It is worth notice that Henry, though furious, did not take out his anger on the incompetent commander or anyone else; despite the vindictiveness so close to his being, he could show a capacity for forgiveness when his moral sense was not outraged which explains much about his successful hold on the political situation. Meanwhile, Sir Edward Howard, one of his favourite companions, commanding the fleet which had escorted the troops to Spain, scored some successes around Brest, and Louis XII began to feel hard pressed. He decided to reactivate the alliance with Scotland, France's ancient device for distracting the English, and, though all good sense spoke otherwise, the temptation to attack across the border while Henry was preoccupied with the continent proved too much for James IV. The consolidation of peace with Scotland, sealed by the marriage of Henry's sister Margaret to the King of Scots, had been one of Henry VII's best achievements; at the touch of pointless ambition it now collapsed in ruins. With a population less than a third that of England, and with an annual revenue of barely £30,000, James would have been well advised to keep the peace. His reign had witnessed a great improvement in the position of the Scottish monarchy, traditionally one of the feeblest and most faction-dominated in Europe; the peace which this had brought had not only augmented the royal treasure but produced also a minor renaissance of the arts in the far north. The finest poet in the island between Chaucer and Thomas Wyatt was not some practitioner of debased Chaucerianism like Lydgate or Gower, and certainly not that idiosyncratic mixture of low vigour, sardonic sentiment, and dubious verse, Henry VIII's poet laureate John Skelton, but William Dunbar in whom native ballad traditions mingled with the genuine memory of Chaucer to produce a very personal form of true court poetry. But the novel claims of cultured excellence could not overcome the attractions of ancient habits, any more than common sense and a liking for the lute prevented Henry VIII from ardently embracing the ancient hatred of France. By mid-1512, Scotland was in effect committed to intervention.

Henry was determined to wipe out the disgrace of 1512 and in any case stood treaty-bound to invade France. Late 1512 brought the Emperor Maximilian into the alliance, at the same time as Ferdinand, satisfied by his gains, decided privately to withdraw while still engaged in signing agreements with his bemused allies. Through the winter of 1512–13 the preparations for the invasion of France went forward, while Surrey was sent north to prepare the borders against the Scots. Although April 1513 yielded yet another disaster in a naval defeat off Brest—the result of chivalrous and unseamanlike rashness which cost the life of Edward Howard—the expedition which finally crossed to Calais in June 1513 was the best equipped and soundest since Henry V's day and a triumph for Wolsey. A splendid army of 30,000 men, sincerely admired by the continental experts for the excellence of its troops, equipment and artillery, efficiently victualled and in very good heart, assembled in the bridgehead to see what glory it could bring to its King who took the field himself, somewhat dilatorily, to display his knighthood and generalship.

The original plan included an attack on Boulogne, quite a sensible idea because the object was attainable and success would have made possible the improvement of the Calais foothold. But sense vanished before the blandishments of Maximilian who wished to use his ally for his own purposes in his Burgundian possessions. Henry was to eliminate the tiresome French enclaves there, so as to safeguard Habsburg interests. The army turned east instead of southwest, to besiege the powerful fortress of Thérouanne. After beating off a hesitant relieving force in the rout known as the Battle of the Spurs, the English took the fortress on 23 August and razed it. Maximilian was still not content, and Henry allowed himself to be further distracted from an intelligent strategy. With the Emperor now attendant upon him in his camp, he invested the city of Tournai, a

French-held island (since 1187) inside Burgundian Hainault. The city quickly surrendered, but for once Maximilian had miscalculated. Instead of handing his conquest over to his ally, Henry resolved to keep it and turn it into a permanent English base—over seventy miles of alien territory from the sea and Calais. Returning in triumph he left behind a governor with a garrison who for the six years that the city was in English hands were to lead miserable lives among a hostile population adept at silent resistance. Even sending, upon instructions from London, representatives to the Parliament of 1514 did not make Tournai feel English.

One notable beneficiary of victory was its chief architect. Wolsey obtained the see of Tournai from a grateful Pope, though he got little out of it except the dignity because he could never divert the revenues from a French bishop-elect whom the local clergy continued to support. The behaviour of Tournai in the years 1513–18 throws doubts on the views of those who claim that they cannot identify nationalist sentiment in the sixteenth century. At least Wolsey did not lose money over the affair, as Henry VIII managed to do. While Tournai was English—the proof of his status as conqueror—it received lavish attention, and the King spared no effort to improve its ramshackle defences. What he had conquered was a city of no strategic importance; what in late 1518 he returned to France was a major modern fortress. Not counting the cost of the campaign, he had spent some £230,000 on the city; yet France paid almost £100,000 less for its recovery. Money that could have been used to repair the grave defects of the Calais defences was simply wasted. The 1513 expedition, spectacularly mounted and much dreaded by the French, turned into a futile sideshow with almost no effect upon the war. Henry had proved his incompetence as a strategist, while care had been taken that the little fighting there was should not endanger his life. The knight of Christendom came as near to being a figure of fun as ever he was to do in his long reign.

While these proceedings absorbed the bulk of England's martial resources, a real war had been fought and won in the north. The whole air of the 1513 campaign which destroyed the Scottish threat was different from the tinsel splendour, the childish display, the tournament effect, of Henry's conduct of war. Surrey, now seventy years old, proved himself to be the sort of professional whom the English army in France sadly lacked. The Scots crossed the border on 22 August and took Norham Castle, but the army which gathered against them, composed of Surrey's retinue, the regular garrisons, and the experienced fighters of the border counties, and supported by an English fleet, prevented both an attack on Berwick and any further advance south while Berwick remained untaken. On 7

September, Surrey encountered James well entrenched on Flodden Edge, and on the 8th, by a daring march across the Scots front, forced the enemy to give battle by deserting their superior and barely vulnerable position. The battle was won by better tactics, a superior use of artillery, and the advantages in close combat of the short English bill over the long Scottish lances. The armies (allegedly 20–30,000 strong each) were fairly evenly matched, but while the English lost some 1,500 men the Scots, prisoners apart, lost well over 10,000 including their King. Scotland was for the moment destroyed—no chance of a threat to her neighbour, but wide open to whatever that neighbour would care to do.

Flodden was a decisive battle (and to Henry's chagrin recognized as such by those who would only smile or shake their heads at his victories in France), but surprisingly little was done to follow it up. Not that Surrey was ever in a position to carry war across the border; anxious to save the mounting expenses, the regency Council in London, content that the frontier was safe, had the northern army disbanded. But with the infant heir to the throne of Scotland in his Tudor mother's hand, his uncle of England should have been able to assert some form at least of indirect control over the northern kingdom and thus consummate his father's policy there. Margaret, however, turned out to be no politician at all, and before the Scottish situation clarified to a point the European situation had once again changed. The events of early 1514 showed up the war for the irrelevance it was to English interests. True, in October 1513, riding the crest of Tournai, Henry and Wolsey once more acceded to a general plan for the invasion of France in the following year. So did Ferdinand, already determined to do no such thing; negotiating behind his allies' backs, he came to terms with Louis XII in March 1514, and Maximilian soon after followed suit. Henry was left alone—alone with the Pope—to hold a singularly unprepossessing baby. Naturally he felt betrayed and was suitably furious, but his futile policy, especially if, in his dealings with men who for years had broken their pledged word with predictable regularity, he had been as trusting as he seemed, deserved no better. It is, however, to his credit and also to Wolsey's that the rage they felt at the behaviour of their allies drove them to outsmart those seasoned double-dealers; before Ferdinand and Maximilian could capitalize on their turned coats, the English had made the most profitable peace of all with France. Perhaps, after all, the fact that they alone had an army in the fields of France (together with the astounding victory of Flodden) gave them a formidable hand to play, but one must not forget the superb diplomatic skill which the emergence of Wolsey added to Henry's equipment.

At any rate, in the summer of 1514, with the active help of the new Pope Leo X (who succeeded in 1513, intent upon abandoning his predecessor's warlike stances), England and France negotiated a treaty which left Spain and the Empire out in the cold. Henry kept Tournai which Maximilian still wanted, and his younger sister Mary, promised to the Emperor's grandson Charles, was married off to the elderly Louis. Thus freed from war in the north, Louis could once more turn his attention to Italy and endanger the control which Ferdinand thought to have established there while his innocent ally of England kept the French preoccupied. Though the war had been futile and though the details of the treaty looked better than they were, the obtaining of this diplomatic triumph by two such beginners marked a very considerable achievement and really put Wolsey and his master on the map of Europe. The peace of 10 August 1514, rather than the expedition of 1513, laid the foundations for the age of Wolsey during which the small and relatively poor country over which he ruled was to seem to dominate the contemporary scene. None the less, the urgent problems of the kingdom had received a serious setback from these three years of war, diplomacy and play-acting during which vast sums of money and much devoted labour had been wasted on pointless enterprises.

3 The Great Cardinal

I

In December 1516, Tierry Martens of Louvain published a short book entitled *Utopia*. Its author was Thomas More, close friend of Erasmus and the brightest star in England's humanist constellation, already well known as the translator into English of an Italian life of Giovanni Pico della Mirandola, and into Latin of some of Lucian's *Dialogues*. *Utopia*, also written in Latin, scored an immediate success on the continent, but it made less impact at home; the first English translation did not appear until 1551. More was thirty-seven when he wrote the book—well into middle age by the standards of the time, and launched on a successful career in the law. Its composition and publication roughly coincided with his move from the life of a barrister and municipal officer in London to public activity at court and in the service of the Crown, so that what started as an academic exercise and private reflection came to acquire the status of a major public pronouncement. *Utopia* incorporated More's view of what was wrong with England and Europe, as well as, presumably, his ideas of what it might take to set these ills to right. But his choice of a vehicle—a piece of indirect and ambiguous fiction—has led to an unending debate about what exactly he thought and intended.

It is now clear that More wrote first the second book of the work in which he described his imagined nation inhabiting the island of Utopia (Nowhere); that he added later the first book in which he provided the occasion for that depiction in a conversation between himself, some friends and a world-traveller called Ralph Hythloday, using that conversation to deploy his criticisms of England's polity; and that lastly he wrote the present conclusion.[1] He went to some trouble to preserve the illusion of reality, as in the prefatory letter to his friend Peter Giles in which he professes himself confused in his

---

[1] J. H. Hexter, *More's Utopia: the Genesis of an Idea* (1952), and 'Introduction' to *Complete Works of St. Thomas More* IV. *Utopia* (1965). For an important contribution on the meaning of the book see D. B. Fenlon, 'England and Europe: *Utopia* and its aftermath', *Transactions of the Royal Historical Society* (1975), pp. 115 ff.

memory of these imaginary conversations; and the details of his non-existent island are worked out precisely, down to the invention of its language and script. It is evident that More had much fun in the elaboration of what seems to have started as a game of wit with friends during his visit to the Netherlands in the autumn of 1515, on a commercial embassy on King Henry's behalf. There are jokes in *Utopia*, as in all More's writings, and the best one is unquestionably the whole concept of the book,[2] but behind the jests More's purpose was serious enough. He was the spokesman of a group, even a generation, of scholars. The many criticisms of society to which Erasmus and his circle had so often given scattered expression were here pulled together, and a possible pattern of a good society was set before the world. *Utopia* constituted a programme of reform.

In assessing this purpose one needs to distinguish between the negative criticisms and the positive proposals. The latter are, in a way, both striking and rather horrifying. In spite of much humane and sensible thought, More expressed a clear preference for a community strictly ordered, ruled on authoritarian lines, given to control by punishment, austere, uniform and essentially drab. Even Utopia has touches of liberty compared with the kingdom of the Polyrites whose totalitarian system, maintained by the lash, received praise from Hythloday. But the realm of Nowhere also is a severe place devoted to the maintenance of a fixed social order in which men live rational lives. Everything is so organized as to minimize or eliminate the play of the individual and assure enforced contentment with one's lot. The essence of Utopia consists in egalitarian fairness applied to the distribution of resources and guaranteed by an immovable structure of hierarchic paternalism. One can see why modern communists should have claimed More as a spiritual ancestor. The roots of More's ideal state should in fact be sought in a curious marriage between the life monastic and Plato's ordered commonwealth; community of goods in Utopia owes more to St Bernard than St Marx, while the dictatorship of his ruling caste

[2]Utopia probably reflects the impact of the great transatlantic discoveries: unknown realms had, after all, turned up, and more such could be waiting for the explorer (as Cortez soon proved). The book may also have helped to inspire More's brother-in-law, John Rastell (a man of ready enthusiasms), to project a colonizing voyage in 1517 which was to employ Sebastian Cabot's expert knowledge. The voyage foundered at Waterford, and the experience seems to have turned Cabot for a time against English expeditions even though such efforts in fact extended back beyond Columbus's first sailing (D. B. Quinn, *England and the Discovery of America, 1481–1620*, 1974). At any rate, his refusal to participate frustrated a typically imaginative venture to the New World proposed by Wolsey in 1521; and the cardinal met a similar refusal from the merchant community of London, despite some urgent pressure applied by the King himself. During Henry's reign, such enterprises thereafter slept, though' an occasional individual (fewer still came back) took ship to the northwest, and though one Bristol merchant at least (Robert Thorne) had enough vision to submit in 1527 a large scheme for government-controlled exploration.

recalls philosopher-kings rather than the proletariat.[3] But that More thought it necessary for the good life to eliminate private property is assuredly true, and from this conviction and its unflinching application stem most of the features which make Utopia so worthy and so depressing an ideal. The fact that the only form of art admitted to the island would seem to be music probably reflects only areas of insensitivity in More himself, as the curious customs touching the sexual relationship certainly reflect some highly personal attitudes.[4] But the general political, economic and social structure of that state, however much it may have been given substance by the author, represented much more than a personal view: here we find the ideal commonwealth of that close-knit group of scholarly reformers, devoid of one thing only—revealed religion. And in 1516, before Luther, the problem they wrestled with was that of the good society, not that of the Christian commonwealth. The Utopians' alleged willingness to accept Christianity appears in the book as a perfunctory afterthought, and More would seem to have held that their conversion neither need nor should have made any difference to their community and its social practices.

When More came to write Book I, he not only greatly improved the whole work by providing a pleasing fictitious framework but also supplied a very necessary explanation for his belief that men could not live good and orderly lives except in so restrictive a system as he had invented for his isle of Nowhere. His criticisms of the England of his day, through the mouth of Ralph Hythloday, extend to all the conventional topics—the evils of enclosure, the malpractices of middlemen, the ruthlessness of public servants, the frivolity of the noble classes, and the wicked policies of kings. More's vivid language has done much to embed these denunciations in the general consciousness; few can forget his once meek sheep now grown so savage that they eat up the men that used to till the land. However, More is no more to be trusted to present a considered or accurate description than academic critics and angry contemporaries usually are; his rage, for instance, at idle noblemen living in luxury on the rents extracted from beggared tenants is a moralistic commonplace, while his outburst against the commercial practices of graziers (alleged to be simply price-raisers) certainly echoes what consumers were saying

[3] It may be noted that More came to regard communism as pernicious. In his *Confutation of Tyndale* (1532) he equates the Anabaptists' belief in common ownership of goods with the common possession of women and a denial of Christ's divinity.

[4] It is well known that More wanted engaged couples to meet naked, so as to avoid disappointment on the wedding night. It seems to be less well known that he, who in one place approved the Utopians' realistic attitude to sexual pleasure, in another likened the carnal act to a bowel-movement or the scratching of an itch. Freud might have had fun with More, but it is more to the point that such notions recall attitudes common among the fifteenth-century extremists called Brethren of the Free Spirit.

but quite misunderstands the economics of cattle-breeding with which the hated 'engrossers' were of necessity quite familiar.[5] More did better with things he understood: his analysis of economic ills is as inadequate as his analysis of bad counsel-giving is acute. But what matters are not so much the details used to illustrate the rottenness of society as the roots of the trouble he identifies. Society is a conspiracy of rich men intent on making themselves richer,[6] and its purposes are all unchristian, from the money-grubbing of merchant and landlord to the warmongering of princes. Humanity is so eaten up with greed that it cannot be made to live rational and healthy lives in the setting ordinarily provided. More explicitly condemned many things against which Parliament had already tried to legislate; clearly, this experienced lawyer put little trust in the power of laws to remedy abuses. The only solution he could respect must remove underlying inducement to the underlying sins of greed and pride. Hence the absence of private property from Utopia where all men always have enough to maintain themselves and no more than their fellows; hence the grey moderation and humility of its social habits. More certainly permits well built houses, properly planned towns, well maintained irrigation works, and so forth, but no accumulation of wealth for future investment seems to be allowed even on the commonwealth's behalf.

What sort of a solution, however, is this? If human society cannot be made worthy except in an imaginary country placed in nowhere, is More offering any kind of answer to the practical problems of the day? Was he proposing that England should turn itself into Utopia? In the jocular pretending of his prefatory letter he may have spoken of people anxious to go to Utopia and wanting to have its location explained, but he, and everybody, knew that the place did not exist; it may be doubted whether he, or anybody, supposed that a state of that sort could exist outside the imagination. In this respect, therefore, *Utopia* expresses despair: the good commonwealth preached and forwarded by the Erasmians, More pointed out, was in this fallen world impossible. Despite its remarkable qualities of thought and lively zest, the book in practical terms testifies to a mixture of conscious and unconscious failure; with its emotional and inadequate analysis, and its rejection of practicable solutions, it altogether fails to offer a usable programme of reform. Once again, an essentially moral stance had led only to the conclusion that men,

[5] The production of beef cattle for the ever-expanding London market, for example, required the timely buying up of beasts for fattening, and they could not be fattened except by intensive pasturing, unfortunately available only on common lands.

[6] It may be noted that later in his life, in his *Dialogue concerning heresies* (1528), More came to a conclusion very different from that famous remark: 'For surely the rich man's substance', he says, taught by experience, 'is the well-spring of the poor man's living.'

being fallen men, could not really help themselves in this world.

Or rather, this would have to be one's conclusion except for one important section of the work—the discussion, towards the end of Book I, of the scholar's duty to enter the service of princes and bring to government the understanding and reforming purpose which he has acquired through his learning. For good reasons this was one of the lively academic debates of the day, and one in which Erasmus had already made his position plain. He held that the scholar's first duty was to his scholarship; all involvement in affairs detracted from his independence and weakened his authority. This is also the conclusion (backed by a conviction of the futility of conciliar service) that More allows his fictional *alter ego*, Hythloday, to pronounce: the scholar would only lose his freedom and gain nothing, for he had no hope of overcoming the power-hunger of the great and the self-seeking of courtiers. For once, however, the all-wise Ralph is not permitted to get his lordly way, and More, speaking in his own name, puts up a strong counterargument. So far as the pages of *Utopia* are concerned, the issue remains effectively unsettled. Instead More settled it in real life when, in August 1517 (shamefacedly failing to inform Erasmus for several months) he accepted Henry VIII's pressing invitation to become a councillor. Unlike his humanist friends, he had been conventionally trained for such a career; like his father, he might have pursued the law to a judgeship, and since September 1510 he had held the office of undersheriff of London, a busy administrative and judicial function. After the fateful embassy which sowed the seeds of *Utopia* he had twice more been employed as the King's representative in commercial negotiations on the continent. There was much logic in his entering the royal service, but for the author of *Utopia* the step involved more than the logic of a career. By taking office More in effect disavowed the despairing message of his book. He resolved to assist in making England a better commonwealth, to promote reforms for the ills he had diagnosed; and his friends, including for a time Erasmus, took the point when they applauded King Henry for his good sense in choosing so wise a councillor.

In 1517, the signs that the humanist statesman might indeed be able to apply his learning to affairs were, in fact, quite favourable. More was not the only representative of the group to follow the summons. His good friend Cuthbert Tunstall, also a member of the 1515 embassy, had become master of the Rolls the year before, and on that occasion More's had been the loudest voice in the chorus of rejoicing. Ruthal, to whom More had dedicated his translation of Lucian, had been bishop of Durham since 1509 and King's secretary for even longer; when in 1516 he was advanced to the keepership of the privy seal, he was succeeded as secretary by another humanist, Richard Pace. Other bishops appointed at this time—Nicholas West (Ely) in 1515, Charles Booth (Hereford) in 1517, John Veysey (Exeter) in 1519—were all respectable scholars (though of the civil law) and favourers of the new learning. Above all, the new master of the kingdom, Thomas Wolsey, not himself a scholar in the mould of Warham of Canterbury, showed every sign of wishing to emulate that aging prelate as a patron of scholars. Wolsey may have lacked learning, but his quick and generous mind responded readily to the teachings and ambitions of the learned. King Henry himself continued to favour the muses and play the part of Maecenas: his court was still a centre of a civilized and high-spirited concern with beauty, with the things of the mind, and with their practical use. The piety of Queen Catherine, eager to improve the Church with the willing assistance of Bishop Fisher, had only increased with the years and her several abortive pregnancies. If the promise of the reign's first years had been blighted by that spirit of adventure which demanded war, the King was now older and more settled, his wars had to all appearance brought sufficient glory, and he might be thought cured of the itch. The calls of reform, it would seem, could be pursued with greater hope of success. That, however, was not the way things turned out.

II

Wolsey consolidated his position in the years 1514–15, when he was already forty-three years old—eighteen years older than his King and by contemporary standards a late arrival in a place of power. His earlier career had been curiously broken and meandering. The brilliant son of an Ipswich butcher, he had conventionally opted for the Church, the best highroad to fame and fortune for anyone born without privilege, and he made a powerful impression as a student at Oxford. Yet though he took his bachelor's degree (allegedly) at fifteen and became a fellow of his college (Magdalen), he never progressed beyond the master's degree and the somewhat lowly positions of bursar of Magdalen and master of its school. One wonders why he did not continue the conventional preparation for a public career by studying the civil law. When eventually he became a bishop he was almost the only member of the bench without a doctorate.[7] According to tradition, Magdalen dispensed with his

---

[7] Hugh Oldham (Exeter) had got as far as BCL; only Robert Sherbourn (Chichester) paralleled Wolsey's MA.

services when he employed college funds for building purposes
without bothering to get the necessary authority: he was always to
love building and to believe in ignoring the rules. By slow stages, in
the service of this or that middling official, he brought himself to the
notice of Henry VII who appointed him one of his chaplains in
1507, a promotion which most clerical careerists would have expected to gain at an earlier age. The breakthrough came with Wolsey's
attachment to Bishop Foxe of Winchester and the accession of Henry
VIII. By November 1509 he was King's almoner and as such a
member of the Council, for the post was at this time always held by
one of the councillors specializing in hearing the pleas of those
allegedly too poor or weak to get justice in the ordinary courts.
Wolsey, who had no law of any sort, performed these judicial duties
with a zest that never left him.

He now also began to accumulate preferments, but it was the war
that made him. Here his immense capacity for work and his
clear-headed talent for organizing things had full play in the
management of the King's armies. During 1513 he began to outrun
his seniors on the Council until even his master Foxe found his pupil
too much for him; early in 1514 he at last achieved promotion to the
episcopate (Lincoln), then obtained Tournai, and, when Cardinal
Bainbridge died at Rome exchanged Lincoln for York, the second
see in the kingdom. Such a rise was possible only to a King's
favourite, and from 1513 it is indeed clear that he had seized the
coat-tails that mattered. Henry's pressure at Rome made his friend a
cardinal in September 1515; in December that year, Warham also
gave way to pressure and surrendered the great seal to the new star.
Wolsey would dearly have liked to exchange York (which during his
years of power he never visited) for Canterbury and thus add the
primacy in the Church to his highest office in the state; but Warham
obstinately outlived him, and Wolsey was forced to achieve his end
by a more dubious method with serious consequences for himself and
the Church. He determined to obtain from the Pope a permanent
grant of appointment as legate *a latere*, that is a permanent transfer
to him of the papal authority over the two provinces of the English
Church, a grant for which there was no precedent but which would
subordinate Canterbury to himself.[8] Though the Pope proved re-

---

[8]Papal legates were officials who exercised the jurisdictional authority of the head of the
Church by delegation. An agent domiciled in the country where he operated was called *legatus
natus*, and both archbishops by virtue of their office held that position which left the direct and
appeal jurisdiction of Rome intact. A *legatus a latere* was a special envoy with exceptional
powers (any such as the pope wished him to have for the occasion), sent from Rome to deal
with a particular matter. Wolsey in effect wanted to convert the commonplace functions of the
former into the most extensive exercise open to the latter by becoming a resident delegate
permanently substituting for the pope in England.

luctant he finally gave way and in 1518 bestowed the title—limited at first but converted into a grant for life in 1524.

For a man of such evident ambition, so justly conscious of his powers, and so clearly an uncomplicated activist untroubled by speculative thought or spiritual reservations, the slow climb to power must have been very frustrating; the impatience, arrogance and upstart contempt which were to earn him so much enmity can be understood, though hardly, since they seriously impeded his work, condoned. Wolsey wanted to get things done: he genuinely believed in improving the condition of England and promoting her outward glory, and he held a conveniently high opinion of her monarch. He had all the energy and much of the competence required, though he lacked intellectual foundations, larger beliefs and bureaucratic expertise; simply and enthusiastically, he always ran at whatever things he wanted to do, regardless of systems, of other people, and of too many realities. He was a eupeptic man, full of simple cheer, ready wit, and charm; he was good company, and more rarely ill than most people at the time. He liked to be friends all round, finding it extremely difficult to refuse the promise of a favour even when he knew that he could not perform it. At the same time he never forgot a slight and paid off all scores, real and imagined. But the chief defects in his character were an uncomplicated greed and a passion for pomp. He enjoyed life recklessly—eating, building, fornicating—and in consequence needed more and more money; too many of his activities were really designed to enlarge his lavish income. Thus he gave many a handle to his enemies, which mattered because he had only one friend—the King whose trust formed the sole base of his power. This fact Wolsey rarely forgot. Like others, he knew how to manipulate one who believed himself always to be in perfect control of all that went on, but those who reckoned that his years of power could be called the reign of the cardinal made a mistake not shared by the cardinal himself.

Though it was domestic administration that had brought Wolsey to greatness, it was the international stage that best enabled him to satisfy his own and Henry's thirst for glory. The treaty with France of 1514 which signalled England's successful conclusion of Henry's early ventures was Wolsey's work. That success lasted less time even than such things usually do. On the last day of that year, Louis XII died, worn out, malice said, by his efforts to satisfy his young and active wife, Henry's sister Mary. The new King of France, in every way Henry's equal as an embodiment of Renaissance splendour, possessed much superior resources. Francis I had no mind to accept the relative defeat in which his predecessor's policy had ended, and from the first he set himself up in conscious rivalry with his brother of England. Two fighting cocks in one arena, both arrogant, confident of their athletic skills, pattern (allegedly) of the modern prince with his feet in both the knightly and scholarly camps; they were bound to clash, and the politics of Europe were bound to be affected by their distrust and dislike. Both at this point overlooked the dimmer figure of young Charles, duke of Burgundy since 1506 and soon, in 1516, to succeed to the crowns of Castile and Aragon.

Francis at once made it plain that the 1514 treaty[9] was dead when he paid no heed to English attempts to transfer his predecessor's widow to himself. This suited Mary who queered the pitch of English diplomacy by secretly marrying Henry's best friend, Charles Brandon, duke of Suffolk, sent to France to arrange for her future there. She claimed to have had a promise of free choice the second time round by way of reward for taking the unprepossessing Louis XII for her first husband, but the clandestine marriage roused Henry's fury which took much appeasing. In the course of 1515, Francis overthrew the earlier settlement and put England under threat. In September, the battle of Marignano restored French ascendancy in northern Italy, and the French-assisted return to Scotland of the duke of Albany, anti-English claimant to the Stuart succession, destroyed any chance of exploiting the victory of Flodden by creating a permanent Anglophil control in that kingdom. Thus there was nothing for it: Wolsey had to renew negotiations with Ferdinand and Maximilian. By October 1515 he had framed an alliance with the former under which England's contribution would be confined to financial assistance; for the present at least neither he nor Henry wanted to engage in any more active war. But even the policy decided upon needed money, and money meant Parliament. In view of Wolsey's first experience, earlier in the year, of managing one, this cast grave doubts upon the prospects of an active foreign policy.

In November 1514 the writs went out for a Parliament to meet in February 1515, and after prorogation in April the assembly met for a second session in November–December. It produced a modest amount of legislation, virtually none of it (so it would seem) of government promotion. A few acts attended to minor problems of the economy and the law. This was assuredly no reforming Parliament. The crown achieved a sumptuary law which had failed to pass in 1512, as well as the much needed supply: the first session yielded a subsidy planned to raise £100,000, while the second added another designed to bring in the more than fifty per cent shortfall of the first and topped up with a fifteenth and tenth. The amount of money demanded was relatively modest. From the point of view of reform,

[9] See above, p. 41.

the only interesting measure was yet another attempt to stop de-
populating enclosure by compelling the restoration to tillage of land
converted away from it since the beginning of this Parliament. This
was a government bill which passed in the first session, but only on
condition that the act should not endure beyond Christmas 1515;
however, Wolsey used the second session to get it made permanent.
His evident willingness to do something about the alleged cause of
all the economic troubles of the realm may have played its part in
persuading Thomas More into government service. We may also
note an act which, initiated by the Commons, gave that House
formal control over its own members by demanding a Speaker's
licence for absence.

However, the real significance of this Parliament did not for once
lie in legislative achievement but in the fact that it provided the
opportunity for revealing the precarious position of the Church's
liberties when confronted with popular anticlericalism and the
power of the Crown. The crisis of the year revolved around the
relations between the *regnum* and the *sacerdotium*, an ancient problem.
In the fourteenth century it had led to the Statutes of Provisors and
Praemunire which delimited spheres of action for the royal and the
spiritual courts, equipped the former with powers to restrain the
latter from trenching on 'the king's regality', and threatened the
papacy with consequences if it interfered with the possessory rights of
crown and nation. The writ of praemunire lay against anyone
invading the rights of the King and the common-law courts; the
elastic imprecision of this definition was made worse by the formidable penalties—permanent imprisonment and loss of movables. The
action, once designed to stop papal aggression, had early become an
ordinary weapon in the conflict of jurisdictions, mostly used by
private persons troubled with the courts Christian; its political
potential, though long dormant, remained great. But crown and
papacy had long since arrived at à happy *modus vivendi*, now embodied in the cardinal/chancellor; it was unfortunate for Wolsey that
at the very outset of his career he should have been confronted with
a forceful reminder that the double basis of his power linked
essentially incompatible claims to supremacy.

The crisis itself grew from two separate events, one touching the
ordinary behaviour of the Church and its relations to the people, the
other directly involving the claims of statute and prerogative. The
first is known as the case of Richard Hunne, the second as that of
Friar Standish.

Hunne's case was a classic *cause célèbre*, a major scandal that roused
immediate passions and enduring memories, so much so that
Thomas More still felt compelled fifteen years later to settle its truth

against anticlerical propagandists and in the process quite plainly neglected the truth himself.[10] Hunne was a substantial London merchant with patent Lollard sympathies, or at any rate a man who believed in people's right to read the Scriptures in the vernacular. His troubles with the Church started in March 1511 when he refused to pay a mortuary fee demanded by the priest, Thomas Dryffeld, who had buried his infant son. After waiting for over a year, Dryffeld quite fairly determined to end this typical lay resistance to clerical exactions by bringing a suit in the archbishop's court at Lambeth, and in May 1512 Tunstall, as Warham's chancellor, correctly (as the law stood) found for the plaintiff. Hunne counterattacked in the King's Bench in the Hilary term 1513, suing a praemunire against the priest and his legal advisers on the grounds that the action in the church court had been an invasion of the rights of the common law. It is hard to see what case he could have had since mortuaries and other spiritual fees were generally agreed to be within the jurisdiction of the spiritual courts. So far as the record goes—the adjournments term by term extended beyond Hunne's death—the action was never settled, though (according to More) it seems probable that the Bench was at last coming round to finding against him; its hesitancy probably reflects no more than the common law's usual reluctance to admit limits to its own jurisdiction.

Hunne had thus reopened the conflict between the King's courts and those of the Church, and if More is to be believed he had done so quite deliberately, intending that his case should become famous in the precedents of the law. However, it was the action of the ecclesiastical authorities, especially of Bishop Fitzjames of London, a noted conservative of cholerically authoritarian views, which wrote Hunne into the nation's memory. Infuriated by this attack on clerical privilege, Fitzjames instigated heresy proceedings against Hunne on 2 December 1514, charging him with possessing a Lollard bible and other forbidden works. Hunne was committed to the bishop's prison and found there, two days later, hanging dead from a beam. Suspicion fell at once upon Charles Joseph, the jailer, and his assistant, though William Horsey, the bishop's vicar-general, was also implicated. In an attempt to hush the matter up, the church authorities acted rashly and foolishly. They maintained that Hunne, conscious of his heresy, had committed suicide, and they proceeded posthumously with the process against him. On 10 December a sermon was preached on his sins at St Paul's Cross; on the 16th

[10] Cf. A. Ogle, *The Tragedy of the Lollards' Tower* (1949); R. J. Schoeck, 'Common Law and Canon Law in their relation to Thomas More', *St. Thomas More: Action and Contemplation*, edited by R. S. Sylvester (1972), especially pp. 23–42; A. F. Pollard, *Wolsey* (1929), pp. 31 ff.; S. C. F. Milsom, 'Richard Hunne's "Praemunire"', *English Historical Review* LXXVI (1961), pp. 81 ff.

sentence was pronounced; on the 20th his corpse was burned for heresy. Naturally this caused an uproar in London where Hunne had friends; few then (and none now) could think well of this macabre treatment. In addition, the Church had been unable to keep out a coroner's inquest, properly convened in this case of an unexplained death, and the jury had had time to view the body and the chamber in which it was found. The jury deliberated into February before bringing in a verdict of murder against Horsey and Joseph, the second of whom had raised suspicion by fleeing the capital in late December but when caught in January had implicated the first. Horsey was arrested pending trial. Whether Hunne was murdered or not has never been settled. More throughout stuck to the opinion that he had committed suicide, but the coroner's report certainly casts massive doubt on this: murder remains the more likely answer. What no one has ever settled or even discussed is why Joseph (the most likely culprit) should have killed Hunne, or why Horsey (as was and is supposed) should have authorized the deed. They had nothing to gain from doing away with Hunne when the heresy trial—which would assuredly have run badly for him—had barely begun. Perhaps one may suspect an unfortunate accident, some scuffle during which Hunne's neck was broken, with Joseph clumsily trying to rig the evidence.[11]

What mattered at the time was the immediate public outcry; the Church's reputation, already enough tarnished by the treatment of Hunne's dead body, came to be involved in the fate of the men accused of the crime. Fitzjames wrote hysterically to Wolsey, claiming that no London jury could be trusted to treat Horsey fairly and seeking the cardinal's assistance in protecting a member of the spiritualty. Wolsey, in great difficulties, could have done without this appeal. At the height of the passion, and before the coroner's jury had finished their proceedings, Parliament had met, to provide both a platform for the people's anticlericalism and the occasion for confusing the case of Richard Hunne with the more far-reaching issue of the rights of the Church.

The case of Friar Standish really took its origin in the Parliament of 1512 which had passed an act—seemingly not one initiated by the Crown—limiting benefit of clergy to men in 'holy orders'. Benefit of clergy was the name given to the privilege enjoyed by persons able to prove that they were clerics who, if accused of felony in the King's courts, could demand to be handed over for trial and punishment to the bishop of the diocese. Since those able to claim benefit included large numbers in minor orders (psalmist, lector, acolyte, exorcist)

---

[11] It seems agreed that Hunne died of a broken neck, but the jury found also damage on his body which suggests that he had suffered injuries in a fight.

who were only technically clerical, and since episcopal punishment
was in practice meaningless, the privilege had become a licence to
what were often professional criminals.[12] The act was not well
drafted, especially in not defining what it meant by holy orders: it
probably intended only the major ones—subdeacon, deacon, priest.
It was also, like so many of the time, limited in duration and due for
renewal in the Parliament of 1515. Some people thought it a worthy
measure in the fight against crime; thus John Taylor, clerk of the
Parliaments, went out of his way to praise it when addressing the
Convocation of 1514. However, in that same year the papal Lateran
Council expressly reasserted the full claims of clerical immunity from
secular jurisdiction which had not been observed for centuries in
England or elsewhere. In 1515 the Hunne case made the issue of the
expiring act more than a matter of principle, as Fitzjames saw
quickly enough: if there was no renewal he might be able to save
Horsey from the trial in King's Bench which was sure to convict
him. That is what is usually alleged: but since Horsey, in priest's
orders, was not deprived of the privilege by the statute, it is more
likely that the bishop meant to go the whole hog, revive the extreme
assertions of immunity, and save Horsey even from being 'con-
vented' (charged) before the secular court. He took two steps to this
end: he used the spiritual majority in the Lords to block the renewal
of the act, and he put up Richard Kidderminster, abbot of
Winchcombe, to preach on the topic at St Paul's Cross on the day
before Parliament assembled.[13]

The abbot's sermon, on the text 'Touch not mine annointed', did
what was intended. He uncompromisingly demanded the exemption
from the King's criminal jurisdiction of all persons claiming membership of the Church, however lowly their orders, and expressly
attacked the act of 1512 as an invasion of the lawful privilege. The
challenge to Parliament was undisguised, and both Houses responded eagerly. As soon as the preliminaries of the session were out
of the way, the act was introduced for renewal in the Lords, but the
bishops apparently succeeded in preventing any further proceedings
upon it. Two days later, nine leading peers were appointed to meet
as a committee with representatives of the Commons to consider
'certain causes touching the temporalty'. They produced an appeal
to the King which asked him to settle the dispute of jurisdictions and
incidentally free the King's Bench for action against Horsey. Henry

---

[12] In the secular court the privilege was proved by the reading of a verse (which could be
memorized), usually the very apposite first verse of the first psalm; a clerk remitted to the
bishop's court was there usually permitted to defeat the charge by purging himself, that is by
bringing ordinarily eight men to swear to his good fame.

[13] The open-air pulpit at Paul's Cross was regularly used for propaganda purposes; the
choice of the preacher belonged to the bishop of London.

arranged a meeting at which, in his presence, experts in the canon law argued the case before the judges. There Henry Standish, warden of the London Franciscans and retained of counsel with the King, defended the act and the general practice of bringing criminous clerks into the secular courts, alleging the custom of centuries. The meeting ended inconclusively, but Standish was now a marked man. The Commons also pressed their purpose: they demanded, in vain, that Kidderminster should publicly withdraw his opinion, and they passed a bill renewing the 1512 act which received two readings in the Lords but was sufficiently delayed there by debate to miss passage before the prorogation.

During the long recess the bigots in the church, Fitzjames leading, went after Standish; in October he was cited before Convocation to answer charges of heresy, drawn out of sermons he had allegedly preached during the summer in support of the views he had expressed at the King's conference. Standish, who knew better than to take his chances with his clerical enemies, instead appealed for protection to Henry. Then, on 12 November, the Parliament reassembled, and the Commons at once revived the agitation for a renewal of the act of 1512. Once again the bishops had no trouble in blocking this move in the Lords, but the attack on Standish misfired badly. A second conference met by Henry's order to discuss the charges against the friar and to seek the opinion of the judges on the claims of the clergy; this time, ominously, representatives of both Houses of Parliament were in attendance. Standish, assured of the one protection that mattered, stood firm, and after much debate the judges delivered themselves of the opinion that his persecutors had fallen into the praemunire by invading the King's regality; they thus stood in danger of life imprisonment and forfeiture of goods, a fate from which only Henry's pardon could save them. The threat sufficed, and the spiritualty hastened to mend its fences. A few days later, at Baynard's Castle, in the presence of all the Lords and most of the Commons, Wolsey knelt before Henry to seek pardon for any offence against the Crown, but also to repeat that the issue of clerical immunity remained open. He asserted that to all the clergy it appeared against the law of God to call a spiritual man into a temporal court and asked that a decision be postponed until a papal ruling could be obtained. This led to more debate, in the course of which Henry showed himself firmly on the side of Standish, the judges, and his own royal rights. At the end Warham also asked for the matter to be referred to Rome, but the King ignored him. Everybody then went home.

The events of that year were important enough to have here been retold at some length, but just what had happened and what did it signify? The clerk of the Parliaments had cause to end the journal of the year with a lament about the conflicts between spiritualty and temporalty; and ever since historians, looking forward, have treated the conflicts as a dress rehearsal for the later battle over clerical privilege and papal power, especially as both struggles involved Parliament and an assertion of some form of supremacy in the King. For Henry allegedly took occasion at Baynard's Castle to speak of kings of England as monarchs who had never had any earthly superior but God alone.[14] Yet there is much danger in interpreting events so determinedly from hindsight. It is, of course, true that both Houses of Parliament displayed a powerful animus against the clergy, and that King and judges defended the powers of the common law over all Englishmen, whether they were lay or spiritual. It is also true that Hunne's case remained in the memory as part of the political folklore of anticlericalism. But despite all the noise the outcome, to say the least, was modest. The act of 1512 was never renewed. Moves in Parliament to aid Hunne's children were blocked by the bishop of London. Over Horsey, the authorities reached a compromise: in return for a heavy extra-curial fine, the attorney general did not proceed with the indictment in the Bench, and though he was removed from the centre of disturbance he was given quite lavish preferments in other dioceses.[15] Standish went untroubled, but despite the royal favour, so manifestly bestowed, he had to wait quite a while for positive benefits. In April 1518, against Wolsey's wish and to the disgust of the clerical party, he was promoted to the bishopric of St Asaph. Wolsey managed to extort a characteristically petty revenge for his defeats when Standish, rashly following common practice, had himself consecrated by the archbishop of Canterbury before his temporalities had been restored and before he had formally renounced any provision in his papal bull of appointment 'in derogation of our sovereign lord's crown and dignity'. Now threatened in his turn with praemunire, Standish acknowledged his error at the bar of the King's Council; not content with this, Wolsey made him come back a fortnight later, this time to

[14] Did Henry really make this famous remark? The evidence comes from the narrative of events included in the volume called *Keilwey's Reports*, a set of law reports mostly from the pen of John Carrell (cf. L. W. Abbott, *Law Reporting in England, 1485–1585*, 1973, pp. 39 ff.). In other words, the narrative is reasonably contemporary. It has been argued, quite convincingly, that it was actually compiled by Standish (Ogle, *Tragedy of the Lollards' Tower*, pp. 154 ff.). However, the most convincing proof of such authenticity is the inclusion, among the law French of the account, of two bits of direct speech in English. Henry's speech is given in French—why? His words fit perfectly with the attitudes he adopted from about 1530 onwards, but very little with his known views on papal authority at the crucial time and years after.

[15] Contrary to A. F. Pollard's statement (*Wolsey*, pp. 51, no. 1) he retained his precentorship of St Paul's until 1531; he died in 1543, never again having made any sort of appearance on the public stage.

kneel and beg the lay lords to intercede with Wolsey who was to sue for Standish's pardon.[16] This childish tit-for-tat will have worked off some of Wolsey's spleen and no doubt humiliated Standish. More important, Wolsey took care to stop Standish from moving further up the ladder; the new bishop ended his days at St Asaph in 1536, and though from 1529 he was out of favour with Henry for new reasons, before that his failed career must have resulted from Wolsey's enmity. To a sixteenth-century clerical careerist, eighteen years in one of the poverty-stricken Welsh sees represented real failure.

The anticlerical vapours of 1515 amounted to neither a notable triumph for the laity nor anything resembling an anticipation of the Reformation. The most interesting thing to emerge from them is the attitude of mind they reveal dominant among the clergy. The whole affair had arisen only because the leaders of the Church were determined to exalt their status and to stamp out heresy. Not only an old bigot like Fitzjames, but a humanist courtier like Warham and an unabashed royalist like Wolsey had taken their stand upon immunity and privilege. Hating all possible deviation and resentful of petty attacks on their 'liberties', they had lashed out at Hunne; infuriated by the popular reaction to Hunne's very unnecessary death, they had quickly involved themselves in an attack on Parliament and common law. In the ensuing confrontation they had certainly come off worse, but—a little public abasement apart—they had lost nothing. Even after the judges had delivered their opinion and the King had signified his agreement, Wolsey and Warham (on their knees) had managed to get the substantive issue suspended to await a word from the Pope (not that this was ever sought). It is evident that clerical arrogance remained high—far higher than the usual talk of royal control and lay dislike of ecclesiastical pretensions would lead one to think. The policy of Henry VII, with its formalized piety, devotion to Rome, and use of clerical councillors in places of importance had helped to create an assurance of safe superiority, and so far nothing that his son had done had given the Church cause to wonder. Its leaders manifestly drew quite the wrong conclusions from the events of 1515—the conclusion that they were safe to go on as before. Talk of reform was pretty common, and commonplace; in 1510, for instance, at a council of the province of Canterbury, Warham and Colet had both in their different ways tried to start moves for the reform of abuses. Nothing came of this, whereas the first opportunity was taken with both hands to reassert a high papalism in defence of so outstanding an abuse as immunity for

---

[16] For the first occasion see the Council transcripts in Huntington Library, MS El 2655; for the second, Public Record Office, Star Chamber Proceedings, 2/75.

criminals only technically linked with the Church. With Wolsey ascendant and Henry still ostentatiously a good and loyal servant of Rome, the Church was really riding higher than ever, not perhaps apprehending a dark future. Meetings of Parliament were to be avoided, and Wolsey determined to do his best to avoid them. Otherwise, the liberties of the clerical estate seemed safe enough. The lesson of 1515 is not that the Church was already fully subjected to the King's regality and supremacy, but that it had the highest opinion of its independence, was incapable of reforming itself, and altogether failed to read the signs aright.

III

The Parliament had been agony for Wolsey, anxious to get on with his plans. However, he also gained benefits: the troubles of the year helped to persuade Foxe and Warham that they had lost their taste for politics, and to persuade Henry that he needed a new chief minister. On 5 December Wolsey at last obtained the great seal, and his episcopal seniors ceased to attend Council meetings. The new chancellor was not slow to tighten the reins of policy, but what he regarded as his first duty in the commonwealth had nothing to do with reform of the Church and little with reform of the major troubles of the state. On 5 May 1516,[17] in a very full session of the Council and in Henry's presence, he held forth at length about 'enormities in the realm' which, he said, arose from failure to administer the law justly. He announced his intention to see the law enforced against the powerful and begged the King to assist, a help which Henry—solemnly expressing himself in favour of justice—said he was very willing to give. Of course, there was truth in Wolsey's charges. Despite Henry VII's achievements, many men still escaped the consequences of illegal actions and violent transgressions because they enjoyed protection and favour, or because the normal processes of the law, with its technicalities and delays, prevented justice from being done. And Wolsey thought that he had an instrument ready to hand to make the law effective; he proposed to revive Henry VII's practice of using the King's Council in the active general oversight of law and order. The reaction against the first Tudor's methods had now sufficiently worn off for such methods to be again acceptable; desirable they had always been, from the point of view of the public interest.

[17] The transcript in Huntington Library MS El 2655 places the occasion in 1515, but since Wolsey is called cardinal (created September 1515) that date must be wrong.

The administration of the English common law did not lack machinery; the network of local courts, with the centralizing super-structure of the King's courts at Westminster which in turn reached into the shires by means of itinerant judges and delegated commis-sions, provided in theory all that the subject, seeking justice or hoping to profit by litigation, could desire. As Wolsey was to discover, he could not hope to secure enforcement of the law, especially of those penal laws that controlled social and economic behaviour, outside the courts of common law. Social legislation usually belonged to the Exchequer, while serious crimes—felonies—were triable only in King's Bench or the local com-missions (oyer and terminer, gaol delivery) controlled by it. Wolsey neither had, nor attempted to gain, any hand in their operations. Instead he concentrated on those tribunals in which, as chancellor, he ruled the roost. In the first place this meant the Court of Chancery in which he certainly sat frequently, dispensing his personal brand of justice to petitioners, but so far we know little about his activities there or his influence on the court's development. He took over a going concern and, apart probably from working it harder, did nothing to settle its organization; he inherited a rather vague set of guidelines designed to remedy hardships or deficiencies in the law and to all appearance did nothing to settle the law administered there. Wolsey was exceptional among the King's non-noble councillors in that he had no law of any sort, neither common nor civil nor canon; for this lack he liked to substitute his untutored common sense and a genuine desire to help people in their troubles. In the sixteenth century, disputes arising out of material for lawsuits were often settled, at least temporarily, by private arbitra-tion if both parties agreed to seek some eminent person's opinion; Wolsey as judge in Chancery seems to have regarded his task as that of arbiter supreme, cutting through the inanities of personal and legal problems with a self-confidence born of ignorance. No doubt he had his successes, but the indications are that he caused as much trouble as he cured, leaving disputes still open and still forced to go to law. The matters brought to the Chancery were often far too technical to be solved by his methods.

The Council's jurisdiction, on the face of it, offered a better opportunity for this type of benevolent despotism, and we are also better informed how Wolsey used it.[18] There need no longer be any doubt that it was he who turned a jurisdiction hitherto intermingled

---

[18] This account rests upon J. A. Guy, 'The Court of Star Chamber during Wolsey's Ascend-ancy' (unpublished dissertation, Cambridge, 1973). See also his articles, 'Wolsey's Star Chamber: a Study in Archival Reconstruction', *Journal of the Society of Archivists* v (1975), pp. 169 ff., and 'Wolsey, the Council, and the Council Courts', *English Historical Review* xc (1976), pp. 481 ff.

with all sorts of other Council business into a settled court, the Court of Star Chamber. By 1520 at the latest everyone concerned accepted the existence of this tribunal as a formal, open and regular place of trial and judgement, separate from the private conduct of the Council's administrative and advisory functions. In name, and also in its judiciary, the Star Chamber continued to be the King's Council adjudicating upon complaints brought before it, but by setting aside fixed days for such hearings, by sticking to the law terms, and by elaborating a regular procedure with regular documentation and regular fees, Wolsey (and the clerks he appointed) created what was for all purposes an ordinary court of the realm. As always, the cardinal's lack of interest in the fundamentals left his creation unfinished; to him Star Chamber meant an active extension of his personality, and he failed to give it the shape which would ensure continued activity without him. It took the organizing bent of the 1530s to round off also this institution, but the full flowering of conciliar jurisdiction in a settled court must nevertheless be put to Wolsey's credit.

Credit is the right word because the court was to do much useful work in bringing order into the administration of the law. In Wolsey's own day, it developed rather differently from its creator's intentions. As he indicated in his policy speech to the Council and in such remarks as that he would teach a high-placed lawbreaker 'the law of the Star Chamber', he planned to employ the weight of Council authority directly upon disturbers of the peace and oppressors of the weak. This noble ideal produced very little practical effect. In the whole of his fourteen years, during which at least 1,700 cases came before the court, fewer than a dozen were initiated by the Crown. The Council's jurisdiction had always been moved by the subject's petition, and Wolsey could not alter this; he discovered that crown prosecutions belonged in the common-law courts where he had no function and little authority. But by revitalizing the Council—which, despite his monopoly of political advice and decision-making, he maintained in full strength and frequent term-time sittings—he immediately encouraged a litigious nation to come in their multitudes. His readiness to hear complaints, based on his conviction that he could do good to the disadvantaged, attracted a rapidly swelling mass of suits. Few of these quite fitted his preconceptions. Most were started by people trying to sort their affairs or advance their ambitions, and too many were frivolous—brought to trouble an enemy, obtain an improper advantage, or cross an action at law which was quite rightly going against the complainant. Wolsey soon lost some of his innocence but never, it seems, his zest; he even abandoned the earlier practice of binding complainants in sureties (to prevent malicious or frivolous complaints), and only his successors reintroduced this very sensible method for sorting the necessary from the unwanted.

Though too many Star Chamber cases ended inconclusively, though too often the chancellor had to repeat ineffective decrees, and though common-sense justice was no better served by Wolsey than by the ordinary courts, he did some good. Now and again his methods paid off, as when in 1525 he ended a dispute between the prior and the city of Norwich that had been going on since 1491 by himself paying for the draining and hedging of a large common at Norwich, a generosity which for a time brought peace. The real effect, however, of Wolsey's idiosyncratic administration lay in the development of Star Chamber's authority over cases of public disorder, contempt of the law, misbehaviour in office, and personal violence—in the creation of a tribunal so exalted that even the powerful came to recognize the limits of their selfish power. Wolsey, that is, turned litigants' purposes to his own intended ends. Though most of the cases heard dealt with property rights (and in consequence always left open the further resort to the common law where alone such issues could be finally settled), the principle that the court had jurisdiction only if some form of physical or other violence had taken place set the Star Chamber on the way to a reform of the criminal law which the country badly needed. Dispensing with the jury, and basing its decisions on the parties' sworn statements and witnesses' sworn depositions, the court developed methods of establishing the truth and attitudes concerning facts and motives which were to help transform the jury trial of the common law. Star Chamber could not deal with anything that threatened a man's life or freehold, and that rule was observed, but such limitations (which excluded felonies and treasons from its competence) still left a vast area of importance where forcible dispossession, corruption of legal process by maintenance or perjury, or the exercise of undisguised power reduced the effectiveness of the law. Unable to initiate action in such cases, Wolsey still, by proclaiming his desire to help, built a large practice increasingly helpful to the law in its efforts to become effective.

The size of the practice brought its problems. It was quickly apparent that even after it had set aside regular days reserved for judicial business the Council could not find time to deal with all that came before it. Backlogs piled up with disconcerting rapidity. Here again Wolsey's lack of interest in fundamental administrative reform produced chaos. He preferred his usual, entirely personal, expedients—in this case the setting up of *ad hoc* and short-lived committees upon which he devolved the less weighty cases. Special committees, duplicating the work of yet another body of councillors, the Court of Requests, appeared very early, in 1517, 1518 and 1520; and throughout his rule attempts were made to get the preliminary stages of hearings dealt with by delegation. But since such bodies either had no power to determine cases or, when given power, felt unable to do so, everything in the end came back to the overworked sittings of the court, and the pile-up continued. At times Wolsey tried to improve organization. In 1523 he added a third clerk to the tiny establishment of the court, picking a young intellectual of humanist tastes in Thomas Elyot who, after a rough time in that office (his seniors gave him the worst drudgery and the least profit) was to make his name as the reign's foremost popularizer of other people's ideas.[19] In 1526–7 plans were drawn up for the reform of the overlarge Council which contemplated devolving all Star Chamber business upon a body of lesser councillors. Predictably (and fortunately, since this reform would have weakened the court's authority) these came to nothing, but the solution adopted—wholesale delegation of cases to the localities where they had arisen, by the use of regional councils in the north and the Welsh marches, and by setting up shire commissions—destroyed the rationale of the court. When Wolsey fell, his zeal for justice and his inability to embody it in efficient institutions had produced widespread confusion. At the centre, the Council was at its wits' end what to do about the flood of often very superfluous petitions; while the emergency measures taken had remitted too many cases to just those places where conciliar authority was weak and where the evils that Wolsey strove to suppress could play freely. This superb amateur in government served a useful purpose by exploiting the possibilities of a fertile mind and a flexible set of institutions, but it was as well that he was succeeded by professionals who knew how to create something permanent, and permanently valuable, out of Wolsey's undisciplined imagination.

In all this activity, therefore, the cardinal was attending to one of the complaints of the reformers (and of *Utopia*), but not in the orderly way or with the happy results that they had postulated. From his own point of view, which in this case coincided with the interests of the state, these activities in Chancery, Star Chamber and Requests further raised some very serious questions touching the cohesion of the social order upon which Tudor government depended. In the first place, so much busy adjudication outside the fences of the common-law courts posed problems to the law's universal rule. Chancery jurisdiction had grown up because the law

[19]See below, p. 161; and see in general S. E. Lehmberg, *Sir Thomas Elyot: Tudor Humanist* (1960), though on Elyot as clerk of the Star Chamber Dr Guy corrects some errors.

did not provide for such common practices as enfeoffment to uses[20] or the performance of unwritten agreements: it had from the first been complementary to the law rather than in competition with it. Star Chamber, too, was thought of as a tribunal backing up the law rather than detracting from its supremacy. The employment of equitable considerations in settling people's disputes and making them observe the rules was, from the first, a filling in of gaps, nor would it be true to say that in the early sixteenth century the ordinary courts themselves were incapable of introducing such principles into the application of the law. However, Wolsey's administration of justice proved so active and enterprising that the relationship stood in danger of altering: the cardinal was accused of using equity to supersede the law, and an equity moreover so personal as to be capricious. Criticism concentrated on the procedural weapons of his court, especially the writ of summons called the subpoena[21] and the injunction which was employed not only to stop individuals from dubious action until the truth of the case was established but also to interrupt the processes of the law itself. Without these weapons, Chancery and Star Chamber were powerless. At a time when the equity courts were dominated by a man who had neither knowledge of nor respect for the common law, conflicts could readily arise over instruments so powerful and so freely used to by-pass the law courts and create much uncertainty for litigants. At his fall, the resentment against Wolsey came out freely and fiercely. However, the debate had before this, in 1523, produced a classic defence of both equity and subpoena from a common lawyer, Christopher St German, whose *Doctor and Student* laid down the lines along which cooperation between the systems was to develop in the future. St German recognized the need for the sort of flexibility which equity preserved in the legal relationships of the people, established its place as an aid rather than a rival to the common law, and accepted the right of the crown to create such new remedies as the subpoena. Despite some occasional rumblings, this remained the leading position on this contentious issue, though it is doubtful if peaceful relations could have been maintained if Wolsey had not been succeeded as chancellor by a series of eminent common lawyers who naturalized his amateur inventions in the law.

The other problem derived from less elevated, more mundane, apprehensions. It quickly became clear that Wolsey's concern for the poor could at times be little more than an animus against the rich

[20]See below, p. 147.

[21]The equity courts summoned parties by a writ of privy seal or great seal which was addressed to the party, not the sheriff, did not specify the details in dispute, and imposed a heavy penalty for disobedience. Though no case of one being exacted seems to be known, the subpoena secured a surprising amount of obedience.

and well established. The cardinal had declared that he would
enforce observance of the law upon those who thought themselves
immune, but too often his actual behaviour smelt more of a vendetta
against individuals or even a whole class—that class of ascendant
men, the political nation, into which Wolsey had not been born and
which took trouble to make him remember the fact. We have seen
how Wolsey used his place in the Council to take his revenge on
Standish; he used Star Chamber even more relentlessly to hunt
down Sir Robert Sheffield who had been prominent in the anticlerical actions of the 1515 Parliament. People soon realized that Wolsey
made a bad enemy. His attacks on the gentry and nobility, advertised as an enforcement of the law from which only evildoers would
suffer, looked justified by what was discovered but derived, perhaps
unfortunately, from a misguided political judgement. No doubt
there was good reason for instructing the judges in October 1518 to
investigate during their circuits 'who be retainers or oppressors or
maintainers of wrongful causes or otherwise misbehaved persons',
and crimes like that committed by Sir Ralph Brereton, member of
the leading Cheshire family, who in May 1516 admitted abducting a
widow under the King's protection, needed remedy. There *were*
overconfident and brutal men in the shires who needed to learn that
the King's law applied to them. But Wolsey appeared to treat these
occasional delinquents as typical of a whole order and to set his
personal authority over them all: it was his arrogance and touchi-
ness, expressed in harangues and insults, that turned proper law
enforcement into intolerable interference. The cardinal's cheerful
and ruthless temperament rejoiced in cutting down the mighty and
devising humiliations for them; and his rejoicing was too manifest.
Capriciously, and often venomously, reaching out everywhere,
noisily proclaiming powers and decisions which vented private
feelings and convictions, Wolsey not only brought home the force of
the state to the rulers of the localities but did so in the most tactless
and abrasive fashion possible. Above all, he did it as a prince of the
Church, flaunting his scarlet, his maces and tapers, his canopies, the
trappings of his mule, in the faces of men who thought themselves
good Christians but socially superior to one whose upstart origins
showed through the pomp bestowed by Pope and King. Wolsey
flouted the basic principles of a hierarchic society. What noblemen
and gentlemen might perhaps have taken from the King—though
we should remember their reaction to the equally intensive if markedly less flamboyant treatment they had received from Henry
VII—they would not accept from his creature. Since among all the
reforms needed a tightening of social controls over potential oppressors stood quite high, Wolsey's purpose was right enough; but if

the assertion of control was not to threaten the social consensus upon which the system necessarily rested, his methods in Council, Star Chamber and Chancery, without Parliament and to the consternation of the common law, were quite wrong.

Moreover, Wolsey, as usual, took away from his sound intentions by his inability to control himself and by his willingness to substitute pretence for reality. The greed with which he accumulated wealth, the enormous household with which he surrounded himself, the lavish palaces he built, and the contempt with which he treated everybody, especially his fellow bishops, left him singularly isolated and very generally hated—hated far more than his positive achievements in interfering with people's behaviour deserved. Despite his political ascendancy at a time of supposed despotism, Wolsey had an appalling press. It is hard to think of anyone who wrote in his praise; his detractors were many and effective. He made the mistake of offending the financial interests of Polydore Vergil, a papal tax-collector resident in England who had made it his life's work to write the history of his temporarily adopted country. Polydore, who did much to ruin for ever the reputations of Empson and Dudley, carried an efficient hatchet which he buried also in Wolsey's skull, though in consequence he had to delay publication until 1534. And Polydore, bringing the new style of Renaissance historiography to England, influenced contemporaries as well as later generations, especially Edward Hall, the ablest of the native historians of the reign, who brought to his view of Wolsey the additional acid of a Londoner's anticlericalism, a lawyer's distrust of Wolsey's chancellorship, and a humanist desire for the church reform the cardinal inhibited.[22] The historians delivered their weighty verdict on Wolsey's greatness; more immediately effective were the poets. Among these, John Skelton also conceived a personal dislike based on financial loss. Skelton was an eccentric semi-genius who employed a good ear and great rhyming skill in the production of a helter-skelter verse that could adapt as readily to tenderness as to irony, to invective as to ribaldry; what it totally lacked was grandeur. The technique suited satire exceptionally well, and he employed it against others, but most powerfully, in 1522, against Wolsey in *Why come ye not to Court?*, a brilliant denunciation of the cardinal's monopoly of power and glory to the detriment even of the King himself. Wolsey's fury did teach Skelton some discretion; he later tried to buy favour with laudatory dedications, but in vain. Even

[22] Polydore, however, lost influence by throwing doubt on the ancient glories of Britain—her legendary foundation by a refugee from Troy called Brutus and her imperial greatness in the days of Arthur, invented (in the main) by that twelfth-century liar of genius, Geoffrey of Monmouth. This scepticism, his best claim to acuity as an historian, condemned him in the eyes of the century's passionate nationalists.

Skelton was less violently personal in his abuse than a later satirist, Jerome Barlow, a nascent Protestant who from the safety of
the continent issued his furious *Burial of the Mass* (1528), a raging
and highly effective attack on this single cause of all the ills in
Church and state.[23] But Protestant attacks of so late a date did not at
the time matter; Skelton's satire, which explained that the cardinal
was taking away his master's outward greatness, could prove a good
deal more damaging.

For as the universal execration grew, generally (it seems) simply
ignored by its victim, it became increasingly clear that he stood on
one narrow pinnacle only, supported solely by the King's trust and
favour. It is not clear whether Henry knew much about his
chancellor's rule: his interventions were always spasmodic and
usually ineffective. He remained content to leave everything to the
cardinal, and Wolsey's one undoubted success lay in his ability to
retain Henry's affections. But he did so too often by pretended
achievements rather than real ones, and this was true even of his
vaunted restoration of order. He did triumphantly settle the one
serious disorder to occur during those early years, the events of 'Evil
May Day' 1517 when some pathological agitators roused the London mob against foreign merchants and had to be put down by
armed force. Wolsey used the occasion in characteristic fashion. He
paid off another score when he compelled the city authorities to
humble themselves; he took the credit for the restoration of order for
which he had not in fact been responsible; and he stage-managed a
scene in Westminster Hall in which Henry could appear as the stern
but ultimately merciful father of his people. In the more mundane
business of really ensuring order and obedience to the law his
achievements fell well short of his claims. In October 1519 he
delivered another of his orations in Council before the King, in
which he praised the good rule of law established in the realm by
Henry's (read Wolsey's) endeavours. In fact, neither then nor in the
next ten years did he get very far in imposing 'the law of the Star
Chamber' upon violent and self-willed men, in spite of all his
imprisoning and pillorying of lawbreakers. He set out to subdue the
powerful laity without resort to the only two institutions for which
they had some respect—Parliament and the common law—and
predictably he failed.

This policy, superficially justifiable, was thus neither in the cause
of true reform nor even by accident accomplished it. It signified far
more a personal fight for power and glory, and it undermined the

---

[23]This dialogue in verse is usually called *Rede me and be not wroth* (from a couplet on the title
page) and ascribed to William Roy; for the correct author and title see E. G. Rupp, *Studies in
the Making of the English Protestant Tradition* (1947), pp. 53 ff.

peace it claimed to be creating. At the same time, however, the troubles of the people also engaged Wolsey who at least began his ministry with some efforts to tackle enclosure, the social problem identified as crucial by writers and poetasters alike. In this, too, he saw only one way—the enforcement of the law. He had no programme and originated no single new step towards reform; there is no indication that he ever thought of drafting an act of Parliament, and none of his proclamations—which reflect his characteristic personal and authoritarian attitudes—contains any innovations. Nevertheless, laws touching these matters existed and needed enforcing if they were to mean anything, and Wolsey's preferred form of activity could have been useful. Unfortunately he proved insufficiently active—too many other things had first claim on his time—and in the only matter with which he persisted the law, as he discovered, was crudely inadequate. In January 1518 he had the Council instruct the judges to review the social legislation touching apparel, vagabondage, the rights of sanctuary, and at least three times during his years of power (1517, 1527, 1528) he issued proclamations calling for the enforcement of the laws in question; but these things he never followed up, and he failed especially to provide any instrument for the systematic enforcement of proclamations. What he did undertake to solve was the problem of enclosures, by searching out and punishing offences against the statutes.

In this concentration on one topic, Wolsey avowedly followed the best advice. He had before him the acts of 1489, 1514 and 1515 which prohibited unlicensed enclosing and ordered that land converted to pasture should be restored to tillage; since depopulation rather than land use or food supply was the grievance, the criterion applied was the destruction of places of habitation and their rebuilding. In 1517, Wolsey set about making a reality of these laws. For three years commissioners sat around the country to take presentments of unlawful enclosing from local juries, and their returns to the Chancery led to some energetic, though spasmodic, action against the offenders denounced who were summoned into ·that court to show cause why they should not be compelled to pull down enclosures and rebuild houses.[24] Not all the returns survive, nor have all the possible cases, extending over at least fifteen years, yet been sought out, but some things are plain. The method of enquiry discovered a great amount of illicit enclosure, while second enquiries and the follow-up in Chancery soon established that inquest juries could be wrong—ill-informed, mistaken, or malicious. A fair number of enclosers were brought to book, but at least as many charged

[24] The best analysis to date is E. Kerridge, 'The Returns of the Inquisitions of Depopulation', *English Historical Review* LXX (1955), pp. 212 ff.

with the offence could prove their innocence or escaped through legal subtleties.[25] On many occasions Wolsey was forced to admit that he had been tricked into proceeding against innocent men.

The real trouble lay with a law that attacked the major agrarian problem much too simply, failed to distinguish the causes of enclosure, mistakenly ascribed rural depopulation to recent times and the single cause of sheepfarming, and penalized some practices that benefited the economy as a whole. The cardinal did not see it that way, nor did anyone whose counsel he might have had: if honest efforts to remedy what everybody agreed was the great social evil of the day failed to succeed, this must be because men used ingenuity and practices to escape the consequences of their deeds. Inclined in any case to dislike lawyers and the landed classes, Wolsey bulled on. If the great enquiry—itself a very impressive piece of administrative enterprise—had turned up so much that could not be proved, he proposed in future to proceed without enquiry and by mere edict. A proclamation of June 1526 ordered the destruction of all enclosures back to 1485 (thus going beyond the tenor of the statutes) or proof of their lawfulness in Chancery within the first fortnight of the forthcoming Michaelmas term (very short notice); another of May 1528 sought to attract secret denunciations against enclosers; finally, in February 1529, all enclosures were indiscriminately ordered to be dismantled. So far as we know, no one took any notice of these increasingly violent edicts, and the campaign against the cormorants of the commonwealth, begun with high hopes and some overconfidence in 1517, fizzled out.

The lesson of this experience is hard to discern, mainly because our knowledge of what was really going on in the countryside is hampered as much as it is advanced by the products of Wolsey's initiative. It is evident that there had been much loss of farmsteads and probably villages in the Midlands from Leicestershire to Buckinghamshire; but since no evidence survives for some of the more obvious open-field counties there is no way of counting totals. The law's reliance on the county as the unit of administration, understandable enough in itself, disregarded the fact that most English counties contain a remarkable mixture of farming areas requiring very different treatment. Emparking, possibly the most damaging form of enclosure, was exempt under the statutes, and the concentration on vanishing places of habitation disguised the more serious problem of the engrossing of holdings for sheep-runs and cattle-breeding; the existence of an inhabited hovel was not by itself

---

[25] For example, the enquiry could be thwarted by showing that the lands in question were enclosed before 1489, or by the accused person's predecessors, or that they were not all held in chief of the Crown (the act of 1515 committed enforcement to the lords of the property, so that crown action applied only against tenants-in-chief).

proof of a prosperous agrarian society. Quite a few alleged conversions to pasture turned out to be that valuable practice, convertible husbandry or ley farming (by which land is put temporarily under grass before reverting to arable), but the juries often failed to make the distinction. Above all, the law failed to recognize that the heavy Midland clays are poor soil for corn growing and yield best returns all round as pasture. In short, the outcry against enclosures, reflected both in writings and in acts of Parliament, mistook far too much and operated against progressive farming practices. Wolsey could have drawn some lessons from his experience in Chancery where for once the problem moved out of the shadows of emotional prejudice into the detailed reality of daily lives. He could have promoted new laws better designed to tackle the real problems, but he never attempted this; his one remaining Parliament in 1523 saw no bill testifying to the experience of nearly six years' involvement with the agrarian scene. And he could have learned that his supposedly wise and generous attack gained only increasing hatred for the regime. Chancery against enclosers joined Star Chamber against breakers of the law in a double-headed war against the possessing classes. This may be thought proof of a commendable social conscience, but it really demonstrates a crass absence of political sensitivity and an unflinching refusal to look reality in the face. If at least the campaign had improved the lot of the rural poor, its political ineptitude might be overlooked; but it did nothing for them, husbandmen, labourers, landless vagrants. All it did was further to annoy the men with power. In his government of England, Wolsey's activity backed his neglect in undermining the security of the Tudor monarchy, and before very long the fact was brought home to Henry VIII who throughout was careful to do no more than give the cardinal a free hand and listen to his songs of self-praise.

It is arguable that the same insouciant lack of realism also informed Wolsey's foreign policy, the area of action in which he felt happiest and for which he is best remembered. But that would be unfair to one who delighted in deviousness and complexity, and who measured triumph by the lack of promise in a situation from which advantage was distilled. Certainly his preoccupation with Europe alarmingly affected his ability to give concentrated attention to the problems of the nation, especially (but not only) in the early years of his ascendancy. The renewal of the Italian wars by Francis I (1515)[26] and the death of Ferdinand of Aragon (1516) altered the balance of forces and overthrew the settlement of 1514. The years 1515–18 witnessed a series of inconclusive manoeuvres largely in-

[26] See above, p. 50.

spired by the papacy and designed to reduce the dominance which
the French had once more established in Italy. In effect it had to be
done without war because for the moment no one could stand up to
the French. The new ruler of Spain, Naples and the Netherlands, the
young King Charles, was in no way yet ready to play his part, and
Wolsey wasted the money he lavished on him and on the Emperor
Maximilian, last survivor from the past and still an active and
pointless intriguer. But Henry could not bear the thought that
Francis had taken from him the champion's title as Europe's young
knight, while Wolsey was determined to enlarge his personal stature
and especially to obtain legatine powers over the English Church
which would subdue the rivalry of Canterbury. The problem was
how to recreate the situation of 1514 with its triumph for England
when no continental ally offered himself to lead the resistance to
France and while France successfully undid the consequences of
Flodden at England's back door.

In 1517 Wolsey's policy received a fearful set-back when his
supposed ally Maximilian came to terms with Francis at Noyon,
England being totally ignored. Severely shaken and justly afraid of
Henry's reaction, Wolsey displayed the resilience which was his
foremost and perhaps his most engaging characteristic. He found
the answer to his difficulties—less predictably than has been
supposed—in the creation of an enduring axis between England and
Rome. Mainly through the good offices of Cardinal Giulio de'
Medici, Leo X's cousin and chief policy-maker, the balance of force
began to shift in 1518. The French, not anxious to put their victories
to a new test, made gestures of peace; Albany for a time left
Scotland; and the Pope began to use the manifest threat from the
Ottoman Turks—whose descents upon Italy's coasts disconcerted
Europe but frightened Leo out of his mind—to refashion the European scene. Wolsey unquestionably recognized the benefits to be got
from a policy for European peace, and in More the Erasmian
pacifists had a representative close to the seat of power: though it
must remain uncertain whether the cardinal really wanted peace or
policy. In the end he achieved both in the greatest triumph of his
career. In March 1518, the Pope, under de' Medici's management,
opened a major campaign for a general alliance against the Turks,
and among the envoys sent out was Cardinal Lorenzo Campeggio
who went to England. Wolsey used Campeggio's embassy with great
skill. First, by stopping him from crossing the Channel for several
months, he at last extorted from the reluctant Pope the grant of a
legatine commission for himself, and when Campeggio at length
arrived Wolsey neatly usurped the role of peacemaker from the
Pope. By means of the papal commission which appointed the two

cardinals negotiators for the intended truce with the major powers of Europe, he organized a universal peace among the princes not as cardinal and legate but as lord chancellor and King's minister. Thus the papal truce became in October 1518 the general treaty of London; Wolsey and Henry stood forth as the conciliators, and therefore the arbiters, of Europe.

The treaty was well intentioned and in diplomatic terms glorious; yet its maker should hardly have supposed that it would prove more permanent than earlier attempts to end the strife among Christian princes. Still, by stealing the Pope's thunder Wolsey had come close to fulfilling the dreams of Erasmus and More, and of many others. He had also obtained a personal power over the English Church which he had been importunately seeking for three years. He had given his King, too, the satisfaction of glory. However, all this he had been able to do only by tying England very firmly to the policy of Rome. From now on, both England's outward relations and Wolsey's personal fortunes were governed to an excessive extent by the close understanding he had set up with de' Medici and Campeggio, successively cardinal-protectors of England at Rome; and to complicate things, de' Medici was also protector of France, while Campeggio held the same position for the Holy Roman Empire.[27] The treaty of London tied English hands by creating a real dependence on the papacy. It has always been thought that this situation was bound to arise with an English chief minister who was also a prince of the Church and determined to make the most of that, and unquestionably Wolsey's personal ambitions played their part in his relations with a Rome that he, unlike other non-Italian cardinals, never visited. It is also true that close ties with Rome suited Henry VIII who still retained much of his youthful devotion to the Holy See. Yet what had been a general inclination became in 1518 a permanent involvement; through the decade that Wolsey continued to direct English policy he never freed himself from having to follow where Rome led. In a sense the real victors of 1518 were, after all, the papal diplomats. And so papalist a habit damaged things for Wolsey in England, too. He could (and did) use his Roman friends to acquire the powers of a legate, great additional wealth, and control over other bishoprics whose revenues went to absentee curial appointees;[28] but in consequence he subjected the

[27] For all this see W. Wilkie, *The Cardinal Protectors of England* (1974).

[28] For financial reasons, Wolsey always held one English bishopric in addition to York—Bath and Wells (1518–23), Durham (1523–9), Winchester (1529–30); in 1523 he also acquired the abbey of St Albans *in commendam*. In addition he effectively administered Worcester (from 1523) and Salisbury (from 1525) on behalf of the absent bishops, Geronimo de Ghinucci and Campeggio, successfully keeping back a large part of the revenues. Though in 1518 he gave up Tournai which had never been securely his, he held the titles and revenues of some Spanish sees by the gift of Charles V.

4 Wolsey: Ascendancy and Decline

I

The treaty of London was in some ways a very remarkable document. The participating powers—who included all the major and several of the minor monarchs of Europe—agreed on a universal peace, forbade their subjects to serve in any conflict between them, guaranteed to protect one another's interests and refused to shelter one another's rebels. It was understood that this new-found amity should result in a crusade against the Turks—so serious a concern for Leo X that he humbly acceded to a confederation which Wolsey had created by snatching the initiative from him. And although no one will read international treaties with the innocence of the idealist, it would also take cynicism too far to disregard the very genuine desire to end the strife among Christians which brought this general accord into existence. In practical terms England—and Wolsey—benefited most, especially from the accompanying Anglo-French treaty which betrothed the infant Princess Mary to Francis I's heir and provided the cardinal with a handsome secret pension. But both in intent and in immediate effect, the general treaty gave full expression to a policy which Erasmus and his followers had urged for years, and to which politicians had frequently paid lip-service. Despite Wolsey's adroit capture of the credit and the glory, it was essentially a papal policy, as indeed it should have been; not only ought the Pope to have presided over an explicitly Christian enterprise, but he alone among the powers could hope for no profit from aggressive war. The days of Julius II seemed happily buried.

Unfortunately for participants and humanists and trusting historians alike, it soon became apparent that the treaty concluded a phase of hopefulness rather than opened an era of cooperative peace. Two events destroyed the system of which it was both the consequence and the embodiment, destroying with it the role of England and Wolsey as leaders of the European concert. Within three months of the triumphant celebrations in London, the death of the Emperor Maximilian (January 1519) totally altered the power balance of Europe. And even while the treaty was being drafted, the consequences of Martin Luther's protest against the sale of indulgences, just over a year old at this time, were beginning to be felt in a growing disruption of that united Christendom to which the treaty meant to give a voice.

In England, Luther's impact came early but at first proved far from overwhelming. The reformer's writings began to infiltrate in 1520 and 1521, and by the early 1520s his ideas were agitating some of the younger scholars, especially at Cambridge. It was here that his leading English follower, William Tyndale, inspired a group who, meeting at the White Horse Tavern and for obvious reasons dubbed 'Little Germany', included a fair sampling of the future leaders of the Reformation. The lead was taken by the warden of the Austin friars (Luther's own order), Robert Barnes; among the interested disputants were Thomas Cranmer and Nicholas Shaxton, destined to be rulers of the Church; its most attractively spiritual member was Thomas Bilney, never a Lutheran but a man who found peace for his troubled soul in a conviction of God's saving grace that alienated him from the penitential system of the Church. Bilney was to convert Hugh Latimer who started as an honest and bigoted enemy to the innovators and became an honest and bigoted preacher of reform. 'Little Germany' made quite a stir in the academic world of Cambridge, but it was not until the mid-1520s that it attracted sufficient attention from the authorities to reach the light of the record.

There is, in fact, no sign that at first anyone was much troubled by contentious debates in a university, far too familiar an experience to bother the men of power. What concerned some bishops much more was the likeness of the allegedly new ideas to the popular heresy they knew so well, Lollardy. It is by now clear enough both that the survival of Lollardy helped to give a home outside academic circles to the newer heterodoxy, and that the Protestant Reformation, even in its early days, added some reviving strength to the beliefs of those secret gatherings of husbandmen and craftsmen in London, Kent, the Chilterns and the Cotswolds where English bibles and Wycliffite tracts, battered and thumbed manuscripts, hidden with care from curate and archdeacon, were reverently read aloud after the day's work was done. The coincidence of Lollard and Lutheran heresy—especially the fact that both attacked the mystique of the Church and the trades-unionism of the priesthood—stood in the way of gaining Luther anything resembling a sympathetic hearing from the leaders of the English Church; in addition, the high papalism to which Wolsey had committed himself, his Church, his country and his King demanded an uncompromisingly hostile reaction when Rome decided to proceed against Luther as a dangerous enemy.

As might have been expected after the experience of 1514–15, the English hierarchy knew of only one method to deal with the situation—the method of violence justified by a brutal assertion of its claims. The persecution of Lollards became more intense: in 1521 Bishop Longland of Lincoln uncovered a nest of vipers in Buckinghamshire and exterminated it, with some burnings and many humiliating recantations; and Wolsey assisted him with a strange circular letter calling upon magistrates everywhere (not only in the diocese in question) to offer their aid. Detections of heresy, examples of which can be found in the church records of the preceding thirty years, multiplied, and Wolsey cannot have enjoyed discovering that his own diocese of York (where German ideas penetrated through the port of Hull) was not immune. The government did not confine itself to calls for assistance to the bishops. In May 1521, Wolsey, patron of scholars, staged a public burning of Luther's books, and futile steps were taken to prevent any more from entering the country. England was among the first powers to come out publicly against the new heresy, partly at least because her rulers were frightened by the continued existence of the old.

It was Henry VIII himself who set the seal upon his government's attitude. Among the King's favourite pretensions his claim to theological learning stood high, and there is no doubt that for a layman, and a monarch at that, he had good knowledge and much interest. He had from the first toyed with schemes to answer Luther, and the tracts of 1520 in which Luther demolished the claims of the papacy made up his mind. Henry decided to enter the lists against *The Babylonish Captivity of the Church*, and in the summer of 1521 his *Assertio Septem Sacramentorum adversus Martinum Lutherum* dropped from the press. The debate about its real authorship is over: it was essentially the King's own work, based on collections of citations and arguments made with the help of experts, and in the last rescension overseen by Thomas More.[1] Although its special fame owed most to the fact that a moderately competent theological exercise was produced by a monarch hitherto thought more familiar with the jousting lance than the pen, it was not negligible in itself. Interestingly enough, Henry accepted the papal supremacy in the Church, which he asserted without qualifications, not so much on the grounds of Scripture or divine law but because it had acquired the respectability bestowed by centuries of general consent. It is possible that in this unenthusiastic conviction we may see the hand of More who later remembered that he had held no high view of papal claims until Henry persuaded him otherwise, and who always, even during

[1] J. J. Scarisbrick, *Henry VIII* (1968), pp. 111 ff.

the later crises, inclined to rely on 'the consent of Christendom' to justify his adherence to the rule of Rome.

The book was not ignored. Its appearance finally decided the Curia to bestow upon Henry the special accolade which, jealous of his French rival's title as 'most Christian king', he had been coveting for years; in October 1521, Leo X (whose reluctance is well attested but hard to understand) decreed that in future Henry and his successors should be called 'defenders of the faith', a title so well earned by the royal hammer of Luther.[2] And the notoriety of being attacked by a crowned head predictably provoked Luther into a savage counter-pamphlet full of insults to the effronterous princeling. Henry fortunately contained his fury sufficiently to forbear further literary production, but he commissioned More to write an answer (published in 1523 under the pseudonym William Ross), while John Fisher entered the war with a work of more theological weight to fill the gaps in Henry's own anti-Lutheran learning.

The King's decision to take a part in the fight against heresy thus testified to the single-minded stand to be taken by all the English authorities, lay and spiritual; more than this, it helped to make Fisher and More, the outstanding Erasmians in England, into the country's foremost anti-Lutherans. The transformation came naturally to Fisher, a man of high theological learning, essentially a Thomist and Scotist of sound orthodoxy, and one in whom spiritual excellence supported a controversial temperament.[3] More was another matter. Henry's order that he should save his King from the Wittenberg bludgeon introduced the great humanist and author of *Utopia* to a new and even then less attractive role. He discovered in himself powers of unscrupulous vituperation which made him one of the less agreeable controversialists in a violently controversialist age, though for a time at least he managed to retain enough of this sharp wit and sense of fun to leaven his diatribes with touches of the real More. However, once persuaded that Lutheran heresy did indeed represent a truly overwhelming threat to the unity of the Church and of Christendom, More proved to be capable of even more determined intolerance than the bishops. Frustrated in his hope that entry into the King's service would enable him to promote the cause of humanist reform, frustrated by Wolsey's political ascendancy which dispensed with all reform, and increasingly frightened by the abyss opening beneath his feet, More turned prosecutor. In doing so he brought into the open what was for England one of the most

[2] *Fidei defensor* was chosen after long discussions and the fortunate rejection of some dull and far from euphonious titles, such as *Orthodoxus* or *Ecclesiasticus*.

[3] Fisher's complex personality—puritan and bishop, laudator of both Duns Scotus and Erasmus—has not attracted the biographers; but see the suitably complex study by Edward Surtz, *The Works and Days of John Fisher* (1967).

serious consequences of the Lutheran advance: it split the ranks of the intellectuals, destroyed the reforming movement of the 1510s, and thus ended the hopes of Erasmianism.

To later generations it was to appear that Erasmus's *New Testament* (1516) with its carefully anticlerical glosses formed a double plank with Luther's protest for the coming Reformation. Certainly, when Tyndale published a translation of the New Testament based on Erasmus (1525) he exploited humanist insights and criticisms in the interests of Lutheran reform. But the Erasmian humanists did not see things in this light at all. Although it was not until 1523 that Erasmus himself made plain his disagreement with Luther, Fisher and More, both members of the circle, had got there earlier and were to be far more outspoken about their opposition to the Protestant Reformation. In consequence, they withdrew from reform altogether. The programme to which they and their fellows had subscribed included the reform of the Church—along moderate and traditional lines which would remove abuses but leave the essentials untouched— together with the reform of the commonweal and the promotion of peace among princes. This programme had united men all over Europe, including quite a powerful party among the cardinals of the Curia. Now, with so different a reform of the Church proposed by Luther which would altogether alter the foundations of doctrine, of church government, and perhaps of the moral order, the humanists found themselves forced either to attend only to the details of social amelioration while defending the institution generally held to represent the worst social abuses of all, or else entirely to abandon reform. In practice they could not avoid the second alternative because men existed who did not see the dilemma—men for whom Luther had added a special force to the cause rather than undermined it. Unlike Fisher and More, the younger generation of humanists and aspirant divines saw in the German Reformation the pattern of reform which would do what was needed in Church and commonwealth alike. For the present, these men—some humanists who came to adopt Protestantism, some religious reformers who accepted the humanist analysis of society—could only discuss and talk and dream, at Cambridge and elsewhere; for the present, power remained with an old order exemplified by Wolsey, protected by Henry VIII, and spoken for by Thomas More. The 1520s thus became a period of failed reform, but also one that incubated a generation of men capable of taking their chance if ever it should come.

The chief ingredient in this rather messy stew, however, was not simple orthodoxy or the deeply troubled mind of Thomas More; nor was it the personal intervention of the King, intermittent but increasingly experienced. The chief ingredient was Wolsey's dominant rule, established in the brilliant diplomacy of 1515-18 and founded upon the concentration of all government action in his own hands. In 1518-19, he would appear to have gone about its final consolidation. He had to face the fact that there was more than one focus of power in the structure. His legateship, though not made permanent until 1524, gave him an unquestioned control of the Church which he used to subdue fellow bishops and enrich himself at their expense.[4] In the state, his chancellorship and dominance of the Council, which seemed to leave him as unchallenged as the King himself, were supported by the care he took over the offices of state. For his control of the royal finances he relied on the loyalty of the lord treasurer, the duke of Norfolk, who had first become his ally over the forward policy of 1511-12; the third duke, who succeeded to title and office in 1524, being less schooled by adversity and far prouder of his noble blood, turned into an enemy. Wolsey further relied on the bureaucratized organization of the Chamber, since 1515 a fully established office of finance managed by Sir John Daunce as general surveyor of crown lands and by Sir John Heron as treasurer of the Chamber—civil servants without political standing and ambition. The ultimate reserves in the privy purse were handled by Sir William Compton for whom, since he remained independent, Wolsey cherished a characteristic jealousy. The cardinal also made sure of the seals. When Ruthal died in 1523 the privy seal, after a brief interlude, passed into the safely clerical and loyal hands of Cuthbert Tunstall, now bishop of London; and when Richard Pace's mind broke down in 1526, another clerical careerist, Dr William Knight, took the signet and secretaryship. The detailed work of supervising and activating the formal organs of government was managed by members of Wolsey's personal household, a training ground for the state's servants (most of them clerks) which during the cardinal's ascendancy proved the 'medievalism' of this administration by taking the place of the King's attendant Household organization.

This engrossing of power and of the instruments of rule concealed one serious deficiency, one insidious threat. The cardinal had no place among those in attendance on Henry; indeed, he so rarely came to court (a ceremonious occasion, every time he did) that one must wonder whether he fully realized how readily Henry could be made to listen to others. At least he understood that he needed to control those who did have the daily contact with the King that he lacked. He was notoriously jealous of the King's secretaries, even though most of them were of his choosing; they knew the need for

[4] See below, pp. 92-3.

constant affirmations of loyalty and frequent protests of innocence when Henry went counter to the cardinal's wishes. Pace and Knight were much employed on diplomatic missions, in part at least for the purpose of interrupting their intimacy with the King. Wolsey never managed to get Thomas More, whom Henry used as a super-numerary secretary, away from court because Henry liked More's company too well, but partly because—as he proved when he begged off the Spanish embassy in 1526—Sir Thomas had no intention of leaving England, Chelsea, family and King. And al-though More scrupulously avoided doing anything that might even look like undermining Wolsey's influence, the cardinal remained suspicious and consistently kept this most distinguished mind in the King's entourage from the real centre of affairs.

Harder to control than the secretaries at court were the people with whom Henry chose to spend the bulk of his time—his wife and his friends. By about 1520, the influence of Queen Catherine had waned, possibly vanished, and it therefore troubled Wolsey little that she never liked him. But what of the group of close companions, the men of Henry's Privy Chamber?[5] By 1517 an odd situation had arisen there. The Privy Chamber remained in the unorganized and rudimentary state in which Henry VII, its originator, had left it; but Henry VIII had added to the companions of earlier years a group of very lively and very fashionable young men, younger than himself, who seemed to be able to do everything with him. Known familiarly as the King's minions, they caused raised eyebrows at court and worse in Wolsey's mind. Their presence became more ominous when in the autumn of 1518 the Privy Chamber was reorganized on the French model and the minions gained a formal and powerful place at court. Partly by the very fact of their existence, and partly because at a time when Wolsey was planning an alliance with the Habsburgs they ardently supported a French policy, they now constituted a threat to the minister. In May 1519 he flexed his muscles and demonstrated where power lay. The four leaders of the young men were expelled and exiled into offices in the shires and at Calais; their places were taken by sober men well affected to Wolsey—two of them markedly older, too. Though Henry may have felt that at twenty-eight he ought to settle down (not that he abandoned jousts, hunting, revelry and women), this action was assuredly initiated by Wolsey and marked his recognition that he needed to control the Privy Chamber as a centre of political power.

In fact, round about this time Wolsey had some reason to fear for his monopoly of power. The first sign, coming perhaps in the wake of

[5] The growth and role of this institution was discovered and worked out by D. R. Starkey (see above, p. 30, n. 9).

Privy Chamber reform, was a long memorial of things that Henry had allegedly decided upon and had ordered Wolsey to carry into effect. If the order had been obeyed, the King would have taken personal charge of his government. He planned, above all, to take charge of all the financial offices by means of quarterly statements of account for his own audit, but he also demanded similar regular reports from all those involved in the administration of justice. Reform of the royal Household was entrusted to a powerful Council committee presided over by Wolsey, and Henry announced his intention to discuss with his Council four major policy issues requiring reform. All of them were real enough. Henry called for the provision of 'equal and indifferent justice'; but Wolsey could claim to be attending to that. Then there was Ireland, indeed a matter too long neglected. Since 1515 the earl of Kildare had again ruled there without any restraint or interference from England, but by the beginning of 1519 Henry had apparently decided that it was time he asserted himself. Further, the Exchequer was to be reformed—a necessary thing if the office was to be rendered capable of serving an active modernized state, but also something of a dream in the face of its entrenched and immobile bureaucracy. In addition Henry expressed a concern for the poor and wished to repair the fortifications of England's frontiers.

Here was royal government in action—except that virtually nothing resulted from these determined words which combined a return to Henry VII's methods of government with a serious programme of fundamental (and necessary) reform. The only part of the administrative programme, so magisterially urged upon the cardinal, to produce any action was (typically) the requirement of a regular privy purse of £10,000 a year to finance the King's private life; and of the issues proposed for consideration only Ireland received attention. In September, Kildare, called to London, managed to make an enemy of Wolsey, and one cannot help feeling that this, rather than the King's desire to improve his government there, had more to do with what happened. Norfolk's son, the earl of Surrey, went to Ireland as King's lieutenant, and Wolsey initiated a forward policy of direct government which bypassed the ascendancy of the great Irish families. Effective rule was to advance from the Pale in all directions; the King's peace and the King's taxes were to cover the whole island. Wolsey used his legateship to manipulate the Church in Ireland; Henry wrote powerful despatches asserting his sovereignty especially over the alien law of the Gaelic parts; Surrey was given some troops and money. Henry favoured a policy of conciliation backed by guile: he wanted the Irish lords to recognize his suzerainty in the full sense of feudal law but did not mean to spend money on war. Surrey, advised by the Anglo-Irish experts of the Pale, recognized the impossibility of this and came to press for a full-scale conquest, quite likely in the knowledge that the cost of this would terminate Henry's interest.[6] And so it fell out: conciliation was never tried, the means did not suffice for the substitution of force, and within two years the failure of activism could not be overlooked. Surrey's recall in March 1522—he was replaced by the earl of Ormond, Kildare's chief rival among the magnates—ended the experiment. For the rest of his rule, Wolsey tried to maintain some sort of control by playing off noble interests one against another, but bastard feudalism continued to rule the earldoms and Gaelic custom the lordships. Like Henry VII before him, Henry VIII and Wolsey, finding the task too formidable, left Ireland to itself. But at least they tried there; the rest of the 1519 memorial vanished traceless. Those who would see an active ruler in Henry VIII and regard him as the real power behind Wolsey can take little comfort from this momentary burst of energy: neither the movement for reform nor the attempt to put some restraint on Wolsey—the two manifest purposes behind that intervention—benefited from Henry's wayward interest.

Wolsey remained unchallenged in the saddle, and the great men of the realm knuckled under to his authority. There is really no sign that he ever encountered opposition in Council or court. Yet there was one man of power who was destroyed in those years, and contemporary gossip blamed it all on the cardinal's jealousy. Late in 1520, Henry wrote a mysterious letter to Wolsey in which he alluded to their shared suspicion of five great noblemen whose reactions to an unspecified piece of news, the King suggested, should be used to test their loyalty. The suspects included Henry's old friend Suffolk, and Henry earl of Wiltshire who early in the reign had briefly been one of his closest associates; also mentioned were two northern magnates, Northumberland and Derby, who played little known part in court affairs. But above all there was Wiltshire's elder brother, Edward Stafford, duke of Buckingham, England's foremost nobleman. By May 1521, Buckingham had died on the scaffold, convicted of treason by a dubious new kind of court, a commission of peers presided over by Norfolk as high steward. He was charged with encompassing the King's death; his motive was alleged to be a desire for the crown stirred up by treacherous prophecies and magic; the evidence was supplied by servants with a grudge against him. There can be no doubt that the charges were at least wildly exaggerated: Buckingham was technically and really innocent, and genuinely bewildered. Nor is there much doubt about the effect of the trial.

[6] B. Bradshaw, 'The Irish Constitutional Revolution, 1515–1557', pp. 68 ff.

Henry demonstrated to himself and others the ease with which he could dispose of even the greatest men—men with a solid power base in their own regions—and learned the advantages to be derived from confiscating their wealth. But why was Buckingham attacked? No one else shared his trouble, especially none of those others of whom Henry had shown himself suspicious a few months earlier: People at the time said that he had dared express contempt for the upstart cardinal who took his fearful revenge. Since that day, historians have usually been inclined to see Henry's hand in the event: Buckingham had a powerful touch of the blood royal, Henry had but one heir and she a girl not yet five years old, the spectre of a battle for the crown did exist and may have been before Henry's eyes. But Buckingham, it would seem, had never wavered in his loyalty to the house of Tudor, nor had he given the slightest grounds for such drastic suspicions; if he had, they would have appeared at his trial. True, he had pride of blood (and may well have insulted Wolsey); he had wealth, a great following, the trappings of power. But he had seemed to lack all political ambition. It is not really possible to answer the question with certainty; for myself, I can believe that Henry's dynastic fears were provoked by distorted or invented stories of the duke's interest in his ancestry and prospects, and that the King here offered the first indication of the extremes to which he was willing to go once he had conceived a suspicion of a man on such personal grounds. Wolsey at the least will not have hindered and may well have done the whispering; certainly he invented some outrageous lies in presenting the story to foreign monarchs.

II

Thus Wolsey made sure in these years where England's rule should lie, but the power he held he used for no constructive purposes, and such purposes as came his way soon had the steam taken out of them. There was much justice in the catalogue of his doings drawn up at the time of his fall in which dozens of important initiatives are listed, always with the words 'we have begun'. Wolsey for ever began things and finished very few, so that even the good and useful ideas to which he frequently lent some initial support came to nothing. The realm, badly in need of a guiding and reforming hand, really marked time while this great activist and man of limitless energy held sway. His inclination to go at everything that came up played its part, but the real trouble lay in his mind—fertile but also sterile, mobile but also unsystematic. The major cause of all this unproductive and lapsed endeavour must be sought in his and Henry's continued involvement in the great affairs of Europe. The maker of the treaty of London could not withdraw from the scene of his triumphs, even when the chance of triumphing again had manifestly gone.

As has been said,[7] the first swell of the Reformation destroyed the intellectual and spiritual basis upon which that treaty rested. The death of Maximilian in January 1519 and the consequences that rapidly flowed therefrom more directly destroyed the system the treaty had tried to erect. Charles of Habsburg, duke of Burgundy and king of the Spanish kingdoms, succeeded to the Austrian possessions of his house and thus united in his hand an overwhelming territorial complex. In July, despite great efforts made by his rival Francis I, he secured election to the vacant title of Holy Roman Emperor. Henry VIII had also briefly been a candidate. It is hard to know how seriously he regarded his chances, but he received powerful encouragement from Rome. The Pope disliked the prospect on the imperial throne of either of the great monarchs who disputed Italy between them, and he therefore urged his favourite son among princes to put himself forward. In reality there was no contest: Charles was the electors' obvious choice, even without the massive distribution of Fugger silver[8] intended to help them over any doubts they might have had. Europe rightly assumed that the new Emperor could not long remain at peace with France. Too many issues, old and new, divided them, from the French domination of Milan (an imperial fief) through disputed territories in the Netherlands to a personal antagonism sharpened by the election. The treaty of 1518 became irrelevant, and England was faced with a sudden testing choice of policies. In addition, Pope Leo X was failing; were he to die, the election of his successor was bound to turn into a test of strength between Charles V and Francis I. But Wolsey had his ambitions, too.

At first sight, Wolsey's and Henry's position promised well. They had set themselves up as the admired peacemakers of Europe, and there was no reason why they should not continue to hold the balance between the parties. Neither Charles nor Francis was prepared to jeopardize the peace until they had made sure of England, and for a time Wolsey continued to bask in the role of the much wooed heiress. He played that game in his accustomed manner—very astutely, with a lavish public display and with a great

[7] See above, p. 74.

[8] Charles V's candidature was financed by the leading German banking house—the Fuggers of Augsburg.

amount of often superfluous deviousness. Charles, who had been in Spain during his election, visited England in May 1520 on his way to his new dominions, and the princes' friendship was well advertised. In the following month, Henry and Wolsey, accompanied by the flower of England's nobility and knighthood, as well as by an army of attendants and workmen, crossed to Calais for a long planned meeting with Francis which turned into the most celebrated junketing of the century. The Field of Cloth of Gold was a truly marvellous spectacle, despite the fact that it seems to have been always either raining or blowing dust. The English, as hosts, built an enormous palace of wood and glass over 320 feet square, on two floors, with state apartments and galleries, while their French guests dotted the neighbourhood with pavilions made out of the precious stuff that gave its name to the encounter. Thousands of beeves and sheep bit the dust, and hogsheads of wine poured into ready gullets, part of them through the traditional channel of hastily erected public fountains. Wolsey, organizing everything, was in his element; and the organization was indeed admirably successful. Feasts, tournaments and poetry entertained the throngs of guests and their wives, and everybody had the greatest fun—except Henry on the occasion that he challenged his brother of France to a wrestling match and finished on the floor. The total cost, naturally, was prodigious as well as very hard to calculate—possibly little short of £15,000 or one seventh of the King's annual income; and that is to count only the expenses incurred by Henry himself. Private people half ruined themselves to keep up with the Tudors and Valois. John Fisher used the occasion for a characteristically sour sermon comparing the evanescent glories of this world with the true glories of heaven, but everybody expected that sort of thing from eminent preachers and no one allowed it to spoil their lavish enjoyment of the event. And why not?[9]

However, the meeting had been arranged to talk policy, and in this respect it proved a disappointment. So little was discussed and even less concluded that one grows suspicious of that earlier encounter with Francis's rival: it is likely that Wolsey's pose as broker between the parties had already lost conviction. After some three weeks of fun at Calais, the cardinal rode off to Gravelines, in the Emperor's dominions, where some real negotiating took place in sober secrecy. England did not come off the fence; on the contrary, it was agreed to call a conference of all three powers at Calais to continue the peace—as soon as possible. So far at least the cardinal maintained the position he had achieved in 1518. Rebellion in Spain, calling Charles away, delayed the meeting, and when it

[9]For a detailed account see Joycelyne G. Russell, *The Field of Cloth of Gold* (1969).

briefly took place, with no princes present, in August 1521, the pretence at neutrality had ceased to be credible. Late that month Wolsey met Charles at Bruges and concluded a treaty against France. Charles promised to support Wolsey's candidature for the papacy, if it should arise, and accepted the Princess Mary (taken from the Dauphin) as his future bride. In return England promised support in money and men for war against France. In November, the French took up the gauntlet in familiar fashion: they ratified a suspended treaty with Scotland and sent back the duke of Albany to lead that country against England. In parenthesis it may be noted that Leo X died in December and that Charles promptly defaulted on his promise, supporting the successful candidate (Adrian VI) in an election in which Wolsey allowed his name to go forward.

Thus less than three years after successfully adopting the pose of sovereign mediator—three years filled with public actions which underlined apparent ambitions to adhere nobly to that line—Wolsey committed Henry (or Henry forced Wolsey to commit England?) to intervention in the forthcoming wars on the side of Spain and the Empire—a total return to the policy of 1512–14, and a manifest surrender of independence. The wars proved thoroughly unprofitable, and the whole policy can in retrospect be seen as leading to disaster for Wolsey and unimagined complications for the King. The country, needless to say, gained nothing from it, not even the dubious pleasure that success at arms had afforded on the earlier occasion. There has been some debate over the question why the Crown should have entered upon so unfortunate a road when no visible English interests were involved in a dispute that looked certain to be fought in Italy. Old views that Wolsey believed in something called the balance of power and switched allies around to preserve it were manifestly mistaken: not only did he choose to throw England's weight into the scale already carrying the heavier load, but he had long since shown that the balancing act he believed in involved standing aside from all alliances. A. F. Pollard, realizing that the policy pursued in 1519–21 matched that promoted by Rome, concluded that Wolsey's dominant motive was the hunt for the tiara which compelled him to pay first attention to good relations with the Curia and show himself the protector of papal interests. However, there are sound reasons for doubting that Wolsey seriously believed in his slender chances of election to the papacy, and for thinking that in devising policy he could not so simply ignore the King.[10] Those more convinced than I can be of Henry's personal control of policy at this date (or most dates) have consequently

[10] Cf. D. S. Chambers, 'Cardinal Wolsey and the Papal Tiara', *Bulletin of the Institute of Historical Research* xxxviii (1965), pp. 20 ff.

found the chief motive in the needs of the Tudor dynasty: seizing on the betrothal of the child-princess to the Emperor, they point out that Henry evidently thought it best to secure England's future by alliance with the Habsburgs rather than risk a Frenchman on the throne.

There is something in this, as there is something in England's commercial ties with Charles's Netherlands and Henry's continuing dislike of Francis I and French pretensions. Nevertheless, it now appears that Pollard hit near the essence of things, even though he overestimated Wolsey's anxiety to become pope. Throughout these years, English policy followed with suspicious faithfulness the moves made at Rome, especially by Cardinal de' Medici who ran Leo X's policy for him. Rome wanted France out of Italy but wished to achieve this without substituting imperial domination; hence Rome always favoured a policy that exploited the pope's nominal spiritual authority over the battling monarchs and tried to create an arbitrating position between them. The only successful effort in that direction, the settlement of 1518, had been achieved by the cooperation of Wolsey, de' Medici and Campeggio; thereafter that triumvirate remained in touch and effectively in control of English policy.[11] To Wolsey, and to Henry too, amity with Rome formed the foundation of English policy. While in 1518 Wolsey had usurped the fame, in 1521 he looked like what he was—the agent of others. Perhaps Henry's hostility to France and concern for a dynastic alliance with the Habsburgs helped to put the cardinal in this fix by reducing his options, but in essence the tune that Wolsey danced to was played at Rome—and played there by the Emperor's party. Power would not for ever be denied, and the outcome of all that diplomacy simply underlined where power lay.

So, in 1522, England was committed to a military effort markedly greater and much more difficult to limit than that of 1512, and committed to making it in support of the dominant ruler in Europe. In the event, nothing much happened; Charles waged his (highly successful) war without help from his northern ally, though at least he had made sure of his sea route from Spain to Antwerp. The old French device of raising Scotland failed, too. Albany turned out to be an altogether spent force and was driven out permanently in early 1524; Flodden was too recent to be overlooked, and France confined herself to exhortations. Though thus safe in the north, the English intervention promised in the treaty turned into something like a disgraceful flop. In May 1522, the earl of Surrey with a powerful (and expensive) force pointlessly raided in northern France, while late in 1523 the duke of Suffolk mounted an attack which, torn

[11]W. Wilkie, *The Cardinal-Protectors of England*, pp. 114 ff.

between capturing Boulogne and advancing upon Paris (in support of an imperialist invasion from the south) achieved some temporary success but had to be abandoned in 1524 when resources ran low. Wolsey on the whole tried to avoid action and to renew moves towards peace—as did the papacy, from November 1523 in the hands of de' Medici as Clement VII. (On this occasion, too, Wolsey had been an unconvincing and unsuccessful candidate). Henry, on the other hand, revived dreams of crowns in France; every time the Emperor's strategy looked like bringing success, he tried to throw in his forces. What put an end to this unprofitable dithering between warlike postures and doubtful diplomacy was Charles's total victory at Pavia (February 1525) which left him the captor of Francis and the master of Europe. The twisting policies of Rome and England had, perhaps justly, come to grief: the Pope was forced to recognize his subjection to the Emperor, and England, her performance in the war having left her with no claim to share in the fruits of victory, found herself without any sort of counter to bargain with.

However, long before Pavia destroyed Wolsey's policy, it had suffered a severe and potentially fatal stroke at home. The renewal of war discovered the inadequacy of Henry's resources—no remaining reserves now, and so much of what should have been available squandered on such displays as the Field of Cloth of Gold. Wolsey needed money for his policy, and he was aware that he would have to face a Parliament. But since he had always thought that subsidy assessments underestimated national wealth, he first determined to establish the nation's ability to pay. Military preparations provided the pretext. The enquiry set on foot in March 1522 was planned to serve two purposes—to ascertain the military potential available and to acquire knowledge of people's financial assets.[12] The programme reflected to the full Wolsey's fertile mind and liking for grandiose schemes, but it also for once achieved considerable success. The military purpose came first. Wolsey meant to reform the militia, mustered by counties from all men over sixteen years of age. His commissioners, who were to collect detailed returns supplied by the constables of vills, demanded to know the names of all such people and their skill and equipment as soldiers; in addition, everyone's wealth in land and movables was assessed, and at least in some parts the commissioners enquired into tenurial relationships and aliens present (with occupations). Some of them went so far as to supply a census of the male part of the nation, with details of social description and employment.[13] The investigation also swept in all

[12] J. J. Goring, 'The General Proscription of 1522', *English Historical Review* LXXXVI (1971), pp. 681 ff.

[13] Few of the returns, which were never digested into a summary, now survive in anything like complete form.

the Church—information on the values of livings and on patronage—nor were religious houses exempt, though the enquiry left spiritual profits alone. By July, Wolsey felt that the commissioners were well enough serving the public purpose—musters—but he distrusted the financial assessments emerging and issued new directions for a second investigation. These second instructions gave the game away. The commissioners were to pretend that questions touching wealth were designed only to establish that the militia could arm itself; however, when the assessment was complete they were to dun all possessed of £20 and over for a forced loan (rated at at least ten per cent of their possessions). The loan was advertised as secured upon a grant to be made by a Parliament that had not then been called.

In itself, the operation may be called successful. The government learned that it had at its disposal a very large potential military force: in the twenty-eight counties for which information survives over 125,000 men could be called serviceable, though by law these were available for duty outside their counties only if they volunteered. No one followed this up: the great inquest led to no reform of the militia, and the information was neglected and forgotten. Money, on the other hand, came in in quantity. On the basis of the new assessments Wolsey extracted from the laity two so-called loans in 1522 and 1523 which raised £200,000, or more than three times the value of the previous parliamentary subsidies; the clergy, mulcted at the rate of 5s in the pound, produced another £55,000. And this was cash, collected at once, not promises—sufficient to send Surrey and Suffolk to France, though not enough to keep them there: the campaigns cost some £400,000, and Wolsey at one point took a step dangerous to himself when he asked Henry to release his private hoard. This further need, together with the promise given that the loans would be repaid, compelled Wolsey to allow the calling of a Parliament which assembled on 15 April 1523 and with a fortnight's intermission sat until 29 July. It turned out that Wolsey's dislike of Parliaments was justified; he could not manage them, and they gave too much opportunity (from his point of view) for criticizing policy and expressing widespread feelings about this rule of priests. Such meetings brought him up against the fact that England was no despotism, an inconvenient reality that usually he managed to ignore.

III

The Parliament opened peacefully enough. For the Speakership the Crown nominated Sir Thomas More who earned the office by his eminence in the law and his place of trust in the King's Council, conventional grounds for Speakership elections in Tudor Parliaments. The opening address, customarily the chancellor's opportunity to shine before King and Lords, was instead delivered by Cuthbert Tunstall, newly promoted to the see of London, who in elegant and unimpeachable fashion reviewed the nature of good kingship, the duties of subjects, the benefits of good order, and the problem of threats from abroad (the real reason for calling the assembly). He also promised reform legislation especially concerning errors in the law and poor justice. To tell the truth, Tunstall throughout his life never gave reason to think that his mind was other than platitudinous. More remarkable was the Speaker's address for privileges which Sir Thomas, deviating from convention, turned into a reasoned plea for the right of members to speak freely to matters before them, without fear of repercussions or victimization. This address has rightly been seen as the first, and classical, definition of the Commons' privilege of free speech, a privilege that Henry was to respect throughout his life even in the face of considerable provocation. However, these auspicious beginnings proved deceptive. The Commons, in particular, concentrated on the ills of the commonwealth and tried to take the promise of reform seriously, but the yield was poor. In the absence of journals for either House we do not know what was proposed; the tally of acts passed included fifteen on various points of public interest, none of them important and none concerned with the real grievances calling for reform. As Thomas Cromwell, whose first experience of Parliament this was, at the end reported to a friend:

> I amongst others have endured a Parliament ... where we communed of war, peace, strife, contentation, debate, murmur, grudge, riches, poverty, perjury, truth, falsehood, justice, equity, deceit, oppression, magnanimity, activity, force, attemprance, treason, murder, felony, conciliation and also how a commonwealth might be edified. However, in conclusion we have done as our predecessors have been wont to do, that is to say, as well as we might and left where we began.

In a way more interesting are the private acts, an unusually large number of them, which fact testifies to the increasing desire of the upper classes to settle their family and property problems by statute. It is worth remembering that much private inconvenience could result from long absences of Parliament.

That leaves one act, that for a subsidy, Wolsey's reason for having a Parliament but the cause of major trouble and of this Parliament's relative futility. Statutory reform meant nothing to Wolsey, and the Commons soon discovered what they were assembled for. Wolsey proposed a levy based on the stringent assessment of 1522, rated at 4s in the pound, which was four times higher than any previous subsidy rating. This the House flatly refused, nor could the Speaker do anything with them. There was much frank talk about the folly of an aggressive foreign policy which was draining the country of its wealth, to nobody's benefit; one of the most striking speeches, it appears, was delivered by Cromwell, a close client of Wolsey's who nevertheless (while professing the greatest respect for King and cardinal) questioned the wisdom of futile enterprises in France and called for a union with Scotland. Wolsey made matters much worse by thinking to overawe the Commons. He moved in upon the House in his full scarlet panoply and attended by his usual throng, harangued the Commons for ungrateful dogs, and ordered them to comply. The House listened in a sullen silence which More, on his knees, was compelled to explain by pointing out that the Commons never spoke in the presence of strangers. The cardinal beat a discomfited retreat, but the damage was done. In the end, More's great efforts secured the passage of the largest grant yet made, though well below Wolsey's demand—four subsidies at 1s in the pound, to be assessed anew for each of the four annual payments.

Wolsey thankfully sent the Parliament home, but he still had far less money than he needed, even allowing for the fact that he never meant to use any of the subsidy money for his advertised purpose of repaying the loans. In the autumn of 1523 he tried to get at least the wealthy to pay immediately, by way of 'anticipation', the first instalment of the grant due in 1524; the resistance he then met should have warned him. Though the first two payments of the subsidy did yield more than previous taxes—some £72,000 and £64,000 respectively—money remained exceedingly hard to come by, and English participation in the war was gravely affected. The revival of positive hopes of success in 1524 drove the cardinal into seeking fresh supply for the coming campaign which was to crown the work, and the investigation of 1522 suggested that the country could indeed pay more than it had yet done. So, in March–April 1524, Wolsey undertook to squeeze out yet another non-parliamentary tax, an old-fashioned benevolence which he dressed up in the novel name of an Amicable Grant. Recklessly he stepped up his demands: the laity were to pay at the rate of one sixth on movable property and the clergy at the fantastic rate of one third. Ever since the commissioners for the 1523 subsidy had started work, news of rebellious murmurs had been coming in from all over the country, and the Amicable Grant terminated obedience. The old loan was evidently lost and the new subsidy was being collected; people decided that enough was enough, and Wolsey had a tax-payers' strike on his hands. He discovered this for himself in London where he put pressure on the city, only to be told that benevolences were illegal by the act of 1484. His furious outburst at being confronted with a law made, as he said, by that usurper, Richard III, got the cool and very constitutional reply that, no matter how evil a man that king might have been, that law was made by the Parliament and therefore perfectly valid. He ought to have listened. Meanwhile he learned that his commissioners could get nothing and that the resistance was beginning to assume the trappings of a physical rebellion. His first reaction was to urge upon local magis-trates the use of force against resisters, but even he could not stand up to such united opposition. Then the King began to hear what was happening; threatened with a serious attack upon the peace of the realm, he showed himself possessed of better political sense than his chancellor. By late May, the grant was called off, and that—a few reprimands in Star Chamber apart—without any attempt to punish men who had talked rebellion. Wolsey tried to pretend that he had obtained the concession and pardon, but no one believed this; and for once Henry's customary arrogation to himself of popular actions, which left to others the odium of unpopular ones, looks to have rested on the facts of the case. The financial consequences of the fiasco extended beyond the loss of the grant. Much of the trouble had arisen from the fact that the subsidy of 1523 had applied a severe assessment to a much larger taxpaying population than usual. It was now thought prudent to relax these conditions, with the result that the last two instalments (1526 and 1527) yielded less than £15,000 between them, about ten per cent of the first two.

IV

The events of 1525 thus destroyed the cardinal's—and Rome's —European policy by setting up Charles V as the master of the continent and by demonstrating to the world that England did not possess the resources (or the ability to mobilize them) which such pretensions to great-power status required. Yet all this did not set Wolsey down. He immediately continued his diplomatic operations, trying to make unlikely profit out of the new situation; even more

significantly, at home he tried to look higher than ever. It is, on the
evidence, quite possible that he was at last falling victim to the
self-aggrandizement he had practised for so long. More and more he
enveloped himself in his cardinalate and legateship, treating the
nobility of England as well as his fellow councillors as manifest
inferiors; and from about 1520 observers noticed a growing tendency
in him to forget who was king. He ceased to be careful to associate
his master with himself in his doings; where once only others had
ascribed everything to him, he could now be found taking the same
line. To all appearance, his relations with Henry remained loving
and secure, but behind the façade the close trust on which his power
depended was evaporating. Wolsey's hold derived from success; with
Henry VIII, failure was always a most difficult thing to recover
from, and the experience of what the minister's arrogant recklessness
could do to the monarchy's hold on the nation was not lost on the
King. For the moment he held his hand; there was no one else to do
Wolsey's work, and as yet there was no reason to terminate an
arrangement which had brought Henry much glory and, more
important, had left him free to live the life he liked.

Wolsey's now almost feverish arrogance found easiest play in the
Church. While the Parliament of 1523 had inflicted a public defeat
on him, he used the concomitant meeting of Convocation to set the
seal on his conquest of Canterbury. By legatine writ he dissolved
Warham's synod at St Paul's and called the clergy to his assembly
convened at Westminster, thus demonstrating his rule over the
Church of all England. He broke with erstwhile supporters like
Richard Foxe and trounced those willing to try resistance, like Nixe of
Norwich and Blythe of Lichfield. Above all, he now elaborated the
machinery of legatine control which had been building since 1521.
Clement VII's grant of the legateship for life (1524) lacked some
refinements and additional powers that Wolsey had desired, but it
sufficed to erect a new structure of jurisdiction. Wolsey's courts and
officials superseded diocesan rights in the administration of probate,
carried out metropolitical visitations, monopolized the profitable
trade in dispensations and licences, and intervened to pre-empt
patronage rights over benefices. After Warham gave up the fight
early in 1523, lesser men had no choice but to follow suit.[14] All was
done in the proclaimed interest of reform, but what actually happened left no doubt that money and the assertion of personal power
constituted the cardinal's overriding concern. One bishop after

[14] For all this see M. J. Kelly, 'Canterbury Jurisdiction and Influence during the Episcopate of
William Warham, 1503–1532' (unpublished dissertation, Cambridge, 1963), pp. 174 ff. As Dr
Kelly says: 'In many respects 1523 marked the high point and the extermination of resistance
to Wolsey from the hierarchy of the southern province.'

another was forced into agreements which transferred the bulk of profits from testamentary causes to the cardinal, and the traffic in dispensations even cut off the profits of Rome by diverting the stream into the legate's pockets. The Pope had reluctantly created an office which long experience had shown was always much disliked in England, and indeed anywhere that papal legates *a latere* penetrated, and he had done so because Wolsey had promised to raise money for Rome from the English clergy; yet the cursory efforts to fulfil this promise came to nothing, as they were bound to do when the clergy were being taxed so heavily on behalf of the Crown and so generally fleeced by the legate. Of Wolsey's effective exploitation of ecclesiastical wealth there can be no doubt at all: to the direct enjoyment of an exceptionally scandalous collection of preferments, he now added what in effect was a regular tribute from the whole bench of bishops and many lesser dignitaries.

Not all Wolsey's activity in the Church deserves execration, though one always feels that any beneficial use of his powers came to him as a secondary consideration. It is worth remembering that his priesthood meant something to him—unlike some of his contemporaries on the continent Wolsey was not a layman dressed up in clerical clothes—and that his generous and scholarly instincts remained available on the ever rarer occasions when other considerations did not overrule them. The livings he wrested from their proper patrons often went to very suitable and even excellent candidates, though it all involved rampant simony and though such undeserving clients as his bastard son Thomas Winter also did well. When, in 1528, Henry VIII for once came into conflict with the cardinal on such a matter, the King was in the wrong; he tried to force a very unsatisfactory abbess with an unsavoury past upon a nunnery, but found Wolsey rightly and successfully obstinate.[15] There was also one item in the humanist programme—a programme Wolsey had always professed to champion—which did receive attention from him. He tried to assist in the reform of education. Although he could not dislodge Warham as chancellor of Oxford, he maintained a lively interest in his old university which came to regard him as its prime patron. In 1518, when an old-fashioned preacher there attacked the advance of the new learning at the expense of scholastic theology and drew the fire of Thomas More, the cardinal's was among the names cited in support of the humanist. In 1524 Wolsey called for the statutes of both universities and talked of reform, though (true to habit) he did nothing further. However, like others before and since, he discovered a way of serving

[15] M. D. Knowles, 'The Matter of Wilton', *Bulletin of the Institute of Historical Research* xxxi (1958), pp. 92 ff.

education which would add glory to his own name: he determined to follow the example of Foxe (founder of Corpus Christi College at Oxford) by setting up a new college there. Being Wolsey, he immediately planned on a grand scale: he would found the most splendid college ever seen and back it up with a grammar school that should become the pride of his home town, Ipswich.

He did not, however, mean to go to the expense himself; the means for endowing such institutions lay ready to hand in the wealth of certain decaying monasteries upon which humanist eyes had been cast before. The 1522 survey may have given Wolsey an indication of where to look, nor was he the first to take over such endowments for educational purposes. As recently as 1524, Bishop Fisher had added the property of two decayed nunneries to his college of St John's at Cambridge. Once again, Wolsey's only innovation was to think big. In 1524-5, proceeding by the correct canonical methods and obtaining papal bulls for his authority, he dissolved some twenty houses and added their property to that of St Frideswide's Abbey, Oxford, the site of his intended Cardinal College. It has been calculated that in effect he disposed of the equivalent of one large abbey—some £1,800 a year confiscated and some eighty inmates transferred to other houses. In 1528-9 he added another seven (worth £200 p.a.) with which to support the school at Ipswich. The work was done by expert agents who encountered more resistance and caused more murmuring than Wolsey had expected; there were signs that despite the decline of monasticism the religious themselves remained attached to their status and the neighbourhood did not want to see them go. Thomas Cromwell, in particular, acquired a bad reputation for the energy and ruthlessness with which he carried out the cardinal's orders.

Cardinal College (1527) was conceived very lavishly, with six professorships attached to it which were to support a system of public lectures long since advocated by reformers and adumbrated by Wolsey himself as early as 1518. Ipswich School was opened in September 1529, on the eve of Wolsey's fall. That event proved fatal to one and nearly fatal to the other institution because Wolsey had been unwilling to transfer the endowments formally to his creations. They were thus found in his possession and therefore forfeit. Nothing could be done about Ipswich, but Cromwell's devoted labours saved the Oxford college, refounded and renamed as King's College (later Christ Church), though rather more modestly. In some ways, Wolsey's purposes in these foundations departed from the humanist stereotype. His Oxford professorships combined tradition with novel learning and placed much emphasis on the study of the civil law; the Ipswich school, though it was planned to use the new textbooks

(Lily's *Latin Grammar* and Erasmus's popular guides to a sound Latin style) as well as the St Paul's school curriculum, was meant to concentrate less on Colet's preference for a moral excellence than on the production of a learned clergy. Like other developments that followed upon Colet's initiative of 1508, Wolsey's purpose was directed towards improving the quality of potential state servants. Trained civilians were needed in the diplomatic service and the administration of equity jurisdiction; and the clergy emerging from the new schools and colleges regularly sought careers in office—in Wolsey's household and through it later in the King's service. The promoters of educational reform had always had these practical concerns in mind, in which respect they differed from Colet though less so from Erasmus, Vives and More. Yet for the present practice diverged from the thought of these leading theorists by still providing an education in the main for the clergy. Some of the laity were putting their children to study, and by the 1540s public life was beginning to offer opportunities to laymen trained in humanist learning, with some sort of a university career behind them. In the 1520s, however, the products of the system still took orders. If William Cecil, of St John's College, was to be typical of later practices, at this earlier date the characteristic university man in high places was Stephen Gardiner, civilian and humanist, whose career began at Cambridge (where he became master of Trinity Hall) but was pursued through service as secretary to both Wolsey and Henry VIII to an episcopate and membership of the Council.

In another way, however, Gardiner was less typical of what was happening: very much the lawyer, he remained firmly opposed to reform when it took the form of Reformation. One unforeseen complication arising out of educational improvements and innovations—unforeseen by More and Erasmus, too—was the growing number of scholars and students who espoused the new heresies. By a neat twist of fate, Wolsey, recruiting for his college among the brighter minds of Cambridge, imported the nascent Protestantism of the White Horse Tavern into Oxford where conservatives were soon raising anguished voices. By 1525, in fact, it became apparent that new developments were confusing the bishops' stand against heresy, and Wolsey once more turned his mind to the struggle with Luther. In December Robert Barnes preached a sermon in St Edward's Church at Cambridge which has caused some to elect that small but attractive edifice as the foundation place of the English Reformation, though in actual fact his words—an incendiary attack on the insufficiencies of the Church and especially the bishops—contained no Lutheran theology. Indeed, Barnes does not at this time seem to have been well acquainted with Luther's thought. His assault on bishops, however, made him a suitable victim. Wolsey, who examined him, treated him gently till he found him hopelessly stiff-necked, and Barnes in the end joined some German merchants on their knees in penance at yet another book-burning staged in February 1526. Subsequently he remained in custody in various places until he escaped to Antwerp in 1528, from where he moved to Wittenberg and conversion to Lutheranism.

Antwerp became the refuge of English reformers as persecution increased. Tyndale fled there when his translation of the New Testament, of necessity published abroad (at Cologne), made him at once into England's leading heresiarch; and he was joined by George Joye (persecuted at Cambridge in 1527) and John Frith (driven from Oxford in 1528). The authorities made some energetic efforts to stop the growth of the new heresies. In London they concentrated on the Hanseatic merchants of the Steelyard, raided twice and in vain by Thomas More early in 1527 for evidence of Lutheranism, but the main strategy aimed to prevent the importation of dangerous books (especially Tyndale's translation, which got through with ease) and to quieten the young men in the universities. Wolsey himself was never forward in such matters; firmly orthodox and in no real sense tolerant, he also lacked the persecutor's temperament. The lead was taken by some of the bishops well experienced in hunting Lollards; by Cuthbert Tunstall whose diocese of London lay particularly exposed to the new wave; and by More who through these years came increasingly to think that by attacking the authority of the universal Church the heretical 'brethren' threatened every form of truth and order. In 1528 More got a special licence from Tunstall to study heretical writings and prepare himself for the role of the champion of orthodoxy. The sporadic persecution looked for a time successful. At Cambridge, with Tyndale gone, protesting voices fell silent as the bishops enforced submission upon such as Hugh Latimer and Edward Crome, ardent and effective preachers both, and extorted a recantation from poor Thomas Bilney, convicted of heresy on very slender grounds. At Oxford, the subversive element was reduced to order when during the investigation some trouble-makers at Cardinal's College conveniently died (in the course of nature and the sweating sickness of 1528), while Richard Taverner, the most Erasmian of England's future Protestants, submitted and Frith fled abroad. But all the time heretical writings were spreading, mostly in manuscript; old Lollard groups were gaining new confidence in contacts with the innovators; the new learning acquired fresh adherents who recognized the connection between reform in general and reform in the Church; and the exiles in Antwerp and Wittenberg developed into a first generation of genuine Protestants—well equipped followers of the new theology. In England, as elsewhere, Luther's uncompromising doctrine of justification by faith alone exercised an appeal which can only be called liberating and exhilarating. If man's salvation and the life eternal were wholly in the will of God, who asked of men only faith in his Word, the apparatus of salvation-ensuring works (such as prayers and pilgrimages and intercessory saints), as well as its agents (the priesthood), became not only superfluous but positively blasphemous. To its followers the Lutheran revolution offered the simple strength (ranging from faith to bigotry) that comes to those who surrender themselves to divine omnipotence. And all the time the total failure to remedy the notorious and ever more publicized shortcomings of the old order in the Church maintained the passions of those who combined anticlerical distaste with a vision of renewal.

V

Wolsey had not the slightest intention of carrying out the reforms in the pastoral behaviour of the bishops, the conduct of the church courts, or the failure of the religious orders to observe the rule for which his legate's bulls repeatedly equipped him. (He did once tackle the orders and ran into resistance from the strict Franciscan Observants who thought themselves better able to judge proper behaviour than a cardinal tainted with notorious sin.) Nor did he satisfy those who wished to see the spreading heresy stamped out. His interest in the Church remained stubbornly financial. As for his fitful interest in general reform, it was revived by the experiences of the years 1523–5 when he had learned how feeble central authority could be in the face of determined local resistance. We have already noticed that at this point he decided to distribute that authority somewhat by delegating cases coming before the Council in Star Chamber to the relevant parts of the realm, more particularly to councils operating in the north and the marches of Wales. This decision was accompanied by some overhauling of the machinery for governing those notoriously difficult regions. Wolsey returned to methods practised by the Yorkists and Henry VII, methods ostentatiously abandoned in 1509 as part of the reaction towards a 'freer' aristocratic society: he planted in those parts members of the royal family as symbols of the crown and equipped them with the large households and personal councils proper to the establishments of major landowners. The Princess Mary, nine years old, went to Ludlow where a council of sorts had continued to administer an ineffective jurisdiction over Wales and the border counties; the real head of the reformed organization was the new lord president, Bishop John Vesey of Exeter. In the north, local rule had been left to the nobility, especially Lord Dacre of Gilsland, whose government of the borders had been severely criticized by the earls of Shrewsbury and Surrey when they visited the region in 1522 and 1523 to prepare for defence against Scotland. Wolsey wanted a personal council here, too, but unfortunately Henry VIII had no legitimate issue except his one daughter; and unlike Charles V he did not believe in relying on unemployed sisters. He and Wolsey therefore found a rather dubious answer in his illegitimate offspring, Henry Fitzroy, the son of Elizabeth Blount. The boy was made duke of Richmond (his grandfather's earldom), endowed with vast properties in Yorkshire, and sent north with a body of administrators and councillors whose names confirm Wolsey's hand in all this. The ecclesiastical administration of the cardinal's archbishopric supplied the financial specialists, while the boy's council consisted of some clerics and some local knights with military experience most of whom were Wolsey's clients. This council for the first time extended its rule also over the wardenships of the borders, while that in the Welsh marches expressly covered all the lordships there. To that extent Wolsey modestly improved a machinery which relied less on regionally competent councils than on the territorial power of a Tudor representative, imitating but superseding the similar powers of non-Tudor magnates. However, nothing really new was here attempted or achieved, even though both councils were equipped with the full range of common law and equity jurisdiction. In the west, Vesey proved a poor choice—insufficiently energetic and easily distracted by business at Westminster and in his diocese. In the north, Wolsey's agents acted energetically enough, especially in the search for money, but their methods provoked much resentment and the pressure had soon to be eased. Above all, these reforms again underlined the clerical dominance over England's government.

At the centre of that government, Wolsey also found time in 1525 to attend to one of the matters raised in 1519: he undertook the reform of the royal Household. In January 1526, visiting Henry (a refugee from the plague) at the Surrey manor of Eltham, he promulgated a comprehensive ordinance for its better order.[16] The seventy-nine chapters dealt in often minute detail with the work of all the offices composing this very large establishment and also, as has been said,[17] proposed a reform of the Council; they did some-

[16] The best discussion of these reforms, throwing new light, is in Starkey, 'The King's Privy Chamber', pp. 133 ff.
[17] See above, p. 62.

thing to promote the ostensible aim of economy; but the core and cause of the operation lay in the problem of the Privy Chamber, newly institutionalized in 1519 and now explicitly reorganized as a third department in the Household.[18] Wolsey's victory in ejecting the King's friends and reducing the size of the Privy Chamber had not lasted long; in the early 1520s, the department again grew rapidly, and some of the men the cardinal distrusted came back into it. The labour of renewed reform took several months and occupied his very personal attention. Part of his problem was that the men he wished to eject now held salaried posts by letters patent, so that he had to negotiate rather than dictate. In the end, by some highly ingenious juggling of vacant crown appointments, he succeeded in reducing the Privy Chamber from twenty-two to fifteen and in getting rid of his personal opponents there. It is quite true that there was need and room for economy in the King's entourage, but the political motive manifestly predominated. There had been occasional tussles before between Wolsey and Henry over the minister's inclination to attract to his presence those who should have been attending upon the King: Henry had several times complained about the dearth of distinguished men about him. Wolsey provided for this by giving him a well organized Privy Chamber staffed by men of lineage who had no obvious political ambitions, and he pretended further to make sure that there should always be sufficient members of the Council at court, though in this respect in fact nothing changed.

The events of the years 1523–5 brought home the need for economy, but the return of political motives can be dated even more precisely. Until the middle of 1525 Wolsey had suffered the reintroduction of his enemies into the Privy Chamber because he had been able to neutralize their influence by compelling them to leave the royal presence on diplomatic and military service. The trick was used consistently from 1521 onwards, nor did it escape notice at the time; and the gentlemen of the Privy Chamber could hardly refuse such honourable employment customary to their rank and station. In August 1525, the treaty of the More (Wolsey's Hertfordshire mansion) ended a diplomatic revolution by making peace with France. Among other things, this event returned gentlemen on active service to the King's presence, so that Wolsey felt compelled to draft, with his own hand, proposals for Household reform, and to conduct in his own person haggling deals over such things as the

[18]The traditional departments were the Household proper (below stairs —responsible for supply and maintenance) under the lord steward, and the Chamber (above stairs —responsible for ceremonial and entertainment) under the lord chamberlain. The Stable (under the master of the Horse) and the Great Wardrobe (under its keeper) usually enjoyed a semi-independent existence.

stewardship of the Duchy of Lancaster and the undertreasureship of the Exchequer, while engaged in rescuing what he could from his ally's inconvenient triumph in Italy.

The battle of Pavia had frustrated all the calculations upon which the Rome–London axis had operated since 1521.[19] De' Medici and Wolsey would seem to have consistently overestimated the power of France and underrated Charles V, as many people did who allowed themselves to be dazzled by pomp and splendour, but as anyone might do who had grown up in an age when Spain and Empire meant Ferdinand of Aragon and Maximilian. Their policy had aimed at creating a stalemate of exhaustion which would remove the French from Italy without establishing imperial and Spanish rule there. England would benefit by ending the French use of Scotland and possibly gain some compensation in northern France for the return of Tournai. Both papacy and Wolsey needed a deadlock between Charles and Francis to make themselves once more effective mediators and arbitrators. Charles V's total victory (in retrospect not unpredictable), together with the pitiful showing of Suffolk's army and the running down of English financial resources, demolished this house of cards. Papal diplomacy at once went into the familiar routine of redressing the balance in Italy by deserting a victorious ally in favour of a defeated enemy, but the first English reaction was different because Henry, not bound to the Roman connection, took a hand of his own. Seeing no reason why he should not cash in on Charles's victory, he toyed with dreams of restoring the English empire in France and proposed a joint invasion of that now leaderless realm so that it might be divided between Habsburg and Tudor. If, as his biographer supposes and as seems likely,[20] the scheme was the King's alone, his lack of any real understanding or political insight is worth notice. Charles, who both needed peace and understood the impossibility of permanently occupying France, made his contemptuous opinion very plain, but Henry went ahead at least to the extent of trying to raise cash for the enterprise. The result was the Amicable Grant and the public pratfall which the King managed to shuffle off onto Wolsey. It was at this point that the Emperor revealed the full extent of his contempt for his uncle of England. Already twenty-five years old he needed to marry and produce heirs; yet his bride was the nine years old Mary of England. He therefore asked that she, and her dowry, be sent to Spain to celebrate and consummate the marriage—an impossibility which indicated his real purpose. What he wanted and achieved was an abrupt repudiation of the contract. However justified his repre-

[19] See above, p. 87.
[20] Scarisbrick, *Henry VIII*, pp. 135 ff.

sentations, and however obvious it had been for some time that the engagement could hardly stand, Henry, who had dreamed of a world empire for his daughter, took the blow very hard.

Thus by the middle of 1525 the road was clear for Wolsey once more to follow the lead of Rome and manoeuvre in the direction of France. He had his own reasons for resentment, for Charles V had twice promised to support him in a papal election and had twice gone back on that promise. However, it does not look as though Wolsey, for once, bore a grudge; he changed direction for reasons less private. Personal considerations of pride and injury moved Henry; Wolsey sought peace partly for the sake of peace and partly because only peace could make penniless England once more into the arbiter of Europe. At the same time Wolsey's policy continued to owe much to his close links with Clement VII and Lorenzo Campeggio. And so, in August 1525, England came to terms with France and withdrew from the imperial alliance.

Though at this point it began to look as though Wolsey, too, was losing his sense of reality, it is more likely that a mixture of his desire to advance papal policy and his need to demonstrate to Henry England's continued power and influence drove him into an extravagant attempt to repeat the triumph of 1518. He set about a diplomacy designed to force Charles into making peace with France, a policy which would extort respect from the Emperor and gratitude from the King who would thus both once more come to recognize the cardinal's mediating role; once more the European amity would be conjured up under his benevolent hand. Since Charles V held all the good cards and had no reason to love either England or Wolsey (or Clement VII), this was not the most promising of lines to take. Still, for a time it looked possible. Francis I returned from captivity in early 1526, released on solemn promises, guaranteed by hostages, which he at once disavowed. Instead of making peace with Spain he determined on revenge, an attitude which played into Wolsey's hands. Later that year, English machinations created the League of Cognac (France, the papacy and the main north Italian states) which renewed war in Italy—so much for Wolsey the peacemaker. To the allies' distress and disgust, England refused to join actively: Wolsey intended to be free to pick up the pieces, and he had no money—and the country no stomach—for war.

By now, however, the cardinal was moving on a stage of his own, barely related to that occupied by the monarchs of Europe. In the spring of 1527 he went on yet .another of his grandiose journeys, visiting Paris, proposing peace to France, promising to go on to Madrid and persuade the Emperor to agreement. He did obtain a formal confirmation of the treaty of the More (and of the sizable pension he drew from France), but a month later, in May 1527, the whole insubstantial structure collapsed around his ears. The imperial army, unpaid, weary and mutinous, ignoring one of its commanders (who died of a heart attack) and forcing the other into compliance (who died in the assault), stormed the city of Rome and sacked it in a fortnight's orgy of looting, murdering, raping and general destruction. The Sack of Rome shocked all Europe, including very definitely the Emperor Charles. Everything else apart, it ended the world of the Renaissance papacy, the world whose relations and diplomacy Wolsey had understood—had indeed helped to create—and had so brilliantly exploited. With the Pope effectively the Emperor's prisoner, that element in the equation upon whose guidance the cardinal had depended was gone. The League of Cognac, Wolsey's instrument for making peace in England's interest, had produced only an even more exalted imperial ascendancy. The Sack of Rome confirmed the message of Pavia, and Italy was to stay Spanish for over a century. Nothing remained of Wolsey's policy which had left England isolated and unable to command anything—gratitude or obligation or need—that could be used to lessen that isolation. The clever move from an imperial to a French alliance, intended to end those hostile confrontations, had turned into a disaster as protests came in from clothing districts worried about the trade with Charles's Netherlands, and as it became plain to Wolsey—much too late—that he had lost the one control that mattered. Henry was about to set an entirely new course the success of which depended on the assistance of a papacy no longer free to please England and the compliance of an Emperor newly hostile to that nation. Henry was seeking to jettison his wife, the Emperor's aunt and for so long the pledge of the Habsburg alliance. He had embarked on his first divorce, and the age of Wolsey was nearing its end.

5 Divorce and Confusion[1]

I

It is not known when Henry VIII decided that he had had enough of his wife. Despite its inauspicious beginnings, his union with Catherine of Aragon had become something of a public wonder and in private an unusually good marriage. At the hunts, the jousts, the feasts and the religious observances which filled their time, the royal couple were always together. The Queen took her share of political labours, too: behind the scenes she used her influence in the interests of the Spanish alliance, and on stage she was permitted to play the part of Queen Philippa to Henry's Edward III in the aftermath of Evil May Day. Henry's extramarital activities were, for a king, almost ludicrously few—two or three known affairs, one illegitimate offspring and another rumoured. To judge by Catherine's pregnancies—in eight years she produced one daughter, five infants that did not survive, and several miscarriages—his marital activities, on the other hand, were vigorous. So far as such things can be established, it looks pretty certain that Henry loved his queen. But she was seven years older than he and, as women who suffered so many pregnancies did

[1] With this chapter the narrative moves into a very difficult sector. While most of the facts are reasonably agreed, interpretations differ widely. That which I put forward some twenty-five years ago ('King or Minister?', *Studies in Tudor and Stuart Government and Politics*, 1974, II, pp. 173 ff.; *England under the Tudors*, 1955, chapter 5) was too simple: I singled out Thomas Cromwell too much and overemphasized the originality of his ideas. I now also think, however, that I accepted too late a date for his first political intervention. Views which argue that Henry was at all times sovereignly in charge (J. J. Scarisbrick, *Henry VIII*) or that nothing very new and drastic was happening (G. L. Harriss in *Past and Present* 25, 1963, pp. 13 ff.) are also too simple. We shall never know the full story, so much of which was played out in private minds and unrecorded conversations, but the intensive work of the past two decades has at least made a subtler and deeper understanding possible. I shall here tell the story as I now think it was, in reliance on the researches of others as well as my own. The best recent account of the Divorce and its circumstances is in Scarisbrick, *Henry VIII*; I shall in particular follow his analysis of the canon law, and while I cannot agree with his interpretation of the years 1529–34 I accept his demonstration of Henry's personal participation as well as other points. The as yet unfinished researches of Mr Graham Nicholson are adding most valuably to our understanding of ideas and policies.

in that age, lost her physical attraction quite early. Moreover, her failure to produce the brood of children demanded of queens even more than of wives in general preyed on her mind; a temperament always sober and pious grew painfully devout, and probably rather tedious. Later events have made it exceedingly difficult to get a clear sight of Catherine of Aragon. Once she had become the wronged wife she was loaded with all the virtues, and since on top of that she stood for one religious party a dispassionate appraisal has become even less likely. She may have been all that her partisans say she was—modest, obedient, intelligent, upright, calm, wise. But an addiction to penitential piety shot through with sorrow, a tendency to withdraw from the bright lights to the embroidery frame, and a serious interest in the edifying discourses of humanists whom her husband liked to patronize rather than heed made her increasingly dull. It also looks as though, those long years of marriage notwithstanding, she had no idea how dangerous the King was.

Against the background of this gradually changing relationship, the political problems assumed an ominous shape. To Wolsey, Catherine had always been one of those alternative centres of power which he did his best to eliminate, and Catherine had always returned his politically charged hostility with a personal dislike proper to a devout daughter of the Church in the face of this incongruous ruler of it. So long as Henry backed Wolsey, Catherine knew trouble; she was to ascribe her later real troubles to the cardinal's doing, though in this she was wrong. All he did was to refrain from arresting Henry's drift away from her. The real reasons behind the break were personal to the King. In the early 1520s Henry began to get very worried about the succession to the throne, and with his only heir a little girl he had cause to be. The efforts to find a politically suitable husband for her testify to his anxiety, as did (whatever other motives may have played their part) the destruction of Buckingham. More pointed still was the public recognition and elevation of little Henry, duke of Richmond,[2] followed by vague plans for marrying him to his half-sister Mary, four years older than himself. Even Henry's very manifest fear of every hint of plague or other epidemics, which has provided much sober amusement for some historians, contained a measure of justified apprehension of what might happen if he were to die with no suitable successor around. Still, his fears produced some odd results, including sufficient insults to the Queen to reveal how far her alienation from her husband had gone. All this took place in the wake of Henry's break with Charles V whose jilting of Mary, in itself pretty well

[2] See above, p. 98.

inevitable, was done so brutally as to leave the King in a lasting cold fury. After the diplomatic revolution of 1525, the Queen stood in a very precarious position—linked to a defunct policy and a hated ex-ally, and personally no longer acceptable to her husband.

So far the situation looked promising to Wolsey who, well aware of Henry's growing desire to discard Catherine and marry a younger wife capable of giving him male heirs, planned to clinch the alliance with France by supplying a French princess in the stead of the now useless Aragonese. Strangely, however, he at first completely missed the really crucial element in the story. It was probably Wolsey's very worldliness that for once let him down: he could hardly believe how serious the King was to be about what looked to him like a commonplace amour. Dissatisfied as Henry may have been with his marriage, it is most improbable that he would have embarked on the problems of a divorce at all if he had not had a successor to Catherine in mind—and he wanted no French princesses. From 1525 onwards he became ever more infatuated with Anne Boleyn, the sister of an earlier mistress and daughter of the courtier Sir Thomas Boleyn who had already earned promotion by his elder daughter Mary's involvement with the King. If the conventional picture of Catherine as the wronged Griselda owed something to partisanship, so do the usual descriptions of Anne as a schemer, a liar and a bitch. Her attraction for Henry is a matter of private chemistry; however, against the tearful tedium of his consort she could put youth, zest, verve and some beauty, as well as a gift to tantalize. She was only eighteen when she captivated Henry, but she was an experienced flirt and knew how to play her cards. Warned by Mary's example she wanted all or nothing—or rather, she wanted all and offered nothing till all was guaranteed. She would be Henry's lawful queen; until that was assured he would never enter her bed. That her resolve succeeded had something to do with the fact that what Henry needed was lawful issue begotten in wedlock, but something also with Anne's personality. There was a lot more to her than the minx and flibbertigibbet of a hostile tradition. From Wolsey's point of view, the King's infatuation was disastrous. It removed the attractive opportunity for using his marriage in the tricky diplomacy then afoot, and it forced the cardinal to work for the success of one whom he disliked and who hated him. Not only had he humiliated Anne a few years earlier when he was told by the King to separate her from an ardent suitor, Henry earl of Northumberland, but in addition all the Boleyns and Anne in particular leaned seriously towards the new reform in the Church. Despite frequent doubts on this point, it is likely that her inclination towards a moderate Protestantism was as serious as Catherine's devotion to the papal Church.[3]   Early in 1527 Henry at last revealed to Wolsey the full horror of the problem, and the immensity of the crisis became apparent at once. The King's brooding egotism had turned these issues of love, lust, discontent and policy into a rooted scruple of conscience and a conviction of God's displeasure which needed assuaging. He had discovered, probably for himself, that his marriage to Catherine was invalid from the first because it contravened the divine injunctions (Leviticus xx, 21) against marriage to a brother's widow; God's wrath at the sin had manifested itself in the deaths of the fruits of the union. The obstacle of prohibited affinity created by Arthur's earlier marriage to Catherine had, of course, been recognized at the time and had received the conventional solution, a bull of dispensation issued by Pope Julius II. Henry now insisted that the Levitical law could not be overridden by any human authority; the bull was invalid and so, therefore, was his marriage. In fact, he was and always had been a bachelor free to marry where he liked, though the fact, which no man could deny, still needed formally pronouncing in the processes of the canon law. He therefore asked Wolsey to take the necessary steps and sat back in confidence that the business would be quickly settled. Instead he found that he had started seven endless years of trouble which were to swallow up not only Catherine and Wolsey but the whole world to which they belonged.

Complex as the history of the so-called Divorce was to be—to the salacious enjoyment and exasperated anger of a continent—the basic legal issue remained simple. Henry maintained two points: the law of Scripture prohibited the marriage to Catherine, and from that law the pope had no power to dispense. He rested his case on the affinity created when Catherine became his sister-in-law, but this existed only (in law) if her marriage to Arthur had been consummated. This Catherine denied throughout, and though Henry for years maintained that she knew as well as he did that she had not come a virgin to him, in the end he admitted that she had spoken the truth. Why he so firmly tied his cause to a lie remains a mystery, especially as an alternative existed to which Catherine had no defence. As Wolsey pointed out almost at once, an unconsummated marriage also raised a legal impediment (called the impediment of public honesty) which needed removal by a papal dispensation—and Julius's bull had inadvertently omitted to dispose of the lesser matter while dealing with the impediment of affinity. A decree of nullity could thus rest

---

[3] See, for example, E. E. Lowinsky, 'A Music Book for Anne Boleyn', in *Florilegium Historiale: Essays presented to Wallace K. Ferguson*, edited by J. G. Rowe and W. H. Stockdale (1971), pp. 16 ff.

on the insufficiency of the dispensation rather than its invalidity. Henry ignored this ingenious solution and pushed on with arguments of which he had convinced himself. Most probably we have here only an example of the King's blind obstinacy once he had fixed a matter in the inmost foundations of his heart; after all, whatever motives may have been playing around his mind, both the first decision to proceed and the astonishing persistence he showed thereafter derived from the transmutation of all arguments into a fanatical conviction which no longer had anything to do with arguments.

Henry needed that conviction because, in actual fact, his case was bad. Against Leviticus stood a verse in Deuteronomy (xxv, 5) which enjoined a man to marry his brother's childless widow—a custom, called the levirate, designed to perpetuate a family—while against his denial of the pope's right to dispense stood centuries of precedents. Henry and his agents spent vast amounts of time, money and ink on establishing the scriptural and legal soundness of his allegations, but at all times the best opinion was against him on both counts. To his fury, his most active and most powerful opponent turned out to be one of his own bishops—John Fisher, who from the first espoused Catherine's cause and relentlessly worked for her, producing at least seven tracts (some of them published in print, and all widely circulated) to affirm the validity of her second marriage. It is really very doubtful whether a genuine enquiry, impartially considering the arguments, could ever have found for Henry, and this played its part in obstructing the quick solution which the King at first believed was available to him. But in fact there never could be any question of such simplicity; Henry's bombshell did not drop into a vacuum. He was asking two things of Rome: to deny a well attested (and profitable) exercise of the papal *plena potestas*, and to do so in order that he might throw out the Emperor's aunt at a time when the Pope was, for practical purposes, the Emperor's prisoner. That Charles V neither would nor could tolerate the proposed insult to his family was certain: his powerful feelings of dynastic obligation reflected not only sentiment but also the necessary foundation of an empire created by family alliances alone. The moment that Henry informed Catherine, to her shock and horror, of his inability any longer to regard her as his wife (June 1527) the situation was plain: what was in prospect was no trial, fair or rigged, of the legal and theological points at issue, but a battle for the Pope between Imperialists and English. And in that battle the former held every card that mattered.

At first, Henry saw no reason to suppose so. Did he not have his cardinal—legate *a latere* and capable of substituting for the Pope?

The very first move assumed that there was no need to involve Rome at all. In May 1527, Wolsey, by arrangement, summoned Henry to a secret court held by himself and Warham—the two metropolitans in England—to answer to the charge that he had been living in sin with his alleged wife. Henry planned to aubmit with public tears of regret to the inevitable sentence of nullity. However, Catherine's reaction when she heard what was afoot, together with the Sack of Rome, put an end to this; it was now certain that she would not accept the secret court's verdict without launching the appeal to Rome for which the law provided, and Rome at this point meant Charles V. It became necessary to alter the international situation so as to free Clement VII for his intended part in the story: he was to set up a court in England by granting Wolsey a decretal commission, that is to say a commission authorizing a judgement unappealable to Rome on the grounds that the Pope had beforehand declared that he would entertain no such appeal. All the negotiations that extended from late 1527 to the summer of 1529 intended that purpose, with successive English ambassadors pressing for the decretal commission, the Emperor's ambassadors preventing its granting, and Clement trying to devise subtle ways which would satisfy the English and yet leave him to do the Emperor's bidding after.

Wolsey knew well that his fate depended on success, and increasingly, as the delays and tricks drove Henry into a mounting fury, he came to prophesy to all who would listen that the whole Church and the English allegiance to Rome were involved in his downfall. Accurate as this forecast proved, it is hard to tell how deeply he believed lamentations clearly used to move Rome for the sake of saving himself; Henry, at any rate, at this time gave no sign that he even contemplated taking his realm into schism. For a long time he continued to believe that one who had so often proved his loyalty and usefulness to the head of the Church would obtain justice from that head, and at intervals he clearly suspected Wolsey, not Charles V, of being the real obstacle to success. He knew Wolsey's feelings about Anne: she made sure that he did. One feels for Wolsey, accused by one side of having started the whole embroilment and by the other of working against its solution. But the man who had always taken all power and glory to himself, and who had landed England in the false position of 1527–8, deserved blame. On top of everything else, the switch away from the Emperor had destroyed Wolsey's contacts with the Curia. Since Campeggio, cardinal-protector of England, was also cardinal-protector of the German Empire, Wolsey neglected him altogether just when he was most needed. The Imperialists not only had an army in Italy but commanded powerful interests around the Pope himself, whereas the

English had to work through residents of little weight and lesser envoys despatched at intervals into the maelstrom.

The first moves were made soon after the Sack of Rome when Wolsey, in France, tried to organize the rescue of the Pope by means of a general peace. Impatiently, Henry went behind his minister's back with a device that reveals his crude ineptitude. He sent his secretary, William Knight, to Rome with the draft of a bull for Clement's seal, a draft designed to solve the problem by pretending that none existed. The bull was to free the bachelor King for marriage to Anne by removing the impediment he had incurred by his relations with her sister;[4] the preamble was casually to mention that there had never been any lawful marriage between him and Catherine. Wolsey discovered the plot but let Knight go on; he knew that Rome would not fall for so obvious a trick. No more it did. The experience did not stop Henry from dreaming up further fantastical schemes. In the spring of 1528 he made Wolsey propose the sending of an Anglo-French military contingent, 2,000 men strong, to protect the Pope and thus free him from his terror of the Emperor. Such extravagances apart, the successive missions concentrated through-out 1528 on extracting a decretal commission to try the case conclusively in England, and to everybody's surprise one was at last issued, to Wolsey and Campeggio jointly. Miserably ill with the gout, Campeggio finally arrived in September 1528, triumphantly waving the precious commission, but carefully concealing Clement's private instruction to prevent it from ever being used. Clement had granted it to be rid of the bullying to which Henry's envoys, especially the impatiently self-assertive Stephen Gardiner, had subjected him; but he had not forgotten whose wrath he needed to fear the most.

Campeggio thought to discharge his private orders best by pro-ducing endless delays. On his initiative, several attempts were made to get Catherine to solve the problem by entering a nunnery; she refused indignantly. In October, a new obstacle suddenly reared up, in the form of a brief of Julius II's, conveniently found in Spain, which supposedly mended deficiencies in his bull but which unquestionably rendered doubtful the powers of the decretal commission, specifically

[4] Henry always argued that while marriage to a brother's widow was prohibited by the divine law and therefore indispensable, the consanguinity of a wife's sister belonged to the papal law and could be dispensed with. His known relations with Mary Boleyn and the impediment thereby created formed part of the general objection to the second marriage in English public opinion. In 1533, when one Sir George Throckmorton was interviewed by the King about his opposition in the House of Commons, he was bold enough to mention that Henry could not marry Anne 'for that it is thought ye have meddled both with the mother and with the sister'. Henry could only mutter, 'never with the mother'; it took Cromwell, who was listening, to add sharply 'nor never with the sister either'.

set up to try the validity of the bull only.[5] The English naturally refused to proceed upon a copy of the brief; the Spaniards as naturally refused to let the original out of their hands. The new delay provoked yet another embassy to Rome (December 1528) which was to obtain new instruments equipping Campeggio and Wolsey with powers to deal with the brief as well; in addition it was to air the possibility of Catherine taking the veil and—a new idea—suggest that perhaps Henry could be licensed for a bigamous marriage. These were signs of growing despair. Then, suddenly in February 1529, a rumour that Clement had died revived flagging hopes of extravagant schemes: let Wolsey be elected. The absurdity of supposing that the powerful imperial interest in the College of Cardinals (which elected Charles's candidates before Charles was even master of Italy) would permit such a thing was made worse by the news of the war, as the French successes of 1528, which had buoyed up Wolsey's hopes and got him the first commission, turned to disastrous defeat before the end of the year. The writing on all the walls within sight was very plain.

Nevertheless, in the end Campeggio agreed to act upon the commission; after all, Henry, by seeking an improved one, had given Rome adequate grounds for repudiating its decision, should this become desirable. On 15 June 1529, the legatine court opened at Blackfriars in London. Henry responded to its summons; Catherine, after one impressive appearance in which she moved all observers but, on her knees, got nothing from her relentless husband, refused to acknowledge the legates' jurisdiction. Her absence meant further delays, and meanwhile at Rome her champions won. On 18 July Clement agreed to advoke (call back) the case to Rome, in response to the Queen's formal appeal. Not yet aware of this, Campeggio on the 31st adjourned the court (on the grounds that it was a delegate instrument of the Roman Rota) for the Roman summer vacations, to everybody's consternation. It never met again: that day's ceremony was—apart from the interlude of Mary Tudor's reign—the last public display of papal authority in England. A week or two later Wolsey learned that everything was lost. On 5 August the French and the Emperor had made peace at Cambrai, so that now there was no means left for either freeing or overawing the Pope. An English delegation, led by Tunstall and More, had managed to assert an

---

[5] It was alleged that Catherine's mother, Isabella of Castile, had in her dying days conceived fears about the sufficiency of the bull and that Julius had kindly put her mind at rest by issuing the amending document. In fact, so far as we know, this second document modified or amplified the bull hardly at all; Henry's real problem was its hitherto unsuspected existence, not what it said. All this tends to support its genuineness, never properly established because it has since vanished: a convenient forgery ought to have more efficiently undermined Henry's case at canon law.

English 'presence' at Cambrai, but it was clear that the real powers cared not a straw for England or Henry, who were totally isolated. This disastrous end to his diplomacy showed Wolsey that he had lost the last chance of getting Henry his divorce and that his career was at an end. The only question remaining touched the size of the penalty that the King would inflict.

II

Wolsey's fall was sudden and total, but not without warning; from the early months of 1529, quite a few people had shown by a new effrontery in the face of his orders that they could scent the coming event. During his summer progress Henry ostentatiously refused to visit the cardinal's house, and when on 9 August the writs went out for a Parliament to meet in November the collapse of his authority was plain to all who understood his attitude to that institution. Besides, the summons was decided upon so immediately after the failure of the legatine court that the King's turning to another tribunal amounted to an announcement of his abandonment of Wolsey. The cardinal tried to delay the despatch of the writs, a stupid and pointless manoeuvre. As late as 6 October he still presided over a meeting of the Council, but on that very day Henry lost patience with obstructive tactics and ordered him to give the remaining writs to the duke of Norfolk. Three days later Wolsey, as usual, opened the Michaelmas term in Chancery, but for the first time in fourteen years he sat alone; the lords and others who had used to throng around him had gone to court to attend the King. The forthcoming Parliament certainly constituted a threat to him, but Henry did not mean to have him wait till then. On the very first day of the term the attorney general preferred a bill against him in the King's Bench which charged him with praemunire for that in despite of the statute of 1391 he had obtained his legacy by bulls from Rome and had exercised its powers in various ways stated, contrary to the law of the realm.[6] After a brief resistance, the

[6] A. F. Pollard, denying that Wolsey was prosecuted by the King for obtaining a papal authority which Henry had himself approved, alleged that he was indicted for actions taken as legate, not for obtaining the office itself (*Wolsey*, pp. 245 ff.). The record (*Letters and Papers . . . of the Reign of Henry VIII* [hereafter *LP*] iv, no. 6035) shows that this is wrong. Wolsey was expressly accused of a breach of the statute committed by obtaining bulls from Rome. Henry may well be condemned for using against Wolsey an action which he had benignly accepted for so long; but moral issues apart, what was the legal position? So far as we know, Wolsey never had any form of written approval or permission from the King. It could be argued that the creation of his legateship by papal authority invaded the King's regality, and this was the

cardinal surrendered the great seal on the 18th, and the introduction
of a second indictment on the 20th (probably because there was
some doubt about indicting a lord chancellor still in office) showed
him that he could not fight the action. On the 22nd he therefore
surrendered himself and all his possessions abjectly into the King's
hands. This did not arrest the suit in which sentence was pronounced
against him on the 30th, just in time to keep him out of the
Parliament to which he had been summoned with the rest of the
peerage. Guilty of praemunire, he was liable to perpetual imprisonment and had forfeited all his possessions, but (as his well timed
surrender proves) he knew perfectly well that everything now
depended on Henry, surrounded as he was by Wolsey's eager
enemies, from the Lady Anne downwards.

Wolsey's eminence had been lonely, and his fall left him almost
totally deserted. Many of his servants hastened to seek other employment, and the leading members of his household entered the King's
service whither Gardiner, principal secretary since 28 July 1529, had
preceded them. Apart from a few personal attendants and menials,
the only one who remained faithful was Thomas Cromwell, 'my only
refuge and aid', as Wolsey was soon to call him. For a year Cromwell spent an inordinate amount of time trying to sort out Wolsey's
very complex affairs; he did much to save the Oxford college and
used his skill and Wolsey's wealth to obtain the pardon which Henry
at last conceded in February 1530. Wolsey, who had from the first
been allowed to retire to his house at Esher rather than face prison,
was restored to York and granted the spiritualties of Winchester, the
see itself for the present remaining vacant in the King's hands.
Cromwell also worked to satisfy the hungry hordes—creditors and
vultures—who descended upon Wolsey's remaining fortune. It is
likely that he also helped to defeat the attempt made by Wolsey's
enemies to use Parliament against him. Not satisfied with his condemnation in the King's Bench, they tried to promote an act of
attainder which would have cost Wolsey his life. On 1 December
1529 a committee of both Houses presided over by the new chancellor, Thomas More, signed a massive list of forty-five articles which
rehearsed the standard grievances against the cardinal's govern-

---

view of the parliamentary committee that drew up articles of accusation against him (Herbert
of Cherbury, *Life and Times of Henry VIII*, 1672, p. 294). Even they, however, were studiously
vague on a point which, because Wolsey surrendered, was never argued. Was there in fact any
way in which Henry could have licensed him? Wolsey evidently regarded papal authority as
supreme and as not requiring royal confirmation, but—had he wanted to be—could he have
been dispensed from the praemunire statute? It is doubtful whether the best opinion would
have allowed a *non obstante* licence against an act protecting the King's regality. In 1535, More
and Cromwell agreed that the dispensing power could not save a man against the Act of
Supremacy.

ment. The document was in form a petition to the King, asking him
not to allow Wolsey ever again to carry any authority, but it was
presented in the Commons and thus evidently intended as a first
move towards parliamentary condemnation. Cromwell, it was later
remembered, spoke so effectively against it that the matter dropped,
but it is also true that Henry did not want any further proceedings.[7]
What saved Wolsey from total destruction was partly the memory of
so many years of trust and friendship but above all the fact that the
King had at this point resolved to be master in his own house. He
had no intention of recreating Wolsey's ascendancy in other hands,
and he would keep the cardinal on ice, just in case he could once
more be useful. As early as 11 November he restored him to the
protection lost in the King's Bench judgement and buoyed him up
with gracious messages.

Wolsey being the man he was, this treatment proved fatal; the
over-ready optimism which had for so long carried him through his
tight-rope exercises on the European stage fed only too willingly on
any sign of favour. His letters to Cromwell (who helped) and
Gardiner (who sneered) were full of lamentations but also always
full of foolish hopes. Totally persuaded that the King would need
him again, he tried to cajole the most unlikely people, until one of
these, the duke of Norfolk, brutally told him to get to his see of York
and attend to his spiritual duties. Squeezing some money out of the
King and borrowing more, the cardinal crossed into his diocese on
28 April 1530, after three weeks on the road from Richmond. After a
bit he got as far north as Cawood, but that was all; his eyes remained
firmly fixed on London—and Europe. Instead of becoming a good
shepherd to his flock he began to solicit local favour, an enterprise
which at a distance looked like the building of a following and a faction. His pomp he abated but little, far too little for Cromwell who wrote
ever more pressingly to warn his master of the dangers provoked by
this continued display. Worse still, Wolsey could not leave his old
world alone; very soon, he was deep in negotiations with French and
imperial agents who, he hoped, could forward his return to power.
How much of his futile and deeply perilous activity was known to his

---

[7] Cromwell's speech is remembered in George Cavendish's *Life and Death of Cardinal Wolsey*
(edited by R. S. Sylvester and D. P. Harding in *Two Tudor Lives*, 1962, p. 116). Pollard
(*Wolsey*, pp. 261 ff.) disbelieved the story, mainly because of the silence of Hall's *Chronicle*. But
Hall made mistakes: he also said that the articles were 'signed with the Cardinalles hand' (p.
768), which is nonsense and a manifest confusion with the other document laid before the
House, namely the surrender of 22 October. The petition of 1 December neither did nor could
bear Wolsey's signature. Acts of attainder were often framed as joint petitions of both Houses;
the extant memorial looks very much like the first step towards that end. Note also that Wolsey
discussed the articles with Cromwell (*LP* IV, no. 6204; manifestly placed too late) and that at
least one man seeking to profit from the forthcoming forfeiture expected to see him attainted
(*LP* IV, no. 6129).

enemies is not clear, but that they had men about him to report goings on is sure enough. Then general talk took a hand: people (unbelievably) began to regret his going, and Henry, complaining about his present ministers' incompetence, loudly remembered other days and better service. The new regime took fright—and action. The charges with which they persuaded Henry to end his gentle treatment of Wolsey—that the cardinal had solicited the Pope to excommunicate the King, and that he was planning to raise Yorkshire in a violent bid for power—were lies, but Wolsey's behaviour gave them colour. On 4 November he was arrested, but on the journey south, to the Tower and a treason trial, he died at Leicester Abbey on the 29th.

Wolsey was gone, little lamented and soon replaced. His achievements died with his greatness because they were so personal and essentially impermanent. The international system he had known so well and used so skilfully had collapsed when the pope ceased to be the pole around which policy revolved. The international world of humanists and moderate Church reformers had before this collapsed into a welter of revolutionary divisions among which Wolsey—still a prince of the Church universal—had no place. He had ruled magnificently and had tried to tackle every sort of problem facing the realm, but nothing had been properly pursued and all the work was still to do. It is often said that by his career and especially by the example of his rule over the Church and state combined he taught Henry VIII the secret of the constitutional revolution that created the schismatic Church of England and the royal supremacy. As we shall see, it needed more than Wolsey's example to bring this about, though certainly the makers of the revolution adapted some of Wolsey's technical methods. Others again take his fall to show that in a sense there never was any revolution—that even before 1530 'the crown, not the legate, held effective supremacy over the English church.'[8] Now it is perfectly true that when he was attacked by the crown's secular instruments—common law and Parliament—he went down without a struggle, unaided by that other pillar of his power, his spiritual office. But what aid was he to expect from bishops whom he had treated like footstools, or from a Pope who, old and sick, saw himself confronted by a King of England suddenly turned nasty? Wolsey himself, and his work, not the necessary facts of the case, had been responsible for creating a temporary situation in which his survival stood solely tied to the royal favour; other prelates were soon to show that they did not read the cardinal's fate as making them mere puppets of the crown. In any case, Wolsey

[8]M. J. Kelly, 'Canterbury Jurisdiction and Influence during the Episcopate of William Warham, 1503–1532', p. 206.

himself had never regarded his papal legateship as a gift held at the mercy of the King or subordinated to the laws of the realm; and he was right. 'My authority and dignity legatine is gone,' he said to Norfolk, 'wherein consisted all my high honour.' We are usually adjured to heed only the duke's reply—'a straw for your legacy'; what Norfolk had respected were the cardinalate and archbishopric which put Wolsey formally above any peer of the realm. But while this was no doubt a typical enough remark for an English noble-man, the fact remains that Wolsey did not see it that way: to him the powers derived from Rome, not those bestowed by Henry, were the crown of his glory. Henry had demonstrated how easily, in the circumstances of 1529, he could destroy the Pope's creation, but that does not prove that Wolsey's greatest prize (and his rule over both provinces of the English Church) was created by anyone other than the Pope. The real construction of a self-sufficient realm remained to be undertaken.

Norfolk spoke for the nobility of England; was Wolsey's fall the product of an aristocratic reaction? When we remember how necessarily careful Tudor kings showed themselves of the political nation's feelings and how large a part those feelings had played in the retreat from Henry VII's methods, the point merits con-sideration. Did Henry throw Wolsey to the wolves because the cardinal had become a political liability? Wolsey had certainly evoked enough hatred and discontent in circles that mattered. The parliamentary attack and such actions as Lord Darcy's embittered collecting of charges against the fallen man underline the nobility's view of the event. But however convenient it was to satisfy men worth keeping in loyal contentment, none of this had anything to do with what happened to Wolsey. Henry did not cast his servant down to please the nobility or perhaps to restore an alliance with it that, so far as he was aware, had never weakened even during Wolsey's heyday. He did assemble a body of notables in October 1529 of which we know neither the composition nor the programme; to read any political significance into that fleeting event is strictly inadvis-able. Henry called a Parliament and thereby recognized the need to consult the realm and especially its great men, but when he had it he asked it for years no questions of importance. He stopped the Lords' assault on Wolsey, throughout was careful to make plain who alone had struck the blow, and showed no sign at all of changing principles or means of government. If there was an aristocratic reaction it appears to have failed to inform the King of the fact.

III

Still, Wolsey's going left a huge gap, in the government of the commonwealth as well as of the Church. The second could, and for the moment did, return to an existence in which legates *a latere* had vanished like the snow in summer. The state needed attention. To begin with, Henry determined to take personal charge of everything. He said so, and for a while he did so. He even sealed some patents with his own hand after receiving the great seal from Wolsey. He decided that the keeper of his privy purse should fill the role of national paymaster which in the previous fifty years had been created around the treasurer of the Chamber, and for some three years the Privy Chamber thus became the central office of the royal finances.[9] For a while the King took on the look of his father, though never all that convincingly. Above all, of course, he assumed the personal direction of policy, especially the policy of the Divorce. It is therefore worth recalling at this stage, before we see how his management faltered and why, that whenever on earlier occasions Henry VIII had taken political initiatives he had shown a penchant for rashness and for crude, obvious and ineffective guile.

However active the King had become (and he soon realized that he wanted another Wolsey, if not the same old Wolsey again), he needed councillors and especially he needed a chancellor. The choice of Wolsey's successor fell, after some difficult discussions, on Thomas More. More, whom Wolsey had allegedly regarded as the only man in the kingdom fit to succeed him, had virtually all the qualifications. For twelve years he had been a councillor and courtier, very close to the King and in his secrets. As chancellor of the Duchy since 1526 he had proved his abilities in law and equity; and he had wide experience of Europe and its diplomacy. He had been jointly responsible with Tunstall for snatching a crumb of comfort from the negotiations which led to the peace of Cambrai. A common lawyer and ex-Speaker of the Commons, he was well placed to soothe the fury which Wolsey had aroused in those two centres of English public life. He was a man of wisdom, sense and fame. But he lacked the major qualification: he opposed the Divorce—as Henry knew he did—and viewed the King's likely future policy with displeasure and dismay. Henry had to exercise much pressure to get him to accept office, though not quite as much as More's friends supposed. For More had reasons for taking on a burden which he could see would be immense. Not only was he

[9]D. R. Starkey, 'The King's Privy Chamber, 1485–1547', pp. 381 ff.

being offered what must have looked like a belated justification for the dozen years of frustrated impotence into which Wolsey's monopoly of power had turned his decision, in 1517, to enter the royal service; he also recognized that the call of 1529 provided an opportunity, uncertain and full of danger though it was, to do what he could for the cause he held dearest. He had watched the growth of heresy with a sick heart and blamed Wolsey bitterly for not stopping it; now he could act. And like everybody else he realized that the conflict developing between the King and the Pope threatened both the Church universal in England and the liberties of the English Church itself: so conscientious and doom-conscious a man could not but agree to serve where he might still be able to arrest disaster. Thus More took the chancellorship with purposes in mind which from the first threatened his relationship with Henry, and the fact that after his accepting the King promised him not to trouble his conscience over the Divorce—a promise faithfully kept for óver four years—speaks better for Henry's generosity than for More's sense of the realities.

The government thus included in the normal place of leadership a well known critic of the King's main preoccupation. This did not exhaust the difficulties that lack of unity brought. In practical terms, the chief place in Council fell to an aristocratic triumvirate of whom only the duke of Norfolk (lord treasurer) had sufficient ability really to count. Norfolk was an ambitious and self-confident man, a good military commander, full of pride of degree and undisguised arrogance. He was also devious, vengeful, foul-mouthed and essentially second rate. His fellow duke, Suffolk, given the titular office (at this time vacant) of lord president of the Council, would have been flattered by being called third rate; but he was the King's old companion and brother-in-law. Even Suffolk (plain Charles Brandon until 1513) looked like old nobility by the side of Thomas Boleyn, viscount Rochford, made earl of Wiltshire in December 1529, who succeeded Tunstall (as the latter exchanged the see of London for that of Durham) as lord privy seal and owed his high place notoriously to his daughter's lodgings next to the King's chamber. These three were generally regarded as the new men of power and certainly dominated the Council, but they were men without original ideas or originating minds—instruments, not leaders, and by no means fully agreed on the issues of the day. Of course, they all supported the Divorce: Norfolk and Wiltshire had cause to like the prospect of a niece and a daughter on the throne. But Norfolk strenuously adhered to orthodoxy while Wiltshire sympathized with the Protestant reformers; and though all three disliked the rule of clerical upstarts they regarded the papal supremacy with varying degrees of respect. All of them sat uneasily around the same table with Thomas More.

Though these arrangements, which put the great and privy seals into lay hands, signified a decision to end the clerical rule of the past two generations, the most promising coming man in the government was, oddly enough, a priest—the King's secretary, Stephen Gardiner, in October 1531 preferred to Wolsey's second see of Winchester. Apart from More, he was certainly the cleverest man among them—an energetic, ranging, fertile mind with an eye to self-advancement. On the Divorce he was 'sound', and as the man who had bullied the abject Clement VII at Orvieto in 1528 he did not at this time hold a high opinion of the Pope or the papal supremacy; but he was an eminent church lawyer and a high clericalist to whom the privileges of his estate mattered greatly. His fellow ambassador of 1528, Edward Foxe, the King's almoner, another man of intellectual stature, had marked sympathies with the Lutheran heresies which both More and Gardiner abominated. From the first, this revised and revived Council was divided along several lines between those wishing to go forward and those anxious to hold back.

The problems facing King and Council in part identified themselves readily enough. For Henry the settling of his marriage naturally continued to come first, and the issue obviously dominated everything else. But there were other things: there was the state of the realm. Wolsey's enemies, of all kinds, had made magnificent capital out of their allegations of all-round misgovernment; they were under an obligation to do better, and much was especially expected of More, writer and thinker and humanist. The first item on any programme was bound to be reform of the Church. Among the cries of the past few years, denunciations of the lamentable state of the spiritualty had been the loudest and most effective. It was in such writings as Jerome Barlow's *Burial of the Mass* (1527) and more particularly Simon Fish's *Supplication of the Beggars* (1528) that the mythology of anticlericalism became codified for all time. This is where we find a handy summary of all the stereotypes—the clergy as 'ravenous wolves' preying in their greedy idleness on the poor commons of the realm, possessed of perhaps a third of the nation's landed wealth, accumulating vast profits from tithe and other exactions, putting people to terrible trouble in their vicious and incomprehensible law courts, corrupting the nation's womanhood, or alternatively its young men in sodomitical monasteries. 'Who is she,' cried Fish more effectively than gallantly, 'that will set her hands to work to get 3*d* a day and may have at least 20*d* a day to sleep an hour with a friar, a monk or a priest?'

In this literature the clergy appear as the sole and total cause of the great number of destitute men in the realm; all social problems can be solved by confiscating their superfluous wealth. In the demand that they be made to labour and to marry, so as to become honest citizens, the old Lollard cry against the special order and pretensions of the priesthood found a voice again, but this time it reached the ears of the one person that mattered. Thomas More might write his witty and violent *Supplication of the Souls* to blast Fish, a common lawyer of reckless temper and foul mouth, but Anne Boleyn showed the offending tract to the King, and Henry liked it well. Modern research has had even less difficulty than More in demonstrating the falseness of many of the accusations: neither was the clergy's wealth so overwhelming (though great enough) nor were all its members proud prelates, mouldy monks, fornicating friars or conniving curates, though few lived up to the strenuous educational and spiritual standards demanded by reformers both humanist and Protestant. The hatred of what was thought of as clerical oppression rose powerfully in the days of Wolsey's rule, and it was a hatred that penetrated several layers of lay society—nobility and gentry quite as much as merchants and artisans, lawyers as much as apprentices, people in the shires and in cathedral cities quite as much as in London. It is significant that both Barlow and Fish made much of Hunne's case, confident to strike chords everywhere. Enough abuses and scandals existed to give credibility to those violent exaggerations. But the violence of all that talk and those feelings could achieve nothing until the King, hitherto the protector of the oppressors, hearkened to the supplications. In 1529, for reasons of his own, he opened the gates and invited the sheep to come in and rend the wolves.

The Church thus had cause to look to its condition, nor was it in a bad state to tackle the problems. The view, once held, that Wolsey had so enfeebled it that it stood no chance against Henry or the reformers cannot any longer be maintained. On the contrary, the very weakness and collapse of the hierarchy in the face of Wolsey's assault gave them the strength to recover now that Wolsey was gone. As we shall see, the confidence of the clerical estate revived rapidly; so far from inheriting a cowed and obedient Church from Wolsey, Henry had to do the cowing himself and found the Church capable of vigorous resistance. Unfortunately for themselves, the leaders of the Church returned not only to a time before Wolsey but also unrepentantly to the attitudes of those calmer days. The Convocation of 1529, for instance, talked a little about reform and dropped it. Warham was old and Fisher totally preoccupied with the fate of Catherine of Aragon, though both could be roused by lay threats to the Church's liberties to man the barricades. The new men promoted in the wake of Wolsey's fall were all careerist lawyers in the Gardiner mould—men like John Stokesley who succeeded Tunstall at London in March 1530, or Edmund Lee who inherited York in the autumn of 1531. They were learned humanist scholars and presumably good-living men, but stiff-necked, conservative, and readily roused in defence of their estate. The end of Wolsey was in no sense also the end of the old order. That Henry should at this time have promoted men of that type throws some light on his purposes and alleged foresight; as his policy developed under other influences, they all proved troublesome. Above all, they were not the men to alter the established ways of the Church.

As for the reform of the commonweal, there are precious few signs that at this point any member of this government, from the King downwards, took any interest in it. Erasmus, and others, expected Utopian reforms from More, but the chancellor's mind was concentrated so furiously on the dangers presented by heresy and schism that he could no longer be counted among the reformers or even the humanists. He did good work in the Chancery itself, beginning that systematic adaptation of equitable principles to the principles of the law which in the end assured the continued coexistence of both, and dispensing rational justice with that serene good sense which always characterized his doings provided there arose no suspicion of hostility to the Church. In both Chancery and Star Chamber More rapidly brought some order into the chaos created by Wolsey; the backlog of cases dwindled fast, specious suits got the treatment they deserved, meritorious complaints received incisive help. But beyond this More had neither the time nor the inclination to promote reform; the fatal split in the reform movement of the 1520s, ever more manifest as Lutheran deviation spread, now prevented all action. What particularly needed attention was the administration of the realm, left in disarray by Wolsey's inspired amateurishness; yet extravagance and disorder characterized these years when Henry was personally in charge. Apart from everything else, he was for the first time really quite poor. Wolsey's policy had been terribly expensive, and his experiments in taxation had left only a clear understanding that the way to prosperity did not lie through subjects' pockets. In the years 1529–31, crown finance was precariously maintained by the pension which France paid under the treaty of 1526. The great Harry, willing to take on Pope and Emperor alike, depended on French complaisance to stave off bankruptcy.

The needs of the realm, quite apart from the purposes of the King, thus called urgently for the sort of help which only a Parliament could give. The one that met on 3 November began by being unusual—the first Parliament of the reign to assemble before Christmas, an interference with the royal routine of hunting and festivities which indicates the state of crisis. It continued to amass records—to pack seven sessions into seven years, produce more and weightier legislation than any Parliament before it or (the revolutionary Long Parliament apart) any after it before the early nineteenth century, and to witness or make (according to taste) a revolution in the English polity.[10] In membership, on the other hand, it was commonplace; all the lords spiritual and temporal received their accustomed summons, and no attempts were made, later allegations notwithstanding, to influence elections to the Commons. Since we are poorly informed about the Commons of earlier Parliaments, no useful comparisons can be made, and it is possible that this one contained an increased number of members sworn to the service of the crown, though the chronicler's disgruntled comment on one occasion, that the House had a majority of such people, is either demonstrably false or means that they had a majority on the day in question. Their presence, in any case, had nothing to do with packing: it rather reflects the increase of the King's servants among the political classes (recently augmented by the absorption of so many of Wolsey's men) and a recognition, new to the best of our knowledge, that membership of Parliament could help significantly in a man's political career at court or in his locality. The most important of the burgesses nearly did not make it. A few days before the opening of the Parliament, Thomas Cromwell was still seeking ways of escaping the consequences of Wolsey's fall which had left him exposed to his private enemies. As we have seen, he did not follow his fellow servants' example by at once transferring to the King, either from loyalty to Wolsey or because he was not yet acceptable. Instead he chose to enter Parliament, an institution he had found interesting in 1523 and knew from that experience to be usable. Through Norfolk he got Henry's promise of good will if he found a place there, while his seat at Taunton he won through the friendship of Sir William Paulet, an ex-colleague in Wolsey's household who had become the King's master of Wards in 1526. As Cromwell told Wolsey's biographer, he entered the House with the intention of becoming 'better regarded'; by a combination of personal circumstances (including choice) he became the first statesman deliberately to build a career under the crown upon membership of the Commons and a managerial role there.

For the first time, too, we know for certain that this Parliament

---

[10] For a full narrative of these seven sessions and the accompanying meetings of the southern Convocation see S. E. Lehmberg, *The Reformation Parliament* (1970). Now and again I find myself differing from Professor Lehmberg on points of interpretation.

contained an opposition group deliberately organized from outside.
Catherine's friends expected trouble. from the assembly; though no
one knew what Parliament might be able or willing to do in
furthering the Divorce, the Aragonese faction thought it wise to be
prepared. There were two centres to this faction, and both turned
their attention to Parliament. Eustace Chapuys, the Emperor's very
able ambassador who down to 1536 acted as the manager of resistance to Henry VIII (to a point well beyond what Charles V was willing to approve), had contacts in the Lords who regularly informed
him of what was going on and took his advice on attitudes and
action. Among them, Bishop Fisher, Catherine's most outspoken
partisan, was naturally prominent, but so were several other conservative peers, especially the earl of Shrewsbury and the aged Lord
Darcy who had not helped to bring Wolsey down only to have worse
follow. More, too, though as ever carefully discreet, was in regular
touch. Since Chapuys was continually calling for armed intervention
from Charles V, these contacts came dangerously close to treason.
The other Aragonese centre formed around some of Catherine's
chaplains, all members of the stricter religious orders, especially
William Peto, warden of the Observant Franciscans of London, and
Richard Reynolds, a Bridgettine of Syon monastery (Richmond).[11]
These men, cooperating with Fisher and others and with More
lending benevolent approval, enlisted the help of probably several
burgesses of the House of Commons. In this way they hoped to learn
of parliamentary moves in time to counter them by public preaching
and propagandist writing; on the other hand, they expected the
group of supporters in the Commons to oppose government measures
hostile to Catherine and to speak in her interest. On several occasions, in fact, voices were raised for her in the House. The King
and his men gradually became aware of this organized opposition,
but in Parliament at least they bowed to the right of free speech.[12]

As it turned out, the first session of 3 November to 17 December
1529 did not suggest that the Crown had any plans to use Parliament
for the King's purposes. The only official measure to pass in that
session was an act releasing the King's debts; that is to say, Wolsey's
loans of 1522 and 1523 were retrospectively turned into a parliamentary grant. This blatant defaulting upon obligations passed with
some difficulty, and Henry was forced to buy favour with a generous
parliamentary pardon for a wide variety of offences. Negotiations
were opened with the Lords over plans to protect the King's revenue

---

[11] In the fifteenth century the mendicant orders had divided into two branches—the
relatively lax Conventuals and the Observants who insisted on applying the rule with rigour.
The Sion house of nuns and monks was well known for the purity of its life and its piety.

[12] For all this cf. my *Studies* I, pp. 155 ff.

from losses resulting from the widespread form of conveyancing known as enfeoffment to uses, but for the present nothing came of this.[13] Otherwise, King and Council had nothing to offer. Sir Thomas More opened the Parliament with a speech in which he announced his own view of its utility, but his words could be (and have been) misunderstood. He launched a measured but angry attack on Wolsey, the great bellwether who had led the shepherd-king's faithful flock astray, and spoke of 'divers new enormities' which had sprung up among the people, 'for the which no law was yet made to reform the same'. This, he added, was the reason for calling Parliament. But More did not have social reform in mind; he was not thinking of the well ordered commonwealth. In the jargon of the day, 'new enormities' meant religious heterodoxy—heretical and schismatical opinions; it was these that the chancellor wished to see legislated against, these that he blamed Wolsey for allowing to spread. He could not have misjudged the mood of the Commons more disastrously, but in any case neither he nor any other crown servant produced any bill against heretics.

Left to themselves, the Commons at once turned to unfinished business—to the familiar problem of the clergy and to remedies for the standard grievances. This could have been foreseen by anyone who remembered 1515 and had kept his eyes and ears open in the last two years of Wolsey's ascendancy, and perhaps it was foreseen by the King who, it is commonly alleged, wished to use popular anticlericalism to put pressure on Rome. But at this stage this is conjecture only: Henry did nothing to stir the Commons or warn the Pope. The outburst of complaints and proposals was spontaneous. The issues that soon crystallized—the excessive cost of probate, undue mortuary fees (the source of Hunne's trouble), and defects among the clergy (especially the farming of leaseholds, non-residence in their livings, and the holding of benefices in plurality)—were among the matters which the Mercers' Company had put on the city of London's agenda in preparing for the Parliament. The bills designed to remedy these abuses emerged from committees of lawyers appointed in the House. In addition to these proposals, the spiritual jurisdiction was attacked in a petition to the King, the traditional form for initiating Commons' legislation which was in process of being superseded by bills drafted in committee. The Commons complained of the use of the canon law as being unknown to the land of England, of the conduct of the church courts, of the proctors (advocates) practising there, and of the general oppressive use of these disciplinary institutions. For the present nothing came of this grievance, but Cromwell, busy in the House to make himself

[13] See below, p. 147.

better regarded and probably, as a lawyer, a member of the drafting committees, preserved the documents for future use.

This effective display of anticlerical passion led to a major clash with the Lords where the spiritual peers still held a majority. Fisher, surprisingly, lost his temper entirely, and his outburst about heretics in the Commons, with memories of Wycliffe and Hus thrown in, provoked a counterblast from men who wished it clearly understood that their hatred of clerical pretensions and exactions in no way lessened their orthodoxy in the faith. They had the support of leading lay peers and, more important, of the King before whom Fisher, now apprehensive about his unguarded language, made out that it was the Bohemians he had called heretics, not the faithful Commons. A joint committee of both Houses revised the bills touching probate, mortuaries and pluralism and non-residence, possibly toning them down a little and giving them the form of officially sponsored measures; all three received the royal assent. Henry had gained something from this unguided unleashing of the widespread feeling that the Church needed reform. The leaders of the clergy had been shown the precariousness of their position and the perils inherent in allowing Parliament to discuss matters touching the spiritualty. Since the King's own policy, however it developed, needed an obedient clergy this sort of lesson had its uses. But what the Commons had done was a very long way from revolution or even from that comprehensive attack on the Church which so many had expected from this Parliament. They had been careful to confine themselves to areas of strictly temporal significance and to abuses often inveighed against by clerical spokesmen themselves; the much hated tithe, a spiritual profit, was not even mentioned, and though the very large issue of the church courts received an airing, nothing was proceeded with. The first session confirmed earlier apprehensions about enemies to the Church, but as reform measures the three anticlerical acts proved only moderately important, while there is no sign that anyone yet knew of any way in which the Parliament could help to overcome the Pope's refusal to free Henry from Catherine. And for over another year at least that same uncertainty continued: during 1530, Henry prorogued Parliament several times, and the Houses did not meet again until January 1531.

The year 1530, in fact, brought into the open the essential conflict of concerns which marred this government's ability to achieve anything. While Henry continued to look for ways to force the Pope's hand, More went ahead to prove that he meant what he had said about the reforming of new enormities, and Anne and her father looked to dubiously orthodox preachers for assistance. Early in 1530, as soon as he was free of the parliamentary session (and of Christmas), More turned his mind and the bishops' attention to a more energetic suppression of heresy. In this he was not at this time going counter to Henry's own convictions, but he was also doing nothing to forward the business that came first in Henry's mind; by reviving the bishops' self-confidence, he can even be said to have hindered the King's purposes.

6 The Battle for Control

I

More had cause to think that the realm was being increasingly exposed to the sweep of continental heresies. Since early in 1528 he had spent much time and ink in taking up and refuting one heretical work after another, only to find that his mop was much too small to sweep back the tide. The flood of publications originated on the continent, out of the King's jurisdiction, but the dangerous books made their way into the country with ease: the secret trade was well organized.[1] Most important was Tyndale's Bible translation (New Testament, in collaboration with William Roy, 1525; Genesis, in collaboration with Miles Coverdale, 1529) which gave currency to Erasmian and Lutheran revisions of such crucial established concepts as *ecclesia* (church or congregation?) and *presbyter* (priest or elder?), and which was accompanied by powerfully reformist prefaces and prologues. Tunstall's attempt to stamp out this dangerous New Testament had greatly amused the reformers who financed further operations out of the money the bishop paid over in buying up the offending edition. In 1528 Tyndale also entered the lists as a theorist of politics when in his *Obedience of a Christian Man* he elaborated Luther's teaching on the subject's duty of submission to his secular ruler in ways highly satisfactory to Henry who read the book with pleasure; next year, however, Tyndale cast himself into outer darkness again by violently attacking the Divorce in a work, *The Practice of Prelates*, mainly concerned to blast Wolsey and the English hierarchy in general. Nearly as influential as Tyndale was the work of George Joye who in 1530 published a Protestant liturgy and work of edification in his *Garden of the Soul* (*Hortulus Animae*), or the writings of Simon Fish who to the explosive vulgarity of his *Supplication of the Beggars* added his *Sum of Holy Scripture*, a compendium

[1] See the bibliography of 'English books printed abroad, 1525–1535', by Anthea Hume, in *Complete Works of Thomas More* (Yale edition) 8, part II, pp. 1063 ff. This lists thirty-one important works before the end of 1531, most of which were readily available in England.

of the faith based on Luther and the Swiss reformers which appeared at Antwerp in 1529 and can be said to have signalled the first triumph of the Reformation when in 1535 it was republished in England. The number of known reformers, many of whom fled to the continent during Wolsey's sporadic persecutions, was growing alarmingly, and so were the characteristic divisions among them. Tyndale in particular grew less accommodating and more curmudgeonly with the years; he quarrelled justifiably with William Roy because he disapproved of the *Burial of the Mass* (which Roy let it be understood was his work), but with Joye he fell out in 1533 over points of the faith. It is worth notice that all these English proto-Protestants quickly developed a predominant interest in moral theology and the resultant demands of secular reform, rather than the more doctrinal preoccupations of their continental friends; the body of opinion that sought to better the commonwealth was ever more closely associated with the radical position in religion.

Those who thought like More could agree with him that Luther's revolt had opened the doors to a lawless proliferation of private whims and fantasies which only a return to strict obedience could cure. More's quarrel with Wolsey derived in the last resort from the fact that the cardinal had used reproof and recantation rather than prison and the stake against heretics who then fled into exile where they could continue to disseminate their poison. Though the fall of Wolsey and the opening of the Parliament encouraged many of the reformers to believe that times were changing, they wisely made no immediate move; and they soon discovered that the first effect of the upheaval was a much more strenuous campaign against them. More provided the definition and the instruments of repression in two proclamations of January and June 1530.[2] Here the King was made to announce his and his Council's determination to extirpate 'the pestiferous, cursed and seditious' errors of the heretics by enforcing the old statutes against the Lollards, and all lesser authorities, from peers and bishops to bailiffs and constables, were enjoined to set to the work. Office holders from the chancellor downwards were to swear a special oath to employ themselves in the detection of heretics and heretical books, but true to his convictions More reserved the actual execution of the laws to the ecclesiastical authorities, the laity being employed in the police work preliminary to trial. The main thrust of the proclamations was against the heretical works already discussed for which they provided a primitive Index of prohibited books augmented by stages as more came to notice. The second proclamation took note of the fact that a good many people showed

[2] *Tudor Royal Proclamations*, edited by P. L. Hughes and J. F. Larkin, I, nos 122 (misdated) and 129.

their desire for an English bible, but it banned existing translations and vaguely promised to provide a sounder one at such time as it might appear to the King 'that his said people do utterly abandon and forsake all perverse, erroneous and seditious opinions'—a time-scale not dissimilar to that fixed by the conversion of the Jews.

Strongly encouraged by the chancellor, who backed these declarations of intent by energetically following up informations and examining suspects, and even rather exceeded his powers when he imprisoned alleged heretics in his house at Chelsea and in the Tower, the bishops responsible for dioceses in which heresy was most evident—especially Stokesley of London, Nixe of Norwich, and Longland of Lincoln—obeyed the call to action.[3] The victims were the first martyrs of the Protestant Church of England, recorded by John Foxe. They included Thomas Bilney—Little Bilney, so influential at Cambridge in the 1520s, never a Protestant but certainly not sound on the mass, who after his recantation in 1527 had fallen into the deepest depression and seems almost to have welcomed his death as a relapsed heretic at Norwich in 1531. They included Richard Bayfield, an important link in the chain which brought heretical books into England (1531), and James Bainham, a lawyer who after abjuring in 1531 was kept imprisoned by More until the next year he relapsed and was burned. Especially they included John Frith, the most promising and energetic of Tyndale's associates who after a daring visit to England in 1531 returned for good the next year to travel around the country organizing a revolutionary movement. He was caught in October 1532 and burned the following July; his residence in the Tower was long enough to enable him to produce several influential tracts against More and against such doctrines as purgatory and the mass which were smuggled out and published at Antwerp. Episcopal registers not used by Foxe, and church court records, testify to a good many more persecutions at this time which, as usual, leave one uncertain whether what was discovered constituted old Lollardy or new

---

[3] The customary absolution from the charge of persecution, granted to More by partisan hagiographers, is contrary to the facts and indeed contrary to what More conceived as his duty. The ruthlessness of his *Confutation of Tyndale* (1532), partly written in office, which contains not one word of sympathy or compassion but only a near-hysterical rage and some rejoicing over men 'well burned', leaves no doubt where More stood on this contentious subject. See especially the savagely unfeeling remarks of his preface which deride the claims of men he had helped to bring to the stake to be thought steadfast in their faith and deserving of respect. More fully accepted the view that heresy, subversive of the terrene order and heavenly salvation, must be rooted out without mercy because one heretic could bring about the damnation of many souls. He was careful to obey the law by leaving the actual trial of heretics to the church courts, but he was the layman most active in assisting these tribunals; for example, he was the only layman who on 24 May 1530 joined a clerical gathering convened under Warham's presidency to condemn as heretical a long series of extracts from various works (D. Wilkins, *Concilia* III, pp. 727 ff.).

Lutheranism, and which also (as usual) resulted in more recantations than burnings, though some people died. Hugh Latimer
got into trouble for his preaching but submitted to Convocation
early in 1532 (not that his penitence lasted more than a few months),
while Simon Fish enjoyed the protection of Henry VIII till his early
(natural) death in 1531; his widow, herself an active Protestant,
married James Bainham.

The impetus which More gave to persecution thus outlasted his
own tenure of office, as did the effect of his writings. Even as lord
chancellor he found time for polemical work of the kind that he had
first massively presented in his *Dialogue concerning Heresies* (1528).
This elicited in 1531 Tyndale's equally violent *Answer to Sir Thomas
More's Dialogue*, which in turn provoked More's vast, and vastly
tedious, *Confutation of Tyndale's Answer* (1532). Confronted with what
he passionately believed to be the work of the devil, More lost his
sense of humour, of perspective, and also of practical effect. His
method—a faithful citing of the adversary in very long extracts,
followed by a detailed refutation—not only made his books unread-
able but also provided a legitimate way of reading the forbidden
books. It is hard to say whether the campaign inspired by More
should be called successful. True, the reformers trembled at his
name, and of the heretics at home a good number collapsed before
the persecution; true also, heretical books were found and destroyed.
At the same time, More could not trust the Boleyns, and many
suspects escaped the bishops.

The persecution, in any case, was not given time enough, for by
early 1531 the situation was changing. The admission to the Council
of Thomas Cromwell introduced a patron of reform into the inner
circles of government, and its supporters took heart. In 1531 Robert
Barnes addressed a *Supplication* to Henry VIII in which he advocated
the free use of the vernacular bible and defended Lutheran tenets on
justification by faith alone, the true Church, the possibility that
General Councils might err, and the danger of superstitious ceremonies; and late that year Cromwell got him a safe-conduct to visit
England and talk to the King. He remained in some sort of favour
thereafter. The early months of 1531 witnessed an attempt to recruit
Tyndale for the King's service. This was undertaken, on his own
initiative, by Stephen Vaughan, agent of the Merchant Adventurers
at Antwerp but also Cromwell's friend and servant; Cromwell
himself cautiously supported the approach, until a look at Tyndale's
Answer to More revived in Henry all his old hatred of the author of
Practice of Prelates, and Cromwell hurriedly put a stop to the negotiations. In the course of the year there also began to appear works
which, while not heretical, yet urgently supported reform at least on

the lines of biblical humanism, such as Richard Taverner's translation of Erasmus's booklet on the virtues of matrimony, dedicated to
Cromwell. In fact, by mid-1531 More had lost most of his power in
the state; his campaign for orthodoxy, pursued unflaggingly, looked
more and more out of joint with the course of events. The fact was
that no policy which did not directly aid the Divorce could hope to
carry on for long.

II

The dropping of Wolsey and the parliamentary session of 1529 had
in no way altered Henry's dilemmas or brought the solution of his
marital problem any nearer. The advocation of the case to Rome
had closed the only road which Henry and Wolsey had thought
possible—trial by papal delegates in England. For the best part of a
year thereafter Henry again concentrated on a single theme: utterly
convinced by now of the legal justice of his case, he laboured to
persuade Rome likewise, in order that a trial in the papal court
should come to the right conclusion. For this purpose every available
talent among canonists and theologians was roped in; the King
collected a fine archive of opinions and tracts in his support, all at
first left in manuscript. There was no question of public statements
or appeals; despite the perplexed or ribald discussion which pro-
liferated abroad and at home, among high and low, with reports
coming in to show that Catherine's growing popularity owed a lot to
contempt and dislike for Anne, Henry insisted on maintaining the
pretence of secrecy. The most spectacular part of his collecting
activity in fact ensured plenty of publicity. From early 1530 onwards, royal agents visited the universities of France, Italy and
Germany to get favourable verdicts from the learned world in
support of the opinions already dutifully delivered by Oxford and
Cambridge; indeed, they went outside the universities to private
scholars, rabbis, soothsayers and charlatans as well. The whole effort
may have been suggested, as tradition alleges, by an unknown
Cambridge theologian, Thomas Cranmer, who supposedly put the
idea before Stephen Gardiner and Edward Foxe when he accidentally met them in August 1529; but this is not all that likely, and
these enquiries ran well in line with the less systematic collecting
pursued for some two years before that. On the other hand, Cranmer, an ex-member of the White Horse gatherings and even at this
early date strongly inclined to a nascent Protestantism, was soon in

the royal service: in October he had an interview with the King as a result of which he wrote a pamphlet in support of the Divorce, and in January 1530 he joined the earl of Wiltshire's embassy which carried Henry's respects to Charles V's imperial coronation at Bologna. While in Italy, he took his share in pressing the universities for favourable opinions, but the accumulated product of the enterprise proved disappointing. Some of the more promising scholars suddenly reversed their views, and in the end Henry could command support only from institutions which were under political pressure to lend it—the English universities and eight more abroad, though those eight included Paris and Bologna, places of high respect. Among those active on the King's behalf were many Erasmian humanists, especially his own cousin Reginald Pole, at this time a king's scholar in Italy and anxious to please his crowned relative.

However, the new accord proclaimed when Clement crowned Charles in March 1530 made certain that there was no hope at all of forcing the Pope to give way to Henry; more than ever the Emperor's client, he at once demonstrated his serviceability by agreeing to the imperial demand that Henry be cited to Rome to answer Catherine's appeal of the case there.[4] In the absence of political power, the submission of an impressive array of opinions (less impressive in any case than the array of contraries) was not going to gain any advantages. Henry was once more at his wits' end, and his advisers also had nothing to offer. The repeated prorogations of Parliament may reveal this disarray in his counsels; they certainly indicate that if there was a way in which Parliament could help him Henry had not yet thought of it. In June 1530 he tried yet another way to persuade the Pope when he got a body of eminent men to sign and seal a solemn appeal to Rome. The meeting which debated and agreed this protest lacked the presence of notorious opponents like More and Fisher, a fact which Chapuys naturally ascribed to jerrymandering but which actually shows that promises made about involvement in the Divorce were being kept. The impressive, though peculiar, body passionately appealed to Clement to do justice and give the King what he asked for; it cited the opinion of the universities and pleaded for consideration of the fact that unless the King could remarry 'the controversy over the succession, ended some time ago at the cost of much slaughter and blood, would open again.' Throughout it uses the most submissive and respectful language towards the Holy See, and the nearest it comes to a threat

[4]Charles wanted a sentence declaring the Aragon marriage valid and ordering Henry to take Catherine back and put Anne away. For this to be pronounced, both parties had to be cited to appear, and though trials at canon law could ultimately proceed in the absence of a party, procedure provided splendid devices for protracting the business. Henry was to use them all.

is a despairing aside to the effect that if the Pope 'leaves us orphaned and deserted, we shall certainly have to put our minds ... to seeking remedy elsewhere.'[5] Read in its own right, this document, about which a good deal of fuss was made, signals a bankruptcy in ideas, a twist in stale and lost devices, not the opening of a new tactic. The true state of the King's helplessness was well enough defined by the fact that Henry had already, in June, effectively accepted the Curia's jurisdiction when he sent envoys to Rome with instructions only to produce maximum delays in the action now opening there.

And then, from late August 1530 onwards, the pointlessness of all these arguments about the Levitical law and so forth was gradually replaced by quite a different set of assumptions and assertions. In the five months down to January 1531, the King's words suggest the working out of a new line moving powerfully towards a policy of ignoring Rome altogether and settling the whole affair in the realm, effectively by royal authority. Henry had discovered a double claim to independence. On the one hand, it was alleged that ancient resolutions enunciated by the early church councils and confirmed by various popes, reserved causes arising in a metropolitan province of the Church for final settlement there, and that Englishmen in particular had a well attested privilege which saved them from being cited to any court outside the realm. Secondly, intertwined with this assertion of immunity was an emphasis on Henry's own imperial authority, an authority, that is, which left him without superiors on earth and not subject to anyone else's jurisdiction, including the Pope's. As early as October 1530, the King argued that his imperial power enabled him to prevent appeals from his realm elsewhere, a point not settled until the legislation of 1533. This imperial authority was doubly derived from Constantine, now discovered to be the prototype of imperial Christian kings—from the fact that Constantine in his day had ruled the Church, and from the fact of Constantine's 'British' origin, the latter for a while tangling with a revival of the Arthurian romance of empire which fleetingly made its appearance in arguments put before Chapuys.[6] The whole complex of notions emphasized the sovereign independence of England and her monarch; it forms one of the foundations (that derived from history) upon which the royal supremacy over the schismatic

---

[5] Professor Scarisbrick (*Henry VIII*, pp. 259 ff.) speaks of a document 'full of menacing hints about turning to other, harsher remedies', but this description hardly fits this appeal which only once refers to possible other action and in doing so is careful to avoid both all indication of intent and all adjectival severity. If the imperial ambassador's information was correct (and several of his regular informants were there), the other ways considered consisted in an appeal to a General Council, not in unilateral action at home (*Calender of State Papers, Spanish* IV, 1, pp. 598 ff.).

[6] This dubious line was abandoned when it turned out that Chapuys had never heard of King Arthur or his supposed empire over Europe.

Church of England was to be erected. At the same time, Henry occasionally hinted at another component in the edifice ultimately built, namely that he had a pastoral duty for the souls of his subjects. It thus looks as though by the end of 1530 the King had arrived at a position fully consonant with that which emerged when three to four years later he broke the deadlock by manifest revolution. He stood there long before he took any suitable action, and (it is alleged) long before one could reasonably suppose that Thomas Cromwell showed him the way out. By this time, we are assured, Henry was not only willing to contemplate full-scale schism but had passed the point of ever being able or willing to return to the papal obedience even if Clement had given in to him.[7]

The trouble is that, words apart, the King showed himself unaware of any new situation until 1532 or even 1533; he *did* nothing. Even the settlement of his marriage, represented as so urgent for reasons personal and national, did not come for two and a half years after Henry allegedly discovered the answer he needed in these claims to national and imperial autonomy. And throughout this time he confined himself at Rome to a very well executed delaying manoeuvre, refusing to surrender to the citation in person or by proctor, and pressing the Pope to return the case to England. In late 1532 he was even ready to abate his high imperial stance to the point of declaring himself willing to have the case tried outside the realm, provided the venue was neutral. After the resounding words of 1530, his language by degrees grew moderate again. Nor would it be correct to say that the 'imperial' argument, when he had discovered it, monopolized the stage; at all times he used and emphasized other points, such as an appeal from Rome to the General Council of the Church,[8] which distracted from the clear-cut claim to autonomy. In

---

[7] This is Professor Scarisbrick's conclusion (*Henry VIII*, pp. 261 ff.). He says (p. 292) that 'we cannot know' where Henry got this body of ideas from, but, as we shall see, it is possible to offer some suggestions. The difficulty of measuring the correlation of ideas and actions is well illustrated by a proclamation of 12 September 1530 which prohibited the bringing into England of any foreign instruments intended to introduce a legatine authority into the realm or prevent the execution of the good (i.e. anticlerical) laws made in the last session of Parliament. This proclamation does invoke the 'high authority, jurisdiction and prerogative royal of this his realm' and has been read as a strong step forward in that it was supposedly aimed at the papal bull of citation (G. de C. Parmiter, *The King's Great Matter*, 1967, p. 140); but the King had already effectively allowed the validity of the citation, and the positive terms of the proclamation show that it was intended purely to prevent appeals to Rome in actions arising out of the new statutes. It was thus well in line with the fourteenth-century legislation and nothing novel.

[8] The question of the General Council, an appeal to which was prohibited by papal law, runs through the 1530s, mainly because Charles V wanted one to settle the Protestant schism, but partly because Henry (sometimes with the support of France) liked to call for one in order to delay decisions and pretend a continued membership of the universal Church. The subject and its ramifications are interesting, but in Henry's mind it seems to me to have so clearly been only a device of propaganda and diplomacy that it does not deserve pursuing in detail in a study of this kind.

the very letter of October 1530 which first provides evidence of the discovery of a new line, the firm assertion of England's immunity was followed by a feeble instruction to gain delays if the arguments advanced should cut no ice. If Henry was clearly so sure of his autonomous rights, and so clearly moving from this early date towards the total breach, his prolonged wait and the ups and downs of his endless stream of instructions become inexplicable.

Certainly the new line came as a surprise to many, so much so that Henry's ambassadors needed several orders before they would put it to the Pope (to *his* great surprise), while a meeting of common and canon lawyers, convened in October 1530 to advise whether the privilege of the realm permitted the committal of the case to Canterbury without any further reference to Rome, returned a straight negative. This reply shows how meaningless earlier threats to settle the Divorce through Parliament had been—mere threats to which no one thought to supply substance. On the other hand, assertions that the King had no superior on earth were not new and had not hitherto been thought useful in the battle with Rome: we have seen that Henry possibly said something of the sort in 1515,[9] and in December 1529 the articles against Wolsey had opened with an assertion of the King's regal power which 'by the space of 200 years and more' had enabled him to 'proceed against the pope's holiness' to prevent such interference as the sending of a legate. That reasonably arrogant statement had found favour with Thomas More, who signed the articles. Even if Henry, unaided, suddenly decided that he had authority and immunity, the grounds of his claim were evidently not yet very certain even to himself. He took some steps, which turned into a farcical flop, to have them better established. His envoys at Rome were instructed to search the papal registers to find proof that popes had before this admitted an English independence of this kind; instead their necessarily cursory searches turned up evidence that England had habitually accepted the authority of popes not only in heresy but also in matrimonial disputes. At the very least it is plain that the new line—the basis of victorious action from late in 1532 onwards—did not at this point command general credence. In consequence Henry did not find it possible either to act upon it at this time or even to maintain it consistently over the years. Though he now held the answer in his hand, he was not sure that it was the answer or could be made to work, a situation which by itself suggests very strongly that the whole concept had not been his discovery but had been suggested to him. We can see no sovereign direction, by a mind fully instructed in the details of the argument, in these long uncertainties and vacillations. What the

[9] See above, p. 56.

facts suggest, rather, is that in August 1530 or thereabouts Henry was presented with a set of arguments and principles upon which something like the later royal supremacy could be erected, that he liked what he heard and tried it out, but that neither he himself nor sufficient people among his advisers were sure enough of their steps on this novel ground to go ahead with the policy implied. In particular, he had not yet discovered any means for giving force to his alleged autonomy, especially not in the legally secure way required if the new marriage was to provide the lawful succession needed.

We do, in fact, know the sources from which Henry drew the arguments and evidences to support his claim to autonomy and immunity.[10] It is found in a series of collections assembled by stages into a comprehensive and well ordered compilation of texts and precedents entitled *Collectanea satis copiosa*; the likely dates of this compiling extend between the early summer of 1530 and the late summer of 1531. New questions thereafter, inspiring new researches, supplied supplementary sections. Here we find the few items ever discovered to support the claim about customs of the realm which allegedly prevented interference from outside; citations from the Fathers (to recur through the pamphlet literature) as well as from Bracton to demonstrate the rights of kings in ruling 'their' churches; Old Testament precedents for priestly monarchy; the classic tests from the early Councils limiting the trial of cases to the province in which they originated; quotations from the Donation of Constantine, from Ivo of Chartres, Hugh St Victor, the fifteenth-century conciliarists, and other authorities, all matter thoroughly familiar to anyone who has ever had to read the propaganda arguments from 1532 onwards. In short, the *Collectanea* contain all the evidence ever alleged in support of the new line and were to be used repeatedly to provide the basis for officially inspired tracts and the arguments for certain acts of Parliament. Henry not only saw but annotated the manuscript—not in the manner of an author, editor or searcher, but rather as a student checking the statements of his instructors. The· impressive research behind the collection would in any case have been quite beyond his powers or time. The man most likely to have been responsible for compiling it is, in fact, Edward Foxe who was to re-use it all in his book on the difference between the King's power and the spiritualty's, the compendium upon which government propaganda and preaching relied throughout the 1530s.[11] The evidence thus overwhelmingly suggests that Henry learned the new

[10] I am most grateful to Mr Graham Nicholson for permission to use the results of his labours which have broken open this secret.

[11] *De Vera Differentia Regiae Potestatis et Ecclesiasticae*, put out by the King's printer in 1534 and reprinted in 1538. Cranmer probably shared in the work.

ideas from others who first realized their import, not that he lit upon
them himself and then commissioned the search for proofs; and that
(as we have seen) is also the most convincing explanation for the
hesitant and ineffective use made of these ideas for several years. It
looks as though a group of like-minded men arrived at this position
by the middle of 1530, drew the King's attention to it, and
then—encouraged by his enthusiasm which supported their research
with such futile efforts as the scrutiny of the Vatican archive—
developed drafts and notes into an ever more comprehensive
catalogue of useful supporting evidence.

When we consider who might have formed the link between
Henry and these followers of a radical scheme of thought, the name
of Thomas Cromwell (despite often expressed doubts) pushes to the
fore. Three independent early witnesses tell of an interview he is
supposed to have had with the King at which he suggested the plan
of action which was to lead to Divorce, schism and royal supremacy;
and while the stories are unquestionably a bit garbled, it may not be
wise to disregard the consensus of such diverse men as Eustace
Chapuys, Reginald Pole, and John Foxe.[12] That Cromwell had a
profound interest in political speculation of an intellectual kind is
now well established; he read and he wrote. Edward Foxe, who like
Cranmer was a member of the reforming circles in Cambridge upon
whom Cromwell was to rely heavily in his transformation of the
Church, had some early connections with Cromwell. They had both
been in Wolsey's household and they shared a leaning towards the
reform which was not otherwise present among the King's advisers
in 1530; it would be strange if they had never discussed such matters.
Foxe did not obtain the promotion for which, as Gardiner's fellow
envoy in 1528, he seemed destined much sooner until Cromwell
controlled patronage;[13] his book was printed as part of Cromwell's
first organized use of the press; in the 1530s, he was a Cromwell
man. We know that Cromwell specially desired and welcomed
documentary and chronicle evidence for 'imperial' claims made by
kings of England.[14] We have a broad hint that he knew the imperial
argument earlier than Henry: in revising the petition against church

[12] In my *Tudor Revolution in Government* (1953), pp. 72 ff., I rejected these stories as reliable
evidence for the manner of Cromwell's rise to power, and in that respect I adhere to my earlier
analysis. However, in the light of what has been discovered in the last twenty years about the
political situation around the King, about Cromwell's intellectual tastes and contributions,
and about the manner in which the body of doctrine that underlay the Henrician political
Reformation came to be developed, I find myself giving credence to the idea that Cromwell
brought the 'autonomy' argument to Henry's attention as early as 1530.

[13] Despite his employment in Divorce diplomacy, Foxe did not gain significant preferment
until 1531 (archdeacon of Leicester), and his elevation to the see of Hereford came in 1535, at
the height of Cromwell's power.

[14] See my *Reform and Renewal: Thomas Cromwell and the Common Weal* (1973), pp. 15 ff.

courts, most probably during the 1529 session, he first inserted and then struck out the word 'empire', applied to the realm of England, thus testifying both to his familiarity with the concept and to his doubts whether so novel an idea should yet be advanced. Lastly, the chronology fits well enough. Throughout 1530 Cromwell was gaining at court, but his known activities offer no real explanation why he rather than better known supporters of the Divorce should have been admitted to the Council of which he was a member before the end of the year. Thus, by the late summer of 1530 a reasoned defence of a new policy was in process of composition, and a new adviser linked to it by the evidence of later actions as well as the opinion of contemporaries can be found arriving in Henry's confidence. There are therefore very good grounds for concluding that at about this time Henry learned from his new servant of a possible line of attack on the Pope which, by asserting the autonomous self-sufficiency of England and the imperial authority of her King, proposed to cut the knot of all the problems created by continued reliance on the Pope's good services.

If this interpretation is correct (and though it has to be in part speculative it best accounts both for the available evidence and for the difficulties of the story), Henry was from late in 1530 in possession of a possible way out of his troubles but neither fully convinced of its feasibility nor exclusively exposed to advocates of its adoption. His leading ministers were the noblemen of high degree and low intelligence who had no solution to offer; willing enough to do all they could towards the Divorce, Norfolk and Suffolk were barren of ideas and merely echoed what the King was saying. The canonists in the Council, led by Gardiner, were stuck with finding an answer involving the Pope's surrender to Henry's demands; anything that made a reality out of the frequent threats to ignore the Pope offended their professional belief in the law and also constituted too much of a threat to the liberties of the Church. They therefore had an ally in Thomas More, or inadvertently formed some sort of a party for him in his efforts to prevent the disaster he could see coming, efforts to which he himself testified years later when he told Cromwell that the King knew his opinions well enough since he had frequently expressed them in Council. From the latter part of 1530, however, these distracted factions were joined in the Council by a group of radicals[15]—Cromwell, Foxe, very probably Thomas Audley (chancellor of the Duchy and Speaker of the

[15] I am aware of the danger involved in using terms like radical, conservative, and so forth, but some descriptive name has to be found for men who were held together by a quite clearly defined programme. By 'radicals' I therefore mean those who advocated a radical solution to the conflict with the Pope, though most of them were radical also about the reform of the Church.

Commons), ultimately Cranmer—who almost certainly had the valuable support of Anne and therefore of Wiltshire. They meant to use the Divorce to take England out of the Pope's Church altogether, a decision so formidable that Henry might well hesitate, however firmly on occasion he used the language of radicalism, before committing himself against so much opinion that either opposed the step outright or could not see how it was actually to be managed.

As the event was to show, the radical faction's purpose went beyond the creation of a schism in the Church. They wished to build a polity capable of undertaking that comprehensive programme of reform that so many people had been talking about for so long, and they therefore needed to get uncontested control of policy. For a time, however, no faction commanded Henry's unwavering allegiance: which is also to say that for a time Henry refrained from imposing his authority on the disputants. Fully aware of, and rather taken with the ideas of the radicals, he preferred to feel his way with caution; uncertain of his ground and told by experts that there was no way in which the radical programme could be legitimately realized, he confined himself to talking about autonomy in the hope that the threat would do at Rome what was wanted. After a fine first spurt he increasingly backed away in an endeavour even now to achieve his main purpose by tradition-hallowed means. Delays at Rome would prevent an adverse decision, and diplomacy—especially the support of France for which he made much play in 1531—would yet bring the Pope to his senses and permit the trial of the case in England. At the same time, the radicals pressed for stronger action, and this too could be useful as a ploy. The years 1530–32 were marked by a struggle of political factions which Henry was unwilling and unable to resolve. Meanwhile, he waited for his Anne, and Anne waited for her crown.

III

The radical programme of reform, which derived from both Erasmian and Protestant roots, included the real reform of the Church, and this in the first instance meant removing the separatist claims to liberty which the Church maintained. From Henry's point of view, whether he persuaded the Pope or ignored him, he was looking for a sentence of nullity pronounced by the Church in England and thus needed a Church securely obedient to himself. Moreover, he knew only too well the shaky state of his finances which was so gravely impeding his freedom of action: he quite simply could not afford a major conflict with the Emperor, which fact offered additional reasons for hesitating before adopting the full radical solution. Whether or not (as rumour alleged) Cromwell from the first promised to make Henry the wealthiest king that ever was in England, he soon proved that he knew where to look for the necessary resources: not for nothing had he shown his hand by squeezing Wolsey's chaplains to get money for Wolsey's lay servants at the time of the cardinal's sudden penury. Thus the first signs that a new and radical line of thought had arrived appeared not in attacks on Rome but in planned assaults on the Church in England.

Not all the legal troubles inflicted on the clergy arose from government action. The 210 prosecutions in the Exchequer deriving from the anticlerical legislation of 1529, which have been discovered for the years down to 1535,[16] show only that private persons and a few professional informers gladly seized upon this addition to the armoury of a man who would trouble his neighbour; that only fourteen ran to a successful conclusion in court is in line with the usual experience, namely that such suits were a form of blackmail intended to compel a settlement out of court. The acts were no dead letter, and the clergy continued to work for their repeal, but these pinpricks had nothing to do with the King's campaign. A brief flurry of annoyance led to the prosecution, under the proclamation against papal bulls, of three leading bishops (Fisher, Nixe and Clerk) in September 1530: they had tried to appeal to Rome for intervention against the pluralities act, so popular with informers. But this, too, meant little: since no court was specially charged with the task, the proclamation (as usual) proved impossible to enforce, and the matter dropped. The episode, however, threw an odd light on the Church's capacity to reform itself. Pluralism was one of the most widely recognized obstacles to an efficient pastoral ministry, though it also helped bishops to provide for valuable administrators and scholars who contributed their own share to the Church's work. No doubt the statute failed to make all the fine distinctions desirable, but it comes as a shock to find three undoubtedly conscientious bishops engaged in so bitter a battle for so doubtful a cause.

The pressure which began in the Michaelmas term of 1530, however, had full government initiative behind it. At the opening of the term, the attorney general indicted fifteen persons of praemunire, for that they had actively abetted Wolsey's illegal legateship. The fifteen chosen were certainly of the conservative party. Among the eight bishops, the appearance of Fisher causes no surprise: from that day, Fisher was rarely out of trouble. The

[16] J. J. Scarisbrick, 'The Conservative Episcopate in England, 1529–1535' (unpublished dissertation, Cambridge, 1955), p. 88.

Divorce was, however, making strange bedfellows. Standish of St Asaph, champion of the King's regality in 1515 and yet a very conservative theologian who had long taken a stand against Erasmus and his New Testament (which had got him into Fisher's bad books),[17] was assigned to be one of Catherine's counsel in 1529 and thereafter joined her party from conviction, against his royal patron. Blythe (Lichfield), Nixe (Norwich), West (Ely) and Sherbourn (Chichester) were all King's men and standard careerists, administrators rather than scholars and of a conservative temperament, but nothing linked them to opposition; several of them had signed the July letter to the Pope, and all in due course managed to accommodate themselves to changing circumstances. John Clerk (Bath and Wells), one of Henry's leading diplomats, at first proved tougher than most in opposing what was about to be unleashed upon the Church, but he quickly made his peace with Cromwell and retained his see peacefully until his death in 1541. The seven lesser clergy attacked also were among the strong men of the Church.

Resistance to radicals clamouring for a renovation in faith and manners was one thing that united the fifteen; another was vulnerability. All those charged had in fact been technically guilty of the offence in that they had concluded agreements with Wolsey to pay him fixed sums in recognition of his right as legate to interfere with their jurisdiction. That these agreements had been extorted from men who had tried to resist the cardinal's autocracy added a cruel irony to the proceedings but meant nothing, of course, in the law. Once Wolsey's surrender had admitted the power of that great threatening cloud, the law of praemunire with its undefined limits, all who had in any active way recognized his legateship stood in that law's danger.

The men picked for attack were thus those strong enough to stand up to Wolsey and thought likely to provide strength now to the Church's resistance to Henry. We cannot be certain whether the move was as deliberate as this sounds: possibly the law-officers, cleaning up after Wolsey (and assisted by Cromwell's inside knowledge?), found useful material for action in contracts they recognized as illegal. Once again, one finds signs that there was nothing very single-minded about Henry's government at this juncture. In October, the Council decided to abandon the prosecutions; as Cromwell told Wolsey on the 21st, 'the prelates shall not appear in the praemunire: there is another way devised.' Yet the law-officers, who pursued the suits with fresh writs right to the end of term, were not ‹

[17] Scarisbrick, 'Episcopate', pp. 347 ff. It seems that over this issue he joined hands with the abbot of Winchcombe whose sermon in 1515 had been the beginning of Standish's troubles with Convocation—a reminder never to oversimplify these factions and attitudes.

aware of this change of plan, and the King's Bench allowed the cases to run on for months until they were closed in the Easter term of 1531 when the accused pleaded the general pardon that had been the outcome of the 'other way'.

As Cromwell told Wolsey, and as Catherine's party also firmly expected, the serious business of subduing the clergy and getting results at Rome was to resume with the reconvening of Parliament, so long delayed by repeated prorogations. However, when the Houses assembled on 16 January there was still nothing resembling a government programme in existence. The only crown bills of the session would appear to be one which punished murder by poisoning with the specially revolting cruelty of boiling alive,[18] and another which tightened up the law against people who evaded punishment by seeking sanctuary. There was the usual spattering of Commons' bills to tinker with the details of commercial life and the technicalities of the law; even the Beggars' Act (Poor Law) of this session, which proposed to suppress vagrancy by whipping, looks like the product of an unofficial bill. And nothing at all was proposed that bore on the fate of Catherine of Aragon: her supporters' apprehensions turned out to be premature. In fact, the government concentrated its efforts this time on the Convocation of Canterbury which reopened a few days before the Parliament with the intention of passing reforming canons. Reform was indeed discussed: there was talk of dealing with clerical dress, simony, the cure of souls in livings appropriated by monasteries—all standard problems—as well as with such familiar lay grievances as the fate of criminous clerks, the excessive number of feast days, the use of excommunication, and the administration of the sacraments without money taken.[19] Convocation spent rather more time on the spread of heresy, examining a number of notorious suspects and growing wrathful over the heretical will left by William Tracy, a gentleman from Gloucestershire—a choice of agenda which again illuminates the clergy's false priorities.[20] Both heresy and reform, however, vanished into the

---

[18] The act (23 Henry VIII, c. 9) resulted from an unfortunate mistake or prank in the kitchens of, ironically, Bishop Fisher; Henry, pathologically afraid of poison (as most highly placed people in the Renaissance were), pressed for the cruel statute even though his enemy had nearly been the victim. Only two persons are known ever to have suffered under the act, one of them the fool whose practical joke had led to it.

[19] M. J. Kelly, 'Canterbury Jurisdiction and Influence', p. 229.

[20] Edward Crome and Hugh Latimer were disciplined; the session began the final proceedings against Bilney and examined a very radical heretic, John Nicholson alias Lambert. As for Tracy, Convocation condemned his will as heretical, but it was the misplaced zeal of a diocesan official which led to his body being exhumed and burned—an unfortunately timed reminder of Hunne's fate. Tracy had a son who, seeking compensation, made sure that the case should not be forgotten.

shadows when the government unmasked its batteries and Cromwell's 'other way' made its appearance.

On 21 January 1531, Warham moved Convocation from St Paul's to Westminster, thus symbolizing a more obvious subjection to Crown and Parliament, and on the next day both Houses learned that Henry wished them to offer a very large subsidy to cover the expenses he had incurred owing to Rome's obstinacy over the Divorce. This effrontery was accompanied by a strong hint that the whole clergy might in various ways have fallen into the perils of praemunire, and within two days Convocation had voted a sum of about £100,000, certainly a large one but based fairly on Wolsey's 1522 census. In turn they asked for a general pardon, to end all those vague threats of praemunire, legateship, and so forth. It looks as though the speed of the concession took the Council by surprise, for Henry had more in mind than cash. He bought a few days' time before accepting the grant by haggling over payment dates, and the Church proved its unbroken strength by using the interval to put forward a petition which demanded three things: their ancient liberties and privileges (from Magna Carta onwards) should be confirmed, the law of praemunire should be properly and narrowly defined, and the anticlerical legislation of 1529 should be modified. This defiance ended the uncertainty manifestly prevailing in the Council; Henry threw his weight behind the radicals, and on 7 February Warham presented the King's conditions for granting a general pardon. He demanded to be recognized as 'sole protector and also supreme head of the Church of England'; and he offered to signify that protection by guaranteeing the peaceful operation of the Church in attending to 'the cure of souls committed to his majesty'. In return he would confirm such privileges as did not offend his regality and formally pardon the clergy for all possible past offences.

These demands left no doubt: if Henry was recognized as supreme head possessed of a cure of souls he was taking the pope's place. That indeed was the radical programme, apparently pushed through in Council by means of the King's financial straits and the clergy's obstinacy. It caused an uproar in Convocation which, to be brief, managed to destroy the real meaning of what it conceded. In the upper house, Fisher led the uncompromising resistance to the new title, while the lower house procrastinated. For three days several of the King's councillors attended the debates in an endeavour to smooth things over, and it appears that they proposed the qualifying phrase—'so far as the law of Christ allows'—which in the end brought a sort of agreement. On 10 February Cromwell appeared in Convocation and had a long private conversation with Warham. Even this did not quite end things, though Warham now knew the time of day. However, on the morning of the 11th, arriving late and breathless from an interview with Henry, the archbishop put to the house a modified form of the concession which was received in a silence that he, according to the old tag, interpreted as consent. The clergy recognized Henry as their sole protector and supreme head so far as the law of Christ allowed, and accepted his aid in the cure of the souls of the people committed to him. The general pardon promised in exchange was embodied in an act of Parliament, and after some difficulty over getting a like pardon for the laity the battle seemed over.

Two questions arise concerning the meaning of these events: what was the charge to which the clergy had surrendered, and how much had they lost? As to the first, the Act of Pardon states that the Church had been accused of praemunire on the grounds that it was exercising a jurisdiction contrary to the King's, that is for having ecclesiastical courts at all, a devastatingly comprehensive basis of attack. However, the chronicler Hall, a member of this Parliament, rather suggests that when the pardon was first seen in the Commons the offence was defined as support of Wolsey's legateship—the offence which had earlier put the prelates in the King's Bench. Convocation was told on 14 March that some of the King's councillors had altered the terms of the document as it had been conceived by the clergy, and it has been argued that these changes belatedly introduced an offence inherent in the clerical estate and independent of anything that Wolsey might have done.[21] There is no way to be certain. The violent first reaction in Convocation and the speed with which the subsidy was agreed suggest that something new—not the stale old charge of aiding Wolsey—had been at issue from the first; but it is also possible that a word in the Commons, pointing out that talk of Wolsey touched everybody, lay and spiritual, introduced a modification.[22] At any rate, in the end the clergy were pardoned for operating their anciently established hierarchy of courts. This was a genuine triumph for the common law and a new note in these debates. We recall that the clerical jurisdiction was first attacked in a petition originally drafted in 1529 and since in process of redrafting in Cromwell's office. We recall the financial gains made from this session. We recall the decisive appearance of Cromwell in Con-

---

[21] Kelly, 'Canterbury Jurisdiction', pp. 225 ff., as against J. J. Scarisbrick, 'The Pardon of the Clergy 1531', *Cambridge Historical Journal* XII (1956), pp. 22 ff. which first demolished the notion that the pardon was for the Wolseian offence. As Kelly points out, Scarisbrick could not have been aware of the 14 March report; and while in general I have followed the latter I think that on this point Kelly may be right.

[22] Kelly argues that while the laity were involved in obeying Wolsey only the clergy could be guilty of using their own jurisdiction; but if accepting Wolsey's legateship constituted a praemunire for the laity, so would their use of the spiritual courts.

vocation. We conclude that we know who stood behind the policy of subduing the clergy by forcing them to buy a pardon and make sweeping concessions. Cromwell really proved the point in May when he managed the parallel surrender of the northern Convocation which added £18,000 to the subsidy voted by the south.

But, as the events of the session showed, there was not enough consistent and unanimous drive behind the King's actions to disguise the profound disagreements among his advisers. It was the radicals who showed up in Convocation—Cromwell, Audley, Anne's brother George Viscount Rochford. What they obtained fell far short of the radical programme first presented. Not only Fisher but most of those involved treated the qualifying clause about the law of Christ—itself potentially a marvellous source of endless debate—and the denial to Henry of a cure of souls as removing the offensive aspect of the new title because they reduced it to a long accepted superiority in matters temporal and saved the pope's spiritual headship. Indeed, Henry himself admitted as much when, in a letter full of subtle evasion, he replied to a protest raised by Tunstall on behalf of the northern Convocation. And there were enough strong men left in the Church to put this interpretation firmly on record. The prelates may have been cowed, but the archdeacons and proctors who made up the lower house proved to be tougher. The lower house of the northern Convocation accompanied its acceptance of Henry's terms with an explicit statement of its reservations, while in May eighteen members of the southern house (acting on behalf of a majority) issued two official protests which could not have been plainer. Nothing, they stated, that they had accepted or might in future accept should in any way be regarded as derogating from the rule of one supreme head over the universal Church or from their obedience to Rome. Most of these brave men found themselves in court, charged with praemunire, but a quick plea of guilty got them their pardons. None of them suffered, except in their pockets, and the position they had maintained was not abrogated by the action at law. It is also worth notice that no more than two thirds of the large grant had been collected in 1534 when the remainder was cancelled in the course of finding more efficient ways to mulct the Church.

Thus the first attempt to put through a radical programme designed to cut the ties with Rome and create a Church ruled nationally by the King as supreme head suffered a defeat, and it did so for three reasons: the clergy proved unexpectedly resistant, the radicals were not yet in control of the King's mind and policy, and the means chosen were relatively clumsy in that they relied on direct pressure and the old law of praemunire rather than legislative innovation. Perhaps we may see in one small victory over the conservatives on the Council some recognition of the place where the real answer could be fashioned. On 30 March, the last day of the session, Sir Thomas More, as chancellor, appeared successively in both Houses of Parliament to make a declaration on the King's behalf concerning the Divorce. He explained that rumours about Henry acting for the love of some woman were false: it was solely the sad scruple of conscience that compelled him to end a marriage in which he had been happy. The opinions of the universities were read out in support. More's feelings as he told this mixture of truth and lies may be imagined. In the Lords, Catherine's partisans tried to start a debate which Norfolk quashed; in the Commons the information was received in silence.

1531 had gained the King neither his Divorce nor his headship; but in one way and another the growing power of those who wished to use the first in order to create the second had become manifest. Cromwell and Foxe, assisted by Stokesley and Cranmer, scored another partial success later in the year when the King's printer put out the first of a long line of officially inspired propaganda works—really an edition of the *Collectanea satis copiosa* with the opinions of the universities added at the beginning; an English translation of the Latin original followed in November.[23] The battle between the Council factions continued. Despite his grasp of the autonomy argument Henry had once more refused to go all the way; there were still strong voices to oppose such drastic action, and he was still not sure that he could get what he wanted by ignoring the Pope and proceeding at home alone.

IV

In March 1531, More was variously reported to be in grave danger of dismissal or so sick of it all as to wish to resign. In fact, though now very heavy-hearted, he stayed on: the causes for whose sake he had accepted the great seal were not yet so lost that he felt it right to retire from a position in which he could still help. After all, the session just ended had vigorously fought Henry to a draw: the Church's liberties survived, though dented. After all, that session had proved the continued willingness of the Church to root out heresy. And Henry's big talk of imperial immunity, of going ahead

[23] *The Determination of the most famous and excellent Universities of Italy and France, etc.*, a title which hides the import of the main part of the book. It drew an answering pamphlet, *Invicta Veritas*, from Thomas Abel, one of Catherine's chaplains. See my *Policy and Police* (1972), pp. 174 ff. and 189 n. 1: it is now clear that this was the book translated by Cranmer. The identification with the *Collectanea* was made by Mr Nicholson.

without the Pope, of appealing to a General Council, of recognizing at best a thin spiritual supremacy at Rome—talk faithfully echoed by Norfolk to the imperial ambassador—had produced not a single positive diminution in the powers of the papacy. The bishops kept their ranks well closed—the only newcomers (Gardiner of Winchester and Lee of York) were no friends to Reformation—and the lesser clergy showed even more forcefully where they stood. From the high assertions to which Cromwell's advice had led him, Henry declined into a feeble holding action, using Edward Carne at Rome to postpone a decision there, but unable to get any further himself. Since Anne was certainly by this time his constant companion (by day at least), the contrast between the pressures under which the King laboured and his inactivity is striking. It would seem that for the moment he had lost faith in the radical solution, perhaps because in March it had fallen so far short of the promised success, even though it was his own readiness to retreat in the face of a determined clergy and a divided Council that had frustrated Cromwell. The country was beginning to wake up to the new man's growing influence—by June it was reported that he did as he pleased in Parliament—but if Cromwell coveted real power he needed to subdue the Church and silence opposition in Council; and, as he knew, he could do this only through Parliament. Since that body did not reassemble until 15 January 1532, the last eight months of 1531 simply marked time, a time filled with attempts to keep France sweet and use her as a sword against the Emperor. The diplomats enjoyed themselves.

The parliamentary session of January to May 1532 proved to be the occasion for the decisive battle. We can trace the new spirit that was entering the King's counsels. In the late autumn of 1531, a long list of matters to be done by Cromwell, which he submitted for the King's approval, included the first extant evidence for the preparation of government bills—a bill for treason (prepared but probably not introduced that session), a bill equalizing export duties paid by natives and foreigners (not passed; this turned into a long contested issue), a bill touching import duties on wines (passed), a bill concerning the King's feudal rights (which led to a lot of trouble), a bill for sewers (passed), a bill touching apparel (which passed a year later). Apart from the prosecution of those protesters of May 1531, the only suggestion affecting the Church was for a bill attacking the revenues of non-resident bishops, but of this move against the Curia cardinals holding English sees nothing more was heard for nearly three years. Though throughout the 1530s we find indications that Henry did not always know what Cromwell was doing in Parliament, he was fully aware of these proposals. For the first time, and under the guidance of the rising minister, he was going to Parliament with positive purposes.[24] The session which opened on 14 January 1532 and turned into the longest yet of this interminable Parliament did in fact pass acts in the traditional area of economic and legal reform which, for the first time, can safely be assigned to government initiative, among them in particular a revised navigation act and the great Statute of Sewers, Cromwell's work, which regulated the management of rivers and drainage for nearly three centuries. In the first session of Parliament which he clearly dominated Cromwell at once signalled his abiding interest in the reform of the commonweal.

However, what agitated Parliament had nothing to do with these mundane questions. The Commons were at once plunged into a major battle over the King's demands for his feudal dues. The problem was this. Tenants-in-chief upon inheriting their lands paid a series of death duties, of which the most important were the relief (for livery of lands to a tenant out of his minority), and the prerogative rights of wardship over the land and persons of minor heirs who, upon attaining their majority, paid a fine called a livery in lieu of the relief. Wardship especially (which put exploitable landed property and the saleable marriage of heiresses into the Crown's hand, often to be sold profitably to interested parties) made a sizable contribution to the King's revenues. For some two hundred years landowners, anxious to avoid these incidents, had developed a device known as the use: a man would enfeoff a body of trustees with all or part of his lands to the use of another (for instance, his heir), so that when he died the tenant at law survived and no death duties arose. It was also in this way possible to evade the legal bar to the bequeathing by will of all land held in knight's service.[25] The common law did not recognize the use but, tied to its doctrine of seisin (the estate created by a lawful enfeoffment) persisted in treating the trustees as possessors; since the arrangement involved the obvious possibility of fraud on their part upon the intended beneficiary who had no standing at law, the Court of Chancery had for a long time undertaken to protect him by compelling the feoffees to carry out their duties. One way and another, enfeoffment to uses proved to be an extremely convenient and widely employed method for settling one's landed property, so much so that large parts of the

[24] Cromwell's role as crown manager in Parliament is defined not only by his preparing and steering of bills in the Commons, but also by the fact that he had now become the man to whom application for licence for absence from the Upper House had to be made; he granted it rarely. By 1534, we find him managing by-elections, themselves rather a novel thing called for by the length of this Parliament.

[25] These are the simplest forms and employments of the use, a very complex system of conveyancing; for a fuller discussion see A. W. B. Simpson, *An Introduction to the History of the Land Law* (1961), chapter 8.

crown estate too were held in this way by feoffees to the king's use; but obviously, and intentionally, it cut severely into the feudal revenue of the crown.

Henry VII had made some attempts to reduce this drain, and in the early 1530s, when once again relative penury was compelling careful attention to all sources of income, the issue revived. In 1529, the King concluded a sort of treaty with the parliamentary peerage by which he would permit them to bequeath by will two thirds of their lands in return for full payment of feudal dues on the remainder. This agreement was meant to be embodied in a statute but nothing happened; actually, there was little sense in confining oneself to a small (though especially wealthy) sector of the landed classes, and no hope of getting the Commons to agree to a bill which would have penalized the gentry represented there. In 1532, therefore, Cromwell proposed to apply the principle to all lands affected but to reduce the exemption to one half of a man's estate. Despite some support from those in the House who could see the advantages of a compromise, the opposition to abandoning any of the tax-evading benefits of the use proved overwhelming, and irate; the bill was dropped.

Unfortunately for the Crown, the Commons extended their displeasure to the consideration of supply. No new taxation had been levied since 1527; and in this session Henry wanted a lay subsidy. We know very little about it; only that the discussions did not go well, were put by for weeks, and then resulted in a grant which the King (perhaps because it was thought insufficient, perhaps for other undiscoverable reasons) refused to accept. The episode remains obscure, but it does testify to the difficulties now growing in the Commons whose members, after three sessions in two and a half years, must have established something of that corporate spirit that such experiences produce and were clearly beginning to feel restive about such an unprecedentedly long commitment to their duties.

While the Commons were getting worked up about money matters, another superficially financial issue was troubling the Lords. This was the bill of annates, really the first serious attack on the papal power in England. Annates comprised the payments—variously based and variously calculated—that the pope extracted from newly beneficed incumbents in livings to which he had provided, especially bishops, abbots and priors. Exaggerated ideas about the drain of money to Rome had for some time run about the country and found credence with critics and pamphleteers. The bill's preamble claimed that something like £160,000 had left the realm in that way (to Rome) since the year 1486. The most careful calculation yet made, avowedly neither complete nor fully reliable, suggests that the actual sum was nearer £180,000, though this might include some items not comprehended in even the loosest definition of annates.[26] Thus it looks as though the drafters of the bill played fair and may even have made quite accurate calculations; the trick lay in giving a shocking impression by using a half century's total, and in passing over in silence what the clergy were already paying the King (about two and a half times as much). In any case, the heart of the matter did not lie in the relief which, it was pretended, the bill was to afford to bishops. It lay in the attack on Rome of which the fiscal element was the least important: the bill provided that if the Pope retaliated by refusing bulls of appointment to the King's nominees for sees and so forth, the necessary consecration should be carried out by English bishops under the authority of the act. It also declared that any possible papal interdict should be simply ignored.

Thus the annates bill unmistakably confronted the lawful claims of the papacy. Attempts were made to sweeten the pill, as in the clause according to which King and country 'be as obedient, devout, catholic and humble children of God and Holy Church as any people be within any realm christened'. The preparation of the bill included a petition against annates, possibly not used, which derived its arguments from the *Collectanea satis copiosa* and used much stronger language than the bill did: if the Pope proved obdurate, the King was asked to break with Rome altogether by means of parliamentary legislation. Of such extremism the bill is innocent, but if either House could have been moved to present the petition they would have given Henry good diplomatic leverage at Rome. The loud opposition in the Lords, immediately known to the imperial ambassador, put paid to any such device; instead Henry conceded the addition of a clause which suspended the effect of the act until confirmed by royal letters patent, time being thus given for further negotiations with Rome.

Even so the bill met strenuous resistance which called for the King's repeated attendance in the Lords and, ultimately, on 19 March, for a division in which the spiritual peers present voted solidly against it. They were, however, in a minority on the day. It is more surprising that the Commons proved very difficult, too. Since it is not sensible to suppose that the House ardently wished the Pope to have his annates, it appears that the organized opposition managed to get across the point that this attack on papal exactions masked a far-reaching encroachment on Rome's spiritual supremacy and the liberties of the Church. According to Chapuys, Henry himself addressed the Commons in vain, till he called for a division (still a

---

[26] J. J. Scarisbrick, 'Clerical Taxation in England, 1485–1535', pp. 41 ff., reckons that total payments to Rome averaged *c.* £4,800 p.a.; deducting non-annate payments from the total, I am left with *c.* £4,500 which, multiplied by forty-five (1486–1531) yields the figure in the text.

rare thing in that House) which carried the bill. The story may be true, though the King practically never attended the Lower House; more usually, and more properly, he summoned a delegation to his presence for instructions. What cannot be doubted is that the first truly anti-papal measure of this Parliament met very strong resistance, a warning to the radicals (and the King) that parliamentary action in support of the Divorce remained problematical. The Lords would be sure to prove difficult; not only were the spiritual peers still firm and united, but as recently as early February, at a meeting of some influential persons, Lord Darcy, supported by a majority of those present, had told the duke of Norfolk that despite the famous arguments from autonomy and immunity matrimonial cases belonged to the spiritual jurisdiction and had nothing to do with Parliament.

One way and another, therefore, the session was stirring up a lot of bad feeling, even though the bill of annates, in its conditional form, got through. From Cromwell's point of view, things were distinctly not going well; so far, his more radical policy had produced nothing but an unhappy Parliament whose lack of enthusiasm for drastic measures was bound to make Henry hesitate even more before he committed himself to the all-out attack on Rome that Cromwell wanted. What was needed was action on the part of the Commons which would seem useful to Henry (whose prime concern remained with the Divorce) and would at the same time advance Cromwell's own policy, that is to say, the subjection of the English provinces of the Church of Rome to the national authority of England alone. He needed yet another manifestation of the Commons' hatred of ecclesiastical malpractices, the one predictable line they could be trusted to follow without swerving. We must turn to the partly obscure, often discussed, and somewhat controversial story of the Commons' 'Supplication against the Ordinaries'.[27]

[27]Years ago I offered an interpretation of these events which suggested that the agititation, spontaneous in 1529, was deliberately revived by 'the government' in February 1532, the emerging Supplication being prepared before the session started but on the basis of the Commons' own first efforts of 1529 which Cromwell kept and worked up (*Studies in Tudor and Stuart Government and Politics* II, pp. 107 ff.). Against this, J. P. Cooper argued (*English Historical Review* LXXII, 1957, pp. 616 ff.) that the Supplication originated without aid in the Commons and was then opportunistically exploited by Henry, while M. J. Kelly ('The Submission of the Clergy', *Transactions of the Royal Historical Society*, 1965, pp. 97 ff.) maintained that there was no planning at all but only a confusion from which the Convocation's surrender emerged almost unexpectedly. I have once more weighed all these discussions and restudied the evidence; and I have also considered the reconstruction of events offered in Scarisbrick, *Henry VIII*, pp. 297 ff., and S. E. Lehmberg, *The Reformation Parliament*, pp. 138 ff. I agree with my critics that I was wrong to use the term 'government' so loosely to cover the King and his councillors with their varying ideas, and that I overestimated the degree of successful planning. My critics, on the other hand, have ignored the possibility that some people were planning what to others came as a surprise; and I think that their interpretations take insufficient account of both the documentary evidence and the setting of events in the developing battle for control of the Church.

Thoughts of the Church's independence had not been absent from the crown's preparations for the session; among the acts passed was one for further limiting benefit of clergy which grew out of an official bill. But this was a very minor matter compared with what began to be debated in the Commons when, probably quite late in February, after weeks devoted to uses, subsidy and commonwealth matters, the grievances of 1529 received a new airing.[28] It is likely that this renewed discussion was engineered by Cromwell whose purposes it suited exceedingly well. He had retained the draft petition against ecclesiastical legislation and jurisdiction which had been put aside in 1529, for pressure of business and because it caused such an outcry from the bishops in the Lords, and he had since worked this up into a comprehensive indictment of spiritual laws and judges, with a few extra details thrown in. The finished draft which was placed before the Commons was either produced in committee or much more probably was in his pocket before the session opened.[29] It differed from the earlier versions in one respect in particular: while attacking the methods of the courts (citations, fees, lawyers' malpractices) it emphasized the Commons' hatred of heresy and desire to see it punished in a way that recalls the avowal of orthodoxy in the annates bill (also drafted by Cromwell) and reflects a similar desire to satisfy the King on this touchy point.[30] The final version also introduced two new matters: regret and apprehension were expressed at the spread of heretical literature (which supports the conclusion that the earlier agitation belonged to 1529, before the proclamations against such books), and the Commons complained specifically about citations from one diocese into another. The Supplication asked the King to provide a remedy by act of Parliament, and that this was what Cromwell meant to have appears from two such bills prepared for use: one that became the Citations Act of

[28] Those who, like Mr Cooper, would date the anticlerical agitation to the start of the session have to explain why in that case it took two months to get the Supplication before the King, an extraordinarily long time by the standards of the day. The Speaker's petition of the same day (18 March) for a prorogation also shows that so far as the Commons were concerned the business of the session was done, which means that at any rate the bulk of bills had passed both Houses. A late date for the Supplication debates also best fits the chronology of events in Convocation.

[29] Apart from the arguments advanced for this in my earlier article, I must emphasize that of the many paper drafts of bills surviving in the State Papers not one can with any likelihood be assigned to parliamentary stages of bills. The corrections on the final version—a careful verbal revision—are in Audley's hand who as Speaker would not have acted as drafting clerk to a committee; but he regularly assisted Cromwell in pre-sessional work.

[30] It has been shown that not lack of faith but justified fears of the strenuous efficiency of the church courts lay behind the feelings that inspired the Supplication: Margaret Bowker, 'Some Archdeacons' Court Books and the Commons' Supplication against the Ordinaries of 1532', *The Study of Medieval Records: Essays in honour of Kathleen Major*, edited by D. A. Bullough and R. L. Storey (1971), pp. 282 ff.

that session settled part of the particular grievance newly introduced, while a second, not used, proposed to subject clerical legislation to parliamentary ratification. The preamble of that draft, which outlined a theory of the body politic of England derived from the doctrine of national self-sufficiency under the King, reveals the stable whence it came. Among the original Commons' grievances, Cromwell had from the first paid special heed to that touching the independent legislative authority of the Church, the only issue in the document which involved profound questions of sovereignty, of the King's power, and of the nation's relationship with its clergy; and he evidently meant to use the pressure of the Supplication and the prepared remedial bill to secure the destruction of clerical independence by statutes resting on a coherent political theory of national sovereignty and the King's pre-eminent authority under God, a destruction which in fact he was to achieve in the subsequent three sessions.

In 1532, however, the time had not yet come: things went differently from Cromwell's planning. On 18 March, Audley presented the Supplication to the King. It is far from clear whether Henry had any previous knowledge of what was coming; Commons' debates were thought to be sufficiently private for some members to have complained, blaming Cromwell, when they discovered that Henry knew of what had earlier in the session been said about uses. The King had at this point little reason to feel especially gracious towards the Commons, and Audley did not improve the occasion by also asking that the Parliament, which had already been sitting for two months, might be allowed to go home. Rightly pointing out that he could hardly dismiss them and at the same time provide a parliamentary remedy for their grievances, Henry demanded a favourable answer to the bill of uses and chose to play the part of dutiful arbitrator between laity and spiritualty. He passed the Supplication to Warham and asked for a reply.

Throughout these events Convocation had also been sitting and had been busy enough, producing a promulgation of reforming statutes that gave this last independent session of the body a fine autumnal glow. The reforms were modest—more drastic proposals once again failed of passage—and strongly reminiscent of the sort of humanist reform that from about 1510 onwards had been achieved in Spain and in some Italian bishoprics, but in bulk this legislation outshone anything done for over a century.[31] This achieved, the prelates deserted Convocation for the House of Lords, to battle with the resurgent anticlericalism of Parliament. On 24 February

---

[31] Kelly, 'Canterbury Jurisdiction', pp. 98 ff.

Warham took a step of great courage and exasperated anguish when he formally recorded a protest against all anticlerical laws made or yet to be made in the Parliament. By this time he had evidently got wind of the Supplication, and he may have had the citations bill (which especially annoyed him) in view. In early March he stirred Convocation once again to attack Latimer, by this time a favourite preacher at court, and when in his absence Bishop Stokesley arrested the proceedings the archbishop revived them a few weeks later. Altogether the old man suddenly stiffened his hitherto pliant back to a point which called for intimidation. It was thought to stop him by threatening him with a praemunire based on his consecration of Standish (in 1518!) before the formalities of royal approval had been obtained, the very offence which had enabled Wolsey to have his revenge on the bishop of St Asaph.[32] There is no sign that this absurd charge was seriously pressed, but Warham began to think himself a likely martyr; his mind ran significantly on his distant predecessor, Thomas Becket, and he prepared himself to resist to the last.

Thus the Supplication dropped into a situation little suited to Cromwell's careful plan: the King unwilling to unleash the Commons without giving the spiritualty a chance to state their case, and the leadership of Convocation, no doubt borne up by the previous year's semi-victory, unwilling to give way any further. Immediately, Warham protracted time; no more was heard of the Supplication before the Easter adjournment on 28 March. Convocation re-assembled on 12 April, two days later than Parliament, and now turned to the Commons' complaints. Their first reaction shows very clearly how independently of King and fellow councillors Cromwell and the Commons had proceeded. The answer returned on the 19th was largely written by Gardiner who had missed the first part of the session, having returned from an embassy to France on 6 March; it contemptuously dismissed the complaints (which it ascribed to the machinations of evil men), upheld the Church's law-making power without qualification, and maintained that there was nothing wrong with the church courts except perhaps an occasional venial lapse. This reply reached Henry on the 27th, and his extreme displeasure greatly shocked Gardiner who seems genuinely to have been surprised to find the King so hostile. Since, as Henry's secretary, he should have known the royal mind sufficiently well, we may take it that Henry had had nothing to do with the promotion of the Supplication and that his pose on 18 March as an impartial adjudicator carried conviction even among his councillors. He showed his mind on 30 April when he once more addressed a deputation of the

[32]See above, pp. 56–7.

Commons. Handing over Convocation's answer, which he coldly
(and justly) described as 'very slender' and 'very sophistical', he
proved his indifference between. the parties by upbraiding the
Commons for the effrontery of some members who had lately—using
the occasion of financial demands—boldly said that there would be
no fear of attack and no need of taxes if the King would but take
Catherine back. As usual, on this theme, he spoke with a mixture of
frankness, embarrassment and anger, but the last just then predominated in his feelings for the Commons.

These bold remarks were the work of the Aragonese group whose
organization has been mentioned before, and they destroyed
Cromwell's plan to break through to a statutory declaration of his
anti-papal and anti-ecclesiastical policy. A few days passed without
either the Commons or the Convocation quite knowing what to do,
until on 8 May the lower clergy in their impatience opened the
floodgates. At their request, their prolocutor (actually Edward
Foxe—so there may have been an arrangement) went with some
members of the upper house to beseech the King to protect the
liberties of the Church. Henry, who was evidently recalling the
methods used a year before when he had tried to force the clergy
into compliance by direct pressure, took his opportunity: on the
10th, Foxe presented ·the royal demands which amounted to the
destruction of the clergy's independent legislative powers—the
target of the first article in the Supplication. New canons were to be
made only with the King's consent, all existing ones were to be
scrutinized by a royal commission drawn half from Parliament and
half from the clergy, and those found good were to be validated by
the King's approval. Though not willing to let Parliament legislate
the liberties of the Church out of existence, Henry stood sufficiently
under Cromwell's influence to accept its cooperation in this reduction of the Church to order. Next day, again moved by Cromwell, Henry backed up his demands with yet another message to the
Commons: he had, he said, discovered that the clergy were, thanks
to the oath the prelates took to the pope, but half his subjects (this, it
seems, was one of Cromwell's favourite remarks), and he asked the
Commons 'to invent some order that we be not thus deluded of our
spiritual subjects'. But Cromwell had no bill ready to deal with any
oaths to Rome; it was too late to return to parliamentary manoeuvr-
ing. The Houses were in fact prorogued on the 14th, a day before
Convocation—after painful attempts to wriggle free—accepted the
royal demands without qualification. There was to be no repetition
of the gallant resistance of 1531. Warham's defiance had oozed out
of his old bones, and Gardiner, defender of the Church's law, was
helplessly out of favour. And anything was better than have the

Commons produce any more bills arising out of grievances which, if pursued, might end the whole ecclesiastical jurisdiction. And so the Church surrendered to the King, in a document aptly entitled 'The Submission of the Clergy'.

The Submission resulted from the Supplication, so that the only beneficiary of that attack on the Church was the King himself, now equipped with power to control the spiritual legislation. Though in theory his relationship to the canons of the English Church was now the same as that in which he had always stood to laws made in Parliament, he had of course established that control by depriving the Pope of his legislative sovereignty in the Church. Neither Supplication nor Submission was used to bring Clement VII to heel; Henry evidently did not regard either as a weapon in his main battle. Indeed, the whole affair looks like having come, by and large, as a surprise to him and some of his councillors; presented with an opportunity to smite the obstreperous Church, he seems to have responded more in a spirit of general and petulant exasperation than for reasons of considered policy. Little practical consequence flowed from the Submission because in this session the clergy had in any case shot their legislative bolt and because the intended revision of the canon law of England occupied a low place on an increasingly crowded agenda.

Yet there was more to it all than a mere insignificant gesture. The hand of Thomas Cromwell is as manifest in these proceedings as the mind of Henry VIII is absent. And though Cromwell had not exactly achieved the end for which he had worked, since he would have preferred a parliamentary statute rather than a submission to the King in person, his machinations had certainly demolished one of the main pillars of the Church. As later on he once noted, he wished to find out how the words 'ut ecclesia Anglicana libera sit' had got into Magna Carta. By then he had removed more of those liberties, but the process had begun with the Submission, even if not quite in the manner intended. And immediately it was even more important that the session ended the struggle of conflicting counsels that had raged around Henry's eclectic head for some three years. The influence of the conservative episcopate, still powerful in the spring of 1531, was gone. Stephen Gardiner, Cromwell's only rival among the up and coming men, was in disgrace and temporarily out of the way. On 16 May, the day after Convocation surrendered, Sir Thomas More resigned the chancellorship. He thereby announced his recognition that the battle was lost: there was nothing left for him to fight for, and the time had come to look to the salvation of souls—his own as well as those of others— a task best undertaken by a private person, away from those corruptions of office that only a

7 The Age of Reform

I

When the author of *Utopia* retired from the public stage, he neither terminated the influence of humanism on England's life and government nor put an end to hopes of reform. On the contrary, a rational and spiritual reform now unhappily required his removal in the wake of which passionate debate shot up like asparagus in May. The 1530s turned out to be the first flourishing age of English printing. During More's chancellorship books produced at home mostly defended the old order as well as Catherine of Aragon: he had seen to that. This conservative production continued for a while. More himself devoted his new leisure to the controversies which while in office he had been unable to arrest altogether; in the next year and a half he produced five major attacks on reformist writers, all printed by his nephew-in-law, William Rastell.[1] Rastell elected himself the chief purveyor of Catholic works, such as a continental treatise in support of the mass translated by More's son John. The mass was also defended by a native theologian of conservative tastes, the Franciscan friar Gararde, while Stephen Gardiner's nephew Germain attracted attention by an intemperate attack on the Cambridge reformers, written from the point of view of a reactionary undergraduate (*Letter of a young gentleman*, also put out by Rastell). Of course, none of this activity of 1533 so far contravened either the law or any settled official policy, but it was increasingly getting out of step with lines of thought developing at court and in Council. It came to an end as the year ran out and as Cromwell took a better grip on the press. Under his patronage a very different body of writers and writings took over the task of discussing the issues of the day; production turned from controversy to constructive thought.[2]

[1] The second book of *The Confutation of Tyndale's Answer*, an *Answer* to Frith's treatise on the sacrament of the altar, *The Apology of Sir Thomas More, Knight* (in defence of his activities in office), *Debellation of Salem and Bizance* (against Christopher St German), and *A Letter impugning the erroneous writing of John Frith.*

[2] The writings are discussed in W. G. Zeeveld, *Foundations of Tudor Policy* (1948) and J. K. McConica, *English Humanists and Reformation Politics*, two books to which this discussion is much indebted. See, however, my *Reform and Renewal* for some modifications and corrections of detail and interpretation.

Where before this one encounters the very occasional treatise
analysing the problems of the commonweal and offering advice, one
now finds a whole generation busying itself with such labours. As the
decade wore on, all sorts of people, discovering in themselves the
urge of often commonplace thought and in Thomas Cromwell a
willing patron of its products, wrote busily on issues real and
imaginary—on the reform of the Church, on the true faith, on the
fortunes of the cloth trade, the price of grain and the problems of the
coinage, on unemployment and poor relief, on the influence of the
stars, the meaning of ancient prophecies, or the impact of recent
history. From the first there were two main centres to this activity.
One clustered around the universities and certain survivors from
Wolsey's household; some of its members attached themselves to
Reginald Pole and for a while lived in that replica of a university, his
household at Padua where he, with the help of Thomas Lupset
(?1498–1530), presided over a coterie of earnest young men debating
the reform of Church and state. Among them Thomas Starkey (*c.*
1495–1538) stood out for learning and intelligence, but the liveliest
wit belonged to Richard Morison (died 1556); both were products of
Wolsey's college. Not all men of this kind went abroad; thus Richard
Taverner (?1505–75), who used Erasmianism in defence of Luther's
teaching, though also one of the Oxford men patronized by the
cardinal until their heterodox opinions became too obvious, was
never at Padua but adhered to the same way of thinking and also
ended up in Cromwell's entourage.

The other centre of reformist propaganda was London, more
particularly a group of three men who had long been associated in a
mixture of commercial and artistic enterprises in their own behalf
and in the King's service—John Rastell, Clement Armstrong and
Richard Gibson.[3] Rastell (*c.* 1475–1536), who had married Thomas
More's sister, fathered that sound conservative, William, who took
over his father's printing business in 1532; he himself, an ardent
enthusiast of little judgement (he died imprisoned for his extreme
views on tithe), allowed his reformist urges to lead him into the
radical camp. By 1531 both he and Armstrong identified in Cromwell the man who, they hoped, would make a reality of their
wide-ranging plans touching the abolition of the Calais Staple, the
promotion of a native cloth industry, the fight against poverty and
unemployment, and the reform of the law. What characterized these
London reformers was a mixture of strictly practical concerns with
the specific ills of the commonweal and a wildly mystical streak of

---

[3] Discussed by A. W. Reed, *Early Tudor Drama* (1926) and S. Anglo, *Spectacle, Pageantry and
Early Tudor Policy* (1969), especially pp. 164–7, 264–5. Again, *Reform and Renewal* contains some
modifications of facts and opinions.

untutored religion which made them hard to live with. Armstrong, so precise in his analysis of a cloth trade he knew from inside, nevertheless saw the real purpose of reform in the creation of a holy commonwealth presided over by the King in the improbable guise of an irradiated saint. Thomas Gibson (almost certainly Richard's son) cherished notions of improving England's towns by creating internal trade monopolies there, but also collected mystical prophecies of a peculiarly vapid kind in order to prove that Henry was chosen by God to lead England towards the new Jerusalem. Stephen Vaughan, a close friend of Cromwell's, was for years agent to the Merchant Adventurers and commonly resided at Antwerp, the commercial capital of northern Europe; small wonder, therefore, that Cromwell hoped to get advice from him on the management of the export trade. But this he much grudged to give, preferring instead to expatiate on the duties of a reform-conscious royal councillor and the splendid ideas of Robert Barnes. William Marshall, another Londoner, who in an endeavour to provide intellectual support for the campaign against Rome published translations of Lorenzo Valla's *Donation of Constantine* and Marsiglio of Padua's *Defensor Pacis* (the latter with Cromwell's financial assistance), also busied himself with the problems of the poor and (probably) produced the most remarkable plan of social reform encountered in the decade.[4] These men appear to have been self-taught, and their learning was sometimes peculiar; their existence—appearing effectively out of nowhere, though they may have owed something to contacts with More's circle in the happy time before More learned about Luther—is striking testimony to the intellectual liveliness of the age.

Two rather more traditional strands contributed to the radical turmoil. There were the common lawyers, especially (but not solely) that prolific pamphleteer, Christopher St German, who in the 1530s turned his attention to the relationship between the secular state and the clergy.[5] Professing to seek peace between the parties, he developed the official doctrine apparent in the Reformation statutes into a political philosophy centring upon the unitary state and the supremacy of parliamentary enactments—a philosophy so like Cromwell's practice that he has been thought of as the minister's intellectual guide. There is, however, no evidence of 'influence' or even acquaintance. St German should be regarded as a thoughtful and able exponent of the views widely held among the practitioners of the common law, themselves—as the only non-clerical group of

[4] See below, p. 226.

[5] *A Treatise concerning the division between the spiritualty and temporalty* (1532); *A Dialogue betwixt two Englishmen whereof one was called Salem and the other Bizance* (1533—this drew More's fire); *A Treatise concerning the power of the clergy and the laws of the realm* (1533—authorship uncertain); *An Answer to a letter* (1535—reply to More).

professional reasoners—an important component of the circles from which government drew its recruits. The profession, which supplied not only attorneys and barristers and judges but also estate managers, auditors, accountants, surveyors, and a large part of the King's civil service, penetrated the ruling elite at all levels and in every part of the country; and while never given to undue radicalism did on the whole entertain certain convictions and habits of thought which suited a government intent upon subduing the Church. In turn they expected, and got, assistance in their efforts to overhaul the law, especially those aspects of it which, by causing massive costs and delays, had transferred much business from the old courts to Chancery and Council. The fall of Wolsey, and even more the rise of Cromwell, abruptly arrested the growing influence of civilians and canonists and revived that of the common law, in a fruitful exchange of mutual usefulness.

The other ever-present profession consisted of the clergy, and here, of course, lay a battle-ground. However, from 1532 onwards the reforming wing increasingly took heart. Though Frith was dead and Tyndale remained in exile (till taken and killed at Antwerp, in 1536, by the Emperor's government at Brussels), Joye temporarily returned to England (1532–42), and Barnes was in Cromwell's employment from late 1532. Variously engaged in government work at home and in embassies to northern Germany during the remainder of the decade, he published in 1534 a revision of his *Supplication* which modified some of his Lutheranism. His work in England, however, consisted in the main of preaching, and this indeed rather than the publishing of books was the preferred activity of the clerical reformers. From 1532 onwards, the number and impact of radical preachers rose rapidly; from all over the country came reports of attacks on excessive ceremonies, on 'superstitious practices' connected with the cult of saints, and especially on the doctrine of purgatory, a man's attitude to which became something of a touchstone in the England of the 1530s. Unable as yet to proclaim the full-blooded Protestantism towards which many of them were secretly moving, the radicals concentrated their assault upon this belief in a temporary state for the dead before they passed to their ultimate fate of salvation or damnation, a waiting interlude which allowed the living to assist the departed with prayers and devotions profitable to the priesthood. The radicals chose to treat purgatory as the typical tenet of an intercessory Church arrogating to itself what belonged to Christ alone and interposing itself between God and man; in response to their attacks the defence of the doctrine became a preoccupation with traditionalists. Latimer took the lead in the preaching campaign, with the assistance of a growing and growingly organized team that included such champions as Thomas Garrett, William Jerome and Edward Crome; further help came from Barnes, from John Hilsey (provincial of the Dominican friars), from John Bale (friar, playwright, antiquary, bibliographer), and from lesser men all over the country; Cranmer and Cromwell offered encouragement, special licences, and on occasion protection. The preachers met with a good deal of resentment and opposition from their hearers as well as counter-preaching from conservatives. The noise rising to the much disputed heavens grew so overwhelming that by early 1536 Cromwell thought it necessary to apply some restraint before the country became too ungovernably churned up: government was always apprehensive of breaches of the peace, though it is worth notice that so far as the evidence goes the disputants confined themselves to verbal violence.

Of course, these various groups of reform-conscious intellectuals did not exist in mutual isolation. Many men can be found whose lives reflect contact with several of them, as two very different individuals may illustrate. Thomas Elyot (?1490–1546), who in *The Book called the Governor* (1531) produced one of the more interesting works of the age, studied at the Middle Temple and went on to graduate at Oxford, though he finished there before the impact of Wolsey's promotions made itself felt, one reason perhaps why he always remained cautiously conservative in religion. His law got him the government service, especially in Star Chamber and on embassies, which in the end proved not to be his preferred mode of life; the university turned him into a fairly typical humanist and writer.[6] Though not really in tune with the events of the 1530s, he had Cromwell's friendship and protection. Except for the doctrines of the faith, Elyot believed in reform, especially of education, sharing the preoccupations of academic humanists like Starkey but also of common lawyers like the three young men who in 1539 produced a comprehensive scheme for the radical transformation of organization and teaching at the Inns of Court. Unlike Starkey and his kind, Elyot was of gentry stock; his estate enabled him to devote his time to the writing of books. His diligent, earnest, essentially unoriginal mind was well employed in various translations from the Greek, and in producing such useful compilations as the medical encyclopaedia he called *The Castle of Health* (1536) or his important Latin-English *Dictionary* (1538). The *Governor*, too, is not high on originality. In the main it expounds a programme for the education of a ruling elite derived from Italian exemplars to which Elyot added a short defence of monarchic rule, probably because he derived his inspiration from republican sources whose influence needed a counterweight.

[6] S. E. Lehmberg, *Sir Thomas Elyot: Tudor Humanist.*

Even more of a bridge between the various groups was that partly tragic, partly bizarre figure, Sir Francis Bigod, Yorkshire landowner, writer, enthusiast, and at the last executed traitor (1509–37.)[7] Bigod touched the reform movement at all points. He was Wolsey's ward from 1515 and in his household; he spent time at Oxford in the 1520s though without taking a degree; he patronized Garrett and Jerome; he collaborated with Latimer and Rastell; he became Cromwell's client. Like others of the day, he combined positive and practical ideas for reform with an enthusiastic temperament and a pre-dilection for mystical dreams. Undoubtedly a Protestant whose chief passion was for the preaching of the Word, he demonstrated the sincerity as well as the eccentricity of his devotion when despite his marriage he tried to get a licence to enter the priesthood, though he was willing to rest content with permission to preach as a layman—just so long as he could gain access to a pulpit. His enthusiasm in the end caused his fall in the wake of the Pilgrimage of Grace when, disappointed by the failure of Cromwell's government to create the holy commonwealth overnight, he revived rebellion in Yorkshire, a mad and sad ending. His contribution to the reform movement was essentially contained in his life and his assistance to others, but he also produced one published book himself (1535), a short treatise attacking the widespread practice of monastic appropriation of livings which left the parish clergy ill provided and the pulpits silent. The little book fully demonstrates his genuine concern for a properly endowed pastoral ministry, as well as the un-disciplined violence of his mind.

Thus the removal of More, the King's anti-papal proceedings, and the approach of an era of great change unleashed a seemingly sudden outburst of intellectual turmoil, devoted to the seeking out of the ills of society and the provision of remedies, which can only be called a movement for reform; and even though the ancestry of the movement has rightly been traced to the age of Wolsey, this complex multiplicity of thought and writing came really as something new. Altogether, the 1530s were marked by an energetic activity of the mind which contrasts strongly with the essentially contained tradi-tionalism of preceding decades when radical thought had been the preserve of the few and had been able to make its mark with the powers of this world only by growing less and less radical.

The new spirit appears also in the arts. Thanks to Henry VIII's attachment to splendour and Cromwell's money-raising skill, this was an age of lavish and, on the whole, remarkable building. Here, too, Wolsey had led the way, especially in his creation of Hampton

[7] A. G. Dickens, *Lollards and Protestants in the Diocese of York* (1959), chapter 3, and *Tudor Treatises* (Yorkshire Archaeological Society, Record Series cxxv, 1959).

Court Palace, but Henry—building Nonsuch Palace, rebuilding St James's and Whitehall (Wolsey's York House), extending Hatfield and Greenwich—as usual went one better. The rebuilding of coastal fortifications from Kent to Cornwall, begun in 1538, employed the latest developments of military science and produced the best examples of the genre found in Europe. And the 1530s also marked an epoch in the development of the English language. In translating the documents of the faith, Cranmer turned out to possess a poet's tongue which Tyndale, with all his plain skill, had lacked; and Cromwell has been discovered to be an innovator and artist in the use of words. As a printer and translator of statutes, Rastell took a leading part in the promotion of the vernacular;[8] another lawyer of learned aspirations, Edward Hall (died 1547), anglicized the new humanist historiography in his impressive history of England from 1399 which was in the main composed in the last fifteen years of his life. Above all, those years saw the heyday of Sir Thomas Wyatt, the greatest English poet between Chaucer and the Elizabethans. The son of a leading civil servant who made a worthy and profitable career under both Henries, Wyatt was naturally destined for the public service and did indeed undertake several embassies. In the main his career was that of a courtier, to his misfortune because he fell for Anne Boleyn at the wrong time and at the last saw all his old friends done to death in the palace revolution of 1536 when Cromwell's friendship saved him from sharing their fate. In 1540 he also witnessed the death of his patron who on the scaffold specially singled him out: 'Wyatt, gentle Wyatt, pray for me.' Wyatt's lyrical poetry, displaying a new freedom and ease learned from the Italians, lies throughout under a rarely dispersed cloud of melancholic despair, genuine enough and indeed understandable. There is no better way to get at the truth of the age's terror, which lies so close to its fierce desire to renew itself, than to read his laments for the victims of 1536 ('Circa regna tonat') and for Cromwell ('The pillar perished is whereto I leant').

II

The printing press was very active in this decade, and the printers flourished, especially that successful entrepreneur Thomas Berthelet,

[8]Howard Jay Graham, '"Our Tong Maternall maruellously amendyd and augmentyd": the First Englishing and Printing of the Medieval Statutes at Large', *University of California, Los Angeles, Law Review* XIII (1965), pp. 58 ff. This reprints (pp. 97–8) Rastell's call for the use of English.

the King's printer, who published the many officially inspired tracts and regularized the profitable publication of parliamentary statutes. But from the point of view of general reform, what appeared in print is less significant than what existed and circulated in manuscript. The literary exercises which achieved publication concerned themselves with theology, philosophy and politics; they were as a rule part of a public argument, often promoted by the moment's needs of government. When they tackled the question of the social order, these writers addressed themselves to a smaller circle—a circle of friends and of men who could help to translate aspiration into action. Some of the (now) best known treatises were never properly completed; some carry the air of current debate among like-minded men. Yet the influence of such unperfected writings must not be doubted; for at least another century people preferred to avoid print when they committed their ideas to paper, as either too undignified or too dangerous, and the truth about these purveyors of ideas must be sought in their unpublished work, often anonymous and un-attributable. The most significant new mode of expounding one's views which appeared in the 1530s was the treatise in the form of a bill in Parliament, the reform proposal put up ready for practical employment. A good few of these proposals turned out to be extra-vagant or much too difficult to carry through—plans for the total confiscation of the Church's wealth, for the creation of a central court to enforce economic regulations and equipped with a nation-wide police organization, for a standing army. Some are really sermons cast in the form of an enactment. But many are real and practicable schemes some of which were adopted. Cromwell's ad-ministration included a planning staff which worked on the ideas of theorists and reformers to produce legislation for submission to Parliament.[9]

What sort of ideas did these practical idealists put forward? Clement Armstrong was probably the most practical among them; his loose and woolly mysticism did not prevent him from shrewdly analysing matters very much within his personal experience, though (together with his bigoted dislike of Parliament, which he thought represented only vested interests) it did stop him from getting much attention from Cromwell. His best effort was a short paper suggest-ing 'how to reform the realm and setting them to work and to restore tillage', written in about 1532.[10] He confidently proclaimed the labour theory of value—'the whole wealth of the body of the realm rises out of the labours and works of the common people'—and established that the basis of that wealth lay in two employments,

---

[9] For all this see my *Reform and Renewal*, chapter 3.
[10] *Tudor Economic Documents*, edited by R. H. Tawney and E. Power (1924), iii, pp. 115 ff.

agriculture and manufacturing industry. He identified the causes and consequences of unemployment and concluded that the chief remedy lay in concentrating the manufacture and sale of woollen cloth—England's staple export—in fixed depot towns in England. This, he argued, would enable the King to organize the trade and control its profits for the benefit of nation and monarch alike. Behind this he visualized a concentrated effort to promote the more intensive production of food. The treatise mingles statistics and demands for precise investigation with furious asides about exploiters and disconcerting touches of religious fanaticism; but its main quality lies in the detailed suggestions for reform which are derived from an instructed analysis of the problem. Armstrong may or may not have been right—some of his analysis is tendentiously naïve and some of his remedies are politically quite impossible—but in him the moralizing inseparable from thought about the good commonwealth was firmly subordinated to specific and practicable reform.

Among the university-trained humanists, Thomas Starkey stands out as the only man to produce systematic and reasonably original writings on reform. An Oxford theologian who got his degree before the invasion of the Cambridge heretics, he never espoused Protestantism, but he fully embraced the 'Erasmian' Christian humanism current in Pole's circle at Venice and Padua to which he belonged for the ten years after 1525. Of all that group he made the most determined efforts to train himself for the service of the state, for (typically) he had none of Erasmus's and More's doubts about the scholar's involvement in affairs. When Pole temporarily returned to England in 1528–30, Starkey spent time in France studying law, and in his reading he concentrated on the great political works of Aristotle and Marsiglio.[11] He returned to England in December 1534, as soon as he learned that Cromwell's commonwealth policies offered him a chance to realize his life's ambitions. Only one of his writings was published in his lifetime—*An Exhortation to the people instructing them to unity and obedience* (1536). The book was printed at Cromwell's insistence, as part of his effort to disseminate the political ideas upon which his reformed polity rested, and its contents owed a lot to Cromwell's conversation and suggestions. Starkey's purpose was to defend the new order and secure its general acceptance, but in the 'process he explained its rationale, that is the idea of the unitary national state and Church subject to the rule of constitutional monarchy and embodying the principle of moderation, that middle way between the extremes of radical reform and con-

---

[11] Though Starkey independently knew Marsiglio, he did not introduce him to the Cromwellian circle; Marshall was busy translating the *Defensor Pacis* before Starkey made Cromwell's acquaintance.

servative reaction upon which the Church of England was to be built in its ultimate emergence in the reign of Elizabeth. The concept of a *via media* depended on the insistence that not all the demands of religion were equally necessary to salvation: some doctrines had universal and mandatory character, while others would vary in their application with time and place. This notion of *adiaphora* (things indifferent) owed something to Erasmus, probably rather more to Melanchthon and Bucer, but was most successfully worked out by Starkey (in response to Cromwell's express demand) who handed it on to the Elizabethan apologists. In the midst of the often crude violence of the early Reformation, it formed an eirenic centre of gravity attracting both unity and obedience; the *Exhortation* is a worthy book, though Starkey was never anything but a moderate stylist.

From the point of view of social reform, however, two unpublished manuscripts of Starkey's have greater significance, especially as both were certainly read in the circle of advisers surrounding the government of the 1530s. The first was a treatise on the ills of the commonweal, with concise suggestions for reform, which Starkey wrote at Padua in 1532-3 and polished further after his return to England. Cast in the form of a dialogue between the leaders of the Paduan circle, Reginald Pole and Thomas Lupset, it unquestionably embodied Starkey's own thought, though this will have owed much to the discussions there.[12] He intended to present it to Henry VIII but was frustrated by events. The other writing is in the form of a letter addressed to the King, though once again it is improbable that it was finished or presented. Written in the autumn of 1536, it discussed the opportunities offered by the political revolution and the dissolution of the lesser monasteries which, Starkey held, had put both power and means at the King's disposal to undertake the renewal of the commonweal that the philosophers had demanded for so long.[13] In these treatises Starkey defined his concept of the true polity, an organic unit of ruler and ruled involved in a dynamic process of improvement in the conditions of life, the ultimate purpose being a perfection of physical and spiritual welfare. He started from the position that under the umbrella of the universal law of nature every community needs to work out a positive law suitable to its local and time-bound needs. In this manner Starkey adapted the rigidity of the Thomist definition of the body politic to the needs of a philosophy which emphasized man's ability to better

[12]The most accessible edition is by K. M. Burton, *A Dialogue between Reginald Pole and Thomas Lupset by Thomas Starkey* (1948); for the making and influence of the treatise see my *Studies in Tudor and Stuart Politics and Government* II, pp. 236 ff.

[13]Long extracts from this letter were published by S. J. Herrtage, *England in the Reign of Henry VIII* (1878), pp. xlviii ff.

his condition by his own action, that action being expressed in the making of reformist laws. Starkey's position evidently owed much here to Marsiglio, but it also accurately reflected the ambitions of the practical reformers who in the early 1530s, before his return to England, were crowding into Henry's government. In some ways the most interesting thing about Starkey is his firm conviction that absolute monarchy equalled tyranny: he wanted his true polity to be monarchical but ruled by consent and cooperation. While he lacked the training and attitudes of the common lawyers, he arrived at a 'constitutionalism' very similar to theirs; it is worth remark that he first attracted Cromwell's attention by these views on the state.

Starkey's actual analysis of what was wrong and what needed doing is less impressive for its content than its manner. Like everybody else he identified unemployment ('idleness') as the chief defect of English society, though unlike the experienced Armstrong he was inclined to seek its cause less in economic than in psychological deficiencies. He denounced gluttony, wasteful expenditure, luxury trades and similar things. However, while he showed himself possessed of the puritan moralism proper to an academic reformer, he knew also that specific ills demanded specific remedy; and he put forward plenty such, a somewhat unorganized catalogue of major reform. He wished to encourage matrimony (among idle young men and especially for priests) as a means of providing both an increase in population and a solid foundation for the social order. He proposed the control of imports, both to stop pointless luxury and to protect the balance of trade. He wished to promote the regeneration of decayed towns and the expansion of arable land. He denounced the 'barbaric' law of England, with its use of a corrupted form of French, hoping to see it replaced by the systematic Roman law of the Italian schools or at least reduced to codified order in decent Latin. There are short references to new laws touching shipping, the raising of cattle, the need for organized poor relief. In his letter to Henry VIII, he worked out elaborate and careful proposals for the reform of education—both an education in letters for the upper classes and a training in skills for the working population—to which he wished to apply the newly transferred monastic wealth. But his chief concern is with what he regards as fundamental—the provision of good government by the careful selection and training of the ruler and the creation of a competent machinery of advice and execution. In his details here Starkey turned unrealistic, opting for an elective monarchy (though he hastened to add that a king so marvellous as Henry VIII was an exceptional blessing produced by the hereditary system) and devising highly academic ruling bodies composed from the various estates of the realm. The general tone of his writings is

practical, directed to real problems which are quite well analysed
and led to their proper resolution in specific reforms. The whole
body of ideas is given cohesion by Starkey's concept of the true polity
and his proposals for responsible government. It will not do to
overrate Starkey, not a thinker of the first rank or teeming with
original ideas; yet he had a good and interesting mind, wrote with
force and instructed passion, proved himself independent and willing
to speak frankly,[14] and added a quite powerful rational dimension to
the turmoil of ideas and demands which burst forth in the 1530s.

Above all Starkey exemplifies the change that had come over
these discussions of the commonwealth. If one compares his output
with More's *Utopia*, his inferiority in literary and philosophical
genius sticks out a mile. But if one considers the purposes of both
writers, the comparison works the other way. Where More had in
effect doubted the ability of existing societies (which yet he despised
and condemned) to remedy their deficiencies, or at least had looked
to a total transformation of the ethical basis of society as the only
hope in improvement, Starkey insisted that things were remediable
in the context of the prevailing order. Reform to him was not a
dream but a rational prospect calling for particular analysis and
systematic action. This was the true, and new, spirit of the age of the
Tudor revolution, the spirit in particular of the man who gave that
revolution reality and direction. As has become plain in this discussion, all the lines put out in those years led firmly towards
Thomas Cromwell.

III

Thomas Cromwell was born about the year 1485, the son of a
clothworker of Putney in Surrey who, like others of his trade, also
kept an ale house. His early life is very obscure, and the stories later
told of it offer little illumination.[15] However, it would appear that in
his teens he got into sufficient trouble to leave the country for a
while, and he made his way through the Netherlands into Italy
where he allegedly served as a soldier, possibly taking part in the
battle of the Garigliano (1503); which side he fought on is unknown.

[14] In 1536, at a time when he was in considerable danger because his friend Pole had lately
revealed his hatred of Henry's proceedings, Starkey was willing to criticize the years 1529–36,
to Henry's face, on the grounds that so long as Anne Boleyn had been alive 'few acts could
proceed, by the conjecture of wise men, which might be durable with our posterity.'

[15] The account given in R. B. Merriman, *Life and Letters of Thomas Cromwell* (1902) I, pp. 5
ff., can be corrected and modified by a few facts discovered since. The evidence is cited in my
'Thomas Cromwell Redivivus', *Archiv für Reformationsgeschichte* (forthcoming).

He then turned to trade, serving a Venetian merchant but travelling back to the Netherlands; he was active at Antwerp in 1514. He had probably come straight from Rome where earlier that year he had stayed at the English Hospice. Shortly after this date he must have returned to England, to marry and settle down. He married money, in a modest way, but also acquired a mother-in-law for whom he provided in his house even after his wife had died. There has been some debate about the date of his entry into Wolsey's service, but it is clear now that he picked up the rising star quite early, being in the cardinal's household by about 1516 and described as of his council by 1519. At the request of a personal friend from Boston (Lincolnshire), he paid a second visit to Italy in 1517–18, in order to help the town get a bull of indulgence from Pope Leo X. He is said to have eased the journey by learning the New Testament by heart, in Erasmus's recently published translation; certainly he knew the Bible well for the rest of his days. Somehow he acquired a good knowledge of the law of England and built up a successful private practice for which much evidence survives, the earliest from about 1518 or 1519. In 1524 he was admitted to Gray's Inn, more a testimony to his standing among London attorneys than evidence of any formal training in the law; he was also soon much in demand as an out-of-court arbitrator. This combination of commercial and legal experience came increasingly to be at Wolsey's command, though his private practice did not cease till about 1532, and in the 1520s Cromwell occupied the place of the cardinal's man of all work, his leading lay councillor. We have already seen how he repaid his master's trust at Wolsey's fall.

Cromwell's riotous and unusual early career—he once said later that he had been 'a ruffian' in his youth—left very definite marks on him. Wherever one touches him, one finds originality and the unconventional, and his most persistent trait was a manifest dissatisfaction with things as they were. He seems to have lacked those natural ties to the past which most people acquire in childhood, question in adolescence, and submit to as they grow older: growing up outside the conventional lines of his day, he remained all his life a questioner and a radical reformer. At the same time, the hard road he had had to tread to worldly success and especially to power—so much more hazardous than that open to the bright child of poor parents who found his way into the Church—had evidently taught him the limits of the possible and the need for patience and adjustment. His life had made him a very political animal, but one equipped with lasting principles, concerned (as he once wrote) always to build rather than to destroy. His acquaintance was as varied as his experience. He had ties with the city of London and especially the Merchant Adventurers, and he knew the cloth trade at first hand. His connection with Gray's Inn, augmenting the effects of his legal practice, gave him personal contacts with many common lawyers and especially the friendship of Edward Hall, the historian. In the 1520s he played bowls at John Rastell's house, and he was well acquainted with Thomas More; they shared a common friend in the intellectual Italian merchant Antonio Bonvisi, long settled in England.[16] Wolsey's household provided an introduction to a large mixed group of men, the middle-rank administrators who ran affairs under the cardinal and were to supply the same service under new circumstances in the generation after Wolsey's fall, as well, of course, as some of the young thinking radicals. As his behaviour in the Reformation Parliament indicated, he learned the ways and the minds of the House of Commons in 1523. Work for Wolsey brought many other experiences and contacts, especially with the realities of monastic lives and economies. Bishops and archdeacons, noblemen and gentry, merchants and lawyers, thinkers and writers, Englishmen and Italians and Flemings, these and more formed the setting of his life; but so did poor men and women, or at least the many people in difficulties who sought his aid. The only area of public life that was unfamiliar to him was the court which he did not penetrate until he made his way to power; there is no indication that he was known to Henry VIII at all before 1530. Acquaintance and experience had made this inwardly exceptionally determined man outwardly flexible and almost invariably affable. He never refused to listen to any petitioner, however dubious; he devoted an inordinate amount of his time to the importunities of those in need of help; and as he climbed ever higher he acquired a justified reputation for never forgetting old friends.

Cromwell was a solidly built man, given to stoutness; his large face with its small eyes, long upper lip and jutting chin concealed more than it revealed. Unlike Wolsey, he disdained pomp and cultivated a plain accessibility which reflected his genuine interest in other people. An exceptionally lively mind hid behind the formidable façade and expressed itself in vigorous and witty speech; his conversation charmed even enemies, and he had great natural gifts as an orator. The spoken word—at court, in Council, in Parliament, in private—was his chief weapon, even as the written word of letters, drafts and memoranda was to be his main instrument of government. Words, in fact, meant much to him, and he took his part in the maturing of the English language that was going forward in his day. Fluent in Italian and probably French, he knew Latin and

---

[16] Bonvisi's invaluable memories of the two great men were lost to us through the obtuse idiocy of Archdeacon Harpsfield (my *Policy and Police*, p. 420).

possibly some Greek, all self-taught. His tastes were those of the intellectual rather than the aesthete; though he seems to have laboured to display a conventional appreciation for attractive buildings and artefacts, he never emulated Wolsey's natural love or eye for such things. Cromwell's major intellectual interest lay in political philosophy—the analysis and understanding of political structures. For a man actively engaged in manipulating and transforming such a structure he was exceptionally concerned to grasp the meaning of what he handled—exceptionally but advantageously, for his desire to elucidate and to act upon principle saved him from the excessive pragmatism and mere opportunism to which both his necessary concern with the immediate task and the self-centredness of the King he served were bound otherwise to drive him.

Cromwell was once thought to have been a conscious disciple of Machiavelli, whatever that may mean, but it is now more likely that he did not read Machiavelli till the later 1530s. So far as one can give a name-label to his political philosophy it could be called Aristotelian. It was Aristotle's analysis he asked Starkey to expound. and he certainly knew the work of that striking Aristotelian, Marsiglio of Padua, whose fourteenth-century writings were to prove so relevant and useful to the architect of the break with Rome. The influence of the common law and a clear grasp of the role of Parliament further helped to shape his mind; as has been said,[17] his administration was to witness the recovery of both from the threat posed by Wolsey's devotion to equity and autocracy. Above all, Cromwell thoroughly shared the anticlerical feelings that in the reign of Henry VIII dominated so much of English public life: he hated 'the snuffing pride of prelates' (as Hall put it), objected to the elevated claims of a ritualistic priesthood, and had conceived a deep dislike of the regular orders. His anticlericalism stemmed, however, from more positive feelings than lay resentment or envy; it stood rooted in his religion. Exactly what he believed remains a debatable point. He once, in 1530, lamented the existence of Luther, but that remark was addressed to Wolsey and meant to please. At his death he claimed to have ever adhered to the Catholic faith, but that was meant only to rebut the charges of sectarian extremism which had brought him down. He probably grew more Protestant as the decade advanced: many people did. To some Lutheran envoys, who had said that 'Christ owed much to him, even as he owed everything to Christ', he admitted in 1538 that on the whole he was of their persuasion but would, 'as the world stood, believe even as his master the King believed'. That mixture of cool conviction and canny care probably comes nearest to the truth. He had in effect become

[17]See above, p. 60.

convinced that only a form of Protestantism could serve the polity he
was building, but his faith was not hot enough to override his
awareness of the political possibilities. As it was (and as we shall see),
it was strong enough to make him drive faster than Henry liked and
to play an important part in his downfall. Nothing, in fact, is further
from the truth than the old prejudice which sees in him only a
faithful instrument to his master. Despite his care to seem always to
be executing only Henry's will, and despite the extraordinarily
fulsome language he used to the King, he left plenty of evidence that
he was ever ready to take initiatives of which Henry knew nothing
and that during his government the active side of politics drew its
inspiration from him.

Cromwell's sober faith took its shape from a sincere devotion to
the Bible, a devotion he shared with such passionate reformers as
Latimer, such genuine Protestants as Cranmer, and such Christian
humanists as Erasmus and the Erasmians.[18] Bible-worship could take
very different forms in the many people whom it alone united. In
Cromwell's case it supplied one of the driving forces to an essentially
political temperament, the principled undertone and transcendental
justification of labours that concentrated upon reforming the earthly
existence of men by reconstructing the state and using the dynamic
thus released (rendered active in legislative potential—that is, in
statute) to remedy the abuses and deficiencies for so long debated
and identified. It was Cromwell's purpose to remake and renew the
body politic of England, a purpose which because of the compre-
hensiveness of his intentions amounted to a revolution, but which
proceeded by using the means inherited from the past. Not only did
the practical statesman in him grasp the political advantages of
introducing major change so far as possible under the guise of
continuity, but Cromwell the thinker also knew about the roots and
long established realities of the polity he wished to transform. These
realities lay in a general order embodied in the common law and in
the making of new law by discussion and consent, not edict. In a
very real sense, Cromwell had a vision—a vision of order, improvement, the active removal of all that was bad, corrupt or merely
inefficient, and the creation of a better life here and now in preparation for the life to come. To Cromwell, the reformed Church was
to serve the purposes of the reformed commonwealth, whereas
more definitely religious minds would have wished to reverse that
order of priorities. It matters nothing that like all practical
visionaries—and, because of the short time allowed him, more so

---

[18] Cromwell, no Erasmian himself, nevertheless respected Erasmus; he just did not find the
humanism of that previous generation, with its acceptance of a universal papal Church,
particularly useful to his task.

than many—he found the path to his ideal stony and its realization elusive.

In Cromwell, therefore, the movement for reform found a man attuned to its call but also singularly able to translate task into action; and the prophets of reform naturally flocked to him. He neither did nor had to 'recruit' them; more commonly he had to withstand their eager rush, though he beat none from his doors and offered material aid to some pretty undeserving cases. Humanists, Protestants and economic thinkers, ardent men and selfseekers and cranks, genuine idealists and men disgruntled by envy and failure, all presented themselves, wrote letters, sent tracts or memorials or bad poems. Often they also sent information and denunciations which, there is no doubt, he needed and valued as much as ideas of reform. Some men he took into his service, some he advanced in the King's, for some he secured gifts or pensions, some few he ignored. With the best of them—with a Starkey or a Morison—his relations were more those of intellectual equals or friends then those of master and servant. He certainly wanted to employ suitable pens in the writing of books and pamphlets intended to defend the revolution on which he was engaged: the campaign of propaganda, exploiting with great skill the potential of the printing press first revealed by Erasmus and Luther and (nearer home) the Tyndale group, was deliberate, designed and competent. But it is clear that he also hoped for intellectual exchanges and especially for positive ideas and proposals of reform; and he got them. However, it would be wrong to think of Cromwell acting simply as the agent of those philosophers. Most of the reforms deemed necessary had been long apparent; what was needed now was their reaction to legislative proposals—the drafting of particular bills for Parliament. Cromwell's office included men engaged in this work; he himself took a very active share in it; his chief assistants came not from the ranks of the reforming scholars but from the real experts, the common lawyers. The most important of them was Thomas Audley who in May 1532 succeeded More at the great seal, first as lord keeper but soon (January 1533) promoted to the full office of lord chancellor. Cromwell's people were demonstrably busy drafting bills from 1531 onwards, years before the best known and most original writers joined his staff. The lead in this age of reform came from the top, from the minister; his work and his reputation attracted the men of ideas until a fruitful interchange of thought and labour emerged in the second half of the decade.

8 The Royal Supremacy

Even before the session of 1532 ended, on 14 April, Cromwell obtained his first office under the Crown, the mastership of the King's Jewels, an insignificant post hitherto very properly occupied by a succession of professional goldsmiths. It did, however, offer access to the royal revenues, and Cromwell characteristically used it to create a central treasureship for himself. In effect he usurped the place that the treasurer of the King's Chamber had held until 1529 and the keeper of the Privy Purse in the Privy Chamber since then by drawing to himself the main reserves, especially the French pension, and allocating their use on the basis of royal warrants which he usually got signed after the money had been spent. At the same time he began a more energetic exploitation of the revenue, reviving some of Henry VII's devices, and breathed much needed energy into the whole administration of the finances.

The new spirit soon manifested itself also in politically more important ways. Cromwell's victory in the Council had derived from the failure of the King's earlier advisers to discover a way of transforming the ideas of autonomy and immunity into the reality of freeing Henry for his second marriage. In the spring of the year, it was reliably reported that Norfolk and Gardiner could counsel only surrender, and the bishop of Winchester at least was thought to be wavering over the Divorce. Such advice ended their influence with Henry whose purpose never faltered, and from May 1532 onwards everything was clearly moving towards the unilateral solution which Cromwell advocated. Audley, in charge of the Chancery, at once procured the release of suspected heretics imprisoned by More; trials and burnings ceased; Barnes received signs of favour. And while official policy appeared to be continuing along familiar lines—pressure on Rome, avoidance of the trial there—in reality the ground was being prepared for very different action. The half-hearted attempts made for three years to enlist French aid against the imperial threat reached a climax in a new defensive alliance concluded in June which was followed up in October with a meeting between the two Kings at Boulogne and Calais. Francis, who undertook to assist Henry at Rome, was thoroughly deceived, as by stages he came to realize: despite their professions, the English no longer wanted to persuade the Pope, but they needed French amity to prevent positive action at Rome and give pause to Charles V (busy at the time with preparation for war against the Turks) in case he should contemplate intervention in England. The real inwardness of Henry's diplomacy was made plain by the company he took to Boulogne. Cromwell was there, for the first time active on the European stage; more important, Anne Boleyn, recently created marquess of Pembroke in her own right, accompanied the King and received full public honours from his French cousin. Francis allegedly (and this is probably true) encouraged the marriage which was wrongly rumoured to have taken place during the visit; what is certain is that, married or not, the pair consummated the union soon after. By late January 1533 Anne was known to be pregnant, at which point a nuptial ceremony was hurriedly arranged.

It is usually said that this event precipitated the decision to separate England from Rome, but this is not so: the causal order runs the other way. The decision to proceed had been taken before Henry went to Calais to deceive Francis into thinking that a conventional solution might still be acceptable. The death of Warham in August 1532 opened the road to a settlement of the issue at home, by whoever should succeed at Canterbury, though steps had still to be taken to make sure that the settlement should look properly legal. The actual replacement of Warham caused difficulties, probably because there were several obvious claimants none of whom could be trusted to be absolutely sound on the Divorce. Very possibly Gardiner would have been chosen if he had not forfeited the King's confidence in April. As it was—true to his procrastinating temper—Henry would not at once make up his mind, but when he did he demonstrated his novel adherence to the radicals. In November he recalled Cranmer, on embassy at Charles V's court (then at Mantua), a man who had never held more than an archdeaconry; when Cranmer arrived, after a seven weeks' journey through a bad winter, he was, on 10 January 1533, immediately appointed to the vacancy. The reformist party had successfully put out their strength. As Henry told Cranmer, he owed his promotion to Anne; and it was Cromwell who had specially sent to hasten his ally's return. Clement VII, still unaware of the way things were going, obligingly granted the bulls necessary for Cranmer's canonical appointment. At his consecration on 30 March the new archbishop swore the conventional obedience to the pope, but before it he had in private issued a witnessed protestation that no oath could bind him to act against the law of God or his obedience

to the King and the laws of England. Thus Henry, looking only for
an archbishop who would obediently end his matrimonial tangle,
put at the head of the Church the man who, already inclined to
Luther, was to preside over the religious Reformation in England.

All this was in hand before there could be any question of
pregnancy or urgency. In September 1532 there also appeared the
first powerful shot in Cromwell's propaganda campaign, a lively and
interesting tract called *The Glass of the Truth*. The King had a hand in
its composition—to the distress of the printer who knew him to be an
awkward and unmanageable author—but the production was overseen by Cromwell and Thomas Goodrich, one of the reformist
theologians now rising to prominence, and the book drew its substance mainly from the *Collectanea satis copiosa*. Its chief purpose was
to popularize the range of arguments for the King's unmarried state
and England's independence that had been current at court since
1530; but Cromwell obtained also the inclusion of a broad hint that
a solution would soon be provided by Parliament. It had in fact been
decided to cut through the whole tangle by giving Canterbury
grounds to proceed and to add a statutory provision which would
block any appeal from a decision so obtained.

The drafting of this act caused difficulties—no wonder, in view of
its import. The first plan was for a simple enactment which would
either relegate the decision in the Divorce suit to a tribunal presided
over by the two archbishops or even more simply declare that the
marriage had been judged invalid in Convocation. But the second
would not have achieved the radicals' purpose of subjecting the
Church to the law made in Parliament; and while the first would
have given substance to Cromwell's view that statute ruled supreme
in England, it seems to have met doubts about the wisdom of so
undisguisedly revolutionary an assertion. Very probably it was the
King who once again drew back, partly because he still wished to
keep more than one road open, and partly because throughout he
tried to avoid any suggestion that in some way his supreme authority
depended on an act of Parliament. He always preferred to deal
through 'his' clergy, very much in contrast to Cromwell whose faith
in the power of statute took time to win Henry's full allegiance even
after the decision to proceed radically had been taken.

The result was a compromise. Cromwell (who was working on the
drafts by September 1532)[1] accepted the advice that the act should
claim to be a development, called for by new grievances, of the
anti-papal legislation of the fourteenth century, should seem to deal
in general with specific legal issues rather than in particular with the
problem of Henry's marriage, and should be careful to emphasize

[1]S. E. Lehmberg, *The Reformation Parliament*, p. 164.

the independence of the spiritual jurisdiction from the temporal. However, in the preamble he took the opportunity to publish the political philosophy underlying the revolution he sponsored. He dug out the unused draft of the previous year of an act for ending the clergy's legislative independence and adapted its preamble to produce the resounding statement of national autonomy which introduces the Act in Restraint of Appeals to Rome. Claiming the authority of 'ancient histories and chronicles' (a manifest echo from the *Collectanea*) it declared that 'England is an empire'[2] containing a 'body politic corporate of all sorts and degrees of people divided in terms and by names of spiritualty and temporalty' and owing sole obedience to 'one supreme head and king'; all problems of the law, both temporal and spiritual, were within the exclusive competence of its properly constituted courts which derived their authority from the king. The statute went on to enact that no appeals could lie to any foreign tribunal in the three types of cases (testaments, matrimony and divorce, and spiritual revenues) which had hitherto been regularly taken from the church courts in England to the court of Rome; a new order of appeals culminating in domestic tribunals was also instituted.

The history of the act's genesis reveals the continued existence of diverse views at the heart of government.[3] Henry tried to use it to claim that the spiritual jurisdiction derived solely from the Crown and wanted a long defence against a possible charge of heresy; opposition from the canon lawyers removed the first, opposition from Cromwell deleted the second. The combination of a powerful manifesto in the preamble and the relatively modest and restricted provisions in the enactment, which has caused some historians to undervalue the statute, resulted from the circumstances which gave rise to it—the decision to turn a particular measure against Catherine into a general act, Cromwell's grafting on of his hitherto unused exposition of his political doctrine, and perhaps especially Henry's continued caution in avoiding irrevocable steps. The bill was not ready when Parliament reassembled on 4 February 1533, being further amended after submission to a body of ecclesiastical experts on the 5th; at last introduced into the Commons on 14 March, it caused some consternation, and the Aragonese faction for the last time rallied their forces. Members of the House expressed

[2] There has been some argument over my assertion that Cromwell introduced the concept of empire into the discussion (*England under the Tudors*, p. 161). The notion that Henry's crown was imperial was, of course, much older; but the description of the territorial realm as an empire (= sovereign national state) at this time occurs, to my knowledge, only three times: in this act, in Cromwell's insertion into an early draft (1529) of the Commons' Supplication, and in a treatise written by Richard Morison under Cromwell's supervision.

[3] My *Studies in Tudor and Stuart Politics and Government* II, pp. 82 ff.

principled doubt whether parliamentary statute could really intervene in these matters of the spiritual law and the authority of the
papacy. However, Cromwell won that victory: the bill passed
without a word being altered, and with its passing England had been
officially declared independent from Rome. Many ties did indeed
remain because what the act actually did extended to so limited an
area of the whole complex connection; it would take more than one
measure to end the arrangements of centuries and reconstitute the
two provinces of the Church of Rome as the self-contained Church
of England. But the opening sentences of the preamble had unequivocally declared the fact of schism and rehearsed the philosophical grounds upon which that schism rested.

Now Henry got the solution of his troubles, as Cromwell had
promised he should. While Parliament was debating the Act of
Appeals, the Convocations had the question of the King's marriage
before them. After some discussion, and under the management of
conservative but loyal bishops, both houses of both assemblies (with
some abstentions) agreed that Catherine's marriage to Arthur, now
stated to have been consummated, constituted an insuperable obstacle in the law of God to her union with Henry. Thus at last the
Church of England—'sufficient and meet of itself' (in the words of
the Act of Appeals) 'without the inter-meddling of any exterior
person or persons to declare and determine all such doubts, and to
administer all such offices and duties, as to their rooms spiritual doth
appertain'—rendered the verdict upon which the archbishop could
act; and in May Cranmer convened his court at Dunstable to try the
issue. Although Catherine refused to accept the court's validity and
would not appear, the formalities were fully observed; and on 23
May Cranmer pronounced the Aragonese marriage invalid and on
the 28th that to Anne Boleyn fully lawful.[4] On 1 June, the new
Queen was crowned, in all her glory, but when, on 7 September, she
gave birth to the child that was to seal her triumph as well as to
justify, by securing the succession, the political origins of all these
upheavals, the long awaited heir was yet another girl, christened
Elizabeth. Henry's disappointment, though in public he managed to

[4]Catherine now became 'princess dowager', as Arthur's widow. She never appealed against
Cranmer's sentence and thus formally the recent act played no part in the final stage of the
Divorce. It was also argued in both Parliament and Convocation that her earlier appeal (*not*
against sentence) of 1529 was invalid by the law of the ancient Church. From all this Professor
Scarisbrick concludes (*Henry VIII*, p. 314 f.) that the act mattered little, but I do not find his
reasoning convincing here, quite apart from his refusal to give due weight to the public
proclamation of the 'autonomous' argument. Of course the act could not be relevant
retrospectively to an appeal of 1529, while an appeal in 1533 would have brought Catherine
pointlessly into the praemunire. That the old law was brought out to reassure opinion in
Parliament only shows that the familiar citations from the *Collectanea* once more did duty in
debate.

hide it, was profound, and Anne never quite recovered from the shock. The King had cause to think that God was mocking him.

The event strengthened his resolve to keep his options open; as usual he wished to skirt commitment to any irrevocable course of action while giving the impression of an iron man. The inability he had shown throughout to act boldly and to follow through dogged him still; in his search for an absolutely secure footing for everything he did, he always hoped to stop every hole in every fence and never burn a bridge. Thus he still avoided admitting to a total breach with Rome and still pursued the negotiations there, except that now he wanted Clement VII to acknowledge that the case had been rightly settled in England. The man who had approved an act which declared that no foreign prince or potentate had any authority in England nevertheless continued to treat the Pope as though he retained some. All this presupposes that Henry meant what he said through his agents at Rome and at the French court. The indications are that he did, even though some calculation of diplomatic advantage also entered into his behaviour: Henry, in his caution, positively refused to see how far he had gone.

In fact it was too late to change course again. In July Clement had issued a sentence of excommunication held over till September; in August Henry replied with letters patent confirming the restraint of annates conditionally enacted the year before. The Pope's sentence was pronounced invalid because he had not gone through all the processes demanded by canon law, and from it Henry appealed to the General Council of the Church. This angered Francis I because it nullified his efforts to make Clement come to terms with Henry's supposed demands, but by late 1533 all these moves were formalistic only. The Act of Appeals and Cranmer's judgement had effectively cut England loose from Rome; the appeal to the General Council was entered only because none was sitting (any that might convene would assuredly give no favourable hearing); however much diplomacy required the employment of traditional devices and a pretence of doors still open, the fact was that the realm had retreated within its own borders. It remained to complete the organization of the unitary state, that body politic that Cromwell wanted.

Before that work, however, could proceed it became apparent that the great changes on foot were encountering increasing opposition in the country. In mid-1533 there began that stream of informations about seditious and disrespectful sayings which was to continue to fill Cromwell's postbag till his fall. People were calling Anne a whore, swearing that they would never take anyone for Queen but Catherine, and using highly-coloured language about King Harry himself—pox-ridden lecher and drunken buffoon. For the present, the law permitted little forceful action against such scurrility, nor was anything done; but the news constituted a danger signal, and the government looked for an opportunity to issue its own warning.

One group among the disaffected was certainly more dangerous than the rest as well as more vulnerable. Ever since the King had opened his campaign against his first marriage, he had been subjected to hostile propaganda from Elizabeth Barton, called the Nun or Holy Maid of Kent. Barton was a servant girl of sixteen, at Aldington in Kent, when in 1525 she went through an hysterical illness with trances from which she recovered thanks to visions of the Virgin and with a belief in newly gained prophetic powers. Archbishop Warham's enquiry thought her likely to be a true mystic. She entered a convent and quickly became famous as a sayer of sooth, a spiritual counsellor and moral tutor. From 1527 onwards her prophecies acquired a political tinge when, under the guidance of her instructor Edward Bocking (a monk of Christchurch, Canterbury), she turned her attention to the Divorce. For years she was active in the cause, exhorting Wolsey, Warham and even Henry to their faces, and sending stern messages to Rome. She greatly impressed all those notable persons, as well as Bishop Fisher; Thomas More treated her with respect but retained doubts about her inspiration and took care to avoid talking politics to her; the only person wisely to refuse all contact was Queen Catherine. The circle that formed around her exercised great influence in stirring up feelings against the King's proceedings, but until July 1533 she was left alone.

By then her protector Warham was dead, and Cranmer regarded her from the first as a dangerous fraud, though the actual moves against her were instigated by Henry himself, at last roused to furious resentment by her continued prophecies of an early death for him if he did not abandon the Divorce. In September 1533, the Nun and a number of adherents were arrested; during the interrogations, the bewildered young woman, an innocent victimized by superstition and intrigue, confessed herself no true visionary and pro-etess, though in truth she had been no fraud, only an hysterical girl exploited by the credulity of the many and the craft of the ambitious few. It was decided to destroy this opposition with every means of publicity and obloquy. In November, Henry staged a lavish enquiry before a body of notables; soon after, John Capon, abbot of Hyde, who by his complaisance earned the bishopric of Bangor, preached a violent sermon at Paul's Cross in which he accused the Nun of every crime from treason to fornication and covered her believers with equal contumely. But the decision to make an example of her ran into difficulties. On the King's instructions, Cromwell first contemplated a proper trial for treason, but because she had told her prophecies to the King's face the judges resolved that she could not be guilty of a conspiracy against his life. Reluctantly, therefore, the Crown proceeded by act of attainder without trial which condemned the Nun and five followers to death for treason. One died in prison; the other five suffered the horrible execution enjoined by the law in April 1534. Several persons, including Bishop Fisher, were attainted of misprison (complicity), for which offence they were condemned to perpetual imprisonment; Fisher was allowed to buy himself off for a fine of £300, some lesser victims soon regained their liberty, and only Catherine's chaplain Thomas Abel, notorious as one of her leading champions, remained in the Tower. At first the bill of attainder had included More, too, as a misprisioner, despite the fact that nothing could be alleged against him. With great reluctance, pressed by his Council, Henry in the end consented to having his name removed. Cromwell expressed his delight, but More rightly judged that delay did not mean the abandonment of persecution. The act, with a preamble that in effect incorporated Capon's sermon, was distributed in printed copies, to counteract the effect both of the Nun's earlier appeal and of her dreadful end.

This drastic action, which contrasts strikingly with earlier long-suffering as well as with the refusal to use terror against such known critics as Catherine's very vocal chaplains, indicates that more was involved than mere haphazard violence. The use of parliamentary attainder, warranted by precedent but very extreme and highly unsatisfactory, was forced on the government when the judges construed the treason law contrary to some fifteenth-century precedents. The experience confirmed Cromwell's determination to bring the law up to date which had been frustrated twice before by failure to get agreement on the drafting of the bill. It is clear that the decision at last to deal with the Nun derived primarily from the new policy and new resolution announced in the Act of Appeals, for the Nun's activities and the propaganda issued by her followers had seriously threatened that policy's success. Beyond these considerations, however, one notes an interesting change of attitude. Hitherto the Nun had enjoyed the protection bestowed by her holy reputation, but to the new archbishop and the new minister this signified only superstition and spiritual corruption. Elizabeth Barton was destroyed not only by the politics of the Divorce but also by the first stirrings of the Reformation.

Cromwell once more underlined the unreality of the remaining traces of hesitancy in December 1533 when he had the Council address itself to the question of fastening the new beliefs upon the country. An extensive campaign of propaganda by preaching was resolved on; the Act of Appeals was proclaimed throughout the realm; and the Council authorized the publication of an avowedly official propaganda tract, *The Articles devised by the whole consent of the King's most honourable Council*, which set out the reasons why the King's doings were just and must command universal approval and obedience. No one had the power to dispense from the law of God, and therefore Cranmer's judgement on the marriage (he being also 'authorized by act of Parliament') was correct. The tract rehearsed the old points about national autonomy, expounded the illegality of the excommunication pronounced at Rome, and explained the legal propriety of the King's appeal to a General Council. It drew attention to God's manifest approval—the early issue of the marriage (divine endorsement for bridal pregnancy?), the recent good harvest, the pacific policies of the European powers towards England (an imaginative distortion), and the absence of plague; and it finished with a violent personal denunciation of Clement, 'a man neither in life nor learning Christ's disciple'. So much for Giulio de' Medici, once cardinal-protector of England. For the first time the pope was called only bishop of Rome. Whatever Henry might say to Francis or the Roman diplomats, his Council made it plain that all dealings with the papacy were at an end.

Thus the next session of the Reformation Parliament (15 January to 30 March 1534) got down to following up the consequences of the constitutional revolution. Even now not all was plain sailing; it is wrong to think that the whole business needed no more than a simple act of will on Henry's part. The King allowed the settlement of his matrimonial affairs to be embodied in the Act of Succession which not only put Cranmer's judgement on record and declared the Boleyn marriage valid, but compelled allegiance to Queen Anne and her issue and made it treason to act to the contrary. Cromwell got some of the treason legislation he wanted, but he could not persuade the drafting committee to make mere speaking against the marriage treasonable: they insisted on an overt act expressed in writing or deed. It is doubtful whether the act would have caught the Nun or the Aragonese preachers. The Act for the Submission of the Clergy marked a double triumph for Cromwell, though he needed to rouse a demand for it in the Commons: the bill was not prepared beforehand but drafted in a joint committee of both Houses, after representations from the Speaker to the King. It incorporated the 1532 surrender of the Church's legislative independence in a statute, as Cromwell had meant to do on that earlier occasion, and it amended the Act of Appeals by putting the ultimate authority in spiritual suits in lay hands (commissions out of Chancery, later known as the High Court of Delegates), a provision which in 1533 opposition from the Church had forced Cromwell to delete. The parliamentary history of this act, so far as we can discern it, shows that there was some conflict between Commons and Lords; it also indicates that Henry, apparently surprised by the proposal, is unlikely to have had a hand in its planning.

What was in some ways the most interesting measure of the session also ran into difficulties which tell us something about the realities of this government. This was the act which abolished all remaining payments to Rome (especially the occasional tax known as Peter's Pence) and transferred the granting of all licences and dispensations to English authorities. It thus deprived the Pope not only of his remaining powers but also of his most profitable privilege, the gains being in the main conveyed to the Crown because licences and faculties for benefices and appointments valued at over £4 were to be issued by the Chancery, only lesser matters being reserved to the archbishops.[5] The bill was drafted by Cromwell who cast it in the form of a joint petition from both Houses and included in its impressive preamble a full assertion of the legislative autonomy of England and the legislative sovereignty vested in the King, Lords and Commons 'representing the whole state of your realm in this your most High Court of Parliament'. It was introduced first in the Commons; in the Lords it encountered doubts, mainly because its drastic provisions harmed those who held papal dispensations hitherto accounted valid. It was therefore considerably amended, the work being done by Lord Chancellor Audley, and thus passed. However, on the last day of the session the Lords added yet another amendment, read that day three times in both Houses, which postponed the effect of the act until confirmed by royal letters patent. Evidently Henry was once more hesitating; still governed by caution, he thought he might repeat the experiment of the conditional Act of Annates in the hope that the comprehensive threat to his purse would at last cause Clement to bless England's schismatic doings. The clause brings out the difference between Cromwell's single-mindedness and Henry's preference for procrastination; its late addition heavily reinforces the other hints in this session that matters went forward in Parliament of which the King knew little. While Cromwell's hand is manifest in all this legislation, Henry's part in it must now be much in doubt. On this occasion Cromwell was not frustrated for long: the King confirmed the act on 7 April.

[5]The main purpose of such licences touched plurality of benefices, but the dissolution of the monasteries (see chapter 10) brought much business to Canterbury and York through the faculties which freed monks from the life religious and allowed them to live as secular priests.

In the first half of April, too, Cromwell sealed his victory in the
King's counsels by formally succeeding Gardiner in the principal
secretaryship, an office he had been effectively exercising for some
five months while Gardiner was once again on embassy in France.
The secretaryship was to be Cromwell's particular instrument of
government; he continued to hold it, though its duties were heavy
and its rewards modest, even after he acquired other, greater places.
In turn, he created out of it the central ministerial position which
was to attach to it thereafter—the control and execution of both
domestic and foreign policy. His domestic policy now involved
making a reality out of the jurisdictional victory over the papal
Church, as well as initiating the long-demanded reforms. As for
foreign affairs, a new element linked to his arrival entered Henry's
thinking late in 1533.

For some fifty years, English policy had revolved around the
conflicts, staged in Italy and the Netherlands, between France and a
Hispanic-Habsburg alliance which culminated in the empire of
Charles V. Wolsey had used the interests of the papacy to gain
England an influential position in the diplomacy arising out of that
contest, but despite his attempted change of direction in 1526-8 he
had not altered the main conditions that governed English policy:
the old enmity with France sealed by the continued English presence
in Calais, and the cloth trade's dependence on Burgundian good
will. As the Divorce came to throw all earlier arrangements into
confusion, Henry at first attempted to attach himself to France as a
protection against Habsburg wrath, but the relationship remained
uneasy, and the progress of the break with Rome increasingly
alienated Francis I who suspected heretical influences in England.
At the same time the Reformation had changed things entirely in
central Europe; in the Protestant cities and princes it had introduced
new actors on the board who from 1530 onwards displayed a
willingness to oppose the Emperor which could be helpful to a king
engaged in a policy so provoking to Charles V. Throughout the
1530s the Protestant League of Schmalkalden formed a significant
new centre of power—but it was Protestant and therefore suspect to
Henry VIII. By the same token it was attractive to Cromwell, fatally
so, as the event proved. In 1533-4, however, there was good sense in
establishing contact with potential allies in opposing Habsburg
power, while the English cloth merchants might conceivably be able
to outflank imperial control of Antwerp by going directly to the
Baltic. English envoys began to open discussions with the League as
well as with Hamburg and Lübeck; there was talk of Denmark,
Poland and Hungary. The men involved were all members of
Cromwell's group—Christopher Mont (a German resident in Eng-

land) and Edward Foxe, Robert Barnes and Nicholas Heath, William Paget and Stephen Vaughan. One can discern the first faint traces of a grand design for a northern confederation —anti-papal at any rate, possibly Protestant. The most extraordinary episode came in August 1534 when Henry, misled by enthusiastic amateurs among his diplomats, formed an alliance with the revolutionary government that Jürgen Wullenwever had set up at Lübeck. In the end, this ill-considered attempt to gain a political and commercial footing in the Baltic profited neither side, and Henry abandoned all contacts even before Wullenwever's fall and death by the axe. Thus Cromwell's arrival in power added northern Europe to English preoccupations without for the moment achieving anything and without removing any of the traditional areas of concern; even Italian affairs continued to remain of interest, and diplomatic relations were clandestinely maintained with a pope whom, as bishop of Rome, the government took every opportunity to vilify and expel. This government rested on a powerful and revolutionary ideological base, but it knew better than to suppose that ideology should control diplomacy.

At home, however, there was neither need nor—in Cromwell's view if not Henry's—any justification for delaying the consummation of the new ideological policy. Politically, the most important outcome of the spring session of 1534 was the clause in the Succession Act which required the realm to take an oath to the lawfulness of the second marriage and to the succession vested in its issue. The act had not specified the form of the oath, but on the last day of the session (30 March) the necessary formula was put before both Houses and promptly sworn to individually by all the Lords and Commons. As soon as Parliament rose, commissions went out to take the oath across the country. They encountered very little opposition and not much reluctance even from people who before long were to resist the ultimate departure from Rome even to the death. A little pressure had to be used to get obedience from some religious houses, but very few people absolutely declined to comply. Unhappily these included Thomas More and John Fisher, called to swear at Lambeth on 17 April. More declared his willingness to agree that Parliament could settle the succession and offered to swear an oath explicitly to that effect; though he had always opposed the Divorce he was enough of a lawyer to accept the power of statute to declare an heir to the throne. But in the oath as tendered he rightly discerned an affirmation against the papal rule of the Church, and to this he could not consent. Both More and Fisher, with Dr Nicholas Wilson, once Henry's confessor, at once found themselves in the Tower which the first two were never to leave again. Henry intended to extort their compliance, not to finish them off, and with Wilson (who in 1537 surrendered and got his pardon) the plan worked; but with the other two, King and minister miscalculated badly. More, at least, knew from the first that the end had come: he could never give in against his conscience, and he knew his master well enough to understand that his refusal would be regarded as nothing better than an obstinate contempt for old friendship and kindness. Henry now began to hate both these great men, and More began to prepare for death, using the months in prison to cleanse his mind and soul of all except charity and faith. In this last phase of his life More not only recovered all the attractiveness of character which had distinguished him before his battle with Luther but acquired a new and saintly serenity.[6]

The oath of succession did not really announce the full extent of the revolution, but in case anyone doubted that More had read its meaning aright the government—with Cromwell determined and Henry now adding the fury of his displeasure—soon demonstrated what was really at issue. While all adult males were sworn to that oath, more positive measures were aimed at the clergy only, for the obvious reason that (as Henry had put it in 1532) they had hitherto been but half his subjects and should be made to affirm their now single allegiance by expressly disavowing the pope. In March and May 1534, the southern and northern Convocations had agreed that 'the bishop of Rome has not any greater jurisdiction than any other foreign bishop', which according to the Act of Appeals meant that he had none. All the secular clergy were required during the rest of the year to subscribe to personal declarations which extended this statement slightly by substituting 'power' for 'jurisdiction'. But the government wanted more from that part of the clergy that they regarded with special mistrust— the regular orders and institutional clergy, seen as cohesive centres of potential resistance in a way that individual parish priests could never be. These were made to take a comprehensive oath to accept the Succession Act, to renounce the bishop of Rome never again to be called pope and declared to be without authority in England, to observe the canon law only in so far as it did not contradict the laws of Scripture and of God and of the realm, and to pray for the King as supreme head and for Anne and her issue. In short, they had to profess full adherence to the royal supremacy in the Church and obedience to Henry second only to Christ, well before the King's position was defined in statute or officially part of his title.

---

[6] More's 'Tower works', especially his *Dialogue of Comfort* and the remarkable letters he wrote to his daughter Margaret, testify to the regeneration worked by the end of all political involvements.

With few exceptions, all the clergy did as they were told; after the battering of three years no will to resist survived among the bishops and the overwhelming mass of the Church, some of whom in any case (it should be remembered) eagerly welcomed the new order. However, some refused, and such opposition came from expected quarters. The binding of the nation to the King's headship of the Church offered an opportunity both to proceed drastically against known opposition and to pay off old scores. From the first days of the anticlerical campaign it had become very clear that the really determined opponents to Henry's purposes were to be found among the members of the most austere religious houses in the realm—men who, unlike their laxer brethren, commanded reverence among the laity. The Observant Franciscans, and more particularly their two houses at Richmond and Greenwich, had supplied Catherine's leading champions, such as William Peto, Richard Risby, John Forest and William Elstow who had fearlessly preached against the Divorce so long as such frank speaking was still possible at all. Cromwell was particularly anxious to get the oath of succession from these enemies of the Boleyn marriage, but he failed; in mid-1534, therefore, their seven houses were ended by transferring those inmates who had not fled abroad to other establishments, mostly (with malice intended) to those of Conventual Franciscans, inveterate enemies to their Observant brethren. Across the river, at Syon, lay the well respected house of Bridgettine nuns and brothers, a community equally distinguished for their learning and their aristocratic connections; here, though all the efforts made for a year to get the oath accepted proved fruitless, nothing dramatic happened, partly no doubt because the inmates of Syon were so well friended in high places (and the government in general rarely persecuted women), but partly also because they commanded genuine regard even from Cromwell, enemy to all enclosed orders. Instead he relied on relatively gentle pressure over time, which achieved nothing before the end came to all monastic institutions. The most serious problem was posed by the Carthusians, most uncorrupted and most ascetic of all monks, who with some justice took the line that they had fully left the world and in return expected the world to leave them alone. In a way they proved to be less prepared for resistance than the Observants and the Bridgettines who had taken an active interest in the affairs of the realm; despite their absolute adherence to the papal obedience, even the London Charterhouse, the most determined of them all, after several refusals would seem to have accepted something like the full profession demanded of religious houses. Their prior, John Houghton, briefly incarcerated in the Tower, led the way in apparent bewilderment

ratify, by way of declaration, the transformation of the *Anglicana Ecclesia* from the English part of the papal Church into the national Church of England, its second part prevented the pleading of customary immunities or exemptions against all exercises of the royal supremacy.

These laws attended to business already settled, pretty much after the event. Three others more positively added to the powers of the crown. The Treason Act, notorious for its severity, in effect supplied the penal provisions absent from the Act of Supremacy. It is quite a short measure, markedly shorter than the rather confused and confusing attempts made during 1531 and 1532 to reform this basic safeguard of the state. It was made treason to practise or plot any physical harm to the King, the Queen, or the heir apparent, or to call the King 'heretic, schismatic, tyrant, infidel, or usurper of the crown'; and the offence could now be committed in mere words as well as in writing or by deed. Aiders and abettors were to be as guilty as the actual traitors, and sanctuary was abolished for the crime. The act was savage, and intended to be so, but it did not constitute a departure in principle from earlier law enforcement. Treason by words alone had on occasion been created by the courts out of the 1352 statute which did not allow for it, and it was certainly better to have the offence defined in law rather than left to be haphazardly construed by this or that judge. The repeal in 1549 of the 1534 act abolished treason by words for the future (though at law it had existed before it was embodied in statute), a conclusion which marks another victory for parliamentary enactment in the sixteenth century. Moreover, the Henrician act explicitly laid down that treason could be proved only by the processes of the common law, thus putting an end to some arbitrary procedures which in the previous two hundred years had quite often been used to convict traitors; and this limitation stood thereafter. The bill encountered opposition in the Commons, though the contemporary allegation that it was this opposition which inserted the limitation that speaking against the supremacy must be 'malicious' before it could be treason is contradicted by the evidence of preparatory drafting which shows the word there from the first. It would seem that serious apprehensions delayed the passage of the bill without in any way altering what Cromwell proposed.[8]

Lastly, two acts took care of the financial difficulties of the crown. One assigned to the King a regular revenue from the Church consisting of the first-fruits (equal to one year's income) of every newly beneficed dignitary and an annual tenth (a ten per cent income tax) levied on every spiritual benefice. This, then, was the

[8] For the Treason Act see my *Policy and Police*, chapter 6.

end of all those protestations that the poor clergy of England were over-heavily taxed by the pope. The King now took approximately £40,000 a year from his spiritual subjects, or about ten times what had previously gone to Rome. At the same time, Cromwell also pushed through a subsidy act the two instalments of which, levied in 1535 and 1536, yielded about £45,000, or something like three fifths of the first instalment alone of Wolsey's last parliamentary tax. The act was less carefully drawn, it affected fewer people, and its administration was less efficient than had been the case with any of the cardinal's subsidies. These facts indicate something about Cromwell's mind. Evidently anxious not to offend opinion in Parliament, at a time when he needed ready support there for the revolutionary measures touching the supremacy, he appears to have been less interested in getting the most by way of cash than in getting a supply bill through at all. What then did he want to prove? The answer emerges from a study of both these financial bills together: the imposition of first-fruits and tenths, and the granting of a subsidy, were both justified on the grounds that the King's government, so immensely beneficial to the realm but also so inordinately expensive to the King himself, merited free and generous support from the nation's pockets. The 1534 Subsidy Act abandoned the principle that extraordinary taxation could be justified only by war and danger of war: when the preamble began by recalling the twenty-five years of wise, virtuous and peaceful rule that the realm had enjoyed since the King's accession, it not only told a lie but announced that peace-time taxation had arrived. As subsequent events were to show, it had come to stay.[9] The enactment of yet another general pardon, barely five years after the last one, looks suspiciously like a *quid pro quo*; but even though Cromwell did not raise much money or raise it easily—while the Church was paying for government he hardly needed to—he had squeezed through what to some may seem his most revolutionary achievement of all.

Parliament managed to rise before Christmas, on 18 December; four weeks later, on 15 January 1535, Henry announced his new style, adding the words 'and on earth supreme head of the Church of England' to his other titles. Though he sat in his Privy Chamber to do so, he spoke in the presence of the leading officers of state: this was a state matter extending well beyond his private or personal capacity. About the same time he delegated the whole authority vested in him by God's grant of the supreme headship to Thomas Cromwell as his vicegerent (deputy) in spirituals. The Church was now fully com-

---

[9] See my 'Taxation for War and Peace in early Tudor England', in *War and Economic Development*, edited by J. M. Winter (1975), pp. 33 ff.

mitted to this clothworker's son, as lay a person and as devoid of spiritual aura as could be found in England. But the victory of the laity, so symbolized, should not be equated with irreligion or heathenism or even mere heresy; representative of a powerful current in the life and faith of the English laity, Cromwell had his spiritual and religious intentions for the newly ordered Church of England.

First, however, he faced the task of translating statements into reality and of employing the weapons which Parliament had created. From 1 February 1535, the day on which the Treason Act came into effect, he had at his disposal all the power he needed to extinguish opposition.[10] He used that power, but with far more care and even consideration than he used to be given credit for, and often enough he stood as a bulwark between the King's wrath and its object.[11] Not that he wished to protect traitors, but he meant to make sure that only those truly guilty should suffer. He worked out a thorough system of supervision, but one that depended entirely on the cooperation—obtained by natural obedience and reinforced by constant reminders—of the hierarchy of countryside and towns. He organized the system in the first of the flood of circular letters that thereafter issued from his office over either the King's signature or his own.

On 16 April 1535, instructions went forth to all persons spiritual and temporal who held authority, ordering the arrest of anyone suspected of continued support for the papacy. All such were to be held in ward while the information, with witnesses' depositions, was to be sent to the Council or to the secretary in person. In either case it was Cromwell who then investigated each case, ordered the release of suspects found to be innocent or accused by malice, and remitted the supposedly guilty to trial by jury in the locality. To make sure that everything was reported, he repeatedly reminded these voluntary agents of police of their duty and kept the penalties for misprisoners (those who failed to divulge knowledge of treason) before everybody's eyes. There was nothing reluctant about his enforcing activities, and where he suspected guilt he was ruthless; but neither would he listen to unfounded accusations or by-pass the processes of the law. In the five years during which he presided over the administration of the treason law, a minimum of 400 cases came to his knowledge; of these something like sixty-five ended in the

[10] Not quite: as Thomas More's case was to show, refusing to speak about the supremacy constituted no offence under the Treason Act, even when the hostile intent was perfectly plain. This loophole was closed by the Act Extinguishing the Authority of the Bishop of Rome (1536), mainly a measure summarizing the work of three years, which made it treason to refuse to answer questions touching the supremacy.

[11] My *Policy and Police*, especially chapters 7 and 8.

horrible execution of the accused. Grand juries refused to indict about sixteen, and some fourteen were acquitted by trial juries. But of the cases investigated close to 200 were abandoned as doubtful or certainly false. An unknown number of people, possibly quite large, suffered various exemplary punishments (mostly the pillory) for seditious behaviour that fell short of treason, but the crucial question whether it required a reign of terror to fix the new order upon the country depends on the treason cases. The evidence is clear: there was plenty of articulate disaffection, dangerous to the government's policy in the absence of a regular police force and in view of the ease with which in Tudor England discontent could turn to violence. Quite enough people got into trouble, some into very serious trouble. Life in Cromwell's England, during the revolution, was uncomfortable and for many dangerous, though many others welcomed what went on and the great majority accepted without thought of pleasure or rejection. But throughout, Cromwell, serving a monarch who increasingly suspected everybody and abominated what he called disobedience, saw to it that the truth should be sought out and the law rule all.

Unfortunately for the reputation of King and minister, as well as for the moral stature of the age, some of the victims were exceptional men whose deaths, however justified in law, burdened the memory of the revolution with blood that should not have been shed. This is not only the opinion of a later day or of popish partisans; it was, for instance, shared by Thomas Starkey who firmly regretted the resort to violence and held that it stained the great achievements indelibly. He was right, but it is also true that the government could not take the risk of sparing people whose example they rightly thought would powerfully support the disaffection which they had reason to fear needed only a lead to become dangerous. Cromwell and Henry knew all about Eustace Chapuys's calls for armed intervention and his promise of a rising against the King as soon as Charles V's forces appeared over the horizon. Wise compassion might have counselled leniency, but—Henry's personal savagery apart—leniency was in the circumstances bound to look like culpable negligence.

The earliest notable victims of the revolution were the monks of the Charterhouse. Resistance had stiffened there since the inadvertent surrender of May 1534, and in April 1535 the government struck by arresting three priors—John Houghton of the London house, Augustine Webster of Axholme, and Robert Laurence of Beauvale. All three were tried for an explicit denial of the supremacy, and there is no doubt that they had so denied it. They refused a pardon (more than was usually offered to convicted traitors) at the foot of the gallows and died with exceptional fortitude, seeking and finding martyrdom. With them died Richard Reynolds, the outstanding father of Syon, and another priest, also for proven treasons. Three more Carthusians were tried and presumably executed in June, apparently with less publicity since on the first occasion this had manifestly backfired; the case remains obscure. These actions cowed all the houses except that of London which continued to withhold the full obedience Henry wanted. Constant pressure by the agents that Cromwell set over them brought the majority to give way in 1537, but the King then refused to accept so belated a surrender as satisfactory and determined to destroy the house. In vain Cromwell risked serious displeasure by trying to save at least the laggard conformists from the royal wrath. Those that had sworn to the supremacy were in May 1537 forced to surrender the house to the King; the others, who continued to stand out, were taken to Newgate and left to starve to death. Whether or not the story, later told, of misery and torture is true (and though some of the most familiar detail is suspect one should credit the main outline), the treatment of the London Carthusians remains the biggest blot on the record of Henry and Cromwell, if only because these monks, so well secluded from the world, were really most unlikely to influence anyone else by their stand. It is quite possible that only the persecution gave them the means of strengthening the resolve of others.

The same cannot be said of Henry's most illustrious victims, John Fisher and Thomas More. They had been imprisoned in hopes of breaking them. Even the availability of the Treason Act did not at first affect the attempt to gain their enforced support, and Cromwell to the last hoped to see More save himself by surrender, partly at least because he clearly liked and respected the man. He had far less sympathy for Fisher who had for some years been so close to the machinations of the imperial ambassador that in his case a charge of treason included much truth. Even if they could not be made to conform, it might seem that in time they would be forgotten, dying obscurely in prison, though no attempt was made to hasten that event by serious ill-treatment. However, it became apparent that their example worked even from the Tower: Houghton's and Reynolds's resolution drew sustenance from the stand taken by More and Fisher, and Henry understood this. In early May 1535, therefore, the effort to break them was resumed. At first Cromwell clearly hoped for surrender and Henry did not mean to go to extremes. However, late that month the King learned that the new pope, Paul III, had made Fisher a cardinal, and this empty gesture drove him into one of the characteristic rages which at intervals drowned his instinct for caution. Thereafter things took their tragic course. The subsequent interrogations were meant to procure evidence usable in a trial, not a difficult thing to do with Fisher who explicitly and repeatedly denied that the King was supreme head and thereby fell into the toils of the Treason Act. More, on the other hand, defeated the act by carefully refusing to answer any question touching the supremacy; his silence, which could not disguise his real opinion, was no treason in the law.

Fisher's trial took place on 17 June, and on the 22nd the old man, a walking skeleton, painfully mounted the scaffold. More was put up for trial on 1 July. He fought to the last in a brilliant display of legal skill, but the jury condemned him on the testimony of Richard Rich, the solicitor general, who claimed that in the course of a conversation More had expressly denied the supremacy. While Rich has always been held to have simply perjured himself by inventing a non-existent remark, the evidence must leave some doubt whether More had not on that occasion failed to guard his tongue as carefully as usual.[12] Rather it looks as though the prosecution managed to exploit a minor indiscretion. After the verdict, delivering the customary speech in arrest of judgement, More left no doubt about his beliefs. At the last he openly declared himself for the universal Church and papal rule, setting the consent of Christendom against the authority of an act of Parliament assented to by one realm only. He died on 6 July, gallant, serene and cheerful to the end.

The news of these executions resounded through Europe and produced a very real explosion of horror. Even Charles V, not given to revealing his mind, spoke to the English ambassador without reserve and with true feeling. Cromwell attempted to present the case in such favourable light as could be found, explaining in letters to France and Rome the long-standing active opposition of both men (contrary to their allegiance), the King's patience, their alleged (and partially true) subversive activities, and their 'crime' of deep ingratitude to a loving master. It did no good: in their deaths Fisher and More won the one victory over Henry VIII which could be won, and that victory has proved enduring. Yet the issue is less straightforward than natural sympathy and revulsion would make it. The English schism and the creation of the lay-dominated Church-state of England were a revolution, at least in the eyes of Thomas More, whatever modern historians may say about antecedents and natural lines of development. And he set himself publicly against it: no matter how carefully he might watch his words and refuse to speak his mind, he had fought actively against it in the earlier stages, and his eminence kept him in the centre of the vortex despite his genuine resolve to stay out of it. Though opinion abroad

[12]*Policy and Police*, pp. 410 ff.

and some men at home united in condemning his death, and though the verdict of centuries has endorsed that condemnation, there were many in the England of his day who agreed with Edward Hall that they could not tell whether he was 'a foolish wise-man or a wise foolish-man' whose jests on the scaffold called his serious purpose in doubt. As chancellor and persecutor of heretics, More had himself accepted the need to kill people in the interests of a higher cause. When Cromwell, during an interrogation, reminded him that he had approved the use of force to compel people to accept the papal Church and asked why in that case the King could not compel people to abide by the law made in Parliament, More could only reply that the cases differed because the first had the support of the whole body of Christendom while the second applied to one realm only. It was not a good answer: as Cromwell was quick to point out, since the result was death in either case, where was the difference? He might have added that the consent of Christendom to the pope's rule was much less unanimous than More pretended. Two profound principles clashed here in inevitable conflict, and so long as both sides accepted death by judicial execution as the proper resolution of such conflicts there was no escaping the consequences.

The destruction of the opposition formed only one side of Cromwell's endeavour to settle the new order in England; he devoted more energy still to positively proclaiming and erecting it. The machinery of propaganda went swiftly into action. In 1534, Edward Foxe published the gist of the arguments collected as long ago as 1530 to demonstrate, in his *De vera differentia regiae potestatis et ecclesiasticae*, that the principles of the royal supremacy rested upon sound scriptural, patristic and historical grounds. At the same time a man of far more conservative leanings, Richard Sampson (dean of the Chapel) in his *Oratio quae docet Anglos regiae dignitati ut obedirent* defended the supremacy on the simple grounds that the King's commands must be obeyed. These Latin books were addressed to the learned and used as a reservoir of arguments by preachers; the *Little Treatise against the muttering of papists in corners* (1534), the product of a suggestion of Cromwell's, elegantly and wittily dealt with the current doubts and contradictions passing in the country. It also apparently introduced the word 'papist' into the public vocabulary where it was to have a long career of evocative vituperation. In 1534 and 1535, William Marshall's translation of Valla's and Marsiglio's anti-papal classics added further ammunition. The most considerable treatise came from Stephen Gardiner whose *De vera obedientia* (1535), written in an effort to regain the favour lost in 1532, comprehensively expounded the 'high' view of the supremacy. Gardiner elaborated the classic concept, first adumbrated in the Act of Appeals, of the unitary body politic, simultaneously Church and commonwealth, comprehending the whole body of Englishmen and ruled over by a single person—head of the Church and King of the commonwealth—to whom obedience was enjoined by God. The book was a real success, pirate reprints appearing swiftly in Strassburg and Hamburg, though to Gardiner's regret it failed to persuade the King of France to follow Henry's example.

This publishing activity apart, Cromwell concentrated on getting the right things said from the pulpits. Circular after circular ordered the preaching of the revolution (described as an overdue restoration to an earlier better state), the proclamation of the King's title, prayers for Henry and Anne and their children, constant attacks on the bishop of Rome. Cromwell took care to prepare standard sermons for use by priests either not capable of writing their own or not trusted to say the right things if they were. In June 1535, successive letters created an interlocking structure of supervision and control: bishops were given precise marching orders for their own conduct and for the behaviour of their clergy, sheriffs and justices of the peace received instructions to keep an eye on bishops and clergy alike, justices of assize went out armed with letters that made them watchdogs over everybody else. Perhaps the most interesting particular order was that which commanded the physical erasure of the pope's name from all service books: attempts to evade it by pasting pieces of paper over the title were severely punished. This decree and its enforcement against all who sought to hedge their bets proves beyond doubt that so far as this government was concerned there could never be any going back. The break with Rome was meant to be total and final. Now the machinery of enforcement existed, employing the established means of social control but giving them a new and newly organized effectiveness; there remained the task of applying it and of building the reformed Church.

Thus in the years 1533-4, the long-standing claims to national self-sufficiency and royal autonomy were rapidly turned into a coherent constitutional structure, the royal supremacy over the Church of England, that Church being understood as the English nation in its relation to God, salvation and a moral life on earth. The official doctrine was simplicity itself: by God's will and appointment, King Henry held office as both king and supreme head, and from him there flowed all authority spiritual and temporal. Parliament did not share in the creation of the ecclesiastical supremacy which all the relevant statutes took for granted as the point of departure for the administrative, political and penal consequences which they enacted. Obviously, Christ's vicar on earth (so far as his dominions extended) could owe his place to no one but God and was responsible to God alone for the exercise of the powers which it conferred. The theory of the royal supremacy as enunciated in the statutes, and echoed in such treatises as Gardiner's *De vera obedientia*, was strictly monarchical, as had been the theory of the pope's rule which the King had simply acquired in its entirety. Of course, like the pope the King was subject to the law divine and—for some people at least, for agreement on this point did not exist—to the General Council of the Church, but these reservations did not trench upon the working absolutism of the dignity. Limited as king by his duty to observe the laws and customs of the realm, and by the need to seek parliamentary consent to taxation and legislation, Henry as supreme head held a personal and unlimited authority over the Church as an institution and over the spiritual concerns of the nation.

However, from the first there were cracks in this monolithic structure; while the King himself and at least some of the bishops subscribed to the unlimited divine-right theory of the supremacy, it looks as though not everyone shared that view. In the first place, all the detailed working out of the new situation was managed by acts of Parliament. To some extent, doing so brought political advantages: the use of statute involved the nation in the King's doings and gave the comfortable air of customary authority to his claims. This political motive is very apparent in such statutes as the Dispensations and Annates Acts which pretended to be petitions to the King, graciously assented to by him. In reality, however, Henry could not have proceeded without Parliament if he meant to make his reform enforceable in the law. While (according to him) it was a sin against God to deny his supremacy in the Church, this availed nothing in practice because no temporal punishment could be inflicted on opponents who by definition could not think themselves threatened with God's displeasure for denying what they believed to be heretical and schismatical. Only Parliament could turn the sin into a crime, punishable in the courts of the realm. The penal clauses of the Reformation statutes could never have come into existence without parliamentary action; Henry and Cromwell did not choose to resort to that institution but had no option. By the same token, the creation of parliamentary penalties to give enforceable reality to the supremacy meant that the King's power, however personal to him, was ultimately active by authority of Parliament; more important still, any change in the settlement, in whatever direction, would again require the use of Parliament so that the order first sanctioned by that body might be amended. From the beginning, the supremacy was absolute in its origin and exercise only for so long as it remained static.

That this vital fact was recognized at the time, despite all the byzantine adulation poured over Henry and all the uncompromisingly autocratic attitudes with which he regarded 'his' Church, is plain enough. In the nation at large, the jurisdictional revolution was accepted less because of God's alleged will than because it was explicitly laid down in acts of Parliament. Perhaps not everybody would have been as high-flown as the man who thought any act of Parliament 'made in the realm for the common wealth' (as for instance, he said, the Act of Supremacy) superior to the edicts of any assembly in Christendom, adding that when Parliament made such acts it worked as much under the tutelage of the Holy Ghost as any General Council of the Church. But such tenets are implicit both in the constant references in government propaganda to parliamentary statutes as the witness of the truth, and in the reaction of people across the country who obeyed because the acts told them to do so. The point was perfectly familiar to Henry's ministers. In the reign of Edward VI Gardiner recalled how Audley had spoken to him in 1543 about the untouchable authority of statute, never broken 'till the same had been by like authority of Parliament repealed'; on another occasion the chancellor warned the bishop that the Act of Supremacy specifically limited 'the King's doings ... to spiritual jurisdiction', so that the statutes subordinating the law spiritual to the common law and acts of Parliament (he meant the old praemunire statutes) remained binding. Thus Audley overrode Gardiner's doubts whether a bishop, holding authority from the Crown, could fall into a praemunire, adding that otherwise 'you bishops would enter in with the King and by means of his supremacy order the laity as you listed. But we will provide, quoth he, that the praemunire shall ever hang over your heads, and so we laymen shall be sure to enjoy our inheritance by the common law and acts of Parliament.'

If that was Audley's view of the matter, we can be sure that the man under whom he operated and whose acts he helped draft thought likewise. Cromwell's whole practice indicates not only a general belief in the force and sovereignty of statute, but a particular concern to use Parliament in the making of the royal supremacy even on occasions where the King, by his papal power, could have acted alone.[13] As against the high episcopal view which transferred upon the King the whole power symbolized by the tiara, we must therefore put the common lawyers' point of view which from the first treated the headship as another facet of kingship, subject to and

[13]The various Acts of Annates, for instance, did nothing that absolutely had to be done by statute: if the King was supreme head of the Church he could by himself decree the use of its wealth and the appointment of the hierarchy.

controlled by the same limitations as applied to secular rule. And this was not only the interpretation which, thanks to the vicissitudes of the mid-century, came to be the true constitutional position in the end, but it also looked the more realistic assessment from the first. Henry might claim to be a lay bishop inheriting the position occupied by Constantine the Great, a claim which effectively spiritualized kingship; in reality he and his subjects behaved as though authority in the Church had fallen to a layman. Nothing demonstrates this more clearly than Cromwell's vicegerency which put him above all spiritual dignitaries: in Parliament and Convocation he sat above the archbishops. High-sounding phrases notwithstanding, the Henrician Reformation signalled the triumph of the laity in the realm of religion. The Church declined from being the spiritual estate of the realm into a specialized profession which, under lay rule, ministered to the realm's spiritual needs; and Cromwell and Cranmer from the first judged more correctly than the King when they inferred from this the desirability of a religious Reformation of the continental sort which would remove the special intercessory functions of the clergy. By making himself supreme head, King Henry, that enemy of Luther, testified strikingly to a belief in the priesthood of all believers.

The Henrician Reformation thus determined the form which authority should take in the new polity. Sovereignty—the ultimate power to make laws which only that same power can unmake —rested exclusively, as Audley said, with the King-in-Parliament. Though centuries of experience and practice stood behind that consummation, only the lay absorption of the Church in the 1530s could actually bring it about. Only after the doubts of lords, knights and burgesses whether Parliament could legislate for the Church had been settled by the demonstration that it could was statute truly omnicompetent and in manner omnipotent. The Reformation Parliament, with its long life and extraordinary labours, witnessed much institutional and procedural development that still remains to be fully understood. It also settled the conventional view of the English constitution so clearly expounded in Thomas Smith's *De Republica Anglorum* (1565) and so hard to find even obscurely stated before the 1530s. Of course, in this mixed sovereign body the King at this time held an ascendant position—was its 'head', as Henry said in 1542, to the 'members' of Lords and Commons—but that detracted nothing from the fundamental constitutional truth. Nor will it do to suppose that the King's ascendancy in any way came close to being a dictatorship—that the two Houses simply did as they were told or acted as mere mouthpieces of the royal will. Even in the making of the Reformation

9 Consolidation and Commonwealth

I

The subjection of the Church formed the most striking but not the sole manifestation of a general policy designed to create the unitary realm of England, under the legislative sovereignty of the King in Parliament and the executive sovereignty of the King assisted by his Council. The first years of Cromwell's administration witnessed an energetic resumption of purposes which over the centuries had at intervals attracted the minds of the Kings of England. By 1536 the feudal suzerainty of the Crown had finally vanished, to be replaced by a universal political rule (even though many of the old forms remained embedded in the new arrangements) and lines had been laid down for settling the structure of all the King's dominions.

In England itself the policy required only the elimination of various forms of particularity which had established themselves, often by royal grant, in the later middle ages. The method employed looked to uniformity of law enforcement. Thus the protection to lawbreakers offered by the existence of exempt sanctuaries was regularly attacked, usually in acts which prohibited it for stated offences but occasionally also by demonstrating that the common law could overrule its claims, though it was not until 1540 that Cromwell obtained the general act abolishing the whole system which he had planned to get in 1536. Sanctuaries (that is, privileged places of permanent refuge) had long been attacked by two bodies whose traditions Cromwell respected—the city of London and the judges of the common law; his intervention typically substituted a general principle of revolutionary import for a piecemeal niggling away at problems which had left their foundations intact.[1] The assimilation of diverse jurisdictions, again something that on suitable occasions had been attempted here and there, was fully accomplished by Cromwell in an act of 1536 which deplored the existence

---

[1]See Isobel Thornley, 'The Destruction of Sanctuary', *Tudor Studies ... presented to A. F. Pollard* (1924), pp. 161 ff.; my *Reform and Renewal*, pp. 135 ff.

of diversities created by royal grants and abolished them at a stroke.[2] From 1 July 1536 only the King could issue pardons and appoint justice of eyre, assize, the peace or gaol delivery. All writs everywhere, even in counties palatine and established liberties, were thenceforth to run in the King's name, and the profits obtainable from enforcing their observance were to come to the Crown. The statutes governing the behaviour of justices and sheriffs were extended to stewards and bailiffs of liberties who were also subordinated to Quarter Sessions. A few exceptions saved mainly the privileges of chartered boroughs, but in general the act rendered the structure of local government uniform for the whole realm, and exclusively royal. By way of a bonus the King also took the opportunity to extend his claims to purveyance and the jurisdiction of the Household Court of the Verge into any liberties that could before this have claimed exemption. The act, with its short preamble and concise clauses, was one of the soberest of the time, a cool cleaning-up operation which terminated centuries of shared authority.

One other activity of the Crown can excite a suspicion that its authority was being extended in devious ways. From 1532 onwards, Cromwell, with the help of the King's legal counsel, was very busy over a massive reorganization of crown lands, and it has been supposed that Henry VIII used these operations for political purposes. On the whole this seems improbable. Thus, for instance, the exchanges arranged in 1532 rationalized estate management when they used the lands taken over from Wolsey's dissolution of religious houses to create the honour of Hunsdon in Hertfordshire. The even more sizable exchanges and purchases of 1536 were either clearly designed to consolidate and improve crown properties by getting rid of scattered pieces, or amounted to a straightforward investment of liquid resources.[3] Similarly the transactions which transferred some of the best manors of the archbishopric of Canterbury to Henry's hands, in exchange mostly for spiritual revenues acquired at the Dissolution, had behind them no motive more distinguished than Henry's greed for places he liked and his passion for developing his country palaces.[4] And even in the north, where the sixth (and childless) earl of Northumberland made the King his heir, so that in 1537 the whole Percy inheritance came to the Crown, political motives seem to have been secondary.[5] All these business transactions

---

[2] 27 Henry VIII c. 24.

[3] 23 Henry VIII cc. 21–7, 30; 27 Henry VIII cc. 29, 31, 33, 50, 52, 53, 61; 28 Henry VIII cc. 19, 21, 29, 30, 32, 33, 35, 42, 49.

[4] F. R. H. Du Boulay, *The Lordship of Canterbury* (1966), pp. 319 ff.

[5] J. M. W. Bean, *The Estates of the Percy Family, 1416–1537* (1958), pp. 151 ff.

belonged to the private concerns of the King as property owner, landlord and palace builder; they played no part in the subjugation of separatist ambitions and were now free of those political and feudal overtones which had still adhered to the handling of the crown estate as recently as the reign of Henry VII.

The outliers posed more complex problems, some of which came urgently to the fore in the 1530s and combined with Cromwell's predilection for fundamental reorganization to produce an outburst of centralizing activity. Wales in particular called for attention.[6] By 1530, the attempt to control the unruly marches and principality by traditional dynastic means—with the officers of the principality acting in the name of a royal prince of Wales, and a feudal council for the marches formally attached to a royal offspring—had clearly broken down. Under the weak guidance of Bishop Vesey, the marches' council failed to bring peace and order even to the English border shires, much troubled by the overspill of the larceny and killing that went on zestfully in the power games played by the Welsh gentry; and it is possible that the obscure treason of a trusted crown servant, Sir Rees ap Griffiths, executed in December 1531, proved the last straw.[7] By 1533 Cromwell had resolved to put that house in order, for which purpose he secured in the following year the appointment of his friend Rowland Lee as bishop of Coventry and president in the marches, with authority over law enforcement also in Cheshire and Wales proper. Lee was a rough and ruthless man, devoid of all graces and (as he himself admitted) unaccustomed to preaching, a curious throwback to the warrior bishops of an earlier age joined to the solid administrator type that served the Tudor Crown. Equipped by several statutes of 1534 with powers to seek out crimes and punish them away from the lawless regions where they were committed, he travelled up and down his bailiwick, hanging thieves, hunting murderers, and forcing juries to give verdicts according to the truth and against favour. Nothing can make Lee an attractive character, and his harshness was long remembered; but it remains true that he stood for justice and for resistance to the arrogance of petty tyrants.

However, the imposition of law and order was for Cromwell only a step towards the real solution which emerged in the act of 1536 commonly known as the Act of Union. Claiming to extend the

---

[6] Earlier studies of Henrician Wales have now been superseded by the work of P. R. Roberts (see bibliography).

[7] He was allegedly charged with having concealed treasonable attempts to provoke an attack from Scotland to avenge wrongs done to himself. Rees had been a trusted man in Wolsey's day and was married to a half-sister of the duke of Norfolk. The obscurity of his disaster may hide political angles involving the Boleyns and the rise of Cromwell; rumour blamed his death on Anne's enmity, but then rumour was inclined to blame her for everything.

provisions of Edward I's settlement of the principality in 1284, it in fact demolished that arrangement by wiping out the distinction between principality and marches, by organizing all Wales in the English manner in shires and commissions of the peace, and by extending the English common law to all the dominion at the expense of local (often anciently Welsh) custom. It further assimilated Wales by giving it parliamentary representation (in 1542 also extended to Cheshire); from 1539 perhaps and certainly from 1542, knights for the Welsh shires and burgesses for the Welsh boroughs sat at Westminster to testify to their country's integration into the single 'body of the whole realm'. Cautious and traditional phrases notwithstanding, the measure did not so much subject Wales to England as profess to end all differences between the two.

Lee was furious. In the best tradition of colonial administrators he protested that Wales was not ripe for self-government, and he feared that the act would put the subverters of the commonweal in charge of the administration of justice. It was indeed the case that the proposals which Cromwell adopted originated with leading personalities in Wales itself. Lee's opposition lost him influence, and his worst fears were never realized; but he was right in prophesying that the act would not by itself provide a settlement. In fact the labours of really establishing the new order for Wales extended down to 1543, and they were bedevilled by divided counsels at the top. Cromwell had recognized the difficulties by including a clause in the act which enabled the King to suspend it or bring it into effect by proclamation; and the work was delayed by strong cross-currents of influence and ambition. The act had turned the marches of east and south Wales into new shires, but it needed commissions of enquiry to establish precise boundaries, to set up hundreds within them, and to sort out the claims of marchers lords now reduced to merely manorial lordship of the familiar English type. The judicial organization, too, needed working out. In its very next session after the passage of the act, Parliament suspended the shiring, and in February 1537 a proclamation put other aspects into cold storage. However, the work went forward. In Wales itself, the transformation was widely welcomed at all levels of society: the 'union' was seen as a desirable enfranchisement and an entry into the greater world opened up by those godly monarchs of Welsh descent, though the full impact of the Tudor myth upon Welsh national self-consciousness had to wait until the reign of Elizabeth.

By 1541, the reorganization was achieved; Quarter Sessions were meeting; and even the special arrangement of four courts of Great Sessions was in being—those circuit courts on top of the shire commissions which alone preserved a separate form of administration for Wales. The massive act of 1543, drafted in response to representations from Wales itself, codified a system that had come gradually into being in the preceding six years. It also gave its first statutory authority to the council in the marches, preserved to provide supervision and equity jurisdiction, and now no longer treated as a feudal baronial body dependent upon a prince of Wales but as a bureaucratic court under a formally appointed chairman. The problem that was not fully settled in this reign touched the degree to which Wales retained a form of separate and distinguishable existence. Was it still a principality, now extended to include the marcher lordships, or was it really just another set of shires? So far as can be discerned, Cromwell intended it to become the second; when the union was first promoted, the King had no son, and even when Edward was born he was never formally endowed with the principality of Wales, as his father and uncle had been. On the other hand, Henry clearly hesitated to abandon the inherited notion that treated Wales as a permanent dynastic patrimony; it is possible that if he had lived longer and had had time to spare for Wales in the 1540s he might, with Cromwell gone, have reverted to the old arrangement which gave Wales a peculiar personal relationship to the Crown. However, beyond evincing hesitation he did nothing, and in practice Cromwell's purpose prevailed. The eleven shires (to include Monmouth, not even formally left in Wales) were in effect fully integrated into the reorganized national state. Representation in Parliament, now withheld only from Durham with its palatine jurisdiction under its bishop, proved the point. Wales was 'Englished' in law and structure, and was generally content to be so for the advantages that reception into the larger whole provided, but its language remained alive, and humanism and Protestantism were in the following century to assist the survival of a Welsh identity.

The device of bringing outliers into Parliament (first tried, rather pointlessly, for Tournai) was also applied to Calais. The problem here was both simple and insuperable. Calais constituted an outpost of English power, an essential depot for English trade, and a listening post for obtaining information necessary to the making of English policy. At a time when England looked likely to be totally isolated in Europe, Calais became the country's front-line defence, as well as a potential danger if infiltrated by hostile or subversive elements. The town and its territory needed to be specially well guarded and governed. In actual fact, its defences were in decay (though from 1532 a good deal of money was somehow found to rebuild them), and under the feeble administration of Arthur Plantagenet, Lord Lisle, its affairs were characterized by incompetence, corruption and absurdity.[8] By 1535 Cromwell had lost patience with the Calais administration and decided to do something; and in August a powerful royal commission crossed over to investigate and to propose reform. Lisle, the central cause of the trouble, eagerly welcomed it in the hope that the burden might pass to other shoulders. The commissioners, who reported finding everything in total disorder, spent nearly two months on their task, and by early November their reform proposals were being discussed in Council. There was some debate whether to impose order on the chaos by royal ordinance or by act of Parliament, but Cromwell's preference for the latter prevailed, with the result that the last session of the Reformation Parliament passed one of the longest acts of the century—eighteen large folio pages in the printed version. This organized the military and civil establishment of Calais, made provision against the purchase of offices, separated the garrison from civilian interference, and attempted to put the finances on a better basis. It is a remarkable and impressive document, and while Cromwell lived a good deal was done to put it into effect. Even so, Calais remained what it had long been—a financial and military liability. Even Cromwell's energy, which had provided the opportunity of reform, had its limits: he could not for ever sit on the local incompetents' backs, though he tried. Why Henry refrained from finding a better deputy for the place is a mystery; Lisle was no special favourite of his. Perhaps remote consanguinity kept him in his unsuitable office; perhaps everyone feared the wrath of Lady Lisle. One really positive result, however—the two parliamentary burgesses for Calais who appeared from 1536 onwards—again underlined the general principle of the reform, the consolidation of all parts in one unified political structure.

And then there was, as always, Ireland, not part of the kingdom of England in any sense but a separate lordship which, even if it had been practical to do so, could not have been assimilated under the pretence used for Wales that existing arrangements were merely being completed.[9] As we have seen, English policy in Ireland had usually fallen back on letting the powerful Geraldine house of Kildare exercise rule, while balancing its hegemony by giving support to the Butlers of Ormond, long loyal to Lancaster and Tudor. In the later 1520s this policy collapsed because a rival claim to the earldom of Ormond arose in a most influential quarter—the Boleyn family who won the lands and the title early in 1528. By way

[8] Lisle, a natural son of Edward IV, is the most touchingly idiotic figure of the day. He exasperated everybody (including his formidable wife), but people could rarely find it in their hearts to speak sharply to one so pathetically conscious of his shortcomings.

[9] B. Bradshaw, 'The Irish Constitutional Revolution, 1515–1557', pp. 101 ff.. constitutes a major historical revision which in the main is followed here.

of consolation Sir Piers Butler received the title of earl of Ossory and briefly also the deputyship, but Wiltshire on the English Council now supported Kildare, as did his ally Norfolk who claimed to be the Council's foremost expert on Irish affairs. Henry hoped to solve the problem by creating his natural son, the duke of Richmond, lieutenant, sending a professional soldier, Sir William Skeffington, over as deputy (June 1530) and giving him a stronger administration independent of all Irish nobles. However, Skeffington's energy cost money, and where Ireland was concerned the King always followed his father's principle: he would spend as little as possible. Thus Kildare's wooing of the English Council soon got him back into the saddle when Skeffington was recalled in July 1532. From this time onward Cromwell's hand is manifest. He was to be involved in Irish affairs throughout his ministry, and his main policy (shaped under the influence of reformers in the Pale) was visible from the first. He meant to end the independence of the feudal earldoms (Kildare, Ormond, Desmond), to reform the government of the obedient parts (the Pale and the earldoms), and to adopt for the time being an attitude of disengagement towards the 'disobedient' Irishry. By May 1534 he had promoted Anglo-Irish reformers in the Dublin administration, added Englishmen of his own choosing, and replaced Kildare once more by Skeffington. The first fruit of his energy was a major rising which, lasting a full fourteen months and costing some £40,000 to suppress, threatened the loss of the lordship and even worse consequences.[10]

The situation deteriorated from early in 1534 when Kildare, reluctantly obeying a summons, came to England, leaving his son, 'Silken Thomas' earl of Offaly, in charge. Soon once again in the Tower, he died there in September from old wounds and old age, but three months earlier Offaly, spreading false rumours of his father's death, had raised the banner of rebellion. Any Englishman found was killed, including the leading professional administrator, Archbishop John Alen of Dublin. Cooperating with the Desmond branch of the Geraldines in Munster, Offaly swept aside the Butlers and occupied most of the Pale, carrying destruction wherever he went; only Dublin and Waterford remained in loyal hands. The rebellion exploited a mixture of motives. At heart it was a strictly feudal uprising against the king of England's suzerainty which Offaly renounced, seeking to place the country under a new lord, either the Emperor or the Pope; and at heart it sprang from the Geraldines' fear for their power in the face of Cromwell's efforts to govern directly. However, Offaly dressed his motives in religious rags, claiming to be resisting Henry's schismatical doings and

[10]S. G. Ellis, 'The Kildare Rebellion, 1534' (unpublished dissertation, Manchester, 1974).

declaring allegiance to the papal supremacy. At least on his side, the negotiations with Charles V were meant seriously; he also tried for Scottish help, but in September 1534 James V allowed himself to come to peaceful terms with England. The appeal of Catholic orthodoxy worked quite well: the rising had the support of the Irish clergy, and the papacy dreamed of reconquering England from across St George's Channel. However, when very slowly the English government set about the task of suppression the end was certain enough. Skeffington arrived with a force in late October, and as soon as it became possible to campaign he systematically reduced the rebels whose successes rested on tenuous military foundations. Kildare's stronghold of Maynooth fell in March 1535, though all traces of rebellion were not extinguished until August. Anxious for bloody revenge, Henry was with difficulty persuaded to use judicious mercy; new excesses would have jeopardized the support of the Pale. In the end, some seventy-five men lost their lives in the immediate aftermath, far fewer than the rebels had killed, often in cold blood. Offaly, now the tenth earl of Kildare, was put in the Tower, to await events.

The failure of the rebellion ended the Kildare rule in Ireland, and Cromwell now had a free hand in the Council because the rising had destroyed the Irish policy of Norfolk and Wiltshire. Old Skeffington died in July 1535, to be replaced by Lord Leonard Grey, Cromwell's rather unfortunate choice. The elimination of the great families removed only one obstacle from Cromwell's path; in fact, it helped to revive the strength of the dominant men in the Pale itself, the Anglo-Irish led by some very determined gentlemen-lawyers. Their first demand, supported by the Irish Council, was for the total removal from Ireland of all Geraldines, and by stages the tenth earl's five uncles were caught and taken to England. In 1537 Henry exacted his favourite revenge when all six were tried and executed for treason; one child, the earl's half-brother, was, however, overlooked, with serious consequences later.

Thus Cromwell resumed his reform of Ireland in 1535, beset by much conflicting advice from Dublin where some wished to use the victory over the Geraldines for a forward policy of reconquest, while others looked to a general peaceful reformation. Neither view commended itself entirely to the minister who resolved to work within the limits set by financial stringency and to confine himself to reforming the settled parts. He determined, in fact, to incorporate the regions of royal rule into the unitary state he was building by applying the model of Calais to the Pale and as much as possible of the earldoms. From 1535, the office of deputy came to be reserved to Englishmen, and a permanent (small) garrison was introduced into

Dublin and some rebuilt border fortresses. These were to be the basic conditions of Irish government for centuries. The deputy's Council now consisted of reliable Anglo-Irish and newly immigrant Englishmen (seconded from Cromwell's staff) who were provided with lands as well as office; but the Irish government was not allowed any real independence, being—like that of Calais—firmly controlled by Cromwell and the English Privy Council. The Dublin reformers, assisted by an English reform commission under Sir Anthony St Leger sent over in 1537, received encouragement to undertake the expansion of English law and manners, to end Irish raids and bastard-feudal attitudes, and to promote the general enforcement of the law. Since Ormond, devoid of friends, had to keep in with Cromwell, the reform embraced the Butler lands, while those of Kildare were being infiltrated by new English; only Desmond, subdued at this time, remained uncertain. For the Irish parts Cromwell laid down no positive instructions, a vacuum filled by Grey's unauthorized efforts to assert himself in futile military raids which alone remained as memories of past quasi-feudal policies.

The first crunch for Cromwell's interventionist policy came when the Irish Parliament assembled in May 1536 to receive and enact the Reformation legislation for the King's other island.[11] Its four sessions, lasting until the late autumn of 1537, proved difficult, but the difficulties were not caused by religion. The gentry of the Pale readily accepted the royal supremacy and raised no objection in principle to the dissolution of the monasteries, but they put up a tough and successful resistance to attempts to secure financial recompense for the costs incurred in suppressing the rebellion and to create an adequate royal revenue for the future. Led by Patrick Barnewall, the new power in the Pale, the Parliament succeeded in unloading the whole burden on the clergy and settled down to exploiting the situation much in the manner of the English laity. Barnewall, who visited England in 1538, favourably impressed both Henry and Cromwell, a meeting of minds which made possible the continued cooperation with the Pale reformers, whose hopes, however, of carrying reform into the disaffected parts were quashed by Cromwell's final veto on the policy of reconquest (February 1539). In many respects, the decision to opt for a limited reform showed signs of paying off.

However, no one ever succeeds properly in Ireland: Cromwell's well defined endeavours were soon undermined by the very people whom he expected to give effect to them. Grey's attempts to coerce some Irish chiefs into nominal submission to the Crown were so inept

[11] B. Bradshaw, 'The Opposition to the Ecclesiastical Legislation in the Irish Reformation Parliament', *Irish Historical Studies* XVI (1969), pp. 285 ff.

as to rouse real fears of a reconquest that no one intended; besides, disliking Ormond (Piers Butler recovered the title in 1538) he foolishly identified himself with a Geraldine revival in Leinster. The damage was aggravated by the relentlessness with which George Brown, Cromwell's choice for the archbishopric of Dublin, carried through the enforcement of the new religious policy; as in England, the great constitutional revolution in the Church passed readily enough in Ireland, but the initiation of the Reformation proper ran into bitter opposition. By mid-1539 Ireland was again in turmoil, and war broke out in September. Under the pretence of restoring the Geraldines, an alliance of mainly Gaelic lords—especially the Ulster chiefs O'Neill and O'Donnell, hitherto irreconcilable—once more carried death and destruction into the Pale. Henry and Cromwell had by this time taken the measure of Irish affairs and refused to be panicked; in particular, they quite rightly wrote off the danger that continental enemies might use Irish rebellion to attack England from her flank. The war of the Gaelic League evaporated in late 1540; its only victim, not without justice, was Grey, recalled and imprisoned in the summer of that year. However, the League had been an ominous phenomenon, despite its ultimate futility. In its aims and composition it in no way recalled the old feudal politics of the earls of Kildare, still so manifest in 1534; uniting Irish and Anglo-Irish, producing an alliance of inveterate enemies, and moved in part at least by opposition to religious changes, it foreshadowed the nationalist and papalist resistance of the future.

In its negative way, therefore, this war confirmed the positive achievements of Cromwell's Irish policy. He had really ended the medieval history of the island when he eliminated the great earls and instituted direct English rule in those parts that could be ruled, though distance and problems of communications always rendered control a good deal less than perfect. The garrisoned shires were meant to be as fully English and under central direction as Calais, with its partly French population and separate council, or Wales with its different legal traditions and its Celts. Ireland, of course, had its own Parliament, in fact revived by Cromwell from a somewhat moribund condition, and this might well make for independence: but for the time being Cromwell made of it an instrument of unification.[12] We do not know whether Cromwell regarded his creation of a reformed part of the island subjected to direct rule from England as a precondition for undertaking the often demanded total

---

[12]By suspending Poyning's Law (1494), which ensured that all Irish legislation must be licensed by the English Council but also that none should be undertaken without prior Irish initiative, Cromwell turned the Irish Parliament into the agent of a full-scale government programme devised by himself.

reconquest or saw his immediate ends as sufficient to themselves. Lack of money accounts for his refusal to countenance a strong forward policy, certainly until the first stage was safely settled. As it was, he achieved his carefully limited purpose and for ever altered the terms of Irish politics and of English relations with Ireland; and he did bring part at least of Ireland into the single realm and empire of his desire. It is also worth notice that what jeopardized his success was not the policy of assimilation and modernization applied to the Pale and the earldoms, but his one departure from principled pragmatism—the reckless enforcement of the Reformation which he had enjoined upon Archbishop Brown.

II

From the first Cromwell had known that he would have to do something about the administration of the consolidated realm. It had not been altogether satisfactory since death removed Henry VII's cold controlling hand, and the reason was plain: efficient government as the old King had devised it required a man like him in charge—an administering monarch. Although a few attempts to improve things had been made in the interval, only Cromwell found the strength and the time, among his other preoccupations, to undertake reforms so thorough and far-reaching that from his surgery the King's government emerged fundamentally altered, whether or not one wants to speak of a revolution.[13]

Despite the reaction of 1509-11 and the modifications introduced by Wolsey, the administration which Cromwell inherited was the product of Henry VII's reforms. Its nerve centre lay in the royal Household which moved and operated the well settled 'bureau-cratic' offices of the Exchequer and the greater seals. These latter carried out essential routines without which the will of government did not become effective, but they contained no originating auth-ority or planning departments. These were found in three developed

[13]The debate about the meaning of Cromwell's administrative reforms, themselves generally accepted as having happened, is no doubt not over. If in essentials I adhere to the analysis I presented in *The Tudor Revolution in Government* (1953), I also recognize the importance of some of the objections raised by G. L. Harriss and P. H. Williams ('A Revolution in Tudor history?', *Past and Present* 29, 1964, pp. 26 ff.). More to the point are the new knowledge and insights provided by Dr Starkey's work on the Privy Chamber, though I cannot agree with all his conclusions. The present account still embodies my conviction that Cromwell's work amoun-ted to a fundamental restructuring on new principles, but (as will appear) in the light of work done over two decades I now see the structure he reformed and the essence of his aims a bit more subtly.

aspects of Household organization, in the inner administration
closely attendant upon the monarch. The vital financial office was,
until about 1529, the treasurership of the Chamber, superseded
thereafter by the keepership of the privy purse, an office held by the
groom of the Stool (or chief gentleman of the Privy Chamber, as he
was soon to be called); the emergence of that new department had
demonstrated the continued vitality and inventiveness of Household
government in the best medieval tradition. The task of embodying
the royal will in formal orders centred upon the King's principal
secretary and the signet, still very much part of the personal entourage. And policy-making as well as most administrative initiative
depended on the large and flexible King's Council whose varied
employment as agents of the Crown (as a whole body, in parts, by
committees, as individuals) had been the real secret of Henry VII's
success. Despite a measure of institutional independence, this Council was before 1509 so much part of the King's domestic government
that it is impossible to distinguish clearly not only between its
various, and variously organized, activities, but even between it and
the councils attached to other members of the royal family: for
instance, that important body, the so-called Court of Audit or
General Surveyors of Land Revenue, included side by side members
of the King's Council and members of the council of the prince of
Wales.[14] Henry VII ruled the kingdom firmly on the principle that it
was his private estate, and his methods reflected that fact. This was
the principle observed by all strong kings at least since the Conquest,
and it is increasingly becoming apparent that Henry VII set up the
most sophisticated form of the system ever produced.

A method of government which depended on the continuous close
supervision of the monarch himself could not endure into his son's
reign when such participation became casual and distinctly intermittent. Wolsey had adapted Henry VII's system by giving better
institutional identity to some of the offices that survived the reaction,
especially the financial organization built round the general surveyors and the treasurer of the Chamber. Thanks to his promotion of
the judicial function of the Council, that body too loosened its ties
with the Household. In the main, however, Wolsey administered by
superimposing himself and his own household upon the King's
administration, removing policy-making and governmental initiative into that replica of the royal organization. (To that extent he
really was *alter rex*.) It was a characteristically audacious undertaking and bound to prove insufficient; even Wolsey could not do
everything himself, and the group of assistants he relied on to

[14] I am indebted to a seminar paper by Miss Margaret Condon for a better understanding of
Henry VII's Council.

manage a control that should have been the King's was too small for the task. The realm was not very well administered in the cardinal's day, especially by comparison with the previous reign. Nevertheless Wolsey had achieved one very important thing: he had really broken the hold of the well entrenched concept which identified the state with the King's private estate. Even his fall demonstrated that under Henry VIII there could be no full-scale return to the father's methods, and the King's attempts between 1529 and 1532 to revive Household methods turned only into a search for someone to take Wolsey's place. More particularly, the Council of those years bore little resemblance to that of Henry VII, being dominated by politicians rather than administrators and quite incapable of exercising the multiple control over policy, action and finance which under the old King's rule his councillors had monopolized.

Cromwell achieved prominence in the Council by means of his administrative efficiency and his willingness to do the work, and it may be doubted whether at first Henry saw in him a successor to Wolsey except in that respect. By 1532 he had learned better, and by 1535 Cromwell's subfusc authority exceeded anything that Wolsey's scarlet had signified. To Cromwell, neither Henry VII's system nor the cardinal's could be satisfactory or even possible. The first belonged to a king, the second to a man willing to create a substitute kingship; after the cardinal's fiasco, Cromwell, not being the former, would have been ill advised, if he had thought of it, to imitate the latter. In any case it is clear that as usual he looked for more fundamental answers and meant to tackle the problem of government nearer the roots. If he intended—as his actions show he did—so to reform the administration as to free it from the accident of the monarch of the day, he needed to do two things. In the first place he had to establish his general control over the system as he found it, a task he managed by working within it, by acquiring a large collection of offices that offered possibilities of supervision and initiative. Since the old system made no distinction, in the government of the King's estate, between offices in the Household and those outside it, it did not matter to him where he found such appointments; as master of the Jewels or principal secretary he held Household office, as chancellor of the Exchequer or lord privy seal office in the settled bureaucracy. What did matter was the use to which he put those offices, and here his second purpose came in: control once established, he set about reordering the system so as to eliminate the Household for good and create (on the foundations of the older bureaucracy) a government for the King's public state, a national government suitable to the reformed polity which emerged in the 1530s.

Of course, these ends could not be pursued in a clear-cut schematic fashion, and it is for this reason that some historians apparently continue to doubt whether they were pursued at all. As
always, Cromwell could only succeed if he worked within the limits
of the possible, and he had to recognize three constraints on his
freedom of action. He could not ignore the King, especially at a time
when he was working towards the elimination of the monarch's
personal control of the administration. Though unwilling to exercise
this in his father's fashion, Henry would never leave everything to his
minister and frequently used the men nearest to him—especially the
gentlemen of his Privy Chamber—to act as executors of his will,
though this rarely cut across the ordinary administration of the
realm. More important, he had a full share of the Tudor canniness,
not to say meanness, with money; he liked to be able to get his hands
on it and would trust no one, individual or organization, with the
storing of the reserves which he let others accumulate. In consequence he maintained the rather primitive system of 'the king's
coffers', a private treasury whose contents he disbursed in person
and for which no accounts survive, so that we know little about it
except that surpluses in the departments were commonly paid into
it. These vestiges of an unbureaucratized private estate administration were markedly less prominent in Cromwell's time, but he
never attempted to remove them; they became more important
again after his fall, though they disappeared altogether in the further
reforms after Henry's death. Secondly, Cromwell could not work to
a comprehensive plan when immediate problems called for immediate solutions, though the steps actually taken throw light on his
principles. And lastly, Cromwell knew that he could not afford to
provide reforms which would weaken his personal control: in the
early stages of such transformations, the guiding hand must and will
prefer to inhibit the full flowering of the endeavour to render
government independent of the accidents of personality. In this case,
the result was that several reforms incubated by Cromwell did not
become manifest until those trained by him completed them after his
disappearance.

These limitations allowed for, Cromwell's purposes nevertheless
showed themselves in his doings. In the administration of the
finances he concentrated on improving the collecting and handling
of revenue by reducing the informality of Henry VII's methods to
controllable order. He did not attempt to do anything extensive
about the Exchequer, a task of great difficulty in the face of its
entrenched bureaucratic traditionalism and at the time, because it
held so lowly a place in revenue administration, of little urgency. He
concentrated on two things—getting rid of Household interference,

and providing efficiently for new revenue. He reduced the Chamber to a well ordered routine within its proper sphere as a court treasury, and he confined the Privy Chamber for good to the administration of the King's privy purse, financed from the surplus in the coffers. The revenue from first-fruits and tenths, which at first had been intended for the Chamber, he kept under his own control through a treasurer who was his personal servant; this arrangement was bureaucratized by the institution of a court (a government department) as soon as possible after his death, in the session of 1541. The model for this reorganization existed in Cromwell's two new revenue courts, that of Augmentations (1536) set up to administer all new land revenue, especially the estates of the monasteries, and that of Wards (1540) developed out of the insufficiently bureaucratic office of Wards to deal with the yield of the King's feudal fiscal prerogative. A fourth such court was finally created in 1542 out of the office of the general surveyors of (old) crown lands, introduced by Henry VII but made permanent and at the same time restricted to a well defined scope by Cromwell in 1536. The older departments of the Exchequer and the Duchy Chamber of Lancaster (in charge of Duchy lands), already sufficiently organized, took their places in this array of offices.

All these departments were intended to stand on their own feet, without reliance on process out of the Exchequer but also without the informalities which had ruled Chamber finance. They had autonomy in gathering the revenues in their charge and in dealing with disputes arising upon the properties committed to them. Grants out of these properties required the authorization of the departmental officers without which the King would not approve petitions, and the departments paid all the charges arising out of their work, including salaries. Surpluses were either at the immediate disposal of government, being paid out upon warrants effectively authorized by Cromwell, or, if left over, went to the king's coffers. Deficits they were expected to cover in subsequent years, though occasionally transfers between offices took care of exceptionally serious shortfalls. The essence of the system thus lay in a recognition (which contrasted sharply with late medieval ideas) of national concerns as quite separate from the King's personal concerns. How efficient it was cannot be readily ascertained. Cromwell's fall removed the controlling hand too soon, and the wars and waste of the next decade undermined all financial efficiency; surpluses became so rare that it often proved difficult to find a treasury capable of paying for even such urgent government matters as an ambassador's diets—though it looks as though much of this shortage was created by Henry's premature insistence on transferring balances to his coffers. Certainly Cromwell's multiplication of revenue courts burdened the Crown with more offices and officers than was wise, and the segmenting of revenue collection may have led to demarcation disputes and similar occasions of inefficiency. But Cromwell set up so many courts because he had to deal by stages with various problems arising, and while he lived he kept them in good cooperative order.

In his reorganization of central control over all the business of government, the same hostility to Household influence made itself felt. In the first place, Cromwell took the secretaryship right out of the Household in any but the most meaninglessly formal sense. He deliberately used the office to make himself chief and universal minister: for the first time, Mr Secretary was the man at the heart of the web to whom and from whom all lines flowed. Cromwell's secret lay in the infusion of personal authority into an office of very secondary importance, and the effect of his imprint endured. Although by no means all post-Cromwellian secretaries carried Cromwell's authority, and although the division of the office into two branches (April 1540) weakened the ascendancy of its holders, no secretary after 1540 ever again reverted to the personal position in the Household which had been characteristic before Cromwell. The full development of the modern secretaryship of state owed much to later statesmen, but the lines were all laid down by Cromwell when he made himself the main executive minister, the manipulator of Council business, the head of a department staffed by men of his own choosing, and especially the controller of intelligence at home and abroad. As an Elizabethan observer was to comment: 'Mr Cromwell ... augmented the commodity and authority of every office that he attained.'

The crux of Cromwell's administrative reforms touched the centre of government, the King's Council itself. What he found was a very large body of councillors, numbering over seventy, all technically alike as councillors, however much personality and standing might create greater and lesser importance among them. What he handed on was a Privy Council of some eighteen to twenty. The reform took place, after some dithering, in the summer of 1536 when Henry, at Cromwell's urging, formed a selection of the large body into what from thenceforth was to be the only King's Council; the remainder, indelibly marked by the councillor's oath, survived without further replacement as 'councillors at large'.[15] The old Council had included office holders and politicians, but also court nobility in general, administrators of the second and third ranks, all the judges and the King's legal counsel (King's serjeants, attorney and solicitor gen-

[15] Cf. my 'Tudor Government—the Points of Contact: II. The Council', *Transactions of the Royal Historical Society* (1975), pp. 195 ff.

eral), and usually some leading doctors of civil law as well. In addition, men of standing in the localities were habitually sworn of the Council, as a mark of favour and distinction; some of them, as for instance some lord mayors of London or the abbot of Westminster, had in fact exercised their function quite regularly by attending meetings. That Council combined the virtues of a governing committee with an opportunity for diffusing authority throughout the realm, but thanks to its size and diversity it had never been an effective committee, requiring the personal guidance and control of monarch or (in Wolsey's case) minister. The new Council was designed to contain only men of political eminence; nearly all its members held one of the newly designed qualifying offices—offices of 'cabinet rank'. The chancellor, treasurer, lord privy seal, lord admiral, master of the Horse, principal secretaries, lord chamberlain, treasurer and comptroller of the Household—these and few more became and remained the Tudors' privy councillors. It is possible that Cromwell paid heed to the proposals for a restricted Council which Wolsey had inserted into the Eltham Ordinance of 1526, but if so it is interesting that he followed the principle of cabinet rank much more consistently by leaving out non-officed noblemen and such lesser officials as the dean of the Chapel or the King's almoner.

The reformed Council differed noticeably from its predecessor. Its small size made it potentially very competent at discharging business, and the restriction in membership also set the whole body clearly apart from the generality of administrators. From this time, the King's councillors became much more eminent, individually and corporately, attracting greater respect just because they were so few and chosen for their special qualities; Cromwell here created the situation so well summed up late in Elizabeth's reign by the Venetian envoy who remarked sourly that 'these lords of the Council behave like so many kings.' These consequences of the reform were reinforced by the rapid provision of better clerical organization and from soon after Cromwell's fall (when the councillors behaved rather like newly enfranchised children coping with the disappearance of a stern but trusted father) of a regular register: by the end of Henry VIII's reign the Privy Council had an archive and a memory. The most striking difference between the old and the new Councils, more striking even than outward appearance and elitist arrogance, lay in their powers. The new Council not only acted in a manner which made the existence of a true first minister both superfluous and usually rather difficult, but it also had means for direct and independent action of which at least no evidence exists before the reform. It seems unlikely to be but an accident that the first surviving

Council letters—those executive instruments to which the monarch contributed nothing—should date from the autumn of 1536, two or three months after the reform. When Cromwell set up the Privy Council he in effect institutionalized his personal authority and mode of government, proving the sincerity of a policy designed to reduce the personal element in government to a minimum. He thus settled the ordinary governing power of the Crown in an organized body removed from the King's personal entourage, even though it continued mostly to meet at court. Nothing did more to destroy the Household potential in government, or to render impossible the personal manner in which Henry VII had used his Council, and nothing in Cromwell's reforms did more to give drive and reasonable continuity to royal government in Tudor England.

As a concomitant to this reform, the by-products of conciliar development also had to be settled. Thus the Council courts of Star Chamber and Requests, really built up under Wolsey, got their final institutional form under Cromwell. For Star Chamber this meant mainly a definition of the bench: since that court was simply the Council in judicial session, the reform of 1536 reduced its membership to the newly defined privy councillors. However, because Cromwell had taken the legal experts out of the Council they had to be specially restored to a place in the conciliar activity which absolutely required them, and the two chief justices, though very rarely privy councillors, were regularly members of the Star Chamber. Councillors at large could also be invited occasionally, here and elsewhere, to ease the work of the overburdened men of eminence. For Requests the problem was rather different because the new Council included none of the specialist councillors sitting there. Thus that court separated finally from the Council in 1538–40, becoming a separate bench linked ancestrally but in no other way with the King's Council; its judges were now always termed masters of Requests.[16] Cromwell appears to have intended the court to act as the recipient of all litigious petitions presented to the Privy Council, but this attempt, like all later ones, to free the governing body's agenda from private men's concerns was wrecked on the determination of suitors to go as high as ever they could. Together with such lesser reforms as the institution of better record-keeping in the Court of Chancery, which Cromwell promoted while he was master of the Rolls (1534–6), these moves all underline the strongly organized, bureaucratic and fundamental character of Cromwell's administrative designs. He tried to bring order, system and permanence into all branches of the government.

[16] D. A. Knox, 'The Court of Requests in the Reign of Edward VI' (unpublished dissertation, Cambridge, 1974), pp. 106 ff.

Cromwell's 'revolution in government' thus derived from his conviction that an administration at intervals refreshed and renewed from within the royal Household could no longer adequately serve the needs of the state. All his positive contributions tended in that direction. So, naturally, did his attitude to the Household itself which he tried to reorganize more specifically for efficiency in its departmental task of running the King's private life and his court.[17] His plans were very large, which makes it no wonder that they also fell well short of fulfilment. By the mid-1530s he had come to terms with the dominant position of the young Privy Chamber. Much as Wolsey tried to do, he sought to gain political control of the department: such an alternative focus of power, so close to the King, posed an obvious threat to ministerial ascendancy. He achieved his aim in the palace revolution that destroyed Anne Boleyn;[18] for the rest of the decade, the Privy Chamber, controlled by his clients, offered no rivalry to his power. In addition, the new set-up rendered superfluous the whole cumbersome organization of the Chamber under the lord chamberlain, now engaged in purely ceremonial functions but still very expensive. The French model, ever resorted to in this reign when Household reform was in question, suggested the reduction of the Household once more to two departments, the lord steward's Household proper and the Privy Chamber under its first gentleman. Cromwell proposed to achieve this by eliminating the lord chamberlaincy, by making the treasurer and comptroller the effective heads of the supply department, and by putting both them and the first gentleman under the rule of the lord steward with the new title (borrowed from France) of great master of the Household.

Cromwell mooted this scheme several times but opposition in Council frustrated him till late in 1539. He then put through a number of detailed reforms, got the great mastership established in the parliamentary session of April 1540, and at the same time had himself appointed to the high but empty office of great chamberlain in order at the first opportunity to sink the lord chamberlaincy in it and thus end the Chamber's independent existence. This would have produced a single bureaucratic organization for the Household, entirely designed to serve its departmental function in looking after the Court. Cromwell's death left these rearrangements unfinished, and in the 1540s the Privy Council by stages, under pressure from office holders, abandoned essential parts of it. The lord chamber-

---

[17]Especially D. R. Starkey, 'The King's Privy Chamber, 1485–1547', pp. 273 ff., which rightly criticizes some parts of *Tudor Revolution in Government*, chapter 6. I cannot, however, fully accept his analysis of purposes and outcome.

[18]See below, p. 253.

laincy came back, after a lapse of time; the Chamber continued to exist, with ever fewer real functions; the great master, deprived of overlordship, again dwindled into the lord steward; at last, quite unpredictably, the dynamic Privy Chamber forfeited all prospects of major importance outside the court because a boy's and two women's attendants were not suitable for it. What was left were the important, mainly financial, reforms introduced inside the Household during 1539–40 which were to serve it well for over 250 years. All this, however, did bring about the departure of the Household from national government, a departure Cromwell had worked for but had been unable fully to secure, partly for lack of time, partly because he here encountered the only opposition put up by Henry in these administrative reforms. The King, willing to permit a Privy Council that exercised so much of the royal office, drew the line at being deprived of the use, at will, of the men immediately around him.[19]

Thus Cromwell laboured persistently and with considerable success at the task of reforming the government of the new polity. Although circumstances prevented him from imposing a totally coherent new order, he sufficiently demonstrated what he had in mind. The transformed body politic could not be managed by methods suitable to the King's estate; it needed, and got, an administration which—and this was true of all Cromwell's reforms—started from novel premises while preserving the appearance of continuity with the past.

III

Since Cromwell controlled government planning and action from mid-1532 onwards, it becomes important to ask whether he used his power in the manner expected of him by those advocates of reform who had found him like-minded and zealous. Did the last four

---

[19]Dr Starkey and I differ as to the degree to which the Household continued actively important in national government during and after Cromwell's time, and consequently also on the nature of Cromwell's policy. He argues that the Privy Chamber remained an essential part of administration, eliminated only by the accident of 1547 which led to the rule of a minor and two women, none of them of necessity equipped with the sort of Household that could practise these 'medieval' methods in government. I would suggest that the Household conclusively lost ground in the 1530s but revived in the 1540s thanks to the accident of Henry's wars and Cromwell's premature departure: 1547 and after could not have had the effect postulated by Dr Starkey if Cromwell had not in good time so reorganized government that the Household potential could finally be dispensed with.

sessions of the Reformation Parliament witness an attempt to put 'commonwealth' principles into action?[20] The question is predictably complicated by the difficulty one has in deciding whether a given proposal or statute emerged from the government and the Cromwell circle or originated elsewhere. Some of the relevant statutes were manifestly promoted by sectional and private interests; some of the more wide-ranging ideas seem to owe nothing to government initiative. However, by comparison with earlier sessions of Parliament the existence of government-sponsored bills, even of a genuine programme of social reform, is also quite manifest. Though Cromwell disappointed Clement Armstrong by not transforming the realm overnight into a replica of paradise, more realistic commonwealth men had to agree that he gave proof of his proper zeal. The measures taken can be classified under four heads, with some fringe interests also present—a serious attempt to control the price of food, a new approach to the problem of rural depopulation, the active encouragement of manufacture and trade, and poor relief. Two general principles stand out in all that was attempted. Even where the precedents encouraged the use of edicts such as court orders or royal proclamations. Cromwell preferred the permanence and legalism of parliamentary legislation, despite the enormous difficulties occasioned by the need to persuade both Lords and Commons. And at all times this government proved flexibly responsive to the demands and complaints of the people affected whose conflicting interests assured that policy could rarely be single minded.

The issue of food prices loomed large from the early 1530s because it was in the 1520s that the general upward movement of price levels, especially in respect of grain and meat, first made itself seriously felt.[21] In addition the harvests of 1529–31 were poor. For centuries prices of foodstuffs had been settled locally, in the main by the action of town corporations, but in Henry VIII's reign the first sign of a more general policy appeared in attempts to give the help of proclamations to local efforts. It was London in particular that urged action: the problem of adequate food supplies at reasonable prices was naturally greatest in this largest, and rapidly growing, community of non-producers. Typically, Cromwell looked for a permanent scheme to replace hand-to-mouth expedients. The solution he favoured aimed to set maximum prices by statutes which delegated to powerful Council committees the right to vary prices

[20] Cf. in general *Reform and Renewal*, especially chapter 5. Some of these topics compel a look beyond the year 1536, but in the main later aspects of the commonwealth policy initiated by Cromwell and fitfully pursued by his successors shall be considered at the right point in time.

[21] All discussion of prices is based on the tables in the appendix to *The Agrarian History of England and Wales* IV, edited by J. Thirsk (1967).

downward by proclamation.[22] He led off with an act for French
wines in 1531 which combined protection for shipping with price
fixing; next year, much the same policy was adopted for butcher's
meat; while in 1533 a more general act created machinery for fixing
the prices of many victuals (mainly dairy produce and poultry)
without actually laying down a statutory scale.

The policy was well intentioned and nearly always futile. The
wine statute fixed retail prices; the Council committee could vary
only wholesale levels which thus got easily out of step with what
traders were allowed to charge. The general statute, much weakened
by parliamentary opposition, lay dormant until brought into use by
Edward VI's Council. Meat prices caused the most enormous
difficulties, partly because the statutory scale was accidentally
affected by the fact that meat happened to be cheap and plentiful in
1532–3 when the levels were set. The butchers of London in particular refused to comply, complaining that the statutory prices would
ruin them so long as the wholesalers (the graziers) charged what
they did. Cromwell did not give up easily; efforts were made for
years to turn the policy into reality. The London butchers suffered a
temporary closure of their shops; control was extended to the
graziers; amending statutes tried to provide better enforcement and
a little more flexibility; proclamations issued in plenty, sometimes
enforcing and sometimes suspending the regulations. Meat prices
called forth four statutes and eleven proclamations in the ten years
that the policy was in being; finally an act of 1542 brought it
conclusively to an end by repealing all the recent legislation. On
wines, the government really surrendered as early as 1534 with an
act which empowered the Crown to suspend the existing law by
proclamation; thereafter, the problem again returned to the attention of *ad hoc* orders.

Statutory price fixing failed. It exemplified a very common-
wealth-type of attitude, namely consumer protection, an attempt
to secure fairness in commercial relations and prevent exploitation by producers. It failed for three reasons, two essentially
extraneous but one fundamental. The extraneous causes of failure
were the great difficulties encountered in getting proclamations
enforced (an experience which in the end drove Cromwell to seek
new statutory powers) and the fact that the act of Parliament proved
to be too rigid an instrument to deal with so sensitive and constantly
changing a public problem. Much the same experience attended
efforts to put down speculators in bread grain, alleged to be exploiting shortages either by illegal exports to the continent (where prices

[22] The fullest discussion of price fixing is found in R. W. Heinze, *The Royal Proclamations of the
Tudor Kings* (1976).

were generally higher) or by market-rigging devices at home. However, behind these deficiencies of an administration not really equipped to manage the details of the economy in the manner desired there stood the more fundamental difficulty (one that government interference has never solved) that one man's justice is another man's iniquity. Especially at a time of population increase and price inflation, giving the consumer what he wanted (and he wanted no change) meant ruin to producer and middleman, with the result that the law was ignored or even that the product disappeared. The commonwealth policy towards prices showed commendable social concern but also that excessive trust in manipulation from above which characterizes radical reformers. At least Cromwell kept a sufficiently open mind to accept the need for altering the provisions and allow himself to be persuaded that the hard-hit butchers and grain merchants were not necessarily the exploiters of the commonweal that doctrine called them.

In any case, he took other steps to improve the supply of food which alone could really keep prices down. Commonwealth thought held that this required redressing the rural balance in favour of arable husbandry, and Cromwell certainly agreed. He was aided by the fact that the height of the boom in sheepfarming was passing; real improvement owed less to any paternalistic action than to the ready response of landowners to higher prices for food (resulting from population expansion) and lower prices for wool (resulting from over-production). That harvests were generally quite good in the 1530s was a boon to a government engaged in a political revolution. However, Cromwell also sought to help with legislation. His addition to the statutes on enclosure (1536) confined itself to making the extensive legislation more effective; the King was given the right to intervene where lesser lords failed to use their power under the law to enforce the removal of illegal enclosures, but whether the policy was actively pursued is at present unknown. It may well be that Wolsey's failure, despite ever more desperate measures, to reverse enclosing taught his successor the futility of the attempt. Another of Cromwell's acts, however, tried a new line. In 1534 he proposed to make sheepfarming less attractive by setting a statutory limit to the size of flocks and by restricting the engrossing of leaseholds, the real agrarian problem of the early sixteenth century. Even though he enlisted Henry's help in the Upper House, opposition there whittled away the second of these purposes. Cromwell used a Commons' committee to reintroduce a modest provision against excessive concentration of farms in single hands, and the Sheep and Farms Act remained a tolerably useful instrument for giving stability to the agrarian scene till it vanished in the Great

Rebellion; but his comprehensive assault, in a bill heavily marked by commonwealth influence, upon the commercial practices of landowners had nevertheless suffered something like a defeat in Parliament.

Rather more success attended Cromwell's efforts to assist the textile industry and especially the export of cloth. Here again he was exposed to contradictory pressures. No one could or did object to the encouragement of a native linen industry, promoted in the act of 1533 which compelled farmers to sow a quarter acre with flax for every sixty acres of arable they possessed. But people were very much divided about the best way to advance England's basic industry, the trade in wool and woollen cloth, in trouble at the start of the decade because of the confusion caused by Wolsey's policy, the uncertainties raised by the Divorce, and probably also plague.[23] Clement Armstrong, experienced in the trade, concentrated on the profitable difference between white (unfinished) cloth and the finished product, demanding that the export of the former should be stopped: it is true that something like two thirds of the final sales price was added in the finishing stages and thus came into the pockets of continental manufacturers. He also wished to end the export of raw cool, blaming the Calais Staple for depriving the realm of the advantage which would accrue if all wool were sold abroad in the manufactured state. In economic theory he was essentially correct, though he did not understand how seriously the old English monopoly of wool, holding the textile industries of Flanders and even Italy in thrall, had been undermined by the growth of wool production in Germany and Spain. In any case, however, economic theory had to take account of political reality which, as the London Merchant Adventurers never tired of explaining, consisted in the unwillingness of continental customers to accept anything except unfinished cloth. Here, too, further disputes arose. The exporters protested that their clients complained of the quality of the cloth exported, while the clothiers and weavers explained that they could not do better at the prices the exporters offered them.

In this mêlée Cromwell behaved with considerable and considerate skill. He left the Calais Staple alone—in natural decline as the foreign market for raw wool continued to contract. He did everything he could to encourage the flow of trade, helping the Adventurers by easing restrictions on export but resisting their efforts to eliminate rivals and allowing foreign merchants (especially the Hanse) to take their share. And he promoted various acts against

[23]The quinquennium 1529–34 witnessed a decline of exports by 6½ per cent as against its predecessor—a unique experience in the first half of the century when cloth exports otherwise rose continuously (J. D. Gould, *The Great Debasement: Currency and the Economy in mid-Tudor England*, p. 129).

fraudulent and insufficient practices which were giving English cloth a bad name. In particular he accepted a merchants' bill of 1536 which fixed a new standard size for cloth, though he also listened to the producers' protests that they could not re-equip themselves with the necessary looms by the time laid down, so that the act was several times suspended by proclamation. Compared with his policy for prices, his support for the cloth trade was based on relative non-interference which allowed normal commercial relations a more or less unfettered play; and it worked. The ten years after 1533 that stood under his management witnessed the biggest expansion yet of this vital trade, an overall improvement of exports by about twenty five per cent.

In addition Cromwell was involved in another dispute occasioned by the problems of the export trade whose need for a free exchange of money with the continental centres of finance conflicted with the theorists' conviction that a free exchange drained the realm of specie. Here his hands were further tied by political circumstances. The main purpose in controlling the exchanges had always been linked to the transfer of money to Rome, both in papal taxation and for the costs incurred by suitors to the Curia. Thus the break with Rome itself counselled a stop to the export of bullion. Furthermore the King himself believed in the bullionist argument which wished to hoard specie in England, while the personal interests of the keepers of the exchanges—officials who profited from the licensing system that control relied on—also stood in the way of freedom, especially after 1532 when the sinecurist share in that office fell to Cromwell's ally Audley. In this confusion of interests Cromwell was at first forced to attempt restraint, total or partial, to the detriment of the export trade; but in the end, in 1538, he cut through the tangle by accepting the advice of the city. The exchanges were freed entirely, greatly to the merchants' benefit, and the dreaded denuding of the realm of its gold and silver did not happen. The theorists had, in fact, got it wrong: an adequate supply of coin and specie depended on the favourable balance of trade which Cromwell's whole policy successfully promoted.

All these details mattered to the commonweal of England; what mattered even more to the commonwealth reformers was the relief of poverty and unemployment. Here Cromwell for once lent unstinting support to very advanced ideas, in the face of formidable opposition from the possessing classes. Their attitude, which dominated both Houses of Parliament, had found expression in the severe Beggars' Act of 1531 which, though it empowered justices to license the hopelessly destitute to beg, mainly concentrated on using the whip and the stocks against what was regarded as the social evil of vagabondage. Neither point satisfied reformist thought which objected to begging altogether, wishing to commit society to the organized relief of those truly unable to work, and believed in finding work for the rest. By 1536, deliberations in Cromwell's group had produced a remarkable reform proposal to tackle the whole problem comprehensively in which the influence of 'Erasmian' thought and the example of various continental cities made themselves felt. The bill prepared for Parliament began with a preamble which carefully distinguished between the impotent and the able, and which recognized that unemployment and poverty owed less to a natural disinclination to work than to circumstances often outside a man's control. It proposed to relieve the former from parish poor chests, fed by voluntary contributions and administered by special overseers of the poor (a new office); the reformist origins of the scheme appear not only in its rejection of begging but also in the insistence that general charity should be regularly stimulated from the pulpits. For those capable of work, the bill proposed a scheme of public works—harbour improvement, road making, bridge building, and such like. This was to be organized under a new ministry, a Council to Avoid Vagabonds, with subordinate officers in charge of particular works and with powers to make regulations; it was to be financed by a general graduated income tax, to be paid annually until 1540 in the first instance; labourers were to be mustered by what were in effect employment exchanges, maintained by wages, and cared for in their health at the public expense. Work, admittedly, was to be compulsory for the unemployed, and three refusals to undertake it when offered made a man a felon—punishable by death. The reformers thus hoped to distinguish between genuine unemployed and genuine vagrants whose existence, and the threat they posed to public order, were recognized as real even by men who refused to subscribe to the undiscriminating condemnation of the poor.

Cromwell accepted this remarkable scheme, though he must have been aware of the difficulties of getting it through. A poor law which added to the powers of central government, created an open-ended right to make law of a sort, involved such a general taxation, and imposed hanging for refusal to work really trod on too many toes. Nevertheless the bill was introduced in the last session of the Reformation Parliament, and Cromwell quite exceptionally mobilized the King for it: Henry presented it in person to the Commons, with a recommendation which was less than whole hearted. It did no good: the bill vanished. In its place an alternative bill, probably prepared in advance for just this contingency, passed into law, a very poor remnant of the great scheme and even so limited only till the end of the next Parliament. The careful analysis of the preamble was replaced by a short reference to the failure of the earlier act to provide work for beggars; the relief provisions were so watered down that, as the act itself acknowledged, the voluntary charity proposed would very likely fail to meet the needs of the case; the whole grandiose scheme for public works and employing the unemployed disappeared. Instead the act tried to improve the penal provisions of its predecessor. Cromwell and the commonwealth men had evidently gone too far; their generous and imaginative ideas suffered a resounding defeat—in and by Parliament. Nevertheless, they could find some consolation in the fact that the important distinction between those able and those unable to work was for the first time recognized by the law, as well as in the survival of parish relief for the latter, however ineffective this was to prove for some decades. The lost bill also influenced Elizabethan thinking on the subject; although no one ever again took up the scheme of works, the better analysis of the problem and the developed system of poor relief which the Elizabethan legislation produced borrowed directly from the discarded proposal.

Cromwell's commonwealth policy thus experienced several notable setbacks, though it also achieved some real successes. In addition to helping settle agrarian discontent and promoting trade, he pushed through measures directly influenced by commonwealth thinkers, as for instance acts to encourage urban renewal (the rebuilding of decayed houses), a sumptuary law which departed from the traditional emphasis on the excessive cost of conspicuous consumption in order to stress the preservation of an organic hierarchical order in society, and measures intended to assist the preservation of natural resources.[24] Considering the solid opposition he was bound to encounter when things were moved that affected powerful political interests, and considering also the vast quantity of major government legislation that resulted from the break with Rome and the Reformation, Cromwell must be said to have tried seriously to justify the reformers' trust in him and to have achieved, even by 1536, enough to show that he meant to reform the commonweal.

Lastly we may note some measures touching the reform of the law which also testify to the political difficulties of reform. The session of early 1536 saw the promotion of two important bills with very different fortunes. In the first place, Cromwell adapted and elaborated a proposal of John Rastell's for securing a fuller registration of

[24]These included the protection of fisheries, the regeneration of woodland (attempted from 1532 but not achieved until 1543), and the safeguarding of agriculture against depredation by rooks. A sumptuary law defines what clothing can be worn by the various ranks of society.

all transactions in land, though he refused to concede the profitable monopoly that Rastell was after. The bill put forward pleaded the need to avoid the uncertainties of title and the consequent 'strifes debates and variances' which resulted from secret conveyancing; it laid down that all dealings in land must be by sealed instruments publicly registered; and it provided for registration officers in every county. The details were worked out with care, but this was another major scheme that came to grief in Parliament in face of opposition from the lawyers (who foresaw a decline in litigation) and from landowners (who preferred the general attraction of secrecy to the occasional advantage of public knowledge). All that survived was a rather petty reform, grandiosely entitled by later lawyers the Statute of Enrolments. This confined registration to a form of conveyancing involved in the creation of trusts and cut the machinery down to the point of ineffectiveness. Once again, all that Cromwell really obtained was the establishment of a principle—the principle that land sales should be readily traceable so as to avoid fraud as well as innocent disappointment—while the land register he wanted still does not exist today.[25]

The other great law reform of 1536 fared very differently, even though it offended even more powerful interests: but then it had Henry VIII's personal support, and he may even have been personally responsible both for its contents and the way it was forced through Parliament. This is the Statute of Uses, the actual outcome of those years of negotiations and debates concerning the protection of the King's feudal prerogatives and revenue against the device which separated the owner of the legal estate in a piece of property from the man who took the income.[26] In 1529 it had been suggested that in return for subjecting enfeoffment to uses to the control of the common law two thirds of noblemen's estates might be exempt from death duties and the restriction on testamentary disposal; in 1532, Cromwell, remembering the financial interests of the crown, tried to cut the free portion to one half but included all landowners. On both occasions the short-sightedness of the gentry had blocked accommodation in Parliament. The statute of 1536 simply removed the advantage of the use altogether by enacting that in future enfeoffment to uses would create a legal estate in the beneficiary, not in the feoffees, and by making no concessions of exempt portions. The gainers were the King, once again assured of his revenue, and the

[25] One reviewer of *Reform and Renewal* (J. M. Kaye in *Law Quarterly Review* XC, 1974, pp. 573 ff.) has expressed the view that the proposed land register would have been futile and absurd because existing arrangements were working so well and everybody was satisfied. It is good to know that lawyer still speaks to lawyer across the centuries, but the evidence of Tudor litigation shows how much harm was done by secret conveyancing.

[26] See above, p. 147–8.

common-law courts since the statutory recognition of the use enabled them to take cognizance of suits arising out of it; the losers were all landowners, intolerably restricted in their power to bequeath after two centuries of growing freedom, and potentially the Chancery.

The profit to the courts possibly assisted the passage of the bill since it would weaken lawyers' opposition to it, but the chief reason for this remarkable, and dubious, success lay elsewhere. In 1534, Henry, thoroughly exasperated by parliamentary opposition, had taken his lawyers' advice that a test case might call the whole practice in doubt, and the death of Lord Dacre of the South had offered an opportunity. The Crown entered process against his last will, and the uses created in it were declared illegal by the Court of Common Pleas. The judgement destroyed the validity of all equitable uses and imperilled the greater part of landed ownership in England; it did not help that in strict law it was entirely proper. Thus in 1536 Parliament found that it could restore security to the arrangements by which so much land was held only in exchange for surrendering the special advantages that accrued from them. The Statute of Uses concluded one phase in the history of the land law by substituting the novel doctrine that title depended on an estate in law, however created, for the ancient doctrine that looked to seisin. In this respect, and in that it recognized what a century of conveyancing had in fact done to the law, it was important and beneficial; but the ruthless refusal (almost certainly Henry's) to alleviate the burden of feudal incidents and to admit that testamentary disposal of landed property had long since become a common and necessary practice was politically unwise and socially unacceptable. The rigorous system set up by the act could not last, nor did it; statute soon led the way in modifying it,[27] and conveyancers followed with devices that exploited the partly inadequate drafting of the law. This harsh act, pushed through by means of a savage legal trick, well describes the mind that Henry VIII brought to the business of reform.

[27] The Statute of Wills; see below, p. 291.

10 The End of the Monasteries

By January 1535, with Cromwell appointed the King's vicar-general and vicegerent in spirituals, and with Cranmer well settled at Canterbury, the party of reform had its chance with the Church of England. Cromwell and Cranmer now dominated, if they did not absolutely control, all ecclesiastical patronage, a power which, as opportunity arose, they used to fill the bench of bishops with reliable sympathizers. One reformer, Thomas Goodrich, had already been appointed to Ely in March 1534. Death and the deprivation of two Italian absentees freed four sees in 1535, all of which went to men of the advanced sort—Nicholas Shaxton at Salisbury, Hugh Latimer at Worcester, Edward Foxe at Hereford, and John Hilsey at Rochester. Not that the reformers always won. When that embattled conservative, Richard Nixe, died early in 1536 to vacate Norwich, room was found for William Rugge; a little later another respected conservative of advanced years, Robert Sherbourn of Chichester, resigned under pressure to make way for Richard Sampson; and neither Rugge nor Sampson, loyal adherents of the royal supremacy, followed the Cromwell-Cranmer line with anything but reluctance. Still, the bench tilted heavily towards reform in those years, even in Wales where William Barlow, a friend of Robert Barnes, got St David's in 1536, and Robert Holgate, urgently pushed by Hilsey, succeeded Catherine's Spanish confessor at Llandaff in 1537.

As vicegerent Cromwell resurrected Wolsey's legatine organization and built it into a regular office which handled much spiritual jurisdiction and superseded episcopal autonomy, though he was careful not to repeat Wolsey's mistake of alienating the bishops by robbing them of their profits. Exercising the authority expressly bestowed by the Act of Supremacy, he undertook a general visitation of the Church during which episcopal powers were automatically suspended, but he also for a while inhibited his subordinates' jurisdiction in probate and other matters. When these powers—those of visitation excepted—were gradually restored by special licence from late in 1535 onwards, the reason given was Cromwell's inability to add such massive further tasks to his other burdens of office, but this restoration itself achieved the end intended: the licences acted as reminders that all episcopal power was now derived solely from the supreme head, a truth sworn to by every bishop at his consecration. The point once made, Cromwell allowed the vicegerency to slip into the shadows, never quite inactive and always available, the physical embodiment of the new order and the sole office to unite the two provinces of the English Church.

Thus the ruling order looked likely to fulfil the hopes of those who had propagated criticisms of the Church and to tackle the problems long since vociferously identified. And indeed, a number of fundamental problems rapidly attracted attention. The law of the Church stood high among them—that law which the Commons' Supplication had denounced as alien and incomprehensible, and which, since it came from Rome, needed reconsidering in the light of the doctrine that only laws made or formally received in England had any validity there. The Act for the Submission of the Clergy had provided for a royal commission of thirty-two—sixteen members of the two Houses of Parliament and sixteen representatives of the clergy—which was to review and revise the canon law; their conclusions were to receive authority by letters patent under the great seal. When no action resulted, Parliament reaffirmed the provision in 1536 and again in 1544, and this last enactment did produce the commission and a report. However, long before this Cromwell had gone ahead without a royal commission when he endeavoured to prepare the ground by means of a steering committee of four church lawyers who completed their gigantic task by October 1535.[1] Such haste did little good: the committee's report was put by, the full commission was postponed, and the canon law of the Church of England remained in a state of uncertainty aggravated by Cromwell's decision, in the summer of 1535, to terminate its study at the universities. Instead of reform this law thus underwent slow strangulation, a fate which probably reflects Cromwell's opinion of it better than the proposed refurbishing would have done.

In any case, the question of the law depended on the fate of the church courts; only if they continued to exist would there be a need for a revised set of canons, and attacks on them had been loud and frequent for decades. In 1534 a popular statute reduced their independence in heresy trials by demanding indictment at common law before proceedings in the bishop's court. Their fate apparently trembled in the balance during 1535. In July and August, several common lawyers in Cromwell's entourage on his instructions discussed problems of the spiritual jurisdiction with leading ecclesiasti-

[1] F. D. Logan, 'The Henrician Canons', *Bulletin of the Institute of Historical Research* XLVII (1974), pp. 99 ff.

cal lawyers, and one of Cromwell's men came out firmly for the total abolition of this rival set of courts. Others wanted at least to transfer a major part of their sphere of action to the common law. In the event, nothing was done, and to all appearance the church courts continued unaltered, retaining their ancient powers over the sphere of life covered by the medieval canon law. This outcome went contrary to the minds of Cromwellian reformers, of common law-yers, and of the large body of opinion that objected to leaving such personal concerns as matrimonial and testamentary causes in the hands of an unEnglish jurisdiction; it clearly represented a victory for the Henrician clergy whose high view of the supremacy had been in hidden conflict with the attitude coloured by common-law and parliamentary preconceptions throughout the creation of the Church of England in 1534. Of course, it would have been almost inconceivably difficult to incorporate all ecclesiastical law and law enforcement in the ordinary courts of the realm, especially at one blow, but it seems likely that the decision to leave things unaltered was Henry's own. As he saw it, he had taken the pope's place in the Church, and he wanted a Church as papal as possible—organized along traditional lines which testified to the God-granted authority that he believed he possessed.

Outwardly, therefore, the Church of England preserved a fully traditional appearance. In practice, the church courts and officers, while continuing to be much involved with the clergy, rapidly lost their hold on the laity; once again, a revolution was disguised behind a face of sameness. Even the ancient grievance over the payment of tithe received no sort of remedy at this time, although there was some pressure. An act of the Reformation Parliament's last session unequivocally ordered that tithe should universally continue to be paid according to existing custom and went out of its way to denounce objectors as planners of 'detestable enormities and in-juries'. It is true that without tithe it would have been difficult to maintain the parish clergy, but it is also relevant that in many places the tithe was already in the hands of lay farmers. Drastic ideas about solving the Church's problem of worldly corruption by confiscating its endowments and putting the hierarchy on salaries were produced in and for Cromwell's office in 1534, but the official line on tithe suggests that no one seriously intended to undertake such mon-strously vast schemes of reorganization.

However, this did not mean that the wealth of the Church would remain immune to the attacks to which it had been intermittently subjected for some 150 years. The transfer to the Crown of new ecclesiastical taxes called for the establishment of a reliable assess-ment upon which that revenue could be levied—one more complete

than Wolsey's abortive investigation of 1522 and more up to date
than the old papal census of 1291. In January 1535, therefore,
Cromwell equipped himself with comprehensive powers: on the 21st
he obtained a commission to carry out a general visitation, and on
the 30th he issued special commissions to survey all church property.
While the first was for the moment put in cold storage, the second
got going at once and worked extremely hard; though few returns
were in by the set day of 31 May, the bulk had arrived by July. Out
of these reports the government clerks compiled the great *Valor
Ecclesiasticus*, a detailed survey of every spiritual preferment from
episcopal sees to village livings and chantries. The *Valor* has
deficiencies, especially for modern historians asking questions about
population and landholding and farming in which the Henrician
enquiry had no interest, but for what it set out to do exhaustive tests
have confirmed its general reliability. Valuations, especially of land
held in demesne, ran a trifle low, which is not surprising in an age of
inflation; property let to rent was naturally easier to assess precisely.
The achievement stands as a monument to Cromwell's concern for
statistical information behind action, and to the ability of Tudor
governments to carry out large enterprises swiftly and efficiently.
And apart from supplying a basis for taxation, it enabled the Crown
to know what might be got if it was decided to embark upon the sort
of confiscation of church lands which had already taken place in
some Lutheran principalities on the continent.

The *Valor* commissions and the task of converting the realm to an
acceptance of the royal supremacy delayed the execution of
Cromwell's visitatorial commission. Pressed by advisers who feared
that further delay would enable evil-doers to cover up deficiencies,
Cromwell unleashed his visitors in September. Although the secular
clergy received some inspection and the general purpose of the
visitation was kept in mind, it concentrated on the religious houses to
such an extent that later opinion, and the surviving evidence, have
created the supposition that the whole affair was concerned solely
with the monasteries and was exclusively intended as a prelude to
their suppression. Certainty, the visitors' formal report (*comperta*) and
the frequent letters in which they informed Cromwell of their
whirlwind progress confined themselves to this part of the Church.
The visitors in question were not many—four main operators plus a
few others doing the odd bit of visiting. Dr Richard Layton and Dr
Thomas Legh dominated the proceedings, especially in the north,
but John ap Rice, a public notary in Cromwell's service, and Dr
John Tregonwell, the leading civilian of the day, were also very
active. Only Layton was in priest's orders, though all four had
graduated in the canon law.

These men have collected much abuse in the course of the centuries, some of it deserved. Layton, a lively and cynical man, too well enjoyed both a dirty joke and the bullying exercise of power, while Legh, a younger man singularly devoid of humour, oozed self-importance at every pore. However, none of this detracts from their intellectual capacity and administrative competence: they were able and clever. None of them was anxious to give the institutions inspected the benefit of doubt or charity, and they knew that Cromwell wanted adverse reports. In the circumstances, the fact that quite frequently they spoke well of what they saw encourages some belief in their trustworthiness. Outwardly they followed the canonical rules for such visitations, but in their haste, and conscious of their purpose, they cut a lot of corners. They went armed with a questionnaire of articles drafted by Layton, and with a set of injunctions to issue to every community authorized by Cromwell. The articles contained nothing that was not customary in episcopal visitations; all the questions concerning the order, behaviour and property of the house and its inmates were entirely traditional. The injunctions, too, avoided the appearance of innovation; at first sight they did no more than impose the rigorous observance of the rule which the institutions professed themselves bound to obey, apart from (naturally) introducing new points touching the abrogation of Rome and acceptance of the King's supremacy. However, demands that inmates should observe enclaustration to the letter, never leaving the house, or that all women (including old serving women and high-born visitors) should be strictly excluded from male establishments, while fully in accord with the ideal, would, properly enforced, have made the running of the houses impossible and were at least in part designed to drive men into seeking licence to leave the life religious. The injunctions can be read as intended to encourage the voluntary dissolution of monasticism, a possibility already apparent in the trickle of departures and spontaneous liquidations that marked the years preceding the great inquest. The least satisfactory features of the visitation were the speed with which it was carried out (dispensing with much customary care as well as ceremonial) and the evident desire to multiply the mutual accusations already too common in many of these no longer charitable communities.[2]

When the last session of the Reformation Parliament assembled in January 1536, Cromwell had sufficient evidence to show that many

[2]For the Dissolution see in particular the latest and best accounts: M. D. Knowles, *The Religious Orders in England* III, a work of great art but also a very careful discussion of the event and its problems; and Joyce Youings, *The Dissolution of the Monasteries* (1971), which poses new questions and clarifies many issues. While I have in general relied on these guides, I occasionally differ from them in interpretation.

things were amiss with English monasticism, and this was employed to secure the passage of an act which dissolved all houses worth under £200 a year and vested their properties in the crown. Heads of houses were pensioned; other inmates had the choice of transferring to a surviving house or taking a faculty (a licence) to live as secular priests. No choice, of course, was open to nuns. The act empowered the King to exempt any house by letters patent, and some eighty of the approximately 300 affected paid for such temporary survival. There was then a kind of halt. The act itself had erected a barrier against further inroads by justifying the confiscation on the grounds that while the greater houses were well ordered the state of the lesser called for drastic action. Many of the survivors continued to behave as though nothing was likely to happen to them; especially they made every effort to establish good relations with Cromwell. However, there were also signs that the operation was not over. The erection of the Court of Augmentations made little sense if its sole purpose was to be the administration of the small properties raked in in 1536; powerful lay interests were pressing upon the assets of the remaining houses; many of these were 'wasting' their properties by so tying them up as to deprive a potential confiscator of much profit, a practice which seems to have been the occasion for a hypocritical circular from Cromwell in 1538, assuring extant institutions that no wholesale destruction was being planned. Yet the stand-still continued for some eighteen months, in part no doubt because the northern rebellions postponed action, though these also brought in a few houses through the attainder of abbots executed as rebellious traitors. The crucial moment came in December 1537 when the great priory of Lewes in Sussex was induced to surrender to the King, its property being very quickly passed on to Cromwell. This transaction was planned as an experiment in dissolution by agreement which included the decision to offer pensions to all the monks. Manifestly it was by now intended that no houses should be left standing for them to go to.

Thus in 1538–40 all the surviving monastic institutions were dissolved individually, by commissioners sent by the vicar-general, and their properties transferred to the Court of Augmentations whose officers surveyed, administered and if necessary disposed of them. A separate campaign against the orders of friars secured a quite extraordinary rapid collapse, in part at least because the friars most likely to resist had been the most prominent in fighting against the supremacy and had thus been weeded out by the treason law. An act of 1539 confirmed all instruments of surrender and the transfer of the property to the Crown, and by January 1540 the operation was over. Some 800 institutions had vanished in four years. The King's

revenues had been augmented, for the time being, by something like
£90,000 a year, and he was gaining great immediate profit from the
sale of jewels and gold, torn from shrines, and from the valuable lead
taken from roofs. Insofar as so violent a deed could be done considerately, it was—a fact which helps to explain the speed and
smoothness of the operation. The Crown took over not only the assets
but also the liabilities of the monasteries—debts, obligations to
corrodians (holders of life annuities), fixed relations with the existing
tenantry. The Court of Augmentations proved surprisingly efficient.
There was very little resistance and even less reluctance than might
have been expected to leave the enclosed life. Very few monks stood
out against the confiscation. Three abbots—of Colchester, Reading
and Glastonbury—suffered death by execution, but it is not at all
clear in each case why. The common supposition that those notorious trials were intended to discourage resistance in others does not
convince, if only because they took place in November-December
1539 when few houses still stood. Only of Abbot Marshal of Colchester can we be sure that he fell victim to the Dissolution: his
refusal to surrender his house led to an investigation which uncovered a clear case of years of treasonable utterances, and these
might have been overlooked if he had not been so stubborn.
Whether Cooke of Reading and Whiting of Glastonbury were
similarly discovered is not known; other people at this time suffered
in this way without the Dissolution being involved. But it is possible.

The speed with which the whole structure of monasticism—orders
of monks, canons, nuns and friars, and the hospitals of St John of
Jerusalem—vanished from the English scene has naturally led to a
well entrenched opinion that it was all planned from the start, but
the closer investigation of recent years has thrown doubt on this
view. Such once current notions as that Cromwell conceived the idea
years before, while dealing with the houses suppressed by Wolsey, or
that the end of Christchurch, Aldgate (London), surrendered to
Henry in 1532 by agreement, constituted a trial run, cannot be
maintained.[3] But it has been suggested that even in 1535 there was
no fixed intention to put an end to the monasteries; the visitors'
injunctions can be read as testifying to a genuine intent to reform
rather than as a cover for suppression; the act of 1536 hindered the
subsequent proceedings whose haphazardly piecemeal character can
suggest a government driven by stages into actions that had not been
planned at all. There is a late tradition, preserved among the
descendants of Cromwell's friend Thomas Wyatt, that the secretary
did not originally favour dissolution by act of Parliament, preferring

[3] Youings, *Dissolution*, pp. 27 ff. The Aldgate house ran out of livelihood and thus out of the
will to live.

to proceed 'little by little' in order to avoid the sort of resentment he remembered from his days as Wolsey's agent. He allegedly said all this in Council but was overruled by others who looked for quick action.[4] The act of 1536, said there to have been the work of Audley and Rich, was certainly no masterpiece and does not look like the foundation of a well planned operation. It must have been drafted in great haste, for the denunciations upon which its allegations of evil living rested can barely have become available before the bill was introduced in the Lords. However, it is equally doubtful whether anyone could have regarded its artificial and meaningless limitations as representing a final step, while Cromwell's supposed advice (and the story has some ring of truth to it) indicated not that he envisaged a partial dissolution but only that he expected to obtain the total suppression of monasticism by persuasion, 'seeing how horrible this kind of religion is, and how odious to the wiser sort of people'. In effect, the course he allegedly advocated came to be adopted, successfully, from late in 1537 onwards.

There are two grounds that make it difficult to suppose that the government seriously meant to stop short at the removal of the lesser houses and contemplated reforming the greater. One, perhaps the less convincing, involves the fate of the monastic property. If, as is widely believed, the Dissolution arose almost exclusively from Cromwell's promise to make the King unprecedently rich, the steps of 1536 cannot be said to have fulfilled that ambition. Even if rather less weight is placed on the financial motives ascribed to Cromwell and Henry, it is plain that others would not have rested content with so small an inroad into the wealth of the Church. The laity's hunger for ecclesiastical lands, which in course of time turned out to be unsatisfied by the vast meal of monastic properties, certainly demanded that meal as the minimum of appeasement. And secondly, we know that by the time of the first assault the whole institution had come under principled attack in Cromwell's own circle. Though one may suspect 'Erasmian' influences here—Erasmus had frequently and forcefully expressed his dislike of all forms of enclosed religion—the indications identify more of a Cromwellian than a humanist evangelism behind the drive. When Starkey wrote his dialogue at Padua he (who knew his Erasmus) thought in terms of reforming rather than removing monasticism; when he came to revise the manuscript in January 1535, the very month that Cromwell settled to the task of overhauling the Church, he inserted proposals for using monastic property (and he specified two 'greater' houses) for the endowment of education. A little later, addressing Henry VIII, Starkey provided the justificatory principle for total

[4] *The Papers of George Wyatt, Esquire*, edited by D. M. Loades (1968), p. 159.

dissolution. Against the argument that the destruction contravened the intentions of founders and thus constituted an unjust invasion of both property rights and testamentary dispositions, he maintained that founders had meant to serve a social pupose, namely the spiritual welfare of the realm, which was no longer wanted in modern conditions. It was therefore right to break their wills since those intentions had been perverted by the present-day users of the property, whereas the original purpose could be suitably served again if the wealth was applied to a form of social amelioration now more desirable, especially education. Starkey, perfectly sincere and by no means original in this argument, thus testified to the fact that the Cromwell group objected to the false use of resources supposedly dedicated to now defunct spiritual ends and wished to find right spiritual ends for them instead.

The monasteries were therefore destroyed in part because the secularization of their possessions was the least that lay demand—royal and private—would rest satisfied with, but also because the government stood under the guidance of men who disapproved of them in principle and had hopes of better uses for so much locked-up wealth. Whether there was ever any prospect of fulfilling those hopes in the face of the former motive is another matter, but either way the end of the whole institution was intended from the first: only the manner of proceeding remained in doubt. I may add that I am not altogether convinced by those who deny that anyone could have regarded the orders as dangerous to the anti-papal revolution. True, their members were as English as the seculars and the laity; true, obdurate resistance to the supremacy was not widespread even among them. Yet the links between the orders, especially those exempt from episcopal supervision, and the international Church remained strong, and the evidence shows that the religious produced more opponents of the King's proceedings than any other sector of the nation. But whether anyone seriously believed that the monasteries formed a bastion of popery, it is clear that those who saw in them an obstacle to the reform of religion, and in the preservation of their wealth an obstacle to social reform, were right: and in 1536–40 these were the people who dominated English politics. The gentry's cry for the lands at first advanced and ultimately frustrated these reforming ambitions.

In Ireland, both the situation and the action taken looked super-ficially different from what happened in England.[5] Though the monastic orders seem to have been pretty moribund, the friars had passed through a recent revival, in marked contrast to their English brethren; the readiness with which so many of these latter moved

[5] B. Bradshaw, *The Dissolution of the Religious Orders in Ireland under Henry VIII* (1974).

into the reformed camp was missing in the other island. Nor was behaviour quite so worldly or so scandalous there; and because the Irish houses owned nothing like so much wealth they attracted far less greedy hostility from the laity. Taken together with the fact that when a suppression bill was introduced into the Dublin Parliament in September 1536 it was rejected out of hand, the traditional view that the Irish nation wanted to preserve monasticism and expressed here its opposition to the royal supremacy becomes understandable. It is nevertheless wrong. The opposition had quite different things in mind—fear that the power structure of the Pale might be disrupted by the intrusion of Cromwell's centralizing administrators, and resentment at the financial demands of the same session. The suppression bill became the means with which the Anglo-Irish hoped to resist Cromwell's policy, and in measure they succeeded. Once Henry had accepted the need to come to terms with Barnewall and the gentry of the Pale and had abated his financial demands,[6] the bill passed quickly enough, in October 1537; and in the Pale at least the dissolution was well under way before that passage was achieved.

During 1538, Archbishop George Brown, an ex-friar appointed to Dublin early in 1536, began an energetic campaign against the friars, and during 1539–40 a serious effort was made to extend the suppression into the crown territories. During the 1540s, the conciliatory policy pursued by the new deputy, Sir Anthony St Leger, even brought some parts of Gaelic Ireland into compliance. However, while all Ireland accepted the royal supremacy before the end of Henry's reign, the dissolution of the monasteries was never carried through completely or systematically. The investigating commissions never even visited nearly half the 140 regular communities and three fifths of the 200 friaries; and visitation was by no means equal to dissolution. The reason for this lay simply in the administrative problem of governing Ireland. Where English rule held sway the orders disappeared; in the independent regions, though ownership of property was often secularized, the communities themselves generally remained in existence, as leaseholders of the new lay lords. This outcome must reflect some attachment to the old religion in Irish Ireland, but neither the judgement that survival of the orders there laid foundations for effective resistance to the English nor the regrets expressed at what was lost in the parts where suppression occurred have found favour with the only scholar who has studied the problem systematically.[7] In the reign of Henry VIII, Irish monasticism was in no state to offer services worth preserving or to invigorate Irish resistance. In the history of Ireland,

---

[6] See above, p. 209.
[7] Bradshaw, *Dissolution*, chapter 12.

the Dissolution constituted not a catastrophe but almost a minor
episode; paradoxically, it seems to have been required there for
improvements in economic conditions and ultimately in Catholic
spirituality, just as national wealth and the Protestant religion
benefited from it in England.

How much difference did the Dissolution actually make in
England? The rapid destruction of so many institutions, established
for centuries in towns and countryside, left obvious gaps both
palpable and intangible. Some of the buildings survived for new
uses. At Tewkesbury, the town bought the priory church for the
parish; some purchasers turned monastic structures into manor
houses; William Stumpe converted both Malmesbury and Osney
abbeys into clothing factories. Nevertheless, it was amazing to see
how quickly venerable buildings fell into ruins, largely because the
removal of the lead from the roofs let in the weather but also because
the builders of the new houses used the walls for quarries. Within
some two generations, the sight of these ruins helped to bring on
feelings of deep regret and real fears of sacrilege, feelings of which at
the time no trace manifested itself. Nearly everywhere, the disappearance of familiar communities and imposing structures was
accepted with revealing equanimity. There were exceptions; in the
north, in particular, resentment flared up here and there, and the
Duchy of Lancaster felt compelled to impose on new owners those
duties of hospitality and guidance to travellers which such houses as
Cockersand and Cartmel had discharged on the lonely shores of the
northwest. But in general the nation's reaction makes it plain that
the monastic ideal and practice had ceased to have any hold on
people's minds and hearts. It is not really possible to determine
whether the termination of the monastic devotion constituted a felt
loss. No doubt there were those who lamented the passing of the
monks and the end of their prayers, but spiritually the English
orders, with the exception of the Carthusians and the stricter friars,
had long been of little worth. Declining numbers, absence of true
vocations, the general permeation of a weak worldliness, had testified to the collapse of the ideal well before its physical destruction.
Genuine corruption existed, though it was not so universal or mostly
so drastic as the legend would have it; what really emerged from the
visitation was a strong smell of embittered internal relations and the
fact that few houses could claim to differ significantly in holiness or
manner of life from the laity with whom their daily relations were so
dangerously close. Those like Cromwell, Cranmer and Latimer who
regarded the whole thing as a stronghold of superstition believed
that the Dissolution opened the way to a revived spirituality, a truer
commonwealth in which there were no specialists in salvation but

only Christians. The monasteries may not have been active hearths of the old religion, but it remains true that the new religion, the Reformation, could not advance until these symbols of salvation by works were out of the way.

In course of those four years, some 9,000 religious, plus an unknown number of lay attendants and servants, were uprooted from home and function. Some, especially the younger and more recent recruits, are known to have welcomed the change, but there is no reason to think that to the vast majority it was anything but hateful and terrible. The official policy of providing either a pension or a chance to take a cure of souls offered a little protection. Pensions fell very unevenly, depending as they did on the wealth of the house to which the pensioner had belonged. Superiors generally did well enough, provided they cooperated willingly in the surrender of their houses, though even here the differences could be striking: the prior of Montacute (Somerset) received £100 a year, in all conscience a reasonable sufficiency equivalent to the income of a middling gentleman, but the abbot of Ramsey (Huntingdonshire) retired on £266 13s 4d. Ordinary monks usually had to make do with sums below £10, the average before tax deductions running at close to £6, while nuns got less and friars nothing. £5 a year constituted just about the minimum for subsistence. The pensions were paid directly by the Court of Augmentations even when the lands on which they were charged had passed out of crown hands, with the result that payments continued regular until the collapse of government finance in the reign of Edward VI. They were, of course, forfeited if the recipient found ecclesiastical preferment. It has proved impossible to trace the fortunes of more than a small number of those who opted for faculties, but there are some indications that they were quickly absorbed into livings and posts of one kind and another. It appears that the onset of the Reformation led to a drastic fall in the numbers of new ordinations during the 1540s, so that only the supply of priests from the religious houses postponed the problem of filling vacancies until the reign of Elizabeth. However, many ex-monks seem to have found refuge as chantry and chapel priests, so that the further confiscations of 1547 (when the pensions assigned ran lower still) came as a very bad blow. Such bald summaries must not hide the miseries of individuals, even though the old stories of destitute fathers dying in ditches were nonsense. The Dissolution obviously devastated, or at least dreadfully complicated, the lives of many men and women, in spite of the fact that it was carried through with some humanity, much careful scruple, and surprising ease. What can be said with some confidence is that attempts to revive monasticism in the reign of Mary met with minimal response.

The Reformation benefited from the Dissolution: did reform? As we have seen, the attack was promoted by men who believed that monastic wealth could be put to better use in Church and commonwealth, but here the direct profit was small indeed. Against the loss of culture and learning which the destruction of much beauty entailed, the gains were tiny. Monastic architecture was among the glories of England, and the greater houses in particular had shared in the recent rebuilding boom; nearly all this vanished—splendid late Gothic choirs, much fine glass, outstanding examples of the jeweller's and goldsmith's arts. Though the new possessors were in due course to supply a sort of substitute in the great houses that arose on much monastic land, this took time; and such equations are in any case meaningless. The Dissolution involved the destruction of many libraries, partly by casual neglect and partly by deliberate attacks on 'popish' books of devotion, theology and law. Something was saved by the labours of John Leland (1502–52), the product of humanist instruction at Cambridge, Oxford and Paris. In 1533 he was commissioned to investigate monastic and college libraries for ancient writers, an enterprise which in the typical Cromwell manner probably combined the search for an historic basis to the new order with a disinterested concern for learning; the experience inspired him to undertake years of arduous travel to rescue invaluable volumes from dissolved houses. A good quantity arrived in the King's library. There is no knowing how much Leland saved; at any rate, driven on by personal initiative and enthusiasm, he did a herculean job, and the revival of antiquarian learning which was to blossom in the second half of the century owed much to him both as a preserver and a student.[8]

The great plans for educational endowment, however, came to very little. It is now accepted that the monasteries of the early sixteenth century played a small part in the supply of schooling either elementary or advanced; they made their chief contribution to learning by maintaining scholars at the universities. Here Cromwell tried to fill a gap when in his Injunctions of 1536 he ordered all clergy possessed of wealthier livings to establish such stipendia at the rate of one scholar for every £100 of income, though the order does not appear to have had much effect. Cromwell, and others, were also privately supporting university students in quite impressive numbers, but it is likely that the Dissolution for a time reduced the supply of studentships. Nor do we know of a single school founded immediately upon the transfer of the properties, though in the course of

[8]For the activities of Leland and his friend John Bale see M. McKisack, *Medieval History in the Tudor Age* (1971), chapter 1, and A. B. Emden, *Biographical Register of the University of Oxford, 1501–40* (1974).

time, from Edward VI's reign onwards, ex-monastic wealth contributed notably to the great wave of educational reform and expansion which by the 1620s had transformed the structure of English
schooling and belatedly fulfilled the ambitions of the Henrician
humanists. Henry himself, urged on by others, did something for the
universities when he used some of the religious lands to re-endow
Wolsey's college at Oxford, finally refounded as Christ Church in
1546, and to augment the endowment of his new college (Trinity) at
Cambridge, created in the same year by throwing together two small
foundations.[9] Private enterprise was in the future to invest in
university education much money that had once belonged to the
monasteries, but the immediate result of the Dissolution was to arrest
rather than to advance the application of ecclesiastical wealth to
educational reform. Cromwell received representations and particular schemes, and he had his own plans, but the pressure of affairs
prevented their immediate realization.

Somewhat surprisingly, the great change-over in ownership made
least difference where one might have expected the most drastic
consequences—in the experience of those who exchanged one lord
for another. At one time, sentimentality supposed that the monks
were especially kindly landlords, content with traditional arrangements, unwilling to squeeze profits from their possessions, considerate to the poor, the widows and orphans. This fond notion
found support in the quickly growing disillusionment after the
Dissolution which cast an evening glow over the last days of the
sweet birds singing in their now ruined choirs. Later, robust common
sense suggested that, like all those who have to act as trustees for
institutional property, the monasteries were bound to exploit the
market with exceptional intensity, a view which drew sustenance
from contemporary complaints before the Dissolution. Sentimentality and robust common sense seem both to have got it
wrong. The facts indicate that no useful distinction can be made
between ecclesiastical and lay possessors: the houses behaved like
everybody else who owed his wealth to landownership. The bulk of
the lands were let on leases of customary length, and exploitation
concentrated on increasing entry fines both on leaseholds and
copyholds rather than on raising rents which generally were in any
case fixed by binding custom.[10] Enclosure and sheepfarming were
practised where suitable, and though the houses, for the supply of

[9] These colleges were the only outcome of intense efforts made by humanist members of the
universities and the Privy Council from 1544 onwards; Joan Simon, *Education and Society in
Tudor England* (1966), pp. 21 ff.

[10] Joyce Youings, in *Agrarian History* IV, pp. 306–55. E. Kerridge's *Agrarian Problems of the
Sixteenth Century and After* (1969) is fundamental to an understanding of all questions touching
landownership and tenancy.

their establishments, retained rather more land in demesne than was usual, they too got much of their food and fuel by purchase in the market. The twenty buoyant agrarian years after about 1505 saw the managers of monastic property join in the general enterprise; thereafter they shared in the relative retreat from development.

The approaching doom had one interesting consequence. Down to about 1535 monastic tenants came mostly from the yeomanry—men farming for their own maintenance and advancement. Thereafter an increasing number of leases, often on rather advantageous terms (long leases at fixed rents), were granted to the gentry, commonly the neighbouring gentry whose good will grew more valuable as the reforming government's intentions became plainer. To judge from Cromwell's postbag, many such gentlemen wrote loyally on behalf of their convenient friends, though in the end it all did no good. When the Dissolution transferred the lands to the King, he found a high proportion securely in the hands of considerable proprietors whose leasehold rights were confirmed in the very acts that arranged the new settlement. What the Crown got at the Dissolution (apart from once-for-all windfalls like lead and jewels) was an enormous fixed rent-roll, rated somewhat below market values, from rural and urban properties, not a vast unencumbered estate awaiting exploitation.

Nevertheless, this was new wealth which might have made the monarchy independent of taxation; as is well known, it was all 'squandered' in a very short time. Precise calculations of the disposal are difficult and in part impossible. Some lands passed more than once through the market. Thus the large estate accumulated by Thomas Cromwell returned to the Crown at his attainder in 1540, to become once more available for sale, and the same thing happened to a good many other properties through escheat and forfeiture. It is not always possible to know whether a grant (all transfers were in form grants by the Crown) constituted a sale or a free gift. From 1547, when all crown lands were united in the charge of the reformed Court of Augmentations and their management was re-organized on a county basis, it becomes very difficult to distinguish ex-monastic property from the rest. The ultimate disposal into new ownership involved innumerable further transactions between private parties which have left very little record in the government archives and only the most patchy deposit elsewhere. Despite the intensive research of recent years—which at least has disproved some confident older generalizations—we still lack anything resembling detailed knowledge for too many regions. In the face of such problems, all summarizing statements are no doubt chancy, but some things have been established quite securely, and in the main they contradict classical views, such as R. H. Tawney's, of the great transfer.[11]

It is, in the first place, perfectly plain that neither Cromwell nor Henry ever meant to retain all the properties in direct crown management. The Crown needed cash in hand, which demanded the immediate liquidation of at least some of the new assets, while the expectations of the landed classes, long anxious to get their hands on all that mortmain property, even received favourable mention in the first act of dissolution. As the duke of Norfolk put it, in September 1536 when absence from court hampered his prospects, 'the time of sowing is at hand, and every other nobleman has already his portion.' This was to exaggerate, but from 28 May 1536 onwards, when Sir Richard Rich, now chancellor of Augmentations, used his favourable position to obtain the first grant of the site of a monastery, the flow of property out of the Crown's hands grew ever more voluminous. By December 1539, when Cromwell announced a more systematic policy by getting a commission to himself and Rich to sell lands to the yearly value of £6,000, altogether 234 grants had been made. Among these early ones, a large number were gifts—rewards to well placed government servants like the lord privy seal himself. Organized selling began in 1539. By 1558 no fewer than twenty-one commissions for sales had issued, a bewildering confusion which no one has yet sorted out. Though Cromwell plainly thought of his commission as a means for controlling the hitherto haphazard outflow, the urgent needs of war finance accelerated activity enormously after his death. The first peak in sales came in 1542–4, and by Henry's death about half the new wealth had been disposed of. Edward VI's minority provided a happy time for greedy courtiers and hangers-on, and when Elizabeth came to the throne she retained at best a quarter of the great estate that had been nationalized in 1536–40. If the intention had been to found the monarchy firmly on the rock of a vast complex of crown lands alone, it was quickly defeated by this 'squandering'. For myself I doubt whether Cromwell ever entertained any such ideas: when the King's income from the new source stood at its height, in 1539–40, he energetically sought a parliamentary subsidy, having to face the obvious argument that after all these recent acquisitions there should have been no need for such taxation. It looks rather as though what was planned was judicious unloading, while the reforming party certainly wanted to use more of the new resources for constructive renewal than ultimately remained available.

---

[11] For the best recent summary see Youings, *Dissolution*, pp. 117 ff.; also the pioneering article by H. J. Habakkuk, 'The Market for Monastic Property', *Economic History Review* 1st series, x (1957–8), pp. 362 ff.

In any case, 'squandering' is not the right term for what happened, at any rate during Henry's reign. Contrary to what might have been expected, the market for land stood up well to the extraordinary supply. Originally lands were sold at twenty years' purchase for manorial and fifteen years' for urban property,[12] the normal terms of the day; as inflation rendered the old assessments of annual value out of date, the sellers easily pushed up sales terms, ultimately to thirty years' purchase. At first all sales reserved to the Crown a yearly rent of ten per cent of the annual value, by way of compensation for the clerical tenth lost when ownership moved from spiritual persons to lay; but here the buyers' market had some effect when these rents were first sold off (also at twenty years' purchase) and ultimately omitted from conditions of sale. The original determination to sell on tenure by knight's service (which subjected the ex-monastic lands to the feudal fiscal prerogative and greatly increased the reach of the Court of Wards) was not finally abandoned despite objections until 1548 when lands came to be granted 'as of our manor of Greenwich', a formula which hid the bestowal of absolute freehold with no strings attached.[13] Down to 1547, the Crown made about £800,000 out of the sales, and in most cases half the purchase price was paid on the nail, the rest being demanded in short-term instalments. Thus the transactions brought cash immediately and in quantity to the royal coffers, a most unusual experience in the sixteenth century. After 1540, outright gifts grew very rare. Generally speaking, then, the sales policy produced very respectable results in massive liquidity, while the revenues of the Court of Augmentations, even apart from sales money, remained buoyant until at least 1546. The real charge of mismanagement must fall not on the sales as such but on the use to which the money was put; wasted recklessly on Henry's wars it did no good, but that is not to say that realization of wealth in this fashion, in any case necessary because of the public demand, was fundamentally wrong. The real disasters happened after 1547 when freedom from royal control ensured that the redistribution should cease to benefit the vendor adequately.

The greatest unsolved mystery attending these events is in fact the ability of purchasers to raise so vast an amount of money in ready cash. That it was done is conclusively proved by the accounts of the treasurer of Augmentations; where it all came from remains unknown. In a land market quite active enough even before the

---

[12] That is, twenty or fifteen times the annual value of the property as assessed by the Court of Augmentations.
[13] J. Hurstfield, 'The Greenwich Tenures of the Reign of Edward VI', *Law Quarterly Review* (1949), pp. 72 ff.

Dissolution, people had become adept at raising the wind, but the investment of the 1540s was so much more enormous than anything ever seen before that one must postulate accumulated reserves and borrowing facilities really beyond anything supported by the evidence. It is no wonder that historians have taken refuge in supposing that massive wealth not derived from land was being released into the purchase of estates; it has been taken for granted that the great transfer achieved a social revolution by infusing into the body of landowners an overwhelming number of 'new men'—merchants, lawyers, perhaps yeomen. Such cases did, of course, occur; when something like a fifth of England's cultivated land changed hands, often several times, in the course of a generation, members of those sectors of the population were bound to take a share of the property. At one time it was thought that the money was invested mainly by speculators who held for a rise in values and thus distributed the drain on monetary resources over the years, but though some occasional speculation of this sort may have happened, the conclusion rested on a misunderstanding. Those supposed speculators were agents who bought multiple (often small) properties on behalf of clients to whom they 'resold' at once;[14] scattered purchasers discovered, in the employment for this purpose of Augmentation officials and London attorneys, convenient savings in expenses as well as the useful mobilization of expert advice. Much of the purchase money may well have come out of the profits of government service, a reflection on the virtues of service under the Crown but also a way of restoring to it what had, sometimes deviously, been abstracted in earlier years.

We do by now know a fair amount about the ultimate new owners of monastic lands, and the general conclusion must be that they were not in any real sense 'new men'. The largest share went to the established landed gentry, often men who as stewards of monasteries had been best placed to know what to buy. Founder's kin took trouble to 'recover' what their ancestors, often very remote and collateral, had bestowed upon the Church. Gentlemen improved their estates by rounding off and adding long coveted neighbouring pieces; often they did this by turning conventual leases into freehold, so that in many cases not even the effective occupation of the land changed at all. In addition, new estates were certainly created, mostly by younger sons of gentle families whom primogeniture would otherwise have forced off the land; lawyers, especially, usually men of landed descent, exploited the opportunity to return to the land, investing there the profits of the law. What happened was

[14] Resales depended on licences to alienate, another source of profit to the crown created by the sales policy.

neither social revolution nor even major transformation, but a
notable acceleration of habits long established. The landowning
classes and their offspring (more numerous now in this age of an
expanding population) had long operated an active market in land,
to extend and consolidate properties or create new ones; the Dissolution and dispersal simply made possible an enormous extension of
activities which in themselves were not new and did not alter the
structure of the lay sector of the landowning classes. Those long-
standing urgent demands for more which the men of property had
uttered over and over again found satisfaction; the redistribution
only very rarely gave his chance to a man who had never previously
been in the way of owning land. This also disposes of the well
entrenched conviction that the Dissolution everywhere introduced
owners who had no ties with land and tenantry—commercially
active exploiters superseding the paternalists of 'feudalism'. If commercial exploitation increased after 1540 this was because inflation
forced lords increasingly to maximize profits; the practices resorted
to—rack-renting, raising entry fines, farming for the market in wool
and foodstuffs, sale of timber and extraction of minerals—were none
of them at all new, having been employed by people sufficiently well
placed to find them useful long before 1540; those socially most
dangerous (threats to tenants' rights) were in addition severely
limited by the force of the customary law.

Nevertheless, the drastic expansion of opportunities had some
effects. Obviously, the great loser was the Church which as a body
ceased to be the largest landowner in England. The Crown took cash
rather than real estate, though it should not be forgotten that the
crown lands acquired a residual permanent addition, too. It was the
whole body of lay landowners who moved into the vacant place of
ascendancy, and here it is significant that though some very large
estates were built up—few permanently, as political fortunes and
economic difficulties took their toll—the main result of the redistribution was to increase the size and number of middling estates.
It is in this sense that the phrase 'the rise of the gentry' has some
meaning: it was in the hands of the greater and middle gentry,
somewhat augmented from below, that the main part of the lands
finished up. There were simply now a good many more established
landowners. And this was quickly reflected in the structure of shire
society, that ultimate foundation of English politics and government.
The Dissolution removed one standard component from that society:
until 1540, the abbots and priors of especially the greater houses had
formed an important part of the county aristocracy, their houses
hospitable centres for local politics and social life. During the
century after 1540 a good many localities witnessed the emergence of

societies dominated by clusters of powerful gentry families, often able to overcome even the traditional ascendancy of a local noble dynasty. Power and influence, and ambition too, became diffused through a larger sector of the political nation. Nowhere do we see sudden or conscious transformations, but subtle shifts occur everywhere as hitherto lesser potentates take a grip on local affairs and organize their newly powerful alliances and enmities on the basis of additional wealth. In the hierarchic pyramid of the sixteenth-century nation, the top rank contracted with the disappearance of so many spiritual magnates, while the layer immediately beneath expanded in numbers, individual wealth, and therefore influence. There was neither decline of the aristocracy nor rise of the gentry, but there was an adjustment within the aristocratic sector away from the predominance of the few to a general power vested in larger numbers. The fact that in an age of inflation the smaller and more compact estates offered better opportunities for profitable exploitation than did the over-extended and often scattered properties of the great possessors reinforced the economic and political consequences of this redistribution of landed wealth. But there was no social revolution.

11 The First Crisis of the Reformation

I

Catherine of Aragon died on 7 January 1536. The inevitable rumours that she had been poisoned may be discounted. Though she had long ceased to play any public role, her death demonstrated her continued involuntary influence on affairs, for it unleashed six months of crisis at the heart of English politics. Henry celebrated the news, dressed in his favourite yellow: 'now we shall not have war,' he said, but 'now I can be rid of Anne,' he thought. His devotion to Anne Boleyn had not long survived marriage; her liveliness turned out to cover a temperament neither peaceful nor accommodating, and she could be both jealous and mocking. Worst of all, of course, was her failure to produce the much desired male heir. In January 1536 she was pregnant again, but she miscarried—of a boy—on the 29th, a tragedy which sealed her fate. The decline of Anne's influence had been apparent to observers for some months, and by early 1536 the King was known to be in pursuit of yet another lady of the court, Jane Seymour, twenty-five years old, the daughter of a Somerset squire with two ambitious sons. To judge from her portraits, she had little enough going for her, but as Anne in her fear grew more strident and tiresome the very lack of colour cultivated by her new rival worked well with Henry who, as so often, could not understand why he should be so much troubled in his private life.

If Anne Boleyn was to go, the political consequences, especially for all the contenders for power under the King, reached far. As Queen, she had only succeeded in adding to the enemies she had gathered during her rise to prominence, but the Boleyn faction was well entrenched in the Privy Chamber.[1] That centre of power, however, also still harboured a strong body of Aragonese supporters. Among the King's ministers, Norfolk had come to resent his niece's

---

[1] See E. W. Ives, 'Faction at the Court of Henry VIII: the Fall of Anne Boleyn', *History* XLVII (1972), pp. 49 ff. I have also had the benefit of reading an unpublished paper by Dr D. R. Starkey on these faction battles which emphasizes the role of the Privy Chamber, and to which this account stands much indebted.

arrogance, while Suffolk, influenced by his wife, hated her; some councillors had never fully accepted the events of the last five years, and she had fallen out with Cromwell. Her approaching fall raised two immediate problems—relations with the Emperor and France, and the question of the succession.

Down to the end of 1535, English foreign policy had been determined by apprehensions of direct action from Charles V, and the Boleyns had always favoured the French alliance which also suited Norfolk who drew a useful pension from Francis I. Cromwell, anxious both for peace and the Netherlands trade, preferred a policy of relative accommodation with Charles, and in early 1536 this became a real possibility. Not only was Catherine gone, so that the imperial ambassador's frequent appeals for military intervention to restore her had lost their point, but it became clear from January onwards that war was about to break out again between Habsburg and Valois, restoring to England something of the freedom of action enjoyed in the age of Wolsey. By March Francis had made sure of war by occupying Savoy and renewing the French claim to Milan. He expected English assistance in recompense for the help he had provided during the crisis of the break with Rome, but this was never on the cards; instead Cromwell, at first under Henry's instructions, opened negotiations for better relations with the Emperor. The story of these dealings has always been told in total reliance on the reports of Eustace Chapuys who displays a perfect trust in Cromwell's confidential conversation that seems a little rash. It is clear enough that Cromwell was serious about lessening the tension and also about drawing away from France, and it is clear too that at a crucial moment he was frustrated by a sudden turn-about on the King's part which took everybody by surprise. But it also looks very much as though Cromwell was using Chapuys, as during these months he was using everybody else, in the most devious and subtle manoeuvres of his career. He was fighting for power, even survival, and he was fighting for the continuance of his policy. He had won freedom for the reform, against many of Henry's entrenched instincts, by allying with the Boleyns; now he needed to extract himself from that alliance, assist Henry to free himself, do all this with the aid of factions fiercely opposed to him and his policy, and yet save the political causes which he wished to promote. The manner in which he did it testifies to the highest political skill as well as to a capacity to act without scruple which actually he used rarely.

The need for such conduct arose out of the second problem, that of the succession. If Anne was thrown over, the infant Princess Elizabeth would no longer be available, and the claims of the Princess Mary, nearly twenty years old and thus capable both of ruling and of asserting a right to rule if the King should die, became realistic. Support for her gathered strength in the wake of her mother's death. The Aragonese faction, especially men of the older generation like Lords Darcy and Hussey, concentrated on the only thing left to it, the promotion of the princess's interests; and the anti-Boleyn factions, including such members of the older nobility as the earl of Northumberland and the marquess of Exeter, rallied to the cause. By February–March, the forces of Anne's enemies were marshalled behind the double purpose of pushing Jane Seymour into the King's arms and reconciling Henry with Mary, in hopes of achieving the destruction of Anne who herself, reading the signs, made an abortive attempt at peace with the much tried princess. But it was only when Cromwell entered the lists that the inept plotting of the factions suddenly became purposeful. He later told Chapuys that he made up his mind to join the fight against Anne when, on April 18th, the King's infuriating change of mind showed him the impossibility of coming to terms with the Emperor so long as the Boleyns and Norfolk promoted amity with France; but though the dates fit after a fashion he was probably (as so often) flattering the ambassador's self-esteem. He had read the situation well before this and made up his mind, but he clearly let action wait until the intensive diplomacy of those weeks should show its outcome.

The easiest and favoured way to get rid of Anne lay in yet another divorce, and in the end, on 17 May, Cranmer pronounced sentence of one, based on the King's earlier relations with her sister which had once more created a canonical impediment to marriage. Thus the stories, so hotly denied when they were used by Catherine's supporters to argue against the Boleyn marriage, were in the end allowed to serve the new situation. But Anne was not merely divorced: she was executed in a sensational scandal that 'proved' her guilty of multiple adultery and even incest, and that made the King appear an unconscionable cuckold. Why? Henry's savagery, which played its part, does not explain everything. Of course, he had to consent to the judicial murder of his consort, and properly handled he could be relied upon to do so. The question is why her enemies pursued her to the death. In part, no doubt, the great hatred she had roused by her triumph over Catherine's virtue and by her tactless and overbearing behaviour in power demanded no less. There need also be no doubt that she would not have accepted a divorce meekly. Even in decline she was far from powerless, and the attack on her could not expect to get away with less than war to the knife. Above all, however, it appears that Cromwell saw a chance of removing from the public scene two strong interests that hampered his ascendancy—the Boleyns, whose attachment to reform now formed an obstacle to proceeding with it, and the old Catholics who would resist it anyway. Cromwell could not afford to do less than remove his rivals for good if he was to survive in power and have the free use of it. Thus he needed to construct a case which would vilify Anne sufficiently to drive Henry into wanting to kill her. Anne's somewhat easy virtue and the free manners of the English court provided the opportunity, and so did the unfortunate inclination of Anne and her friends to mock the King behind his back.

The assault began openly on 24 April when a commission was appointed to investigate the conduct of the Queen and of certain courtiers. Three days later, less than a fortnight after the dissolution of the Reformation Parliament, writs went out summoning a new one which (as was stated at its opening on 8 June) was intended to deal solely with the fall of Anne and its consequences. By 27 April, therefore, before the so-called evidence was obtained, Henry and Cromwell knew what the outcome must be. The terror struck swiftly. Between 30 April and 6 May, all the suspects went to the Tower; interrogation was perfunctory, though Cromwell seems to have got something out of the weak link, the court musician Mark Smeaton, by threats of torture; the commoners were tried on the 12th, Anne and her brother George Lord Rochford on the 15th; five men died by the axe on the 17th and the Queen by the sword on the 18th. All were sentenced for treasonable adultery. There died Lord Rochford (who defended himself brilliantly against the preposterous charge of incest and even on the scaffold refused to speak the conventional words of repentance), Henry Norris, Sir Francis Weston and William Brereton, all prominent members of the Privy Chamber, as well as poor Smeaton, a pawn in the game. Anne herself to the end preserved her individuality in a way that makes one feel a much higher respect for her than all the things she did in the days of good fortune: sometimes hysterical but at heart deeply contemptuous of the plotters who had brought her down, she went to her death with a brittly gay display of stoicism. It had no effect on Henry who concluded a formal betrothal with Jane Seymour on the day after Anne's execution and married her on 30 May.

The crisis, however, was not quite over. The alliance which had destroyed Anne demanded its reward. Cromwell, promoted on 8 July to the peerage as Lord Cromwell of Wimbledon, inherited Wiltshire's office of the keepership of the privy seal, and his servant Ralph Sadler took Brereton's best estates. On the other hand, the conservative conspirators, who wanted the restoration of the Princess Mary, got neither this nor anything else. In May Cromwell took charge of the efforts to make peace between her and her father, but no one had reckoned on her principled obstinacy. She refused to sign

several letters of submission, sticking always at the acknowledgement
of the royal supremacy with its implications for her mother and her
religion. As usual, such 'unfilial' behaviour infuriated Henry who
finally insisted on total and abject surrender. On 15 June, much
battered, advised even by friends that resistance was pointless, Mary
gave way, though she never forgave herself for thus denying every
principle she believed in; for the moment Henry graciously accepted
her. Her last stand, however, had caused further ructions at court.
To observers it looked as though all Mary's friends were being held
responsible for her resistance: Exeter and Fitzwilliam were forbidden
the court, her attendant Lady Hussey spent a spell in the Tower,
leading courtiers like Sir Nicholas Carew, Sir Anthony Browne and
Sir Thomas Cheyney felt their heads loose on their shoulders.
Chapuys understood that Cromwell also feared for himself, but
Cromwell, on his way to peerage and privy seal, once again deceived
the ambassador. He certainly had involved himself quite generously
on Mary's behalf and was exasperated by her stubbornness. On the
other hand, he superintended her surrender and manifestly never
lost the King's confidence. In fact, this crisis of June 1536 signified
the break-up of the anti-Boleyn alliance. Having used Mary's
supporters to dispose of Anne, Cromwell now used the difficulties
over Mary to push down his temporary allies; he emerged the sole
victor of six months of struggles and at once set about constructing a
court faction for himself, based on a following in the Privy Chamber.
The Marians had been outmanoeuvred, but for the moment they
survived, though powerless to stem the tide of reform.

Mary's surrender had come only just in time for the work of the
Parliament which met on 8 June. In opening it, Lord Chancellor
Audley went peculiarly out of his way to praise the King: who else,
he said, would after two such marriages venture upon yet a third,
except this great sovereign who yielded reluctantly and from no
carnal desire to the urgings of his nobility, much troubled by the
uncertainty of the throne? The urgency of the Parliament had left
things somewhat unplanned. The Commons had to ask for an extra
day to elect their Speaker, as though for once the Crown had not
been ready with a candidate; however, they duly chose the official
nominee, Sir Richard Rich, chancellor of the Court of Augmentations. Sittings were strangely dilatory—only twelve in the
first three weeks; and though business in Convocation, which was
debating the establishment of a formulary of the faith, helps to
account for these delays, lack of preparation also had to do with
them. The bulk of bills passed touched private matters; Cromwell
and Audley took advantage of a Parliament without much public
business to get through a large number of royal estates bills, and

private persons followed suit. Public bills nearly all confined themselves to continuing or slightly amending existing legislation, a clearing-up operation after the hectic days of the Reformation Parliament. At last, on 30 June, Audley was ready with the new Succession Act which passed in four days. It repealed the act of 1534, confirmed the attainders of the Boleyn faction, settled the crown upon the descendants of the Seymour marriage, devised a new oath of succession, and refined the treason law. But since so far there were no Seymour children, a drastic clause empowered the King—only in the absence of legitimate heirs—to determine the succession by letters patent or by his last will. Henry in fact at this point had three illegitimate children—Henry duke of Richmond, Mary and Elizabeth. It was widely thought that he would leave the throne to the first, but the boy died in late June, leaving only two bastardized offspring, both girls. This may have been why nothing was done to follow up the empowering clause of the act, even though there was to be no legitimate heir before October 1537; for some fifteen months the succession remained in a dangerously uncertain state to which Henry's marital policy had condemned it. He trusted his luck and it held; but it was not a happy situation.

Perhaps the most significant thing about the Second Succession Act was that it confirmed the defeat of Mary's partisans. They had hoped by overthrowing Anne to secure the legitimation of the Aragonese marriage; in this Parliament they learned that the normal politics of the day, revolving around the factions of the court, could not undo the past, and that their plotting had only succeeded in making Cromwell all-powerful. The shock of this recognition was to have wide-ranging consequences.[2]

The other bill to arise out of these problems, which was brought in by Audley on the penultimate day of the Parliament and passed rapidly through both Houses, looked like posing a greater danger to parliamentary sovereignty than any other act of the reign. It enabled a king who succeeded as a minor to annul, by the prerogative, all legislation passed before his twenty-fourth year. Because it was repealed in 1549, as soon as it became relevant, the purpose of this attempt to protect the Crown from manhandling during a child's rule has never been much considered; despite its drastic implications it was, like all such attempts to bind the future, quite possibly without meaning.[3] The only important bill to come from the Commons, the work (as the preamble proves) of Cromwell, com-

[2] It is possible that the difficulties over Rich's Speakership reflect a last conservative attempt to disrupt the government's policy.

[3] The Second Succession Act also contained an extraordinary clause intended to protect it against infringement either by judicial interpretation or by future legislation. The best comment on this is the Succession Act of 1543.

pleted the creation of the self-contained Church of England by a further violent denunciation of papal claims to authority, maintenance of which was now made treason. The act also closed the loophole which More had exploited: it was now treason to oppose silence to demands for adherence to the royal supremacy.

Thus when Cromwell, lord privy seal, on the last day of the session presented his writ of summons in the Upper House and was admitted, he, the junior baron of England, stood unchallenged in the seat of power. All rivals had fallen, some to the headsman and others to fear of a like fate. For the moment the man who had achieved all that his master wanted ruled everything under the King, and he was already deeply involved in proving once again that he would use his power 'in edification and not in destruction'. But though the exceptional nastiness of the fate inflicted on Anne and her followers owed much to the blindly bigoted temper of the King, and even though the victims have never easily commanded anyone's sympathy, it remains true that in order to get to the top Cromwell had willingly become the instrument of lying and corrupted proceedings.

II

By the end of 1535, the amount of contentious preaching disturbing the pulpits had began to trouble the men in authority, and on 7 January 1536 Cromwell took some much needed action. A circular in the King's name, backed by a covering letter from the vicegerent, went to all the bishops, exhorting them to stop extremism on either side, to promote the middle way, and to beware of Henry's anger if they neglected their duty and failed to keep the peace. But exhortations, however eloquent, could not succeed with men whose chief problem was to know what novelties might be acceptable and where the changes would stop. The Church of England badly needed a definition of the true faith, to set a limit beyond which lay the preaching of heresy or sedition. The production of such statements and summaries marked the century of the Reformation everywhere, but nowhere more so than in England. The attempts to end the uncertainty began in July 1536 when Convocation, presided over by Cromwell and assisted by the King's theological learning, produced a list of Ten Articles. Cromwell had contemplated going much further towards accommodation with the Lutherans: in 1535 and 1536, English emissaries led by Robert Barnes and Edward Foxe had held conversations at Wittenberg from which emerged proposals for a distinctly Protestant formulary. With this the King would have nothing to do: the Ten Articles, in form a pronouncement of the supreme head's, show the limit of what he was willing to accept. In the main a rather conservative document, they asserted in essence the traditional doctrine on three sacraments (baptism, penance and the eucharist) and advocated a reasonable use of ceremonies, images, prayers to the saints and prayers for the dead. But in several points the formulary significantly deserted strict Catholic teaching. Four of the seven sacraments (so eloquently defended by Henry in 1521) were simply 'lost'—not mentioned at all—and every article contained attention-arresting touches of Lutheran teaching which were no accident.[4] In discussing saints and ceremonies, the document asserts the propriety of honouring the established practices of Christ's Church but emphasizes the point that they must never be used in such a way as to distract from God's monopoly of grace or the sole sacrifice and intercession of the Son. One hears echoes of the adiaphorism promoted by Starkey (and Cromwell). The last article, on purgatory, struck a delicate balance, again with a slight bias towards the reform: it declares prayers for the dead to be 'a very good and charitable deed' (on the somewhat surprising testimony of the Book of Maccabees and of 'divers ancient doctors', a phrasing which slides over the notorious absence of scriptural authority for such prayers), but since the place where souls departed may dwell 'be to us uncertain by Scripture' the developed doctrine of purgatory is denied with a sideswipe at papal claims to be able to deliver the dead from thence for the prayers (and the money) of the living.

This then is the *via media* at its inception, rather mechanically constructed by infusing tradition with a dissolving dose of the new teaching. As the first beginning of the Protestant Reformation in England the Articles met some incomprehension and more resistance; they needed pressing upon the hesitant and impressing upon those impatient to go much faster and further. That need was fulfilled in the Injunctions which Cromwell, as vicegerent, issued in August 1536, for the remedy of abuses and the advancement of improvement. Naturally enough, Cromwell began once again by calling for obedience to the supremacy and for preaching against the pope's 'usurped power and jurisdiction'. He went on to the Ten Articles, which the clergy were to expound to the people; their effect received elaboration in paragraphs which initiated the reformers' active campaign against the 'superstition and hypocrisy crept into divers men's hearts'—the use of images, prayers and pilgrimages to 'buy'

---

[4] P. Hughes, *The Reformation in England* I (1950), pp. 350 ff. For example, the article on baptism, though mainly concerned to deny the views of Anabaptists and Pelagians, cites St Paul in a darkling hint that justification comes by faith alone.

grace and salvation. This was to attack the heart of the degraded popular devotion of the later middle ages. Instead the clergy were to teach the faithful the Lord's Prayer, Creed and Ten Commandments in English, and to provide for the competent and reverend administration of the sacraments. The Injunctions contained the customary strictures on inadequate clerical behaviour—tavern-haunting and card-playing, for instance—and the equally customary orders for the maintenance of church buildings. The demand that the wealthier clergy should support undergraduates at the universities has already been noted. The Injunctions impress by their ordinariness rather than by any revolutionary or even elevating characteristics; they constitute a move in the direction of long-demanded reform and concede little enough to Reformation.

However, between them the Ten Articles and the Injunctions form the first stage in the weaning away of the English Church from the Catholicism of the past—gradual and cautious, by insinuation rather than proclamation. The product of much necessary compromise not only between the leaders of reform and the conservative bishops but also between the episcopate and their idiosyncratic supreme head, they could hardly speak more firmly. From Cromwell's point of view, no doubt, and certainly from Cranmer's or Latimer's, this was a minimum programme, a mere start. Even so, they met resistance. Some priests continued to celebrate forbidden holy days; others refused to obey the order to read out the Injunctions from the pulpit; others affirmed the existence of purgatory; above all, of course, clerical morals were not mended overnight. Indeed, the signs are that in dioceses which enjoyed the attention of reforming bishops of the old order their successors at first presided over a real decline in standards. However cautious Henry and Cromwell might be, they had done enough to interfere with entrenched observances and popular beliefs to cause more than a ripple of disquiet to run through the villages of England, and in the consequent disturbance behaviour often grew lax and attention to spiritual duty flagged. We need not doubt that the promoters of the reform knew well how much work would be required to make a reality of their dreams. At the same time, these efforts to establish an official line also failed to silence the zealots who, in various ways, wished to 'purify' Church and commonwealth overnight.

The first half of 1536 had witnessed the closing of yet another door upon the past when Reginald Pole, in earlier days a devoted admirer of his princely cousin, finally came out against him. Henry had for years tried to get his learned relative, for whom he entertained much respect, to return to England and offer his reputation in support of the schism. Throughout 1535, Starkey, now in the King's service, had on Henry's instructions been urging his old mentor to express himself in favour of the royal supremacy, and Cromwell had personally backed these appeals. Always reluctant to take up a public position, Pole had temporized: though the death of More and Fisher shocked him profoundly, he continued to write and receive conciliatory letters. Finally, in January 1536 a copy of Sampson's *Oratio* arrived, intended to win him over; instead it persuaded him that he owed the world an answer. The news that Pole was writing on the Henrician schism caused much excitement among his friends and acquaintance who wished to see their patron honoured in his native country. Thus when the manuscript of *De Unitate Ecclesiastica* became available—Pole sent Henry a copy in May—the shock was great; Starkey, losing all influence with Henry, feared worse from which Cromwell guarded him; and Henry rose up in typical fury. *De Unitate* not only uncompromisingly asserted the papal primacy but did so with so much passion, violent denunciation of the King, and merely abusive language that it made the breach irreparable. Pole, not the most worldly of men, never understood why Henry should so resent being called murderer and robber and wild beast; his first sight of the Ten Articles suggested to him that reconciliation was still possible. But in truth he had done the unforgivable thing. More's great admirer and Fisher's could not have spoken otherwise in substance, though he might have used less frantic fury in doing so, as good friends kept telling him who saw the drafts of the book. *De Unitate* earned Pole the cardinal's hat from Paul III in December 1536, a fitting symbol of the end of the affair. Another link was gone between the Henricians and that humanist past which had promised so fair for reform and amity (and had done so little); the year 1536, which saw also the death of both Tyndale and Erasmus, marked a well notched caesura in the intellectual progress of the English Reformation. Those like Starkey and Morison, who could trace their spiritual pilgrimage back to the beneficence of Wolsey and the influence of Pole's circle at Padua, now cast off from their moorings, but in doing so they remained humanist scholars and promoters of reform, only now in an environment which had replaced peace by conflict and talk by action.

Before anything, however, could be done of the patient day-by-day labour which alone could transmute declarations of purpose into established practice, the whole work, and possibly the very existence of the Tudor monarchy, were imperilled by sudden uprisings in which the defence of traditional religion played its part. On 1 October 1536, a riot at Louth in Lincolnshire opened weeks of rebellion which convulsed the north and threatened to swallow the whole country.

III

The story of events between October 1536 and March 1537 is clear enough; its inwardness and import are quite other matters.[5] By late September, three sets of official enquirers—royal commissioners for the subsidy of 1534, the vicegerent's Dissolution commissioners, and Bishop Longland's agents for the enforcement of the Ten Articles and the Injunctions—were busy in Lincolnshire, to the manifest disquiet of the people. Rumours were springing up everywhere threatening fresh exactions, with new taxes on livestock, confiscation of church plate, and so forth. On 1 October, a sermon at Louth roused the town; similar riots broke out at Caistor and Horncastle; within a few days most of the shire was up, riots coalesced into a rebellion, and a programme appeared which demanded an end to peacetime taxation, the repeal of the Statute of Uses, the restoration of the Church's ancient liberties, an end to the dissolution of abbeys, the removal of heretical bishops, and the punishment of base-born councillors like Cromwell and Rich. Leaders emerged, especially the shoemaker Nicholas Melton who called himself Captain Cobbler. The mob killed the bishop's chancellor and one of Cromwell's commissioners, and the gentry of the shire, led by Lord Hussey, professed themselves forced by fear to let the commons have their way. However, Henry stood firm; the duke of Suffolk was despatched with very inadequate forces to restore order, and despite its noise the whole affair collapsed suddenly; by the 18th everyone had gone home. Some 140 men were held in prison; the rest of the shire received a royal pardon on 14 November.

Yet this was only the beginning. On 4 October, Robert Aske, a lawyer and gentleman from the East Riding of Yorkshire, had (allegedly) been captured by the rebels as he travelled through Lincolnshire and been forced to take their side. Returning north, he had the whole East Riding up within a few days, and after this the rebellion spread with quite astonishing speed. Aske apparently invented the name by which it has ever since been known, the Pilgrimage of Grace; and the pilgrims, to signify their supposed religious motives, marched under a banner with the five wounds of Christ. On the 16th Aske occupied York against feeble opposition; on the 21st Lord Darcy surrendered the vital castle of Pontefract after what can hardly be called even a token resistance; by the 24th the forces of the East and West Ridings, between 20,000 and 40,000 of them according to various reports, had assembled in a great camp

[5]For the interpretation here advanced see my 'Politics and the Pilgrimage of Grace' in a forthcoming volume in honour of J. H. Hexter; this also reviews earlier work on the topic.

at Doncaster. The rising quickly engulfed the rest of the north. In Durham and Northumberland, roving bands of rebels brought in one gentleman after another, sworn to the pilgrims' oath and soon in command of the campaign. Lancashire was stirring by 10 October; the northwest rapidly followed suit. By the end of the month, virtually all England north of the Trent and Ribble was in rebel hands; only Scarborough, Skipton Castle, Berwick and Carlisle remained loyal. The King's countermeasures were necessarily far slower and feebler. While the earl of Derby was set to watch Lancashire and the earl of Shrewsbury gathered forces in the north Midlands for a move against Yorkshire, the duke of Norfolk, brought out of virtual retirement, rode north with speed, collecting troops as he went, to encounter the rebel host on the Don on the 26th, with a force probably not more than 8,000 strong. There was nothing for it but to temporize: Norfolk promised the rebel leaders—identifiable now as Aske, Darcy, and Sir Robert Constable—that he would present their grievances to the King, and a lull ensued while these were formulated in a meeting at Pontefract marked by the sort of exultation that testifies to the scent of victory. But those talks also weakened the impetus of the rising; it was almost as though the leadership could hardly believe in their success, and November went by without further action. At last, on 2 December, the Pontefract articles were agreed, and on the 6th Aske met·Norfolk at Doncaster for a discussion which satisfied him of the King's good will. Aske, who for weeks had laboured to keep the rebellion in being, now with some difficulty persuaded his followers to accept the duke's promise of a pardon, and within a few days the great host had disappeared.

Unrest, however, could not end so easily; the rebellion simmered on in Lancashire and the northwest, and soon new rioting occurred which was to have fatal consequences. Norfolk took longer to return from discussions with the King than had been expected; some leading gentlemen of the north were being summoned to London; the things complained of (especially the collection of clerical dues) continued unabated. The commons, as was their wont, soon thought themselves betrayed, and Aske found that he no longer had authority enough to impose patience and peace. As Norfolk moved slowly north again to restore order among the pardoned shires, news came in of a battle at Carlisle in late January in which a band of borderers had beaten back a force of peasants besieging the town, while in the northeast two men whom only bitter despair united, John Hallom, a yeoman, and Sir Francis Bigod, had suddenly attempted to renew the Pilgrimage with attacks on Hull and Scarborough. Though all these last twitches of the fever ended quickly, they gave Henry the pretext he wanted to break his promise of a pardon. He had never meant to submit tamely to dictation by rebels, however loyal they might profess themselves to be, provided only he obeyed their command to govern the realm in a fashion agreeable to themselves.

The King's vengeance, though surprisingly moderate by the standards of the time, was grim enough. The worst happened at Carlisle where Norfolk displayed the royal banner so as to be able to deal by martial law with rebels taken in open battle: here he hanged seventy-four of the commons. Elsewhere the duke used the common law, and not surprisingly some men guilty in fact were acquitted by juries. Nevertheless, the gallows were busy as he moved through the north. The alleged leaders were brought to London for investigation and trial in May; executions followed in both London and Yorkshire. On 25 May there died at Tyburn Sir John Bulmer, Sir Stephen Hamerton, Nicholas Tempest, Friar John Pickering and two ex-heads of religious houses—John Cockerell of Guisborough Priory and William Thirsk of Fountains Abbey. On the same day, Lady Bulmer was burned for treason at Smithfield. On 2 June they were followed by Sir Thomas Percy, Sir Francis Bigod, George Lumley, and two more monks, Adam Sedbar, abbot of Jervaulx, and William Wood, prior of Bridlington. The King was slashing the heads of the thistles. That left the men whom the government accused of having been the real cause of all the trouble. Darcy and Hussey suffered in late June, after weeks in the Tower under sentence of death; Aske and Constable were sent back to York and Hull respectively, to hang in chains to the terror of the country. In the north, too, the trials touched men of some eminence; thus Sussex and Derby, settling Lancashire, concentrated on monks rather than the peasantry. In Lincolnshire, on the other hand, the commissioners hanged virtually only the commons. Nearly fifty victims died there (though a larger number were pardoned), while the Pilgrimage proper cost the lives of over 130. Especially since the pilgrims themselves seem to have caused the death of nobody, these are sad enough figures; yet a total of well below 200 people executed for raising a vast rebellion covering seven shires and threatening the safety of the whole realm—200 out of perhaps 40,000 involved—is really astonishingly low, especially when it is remembered that over seventy of them were the victims of Norfolk's one act of savagery at Carlisle. It is really the number of greater men killed that has created the impression of a holocaust. As so often in the reign of Henry VIII, it was the ruling sort, involved in politics, who paid the price in numbers disproportionate to their total.

By March it was over; what had it been, and why had it happened? The common view sees the rebellion as the protest of a whole community—'northern society'—against the breach with Rome and especially against the Dissolution of the monasteries, against the new learning and the King's autocracy, complicated by the social and economic grievances of its various component parts. The Pontefract articles, which most fully sum up the aims of the movement, range comprehensively enough. The largest set of demands touched religion: they denounced various heretical writers, asserted the pope's spiritual headship, called for the restoration of dissolved houses, threatened death to heretical bishops and laymen, and called for the return of all ecclesiastical liberties including benefit of clergy and rights of sanctuary, a full catalogue of very conservative reaction. Secondly, the pilgrims passed their verdict on the King's government: they demanded that the Princess Mary be declared legitimate and restored to the succession, that Cromwell, Audley and Rich be removed from office and punished, that Parliament be free again of electoral and managerial influences, that the act permitting the King to bequeath the crown be repealed, and that all debts incurred during the commotion be cancelled; and they called for a 'free' Parliament to meet at Nottingham or York and do all that was required. A number of statutes (especially Uses and Treasons) came under specific attack; and there were complaints against interference with the course of the common law and perversion of custom. Economic grievances made the least noise, though there were some complaints against the exploitation of tenants (excessive entry fines and the like), against enclosers, and against heavy taxation.

There must, however, be grave doubts whether the articles constitute anything like a representative programme, and worse doubts about the extent to which the rebellion as a whole arose from the issues they enshrined. It has always been recognized that the different parts of the north did not all rise for the same reasons, but the full significance of this has not always been brought out. Thus the complaints against enclosers and oppressors of the tenantry explicitly applied only to Westmorland, Cumberland and the Craven district of the West Riding; they were directed mainly against the earl of Cumberland and had a prehistory in recent rioting not paralleled elsewhere. The royal supremacy as such escaped attack altogether, and Aske admitted that he alone was responsible for the reference to the pope's spiritual government of the Church. The points touching Parliament were contributed by a burgess of the Reformation Parliament who resented Cromwell's management of the Commons and abominated the policies put through by means of it. Certainly in Lincolnshire but to all appearance in Yorkshire too, the rebel bands needed to have their enemies pointed out to them: it was the gentry leaders, not the commons, who singled out the hated ministers of the

crown, and one wonders whether the peasants had ever heard of
Cromwell, let alone Rich. Virtually all the complaints against
statutes and legal practices also were of no interest to the lower
orders, though the West Riding weavers (like weavers elsewhere)
resented the recent act setting higher standards in cloth manufacture. The crucial issues gather around the monasteries because it is
usually held that the Pilgrimage was above all a protest at the
Dissolution and a vote of confidence in the holiness and usefulness of
the northern houses of religion. The monks, it is true, had retained
more popularity in the north and especially in Lancashire; but no
houses were restored in Lincolnshire and few in Yorkshire, anti-
monastic sentiment of the familiar kind made itself heard there too,
and the truly popular rising in the northwest made no issue of the
Dissolution. It was Aske who emphasized the cause of the abbeys,
more ardently than their inmates themselves most of whom stood
aside from rebellion. The list of heretical writings is peculiar: it
includes some prominent English and continental reformers, but also
men who, while in various ways supporting social amelioration, had
published no heresy. The presence of London lawyers of conservative
tastes (Aske among them) comes through here and elsewhere in the
articles; evidently, to some extent the Pilgrimage was bred at the
Inns of Court. But on the evidence it is not really possible to agree
with those who have seen in the risings a predominantly religious
movement, though Aske, who really wanted to lead one, deliberately
created that character for them.

Indeed, how spontaneous was the outbreak? After the event, it
was generally represented as an uprising of the commons who had
allegedly forced their betters into compliance; even Aske, the great
captain, claimed to have been coerced by peasant rebels. Here and
there the palpable attempt to shift the burden of guilt may have
been justified. The Westmorland and Cumberland rebels rose of
their own volition against their landlords, but in this they were
exceptional. There was some independent trouble in Lancashire
before Aske's emissaries spread the major rebellion there. The riots
in Lincolnshire, the start of the whole affair, looked spontaneous
enough, with popular leaders heading mobs gathered in fear of royal
exploitation, but a closer study dispels most of this appearance. From
the first, the real lead came from the local gentry, alienated from the
court by the duke of Suffolk's energetic attempt to create a Brandon
interest in the shire. As soon as they realized that things had got out
of hand they withdrew their support: hence the astonishingly rapid
collapse of the movement there. The commons of Yorkshire and
Durham rose as a rule where their lords offered guidance and
encouragement; adjacent parts, dominated by gentry or nobility

who refused to come in, remained undisturbed. Too many gentle-men who later claimed to have been coerced proved the sincerity of their surrender to threats by becoming the energetic leaders of rebellion, and they had no answer to the question why they should have been so very scared when not one case was known of a gentleman suffering physical damage at the rebels' hands. Edward Lee, archbishop of York (who did try to dampen down passions), and other members of the Council of the North fled to Pontefract, into Darcy's arms, rather than to the safety of Scarborough, and then played a very active part in the debates and planning there. Darcy's rapid surrender of Pontefract was put into perspective by the easy defence of Skipton Castle and Scarborough, both less powerful fortresses. In fact, it cannot any longer be seriously doubted that the main part of the rebellion was led and presumably incited by the northern gentry; so far from there being a spontaneous rising of the commons—a peasants' rebellion of any sort—the pilgrims' host was brought into existence by the natural rulers of the region who used the official machinery designed to muster the tenantry for war against the Scots.

The ruling order of the north did indeed have cause to resent much that had happened. Of the great families only Clifford had done well of late, and that family remained loyal, holding Skipton, Carlisle and Berwick. In 1534, Lord Dacre, warden of the west march, narrowly escaped conviction for treasonable dealings with the Scots which were really no more than the ordinary private arrangements of the borders (unfortunate, no doubt, in one who held his office); his ascendancy much abated, he was widely expected to take any opportunity to restore his fortunes. Though the Nevills were a much reduced force, and the earl of Westmorland kept out of the commotion as he kept out of everything in the reign, members of the clan dominated the Pilgrimage in Durham and north Yorkshire. Above all, however, the Pilgrimage can be made to look like a battle for Percy. That great house had greatly declined under the in-effectual sixth earl who sealed his doom when in January 1536 he made the King heir to all his lands. His disinherited brothers, Sir Thomas and Sir Ingram, played a very prominent part in the rising in Yorkshire and Northumberland respectively. Percy officers ap-peared everywhere as leaders of the rebellion: Aske himself had been a Percy man. The gentry in general, apart from these magnates, had obvious grievances of which the Statute of Uses with its prohibition of all bequeathing of land was the foremost, and though feuds among them helped to assign some men to loyalty and some to rebellion the general air of a society still feudally ordered which rose in resistance to centralizing government and the intrusion of London-supported new interests is strong. Thus the Pilgrimage is usually interpreted as a mixture of religious reaction and neo-feudalism.

Yet if the first of these elements has been manifestly overstressed, the second also looks less than convincing. It was surely a strange feudal counter-attack which involved in person none of the greater nobility. Not only did the earl of Westmorland stand aside and the earl of Northumberland deliberately withdraw from the north at the crucial moment, but even Dacre, contrary to all expectations, never stirred. Family cohesion sometimes worked and at others failed: Darcy's sons and Aske's brothers, the close relatives of the outstanding leaders, remained true to the King. Some of the most actively troublesome gentlemen—Sir Robert Constable in the East Riding, for instance—had no Percy connections; others, like the King's councillors in the north, were just the kind of 'new men' intruded by government against which one would have expected a feudal outbreak to direct itself. No doubt all this underlines the very mixed character of the rising, pulling in a great variety of exasperations, fears and people, some genuinely attached to the old religion, some passionate for Nevill or Percy or Lumley, some devoted to monasteries, some stirred to fury by the many signs of interference and the many rumours of more to come, some taking initiatives and some loyally following the call of their traditional rulers. But this confusion also underlines the fact that by itself it does not explain what happened.

The idea of a spontaneous combustion which then brought in the existing inflammatory material to set the whole north ablaze is not in accord with the facts; it is necessary to regard the evidence of manifest advance planning. Was it pure coincidence that Aske, after weekending with the Ellerkers, should happen to cross the Humber three days after the Lincolnshire rising had begun, that he should have been 'taken' by the rebels, and that he should have returned to Yorkshire rather than continue his alleged intention of making for London for the beginning of the law term—his return being followed immediately by the outbreak at Beverley? Cromwell also had a very good point when he asked Darcy how it had been possible to produce thousands of the badges of the five wounds virtually at a moment's notice if, as the pilgrims claimed, the idea of using such badges had occurred because of the accidental killing of one of their number by a friend who mistook him for a King's man. Even in Lincolnshire, where the first stirs were provoked by rumour-spreading clergy, there is evidence of rioters being paid for their work—and that money must have come from somewhere.

In short, the Pilgrimage, though it had its spontaneous moments, was in itself no spontaneous event but in great measure a planned rising; it is quite likely that one cause of its failure lay in the intercutting of plotting with disconcerting spontaneity. The point is proved by a look at the real leaders who did not come from either the commons or the great northern families. The three chiefs were Darcy, Constable and Hussey, with Aske providing both a cover for them (so that they could claim to have been merely coerced) and an ideological inspiration. All three had been involved in opposition politics since at least 1533; they had been regularly in touch with the imperial ambassador and had frequently avowed their dislike of heresy, hatred for Anne Boleyn, and more recently disdain for Cromwell. In 1534 Darcy had offered to raise the north provided the Emperor sent at least token support; kept at the time in London by a suspicious government, he did not return to Yorkshire until the summer of 1535 by which time Charles V had made plain his unwillingness to intervene by force. But it was still a time to plot. Darcy and Hussey seem to have persuaded Chapuys that they were northern magnates with great authority on the Scottish border, but that was nonsense. Both were the first noblemen of their titles, created in 1505 and 1529 respectively. Darcy, nearly seventy years old at this time, had served the Tudors faithfully as a soldier; his northern influence depended entirely on his captaincy of the royal castle and honour of Pontefract. Hussey, about as old, was essentially a courtier *pur sang* who in 1533 became the Princess Mary's chamberlain and whose wife in 1536 earned imprisonment by her loose tongue and her loyalty to Mary. These were the men who really organized the rising—the remnant of the Aragonese party who had thought themselves close to victory in May 1536, only to find themselves again outmanoeuvred by Cromwell. No wonder that the restoration of Mary, the repeal of the Succession Act, and the destruction of Cromwell loomed so large in the rebels' demands.

Thus the Pilgrimage originated in a decision by one of the court factions to take the battle out of the court into the nation, to raise the standard of loyal rebellion as the only way left to them if they were to succeed in reversing the defeats suffered at court and in Parliament, and in forcing the King to change his policy. In the plotting around Chapuys this leadership had not been alone; the ambassador compiled long lists of allegedly disaffected noblemen willing to join in rebellion against Henry. In the upshot, none of them did; several of those that Chapuys particularly relied on— Derby, Norfolk, Rutland, especially Shrewsbury—sealed the rebels' fate by accepting the command against them, while the west country group of Courtenays (the marquess of Exeter) and Poles stood apart, hesitant and ill prepared. In fact, the conspiracy did not at all go as planned. It is evident that Lincolnshire rose before Darcy was ready (hence, very likely, Aske's visit of inspection), while the equally premature collapse there ended all hopes of carrying the rebellion further south. The great variety of issues that agitated the seven shires made the movement much more formidable but also far less suitable for achieving the primary purpose of ousting Cromwell, reversing religious policy, and restoring the Aragon succession. Darcy had meant to apply the persuasion of a modest protest backed by force; instead he found himself in the midst of a storm from which either he or Henry, but not both, could hope to emerge. In particular, the strong reaction from the commons, while very useful in supplying power to the machine, also raised the spectre of a true popular uprising with memories of peasants' wars, a thing which no one in the organizing order wanted to see and fear of which cooled the rebellious ardour of the Lincolnshire gentry inconveniently early.

At Doncaster, Aske and Darcy were in manner as baffled as Norfolk. They had military superiority, but what use was that when no one moved in the south and when any actual campaigning would have to start in mid-winter? Besides, they did not want civil war; they just wanted Henry to give in to threats. They consistently proclaimed their loyalty to the King whom they wished only to liberate from evil counsellors—an accurate description of the faction leaders' purpose as well as a necessary ploy which was bound to lose them the initiative as long as Henry's nerve held. And hold it did: threatened by rebels in his own realm, he at once threw all his power and energy behind Cromwell. If, as has been suggested, Darcy remembered Henry's surrender to the taxpayers' strike of 1525 he miscalculated entirely: acceptance of the pilgrims' demands would have implied a vastly more devastating defeat than was involved in the conciliatory action taken on the earlier occasion. The campaign against the rising was conducted by Henry in person, and his skill emerges particularly in the lordly orders sent to Shrewsbury, Norfolk and Derby to proceeed at once to suppression. Henry knew quite as well as his generals that they did not have the necessary forces, but he also knew that one touch of temporizing weakness on his part would decide those wavering loyalists—all enemies to Cromwell—to join the other side.

Thanks to the King, the tightrope held. He had further good fortune in the abysmal timing of the Pilgrimage, in part at least a consequence of the fact that the conspirators could not control the forces they had unleashed. The marquess of Exeter later thought that Darcy had badly mismanaged the whole thing. In November 1536, Charles V, deep in his war with France, left for Spain to prepare his next campaign. Nothing was further from his thoughts or from practical politics than armed support for the northern rebels. They could not even try to enlist Scottish aid without at once losing all support among the borderers. True, Paul III hoped to exploit the rising, but he was frustrated by its short duration and the time it took to hear of things. When he sent Cardinal Pole on a mission to organize aid—the one positive piece of policy to result from all Chapuys' plotting—he got him going much too late (February 1537). From first to last, the pilgrims were left on their own, reliant upon coercing a distant King against whom they neither could nor would raise any real threat of deposition.

Neither the plot which in the last analysis lay behind the rebellions, nor the actual unrest of the north in its various manifestations, was ever anything but a futile attempt to arrest the power of the revolution to which Henry had lent his countenance from 1533 onwards. Well aware of what had been going on, the government nevertheless took care to tailor its revenge to need and to the prospect of pacification, and most of the gentry tainted with suspect activity were permitted to ride off on the incredible tale that they had all been forced in by their tenants. This sort of clemency paid off, for in the main the rulers of the north returned sheepishly to the fold and to the profits of secularized lands. The leading conspirators were bound to die. Old Darcy, to whom loyalty had become the necessary cause of treason, old Hussey, embittered by the faction struggle, Robert Aske, not quite the shining hero of tradition but yet the one man among them for whom the cause of true religion came first, deserve posterity's pity, for what that is worth; but they knew from the first that they were gambling with their lives. It is less easy to forgive them for drawing thousands to treason, however ready those thousands were to be drawn.

The Pilgrimage collapsed really far too quickly to justify the common view of it as a genuine mass movement eager to overthrow a whole system and policy; only in Lancashire, where religion sincerely drove on rebellion, and in the northwest where the commons genuinely felt grievances of their own, did the end not come the moment the gentry decided that they had gone too far. This was also what the investigations revealed to Henry and his ministers. The King might call Lincolnshire one of the 'most brute and beastly' shires of the realm and profess to believe that the rising was the work of mere peasants, but neither he nor his Council acted as though they credited this: they knew what was happening. And the executions in the north, the Carlisle victims apart whose case was special, also indicate that no one thought he was confronted by either a peasants' war or a feudal conflict or a religious resistance movement involving a whole 'society'. Even the clergy, so prominent in stirring up trouble, escaped very lightly; Archbishop Lee, his lame excuses accepted, went back to promote the reform at York, and Bishop Tunstall, who during the troubles had hidden himself from both rebels and King in a suspicion-arousing manner, even accepted the government of the north. Advantage was taken of the involvement of some monks to get hold of a few houses by charging their heads with treason, and the Lincolnshire clergy, responsible with their rumouring for originally setting fire to the tinder, suffered some attenuation. But as far as the gentry were concerned, once those too obviously in the van of rebellion had been eliminated and the Marian conspirators weeded out, there was no question of pursuing the sort of vendetta that would have been called for if 'the north' had needed modernizing. However they had behaved during the risings, they had to be lived with and worked with still like the gentry everywhere, as the only possible means to keep the region in its normal state of political equilibrium.

It follows that it is a mistake to regard the Pilgrimage as the protest of an older style of society against change and transformation. No doubt there were some touches of this in the outbreak, especially in the attachment to the old religion that here and there was genuine enough among gentry, clergy and commons. In the far north, some ties to the great border families survived, though they played little enough part in the troubles. But in Yorkshire and Lincolnshire, the heartland of the rebellion, the situation pointed much more to the future than the past—to the creation of alignments among the gentry which had nothing to do with feudal allegiance and a great deal to do with the struggles for power and patronage centred upon the court. When Willoughbys and Dymmocks—earlier beneficiaries of Tudor favour—used popular apprehensions (the sort of thing that elsewhere led to readily suppressed minor riots) to resist the advance into Lincolnshire of Brandon and Blount interests; when Tempests and Bowes in Durham or Ellerkers and Constables in Yorkshire mustered their tenants to resist the advance of new courtiers into the Percy inheritance, they were not testifying to the backward difference of the north but anticipating the kind of reaction that in the course of the century was to create 'court and country' divisions in so many shires. Here the England of the seventeenth-century civil wars can be seen emerging from the England of the fifteenth-century magnate struggles, and the transformation had already gone much further than has commonly been supposed. Though the intervention of idealists like Aske and Bigod complicated the issues, and though the political ambitions of Mary's party gave a singular character to events, the materials they all worked with were the grievances of a distant, not a

different, part of the realm, much disturbed—as others would come
to be—by the progress of centralization and reform.

Thus the settlement of the north called not for full-scale reconstruction but only for some administrative repairs. The death of
Northumberland, only thirty-five years old, in June 1537 not only
gave the King his lands and eliminated the Percies for a generation,
but also left the wardenship of the east and middle marches vacant,
while the west march needed attention because Cumberland had
proved his inability to exercise the office effectively. Though the
duke of Norfolk believed it to be essential that the King should on
the borders be served by noblemen, Henry (having vainly tried
various unlikely peers) accepted Cromwell's policy of using the best
men available, among whom there happened to be no men of noble
lineage. The King formally took over the wardenships himself and
appointed deputies from the local gentry to execute the office. All
this did not imply some new policy of ending the ascendancy of
dissident feudatories who in any case did not exist; as soon as
possible, the wardenships reverted to local men of peerage status.[6]
But while in reality the product of necessity—the dearth of
magnates—the policy nevertheless confirmed the change that had
come over even the borders where to cry Percy or Nevill or Dacre
had really ceased to be of use since no members of those ancient
houses stood willing to answer. Henry's appointments did not signify
a change from aristocracy to gentry, but they did demonstrate that
the social structure even of the far north was by this time much more
like that of the rest of the realm than had been true even fifty years
before.

The government's main attention turned to the Council of the
North which not only had failed to prevent the rebellion but had
contributed so many allegedly reluctant leaders to it. Norfolk,
anxious to return south, laid down the lieutenancy in September
1537, but even before this Cromwell had taken the opportunity to
reform the northern administration on lines familiar from his other
work on institutions of government. The young duke of Richmond,
nominal head of the earlier council, having conveniently died in
June, the fiction of a northern magnate council was replaced by a
proper bureaucratic body, a mixture of harmless noblemen, leading
local knights, common lawyers and civilians among whom the
professional element firmly predominated. Tunstall, under protest,
accepted the presidency, but within a year he was replaced by a

---

[6] There has been some debate over all this between M. E. James, *Change and Continuity in the
Tudor North* (Borthwick Papers XXVII, York, 1965), and M. L. Bush, 'The Problem of the Far
North: a Study of the Crisis of 1537 and its Consequences', *Northern History* VI (1971), pp. 40 ff.
Though in general I agree more with Dr Bush I think he has underestimated the significance
of the switch from the old to the new nobility.

reformist churchman, Robert Holgate, bishop of Llandaff. The use of episcopal presidents by-passed the rivalries of local claimants. The council's area of competence was extended from Yorkshire to the marcher counties;[7] only Lancashire, where the Duchy had its organization and claims, was left out, with the unfortunate result that that county remained unmanageable and unreformed long after the rest of the north was well settled. Equipped with the powers of common-law and conciliar jurisdiction, and instructed to follow a regular routine of sessions held at York, Newcastle, Hull and Durham, the Council of the North became an efficient instrument for government in the King's interest, as well as a useful and much employed institution for resolving local litigation and disputes. Efficiency was not the product of a moment, but Cromwell kept his eye on things, and the new administration soon settled in quite well.

---

[7] In 1541–2, the renewal of war with Scotland again removed the wardens of the marches from council supervision.

12 Cromwell's Rule and End

I

Henry had weathered a storm—no doubt of that, whatever the storm may be judged to have signified. But since the rising had in particular been an attempt to unseat the leaders of the reforming party, the victory was also Cromwell's, a fact demonstrated to the world when, on 26 April 1537, he took Darcy's stall in the Order of the Garter. Sir Thomas Cromwell, Lord Cromwell of Wimbledon, KG—some way to come for the shearman's son and, by the standards of the day, a cause of legitimate pride. Nevertheless, one hopes that he himself, walking in procession in lieu of the old soldier who had hated him so, saw the incongruity.[1] The party of reform emerged from the turmoil if anything stronger than before, nor were there any signs for the moment that Aske and Darcy had managed to raise any doubt in Henry's mind over the direction which policy was taking in Church and state. The birth of the ardently hoped-for heir, christened Edward, on 12 October 1537, set the seal on the King's triumph and confirmed his conviction that at last he was earning the reward of his personal goodness. Cromwell had certainly remained fully in Henry's confidence throughout the troubles; his propaganda machine had worked overtime to produce the widely distributed official *Answers* to the rebels' demands and two violent pamphlets by Richard Morison to counteract the claims of rebellion. About the middle of 1537 there appeared Morison's *Apomaxis*, a Latin defence of everything done since the first moves against Rome which was intended as the regime's official apology abroad. As soon as peace was restored, Cromwell thus felt able to resume the work of reform, more particularly that transformation of the Church of England in a Protestant direction which he had initiated in the summer of 1536.

Much of this work amounted to enforcement—the seeking out of

[1] For the installation Cromwell borrowed the collar and George of the earl of Wiltshire, bereaved father of Anne and George Boleyn!

dissidents and the maintenance of conformity; but, as usual, the vicegerent also pushed on with constructive proposals, increasingly assisted by Cranmer who now began to emerge into a position of spiritual leadership, though he never ceased to leave the initiative to his much more single-minded and positive friend. The King did not regard the Ten Articles as a conclusive statement of faith, and indeed they were too brief for that and sounded too uncertain a note; he therefore pressed for further work along these lines, and from February 1537 onwards Cromwell and the bishops were intermittently engaged in drafting a formulary which might become the doctrinal basis of the Church of England. The debates reached a climax in June and July when the disputes between conservatives and radicals consolidated around the nature and number of the sacraments. Cromwell tried his best to force the bishops into accepting the radical line first hinted at in the Ten Articles, but the outcome, predictably, was a compromise, the book called *The Institution of a Christian Man*, published in September 1537. The King tried his hand at revising it, only to find that Cranmer's belief in obedience stopped short of accepting dubious theology and bad grammar, and he refused to license it; thus what became known as the *Bishops' Book* lacked the official authority of the supreme head. Though the *Bishops' Book* singled out the three sacraments acknowledged in 1536 as those solely instituted by Christ and therefore superior, it accepted all seven and thereby marked, if not a retreat, at least a failure to advance further towards the Lutheran position. This vacillating and unlicensed commentary on the faith, however submissive to the King's authority in form and however anxious to emphasize order and obedience, could not heal the growing divisions in the Church.

Cromwell, in any case, was much more concerned with yet another reformist move. He had long been a believer in giving the Bible to the people, and now, firmly in the saddle, he resolved upon a very drastic departure from the earlier policy of keeping the Scriptures the preserve of the learned, a policy which More had formulated and which always remained more agreeable to the cautious King. The story of the English Bible in the 1530s provides very clear proof that, notwithstanding his careful professions of subservience, the vicegerent was quite capable of pushing on reforms not altogether pleasing to the supreme head and of doing this by disguising the truth of events from his master. Before he could compel the realm to read the Bible he needed a suitable version, and this inevitably meant that he had in some way to rely on the work of Tyndale, a man whom Henry abominated, transmitted through others whose beliefs were at least likely to lean towards what Henry still regarded as heresy. This reliance became inescapable when Cranmer's plan to obtain a translation by distributing sections of the Bible to assorted bishops came to nothing in 1535. Instead there appeared in the same year the first complete translation (by Miles Coverdale), a remarkable work of carpentry which used Tyndale, Luther and Zwingli to help out the translator's lack of skill in the ancient languages but improved on its models in mellifluity and elegance. Since Coverdale, a peaceful man, omitted those prefaces and notes which always caused the real disputes among the faithful, Cromwell would have been content to use his version, but Cranmer and other divines deplored its inadequate scholarship and consequent inaccuracy. They approved instead the translation ascribed to a fictitious Thomas Mathew, actually Tyndale's work completed by his friend John Rogers, which, carrying some of those troublemaking annotations, became available in 1537 and at Cromwell's instance was licensed in August for sale in England. Cromwell was soon to prove that he thought it a poor second best, but at least he now had a vernacular bible to offer to a nation to whom he wished to teach the truth of God's word in a language they could understand. While Cromwell was in charge, all those reservations with which his predecessors and successors hedged their willingness to let the people read the Scriptures were noticeably absent.

The energetic euphoria of the summer of 1537, culminating in the celebrations of Prince Edward's birth, came to a sudden end twelve days after that event when Queen Jane died, a victim to sixteenth-century medicine. Henry showed some short-lived sorrow but soon decided that his freedom to remarry constituted a first-class diplomatic asset; only in course of time and further disappointments did the memory of his third marriage, to the most colourless of all his wives, assume a posthumous halo of heartfelt attachment that owed something at least to its brevity. From Cromwell's point of view there was some gain in the fact that the Queen's death arrested the build-up at court of a powerful Seymour faction, but the complications arising from Henry's search for a replacement nullified this. Even a man of Cromwell's phenomenal powers of work found that those often idiotic and always time-consuming machinations reduced his ability to press on with the reform. The history of his remaining two and a half years in power is a web woven of the King's wife-hunt, the revival of threats from abroad, the efforts to continue reforming the realm, and special complications introduced by the fact that the beginnings of the Reformation released activities more radical than Cromwell's and far too radical for Henry's continued trust in his servant.

The confident mood of 1537, produced by victory over domestic rebels, owed a good deal also to an international situation that freed England from all apprehensions. Reginald Pole's mission on behalf of the Pope, in February 1537, not only started much too late to exploit Henry's troubles at home but his ostentatious rejection by both Charles V and Francis also showed up the futility of the papal reaction. The cardinal was forced to twiddle his thumbs for months in the backwater of the neutral bishopric of Liège before disconsolately creeping back to Italy in August by devious routes designed to save him from the threat of assassination by Henry's agents. Throughout the year, the desultory war continued between the French and the Imperialists, and England could comfortably attend to its own affairs. The Council called by the Pope to meet at Mantua in May 1537 was easily ignored by a monarch who had for years been declaring his willingness to submit his cause to just such an assembly. But this contented isolation was ended by Queen Jane's death, mainly because Henry now wanted to marry no more Englishwomen but meant to demonstrate his greatness by seeking a worthy wife abroad. This ambition suited Cromwell who could see no profit in the promotion of yet another aristocratic connection at home and could hope to use the King's marriage for the purpose of creating alliances which might free the country more securely from the recurrence of foreign danger. The trouble was that Henry turned out hard to please, but also that not many foreign princes wished to commit sisters or daughters to the bed of one who had become something of a legendary monster. In the course of 1538 and 1539 no fewer than nine candidates were seriously considered and more still given brief glances. Embassies travelled the continent, almost reviving the splendid (and expensive) days of the Divorce when English envoys were to be met in every corner of Europe; the King's great court painter, Hans Holbein the younger, was for ever on the move to commit yet another young lady's features to paper for his master's solemn study; Henry planned a beauty parade of French princesses at Calais. The King's almost childish crudeness and selfishness caused a number of scenes, much wonderment, and some disgust. The candidate favoured longest was a young member of the house of Guise, the widowed duchess of Milan, but it is clear enough that the lady herself was entirely unwilling.

Thus Cromwell decided to exploit the possibility offered of renewing the proposal for an alliance with the League of Schmalkalden which had fizzled out in 1536. His German experts, Christopher Mont and Robert Barnes, got busy once more, and in May 1538 envoys arrived from the League. The negotiations dragged on until October but it is far from clear how serious Henry was about them. Certainly he refused to contemplate the doctrinal concessions demanded by the Lutherans, concessions which Cranmer would have welcomed and Cromwell strongly hinted would suit his views. Even the ominous truce which Charles V and Francis I, at the Pope's mediation, concluded at Nice in June, followed by a conference at Aigues Mortes at which they agreed to join in the defence of Christendom against its enemies (the Turk, the Lutherans, and the King of England), failed to panic Henry though it manifestly troubled his minister. Throughout the summer Cromwell was pressing on with his efforts to advance the Reformation; the Dissolution progressed rapidly now, the friars' orders came under attack, the campaign of preaching especially against relics and pilgrimages—hallmarks of the old religion—intensified. In September, the famous shrine of Thomas Becket at Canterbury was destroyed by the orders of the government, several carts being required to carry off the loot. Becket, champion of the Church who had humbled a king, needed exorcising from the consciousness of a people who for centuries had treated him as the national saint,[2] and much effort was devoted to vilifying him; the speed and ease with which his cult vanished do, however, tell a good deal about the depth of traditional piety in Henrician England.

In September, Cromwell consolidated the advance in his second Injunctions, intended as elaborations and enlargements of those of 1536. He once more tried to prevent too violent a pace of change and especially reasserted the lawfulness of tithe, but the two most significant clauses testify to his continued reforming zeal in Church and state. A Bible 'of the largest volume' was to be put in every church, the cost being shared between the parson and the parish; and every incumbent was to keep registers of all baptisms, marriages and burials performed by him. Neither order could be executed very well at once. There still existed no acceptable translation of the Scriptures ready to be licensed for universal use, while parish registration met with both inertia and much suspicion since all such census-taking roused apprehensions, unjust in this case, that it would in some way result in taxes. However, Cromwell did his best. The Great Bible, which made the enforcement of his injunction possible, was of his promoting. Since the edition, prepared by Coverdale, was ready by mid-1538 he had expected to have it in print by September, but the work ran into serious delays, efforts to print in France were interrupted by the ecclesiastical authorities there, and in the end copies (after all printed in England) did not become available until November 1539 when Cromwell obtained letters patent giving him a monopoly of bible-licensing. The splendid title page of the Great Bible shows the King handing the Word of God to

[2] Both Cromwell and Cranmer owed their baptismal names to Becket's popularity.

his archbishop and his vicegerent who reappear lower down to pass the precious gift to clergy and laity respectively.[3] There should be no doubt about Cromwell's responsibility for this fundamental reform or his sincerity in promoting it. Parish registers also began to be kept, though few now survive before the reign of Elizabeth; for the first time it became possible to provide reliable information about the people of England, their numbers, ages and fortunes. Cromwell defended registration on the grounds that it would prevent much dispute over descent and inheritance; he thought of it as a basic reform which would bring order into social relationships.

All this activity, backed up by frequent circulars to justices of the peace and the like—activity always carried from intention to execution—did not, however, help to relax tensions which continued to build up through the year. The development most dangerous to Cromwell was the appearance of unwanted allies—reformers far more extreme than himself and much less acceptable to the King. The year 1538 witnessed the arrival in England of the so-called radical Reformation—sectaries of the Anabaptist stamp and the followers of Zwingli dubbed sacramentaries on the ground that they denied the real presence in the sacrament of the altar. Doctrinal revulsion received force from fears of social subversion: the existing order identified all such extremism with the well publicized horrors of the Anabaptist kingdom of Münster (1535) and more sensibly with the populist Lollardy which the Church had known for so long. Actually, there were very few true sectaries in England and most of them immigrants, but fears rose high when infection was discovered at Calais, always a place sensitive to dangers of subversion. Neither Cromwell nor Cranmer wished to protect sacramentaries, and Cranmer in fact proceeded against one such, John Lambert alias Nicolson, burned for heresy in November 1538 after a trial in which the King had personally displayed his theological learning as well as his readiness to bully his victims. November altogether brought signs that the Reformation was beginning to run into difficulties. On the 16th, the King issued a major proclamation of the drafting of which he had for once taken charge himself. In the main it was an attack on Anabaptists and sacramentaries, rightly thought to be mostly foreigners: those already taken were to be dealt with as heretics and all others were expelled the realm on pain of death if caught. Henry took the opportunity to proclaim also his particular, and strangely personal, opposition to clerical marriage, one of the issues that prevented agreement with the Lutherans. The proclamation protected acceptable practices and ceremonies against those who were taking the campaign against 'superstition' further than the King

[3] After Cromwell's fall, his coat of arms but not his figure was removed from the page.

approved; it also initiated the censorship of the press in England, though for the present it confined licensing by the Privy Council to the Scriptures.

In general, therefore, Henry was giving a warning that change had gone far enough, but even this very proclamation demonstrated the limits of his autocratic control. Before it was issued, Cromwell obtained the addition of two clauses one of which (laying the stress on the Protestant preference for the preaching of the Word) weakened the reaction by re-emphasizing the distinction between decent ceremonies and 'superstitious abuses and idolatries', while the other set out the official line on Becket's evil behaviour which made him no martyr or saint but only a traitor. Several unhappy Dutchmen suffered death as the consequence of the proclamation, but the persecution petered out before it had really got going: in late February yet another announcement not only pardoned all sectaries provided they mended their ways but gave a detailed justification for ceremonies which turned them into nothing but aids to preaching and faith. At this stage the reforming party was well in the saddle again, for reasons which had to do not only with Cromwell's zeal but also with developments on the European scene.

The progress of reform throughout 1538 effectively put an end to hopes at Rome that it might still be possible to bring England back into the fold. These had been unrealistic for years but received nourishment both from English diplomatic finesse and from the northern risings—hence Reginald Pole's first mission which, as it turned out, succeeded only in bringing disaster to his family and friends. Through 1537 Henry and Cromwell kept in pursuit of him, though it is never clear whether they meant to assassinate him or win him over; probably they kept both options open. Once again Henry's friendly regard for a protégé had turned into undying hatred, and when Cromwell found that he had been tricked by double agents really working for Pole he threw himself wholeheartedly into the business of destroying what Henry regarded as a nest of traitors. In August 1538, Reginald's younger brother Geoffrey was arrested, an unstable and unhappy man who saved his life by revealing all he knew (and perhaps more) about the opinions and activities of his family and the Courtenays. In November, the elder Pole (Henry Lord Montague) and the marquess of Exeter were arrested; trials and executions followed in which altogether some sixteen persons, all of standing, died; and Pole's mother, the old countess of Salisbury, daughter to the Yorkist duke of Clarence followed into prison, to be condemned by act of attainder the year after, though she survived in the Tower till her belated execution in 1541.

It is usually said that the government produced no convincing evidence of treasonable conspiracy; it was—and is—widely held that the tragedy represented only the King's bloodthirsty suspiciousness, Cromwell's hatred of the old nobility, and perhaps the final removal of the so-called 'White Rose', the Yorkist remnant, for the sake of Tudor dynastic security. This, however, is too simple a view; more lay behind these events than has been recognized. True, the charges brought against the Pole-Courtenay group, while constituting treason by words under the act of 1534, do not amount to proven conspiracy, but they include (and these matters were admitted) a mass of highly suspicious dealings with the cardinal during his stay at Liège, dangerously illegal plans to flee the realm without licence, broad hints of dynastic ambition, and plenty of evidence that treason was contemplated even if not plotted. A dispassionate assessment leaves little doubt that the two families were not only disaffected but revolving ways of giving disaffection teeth, however incompetently they went about things. Moreover, it is a mistake to treat the events of 1538 in isolation. A clue is provided by the inclusion among the victims of Sir Edward Neville and Sir Nicholas Carew, neither of whom had any blood relationship to Pole or Courtenay. Both, however, were gentlemen of the Privy Chamber—the last survivors there of the Marian Court faction of 1536 whose leaders had fallen in the executions of 1537. Exeter had been of the Privy Chamber until turned out by Cromwell's campaign for control of that body; like Darcy and Hussey he was an alienated courtier. It looks very much as though this rump of opposition did mean to use Pole's mission for yet another attempt against Cromwell and the innovators. We need to remember the long-standing and serious plans for using Pole. As early as 1533, Chapuys had thought that the Emperor would do well to secure the person of this Englishman living in Italy because he would make the best Imperialist candidate for Henry's throne; and the pilgrims of grace had talked darkly about 'princes of the blood' who ought to be in power around the King. None of this was news to Cromwell or Henry, and taken in conjunction with the wild talk reported of Montague and Exeter it created a convincing impression of a major danger at home even as the possibility of danger from abroad was becoming urgent again. The events of 1538 really formed the final stage of the power struggle that had started with the rise of Cromwell and the conflicts of policy. The strange thing is that these conspirators, whose influence could have raised Devon, Dorset, Wiltshire and Hampshire, should have failed to coordinate things with Darcy in 1536: for the evidence of close contacts between them is quite conclusive. To all appearance they were taken by surprise by the northern rising, and Montague in fact later put the blame for mismanaging the rebellion on Darcy. Insufficiently prepared, they played for safety, with the result that the government was able to destroy the opposition by stages. However, the manifest incompetence of the plotters, while it adds to one's pity of them, does not disprove their intention to plot. Henry's reaction was predictably savage, and Cromwell's predictably thorough, but they had a reality to react against.

These events also confirm, as the north had done eighteen months earlier, that talk of a feudal reaction distorts. The Percies had vanished without a shot or a shout, and the Courtenays' disaster equally roused no outburst of regional loyalties. Nevertheless, Cromwell thought it wise to take a firm hold on the southwest where he employed the tried device of a local council.[4] In March–April 1539, a body analogous to the Council of the North was set up, under the presidency of Lord Russell, to administer Exeter city and the shires of Devon, Cornwall, Somerset and Dorset. It sat only for two brief months between September and November that year and vanished quickly at Cromwell's fall. The council, as it turned out, was both superfluous and expensive. Neither political troubles nor even massive lawlessness justified its existence. It came into being rather precipitately, in the wake of the general reorganization of the coastal defences which Henry set in motion early that year; Russell, an old courtier and a privy councillor, was elevated to the peerage and equipped with a sizable local estate only a few weeks before he took up his duties, and his instructions, modelled too faithfully upon those issued for the north, used terms and mentioned administrative concerns quite inappropriate for the southwest. Evidently Cromwell, who had displayed an earlier interest in the better government of the region, took the opportunity to extend his favourite system of bureaucratic boards in a new direction, but lack of need as well as the heavy cost doomed the experiment.[5] The story provides yet another, and a strange, example of the independent initiatives that Cromwell was willing to take in government without consulting the King's wishes, but all that he left behind in this case was the establishment of the Russells as the dominant family in Somerset.

Defence against foreign threats had opened the way for this abortive move, and defence was indeed the King's first pre-

---

[4] Joyce A. Youings, 'The Council of the West', *Transactions of the Royal Historical Society* (1960), pp. 41 ff.

[5] Professor Youings suggests that Cromwell's fall saved the realm from being covered with a network of bureaucratic institutions; perhaps so, but the problem of controlling local government remained. The growing tension between unitary centralization (Cromwell's ambition) and the power of local people and groupings was to be temporarily tided over by the use of aristocratic lords lieutenant: but this compromise did not prevent the civil war, and I suspect that Cromwell would have thought it inadequate.

occupation as 1538 turned into 1539. In November 1538, Paul III put the suspended bull excommunicating Henry into effect, and in January Pole, now driven on by justified hatred as well as religion, once more went on a mission to the powers, to seek aid against England. He even visited Charles V at Toledo, after preparing the ground with a long address (his *Apologia ad Carolum Quintum Caesarem*) in which he gave his version of English history since the Divorce and put all the blame on Cromwell, that offspring and servant of the devil. The second mission proved even more pitifully futile than the first, but initially it seemed to presage danger. Henry reacted with vigour. He himself journeyed rapidly along the coasts to survey defences and urge on the work of construction, an amount of travelling that can have done no good at all to his ulcerated leg and therefore his temper. Cromwell thoroughly overhauled the shire musters, an effort which produced a major census of able-bodied males but also discovered the inadequacies of the military potential and of the organization designed to mobilize it. The danger grew more urgent in the early months of 1539 when both Spain and France withdrew their resident ambassadors from England. Cromwell saw the chance of reviving his scheme of a Lutheran alliance; yet another Saxon embassy was solicited which arrived in April, but despite a cordial reception from King and minister it left after a few weeks without any agreement being reached.

In any case, Henry was now looking into a slightly different possibility. His search for a wife narrowed down to Anne, the sister of William, duke of Cleves, whose territories commanded the vital route down the Rhine which linked Charles's Burgundian and Italian possessions, and upon which any imperial attack on England depended. The duke, who had just inherited Gelderland upon which Charles had claims, was no Lutheran, but he had withdrawn his Church from the papal obedience and was connected to Protestant Saxony. Thus Cromwell's grand northern alliance against Rome and the Catholic powers showed signs of materializing. However, the situation, as usual, changed again very quickly. In March, a new French ambassador arrived, while Gardiner, who in September 1538 had been replaced by Edmund Bonner after three years at Francis I's court, was back in England to intrigue against Cromwell and promote the French amity as a better way to counter the foreign threat. Henry, in fact, refused to believe that the friendship between Charles and Francis would endure, in which estimate he was perfectly correct. Preoccupied with Germany, Gelderland, the Turks, and (soon) a rebellion in Ghent, Charles could spare no thought for the crusade against England. Cautious as ever, Henry wished to avoid any positive commitments, and Cromwell's bolder line, driven forward by his desire to consolidate the Reformation, increasingly moved him out of step with his master. By May only the marriage negotiations at Cleves remained active, and they not very much so. Henry was told that the lady lacked polite accomplishments and seemed rather shy, but she was said to be handsome; and Holbein's portrait confirmed that her face at least did not disgrace her in the gallery of Henry's generally rather unattractive wives.

II

Putting the country into a posture of defence cost money—a lot of money, more even than the crown's improved revenues could cover. One result, late in 1539, was that Cromwell accepted the need to organize the profitable liquidation of part of the new crown lands, but in addition he wanted a subsidy. None had been demanded since 1534, and the country had been free of tax-collectors since late in 1536. In any case, the troubles of the last few years had prevented the calling of a Parliament, and the delay had piled up unfinished business both public and private. The time had come to call one again; the writs went out on 1 March and the Houses assembled on 28 April, to sit for about two months with a prorogation over Whitsun. Cromwell had worked hard to manage the elections: this (so far as we know) was the first Parliament for which the influence of councillors was mobilized and coordinated in shires and boroughs. In Hampshire, Cromwell's secretary Thomas Wriothesley overcame the influence of the bishop of Winchester but in general the operation aimed to secure worthy and amenable members in the King's interest, not Cromwell's. The vicegerent was not trying to build himself a parliamentary party, not in any case a thing conceivable at the time, but only (as he explained to Henry) to obtain a Parliament more 'tractable' than its predecessors. Management for general government ends is what he had in mind, not perhaps corruption or oppression. He also found that like most parliamentary managers down to the rise of modern parties he had overestimated the Commons' tractability, and he proved unable to prevent Council divisions from manifesting themselves in the Lords. The meeting of Parliament had for him the disadvantage that it enabled—indeed compelled—his enemies to foregather at Westminster. Norfolk hastened up from his county and Gardiner from his diocese, and from the first things did not look too good for the lord privy seal when the Commons elected as their Speaker Sir Nicholas Hare, a client of the

duke's. Throughout the session, in fact, Norfolk was to out-
manoeuvre Cromwell, obviously because Henry was drawing away
from the vicegerent's radical policies and backing the conservatives
on the Council.

The Parliament started hesitantly, with only four sittings in twelve
days. Cromwell did not attend these, partly because he was ill, but
the real reason was different. The lord privy seal had no mind to
take his lowly place as the next-to-junior baron, and the first business
of the parliament was to pass a bill which altered the sitting order of
the Lords so as to put the King's vicegerent in the first place, above
all archbishops and dukes. As soon as this bill was through, before
the Commons had even seen it, the House rearranged itself and
Cromwell promptly recovered from his illness. But his absence had
been unwise, for during those days Norfolk and Gardiner wrested
the initiative away from him. The Parliament was called for several
reasons—money, the clearing up of past events like the surrender of
abbeys to the King and the various executions of 1537–8 (for which
confirming statutes were passed), and so far as Cromwell was
concerned further measures of social reform. But (as Cromwell knew
well) its chief end lay elsewhere, in the settlement of religious
divisions. On 5 May, Audley announced the King's desire that the
Parliament should turn its attention to providing a measure which
would end religious disputes in the country, and this issue was to
dominate the session. Immediately the Lords nominated a committee of eight to consider the problem, and though Cromwell (still
absent) was naturally, as vicegerent in spirituals, put in charge, he
found that he had on it three radical allies (including Cranmer) and
four conservative opponents. His enemies had neatly blocked any
hope he might have had of using his spiritual office to direct the
settlement which Henry's insistence made into the first concern of
the day.

Reform, in fact, achieved not very much in 1539; several important bills failed for lack of time, though some of Cromwell's plans got
through. One of the chief hopes of the reformers received support in
a short act which authorized the King to create new bishoprics by
letters patent, endowing them out of monastic property. The act
emphasized the needs of spiritual administration and especially of
support for learning; it reflects the ambitions so frequently proclaimed in the Cromwell circle for a proper use of the new wealth.
Henry himself took a considerable interest in the working out of the
proposal, helping to produce a scheme for thirteen new sees and the
conversion of monastic cathedrals into sufficiently endowed secular
establishments. This second intention was carried through, but in
the end only six new sees were created between 1540 and 1542—

Westminster (abolished in 1550), Oxford, Chester, Peterborough, Gloucester and Bristol—though this was still a notable reform. Not only were the unmanageably large dioceses of Lincoln and Lichfield broken up into potentially better governed units, but the new foundations were specially charged with maintaining grammar schools and with supporting large numbers of King's scholars at the universities, while Westminster came to be responsible for underwriting readerships at Cambridge and Oxford in Greek, Hebrew, law, divinity and medicine. Educational reform was altogether much discussed at the time; schemes were prepared to create a special institution for the study of civil law at Cambridge and for a humanistic reform of the common law at the Inns of Court; but the 1540s, with war and inflation dominant, proved barren ground for the more grandiose ambitions. As it was, the creation of the new sees constituted a useful and worthy reform, very much in step with advanced thinking in all the Christian churches of the day, which does not deserve the contempt often bestowed upon it. It was, after all, probably all that England could afford to do, both financially and administratively.

Cromwell's major reforming bill of the session, however, caused difficulties at the time and has continued to trouble historians ever since. As we have seen, he had for nearly a decade been engaged in remedying the deficiencies of the body politic, and he had tried to do much of this through statutes applied and varied by royal proclamations. He had also found the labour both overwhelming and frustrating, mainly because it proved virtually impossible to enforce proclamations against passive resistance and evasion. Moreover, his energetically active policy had drawn attention to the prerogative power vested in proclamations: the nature and limits of their functions had become matter for legal debate. Thus in 1539 he decided to solve the outstanding questions by an enabling act which would confirm the general constitutional basis for proclamations (by converting judicial opinion into parliamentary authority) and would set up machinery for their enforcement. The bill came under much attack in this 'tractable' Parliament; thoroughly amended in the Lords, it was in the Commons replaced by another bill which included a new clause protecting life and freehold from invasion by the prerogative. The act as passed authorized the issue of proclamations which were to be obeyed 'as though they were made by act of Parliament', and provided a large conciliar body (the Privy Council augmented by the inclusion of a good many ordinary councillors left out of the reformed board in 1536) to hear and determine actions arising from them.

This statute, and memories of the opposition it aroused, have

induced various historians, at different times, to believe that what
Cromwell had planned, until a vigilant Parliament stopped him, was
the creation of a prerogative power to make law which would
supersede parliamentary statute. This is not so, and the suspicion
deserves to be interred. Though the original bill, no longer extant,
may have tried to equip proclamations with more extensive powers,
the preamble of the act, which was taken over from the official bill,
set out a policy entirely in accord with the limited purpose of the act
as passed. This simply codified the common-law interpretation of
proclamations along lines laid down by the judges in 1531; its
purpose throughout had been to provide machinery for the execution of Cromwell's 'commonwealth' policy and not for a legislative
despotism; it preserved and indeed increased the supremacy of
statute over the prerogative; and it falls straight into line with
Cromwell's constitutional practice throughout his administration.
The act was repealed in 1547 (not because it was oppressive but
because the court set up in it did not work well); during its existence
proclamations were used exactly as they had been before; it was only
in the reign of Elizabeth, when proclamations once more rested
solely on the Crown's common-law prerogative, that they began to
offend against the principle of the clause that the Commons had
inserted in 1539. The new judicial machinery proved too cumbersome and was reformed in 1543; though the special council heard
cases and made some efforts to give effect to proclamations, enforcement remained the unsolved problem of these necessary and flexible
instruments of policy. Manifestly the Parliament of 1539 showed
itself alert to dangerous possibilities, and this is a fact worth ponder-
ing in any assessment of Henrician Parliaments, but nothing in
Cromwell's well attested practice justified their fears or historians'
strictures. In fact, the act was a major achievement of law reform
and deserved a better fate, even though its administrative clauses
failed to solve the problem of enforcement. It may stand as one of
the crowns, though temporary, of Cromwell's work, clearing the
ground for effective and renovating management, under the authority of Parliament, of the nation's secular and spiritual affairs.[6]

The history of the Proclamations Act made plain that this
Parliament would be engaged upon a small number of major bills
rather than deal with the general programme of reform which
Cromwell had prepared. What really frustrated his plans was the
King's demand for a settlement of the faith, a matter in which he
could only lose. The committee under his chairmanship never acted

[6]For the fullest account, which sets the statute into the context of practice, purpose and
debate, see R. Heinze, *The Proclamations of the Tudor Kings*; this also reviews the earlier
controversies.

at all, so that Norfolk could launch his attack on the vicegerent with a good show of just exasperation. On 16 May he complained of the failure to heed the King's request and presented to the Lords six major doctrinal issues in the form of questions so framed as to demand strictly traditional answers: could the sacrament of the altar be the body of Christ without transubstantiation, was lay communion in both kinds necessary, were vows of chastity binding for life by the law of God, were private masses enjoined by that same law, could (by that law) priests marry, was auricular confession necessary according to the law of God? It quickly became clear that the outcome had been agreed with the supreme head. On the 20th Norfolk again intervened to press for a discussion of doctrine and demand that the debate on the subsidy be postponed: evidently Cromwell had been working on this through the Commons in the hope that Henry's desire for money would distract him from the religious controversy. Norfolk won, and the Whitsun prorogation, also engineered by him (probably on Henry's instruction),[7] was used to arrive at decisions. When Parliament reassembled, Audley announced that the King, having taken spiritual advice, now wanted an act which would answer Norfolk's questions in the positive sense and would enforce this orthodoxy as England's faith. The radicals put up a token resistance by getting two drafting committees appointed, one reformist and one reactionary, but the bill introduced on 7 June embodied only the views of the latter. The Act of Six Articles passed swiftly enough, though hurried drafting called for some belated provisos and, after the bill had passed both Houses, for an amendment which postponed the date by which married priests had to put away their wives from 23 June (yesterday, when the amendment was introduced) to 12 July.

The six articles of the faith settled in the statute all represented crucial points of divergence between Catholicism and Reformation; the traditional view that total orthodoxy was here reasserted and the reformation firmly arrested must be accepted. The statute caused consternation among reformers both English and continental; Latimer and Shaxton felt compelled to resign their sees of Worcester and Salisbury; but Cranmer and Cromwell, true to their principle of submission to the authority of both the supreme head and the Parliament, abandoned opposition and put a brave face on defeat. The statute was, as Henry had demanded, a penal act: denial of transubstantiation became heresy punishable by burning, while

---

[7] Formally, the prorogation was requested by Parliament but the move came from Norfolk and· was in fact so inconvenient to both Houses that they felt compelled to agree that bills unfinished in the first session should exceptionally be continued into the second as though there had been no prorogation.

offences against the other five articles were variously subject to the penalties of praemunire and felony. Special care was taken to dissolve the marriages of late entered into by clergy who had jumped the gun in hopes of further reform: the act's insistence here faithfully reflects Henry's particular abhorrence of broken vows of celibacy. Moreover, the act created machinery for enforcement, adding county commissions with inquisitorial powers to the ordinary process of the spiritual law. It was a savage and formidable measure, and it had its victims. But like so much else in Tudor legislation and policy it worked only if spontaneously supported by the lay rulers of society, and it was never enforced with the vigour and consistency intended. Cromwell, dangerously to himself, from the first used his authority to hamper its application, an activity in which he was assisted by the death, late in 1539, of Bishop Stokesley of London, the one bishop who tried to make a reality of the reaction. Yet the doctrine of the Six Articles remained the official truth of the Church of England while Henry lived; now there could be no question of importing more of the continental Reformation. The conservatives may have hoped to use the act to wipe out the reforming party in the clergy altogether, and if that was their intention they and the act certainly failed, but this does not alter the fact that the Parliament which Cromwell had meant to use for the consolidation of the reform instead put an end to it. At the very least he had suffered a major defeat, and he must have realized how uncertain his position of power really was whenever he got out of step with the King. It tells a good deal about his temperament and determination that so far from accepting this lesson he quickly reacted by re-establishing his control and resuming his perilous policy.

III

In fact, Cromwell had throughout this Parliament played his losing hand with great skill; he had ridden some very telling punches, and before the Houses rose on 28 June he had recovered the management of affairs. He now obtained his Bible-licensing monopoly, resumed the supervision of law enforcement in the realm, and decided to exploit the international situation by freeing England from the dependence on French friendship which Gardiner and Norfolk were advocating. Assisted by renewed peace moves among the great powers he at last brought Henry to a point; on 4 October 1539, his agents signed the marriage treaty with Anne of Cleves. The lady arrived in England in December, to be received with great pomp and great hopes, but her first meeting with her intended husband proved utterly disastrous. Anne was not plain, but she was heavy, ordinary and dull; she spoke no language other than her own, and her accomplishments were modestly domestic. Henry disliked her on sight and expressed his furious disappointment, but Cromwell made it plain that there was no way out. The marriage was celebrated on 6 January 1540; on his way, the forty-nine year old bridegroom said to his minister, 'My lord, if it were not to satisfy the world and my realm, I would not do that I must do this day for none earthly thing.' This unpromising start set the scene: Henry found himself unable to consummate the marriage, even after Cromwell had given Anne some dubious instruction in technique, and before many days had passed he demanded to be freed once more. Not unnaturally he relied on the man who had already removed two inconvenient wives to achieve yet a third miracle, but Cromwell soon knew that the way was not easy and that he had made a mistake of monumental proportions. The Cleves marriage did not by itself sink him, but it fatally tied his hands just when he needed every liberty of movement to withstand the renewed assault of his enemies. Before the end of 1539, the lord privy seal was aware that an anti-Cromwell faction was rebuilding at court which included influential members of the Council and the Privy Chamber—an ominous revival of the grouping he had smashed in 1536–8 and even more dangerous than its predecessor because it was not tainted with disloyalty to Henrician rule in Church and state.

From the minister's point of view, the trouble with the projected divorce was not so much the affront to Cleves and the consequent collapse of the anti-papal alliance—these he could evidently absorb as he had absorbed Henry's surprises in foreign policy before—as the person whom Henry had chosen for wife number five. From early in 1540 everyone knew that the King's eye had lit upon yet another young lady of the court, Catherine Howard, Norfolk's niece, a twenty year old girl of great vivacity and exceptionally loose morals, Though the ending of an unconsummated marriage posed for once no legal problems, all it would achieve would be the triumph of the Howard faction at court. So Cromwell procrastinated in the face of Henry's growing urgency, a dangerous thing to do when the lust of an aging autocrat was driving things on. At the same time he also again lost some political ground. In February Norfolk went on a special embassy to France from which he returned with messages of good will and possibly with hints that relations would be immensely improved if Cromwell were removed. In March Gardiner found a fresh opportunity to assail the minister when Robert Barnes

preached a sermon which brought him in danger of the Act of Six
Articles. Barnes was followed in the same vein by William Jerome
and Thomas Garret, notorious adherents of the reform. A flurry of
accusations, defiances and recantations, carefully played up by the
bishop of Winchester who not for the first or last time proved how
well he could employ the pose of a bluff honest man, drew the King's
scandalized attention to this outrageous example of the public
divisions he had meant to end by the act, and by early April the
three preachers were in the Tower. Yet Cromwell avoided public
involvement in the disaster that befell his reckless protégés. He made
a great show of friendship with Gardiner and strengthened his hand
on the Privy Council by surrendering the office of secretary to two
members of his staff, Thomas Wriothesley and Ralph Sadler, both
immediately sworn of that body. He needed supporters, for Henry
now readmitted Gardiner and Sampson of Chichester to the board
from which Cromwell had secured their exclusion a few months
earlier.

Thus the politics of power oscillated in conditions of highly
confusing uncertainty: one of our difficulties is that they much
confused our ambassadorial informants whose reports are not to be
trusted. That there was a struggle cannot be doubted, but we shall
never know just what was going on. Peace temporarily returned
when Parliament reassembled on 12 April. Cromwell was still very
manifestly in charge; indeed, this last parliamentary session of his life
proved something of a triumph for him. On the 18th he obtained his
highest glory—elevation to the earldom of Essex and the high dignity
of the great chamberlaincy. All the signs are that at this point Henry
sincerely meant to express his continued trust in his greatest minister,
and the way in which he chose to demonstrate it was particularly
galling to the hostile faction with its contempt for the upstart and
outsider. Yet all the time, wherever the swinging balance settled, the
time-bomb of the Cleves marriage was ticking away as Cromwell's
failure to deal with it jeopardized Henry's trust and reliance.

Meanwhile Cromwell resumed his proper life's work in
Parliament. The session of 1540 witnessed a massive programme of
reforming bills; though as always more was projected and introduced
than reached the statute book, the acts passed picked up quite a few
earlier plans and attempts, and some long-standing intentions
achieved realization. The session completed the Dissolution by confiscating the properties of the Knights of St John; under the guidance
of Lord Chancellor Audley several important law reforms were
pushed through, though Cromwell's dream of a comprehensive
overhaul of the legal profession got nowhere; sanctuaries were
abolished; a major navigation act promoted shipping and trade;

another statute laid the foundations for a proper organization of the medical profession. The Statute of Wills, which permitted a man to bequeath two thirds of his landed estate, removed the objectionable rigour of the Statute of Uses and completed the fundamental reform of the land law. Cromwell himself concentrated on two things—the subsidy, and unity in religion—and in both he allowed his inmost convictions to appear. He devoted great care to the preparation of the subsidy bill whose preamble justified this further example of peace-time taxation not only by the costs incurred in defence and social policy but emphatically on the grounds that the nation owed Henry deep gratitude (and money) for leading it out of the shadows of popish thraldom to the shining uplands of the true religion. As for unity, Cromwell opened the session with a major speech in which he called for an end to strife and elaborated his favourite theme of the middle way; conveying the King's desire to see the work of pacification continued, he obtained the appointment of two committees of bishops (biased on the conservative side) to formulate a definition of doctrine and draw up a book of authorized ceremonies—the first hint of a reformed liturgy which in the end was to result in the Book of Common Prayer.

Determined though Henry was on the suppression of theological disputes, and passionately though Cromwell advocated the *via media* between heresy and superstition, nothing in fact came of all this except a short enabling statute looking to future decisions. The money grant, on the other hand, passed readily and—despite a feeling that a Crown so recently and so lavishly enriched might be able to live of its own—was a substantial one of two subsidies and four fifteenths and tenths. The subsidies each yielded twice what had been collected in 1535–6, so that approximately £160,000 came to the Exchequer in 1541–2, with another £60,000 in the two subsequent years.

It was at this point that Cromwell, triumphant in Parliament and more secure in Council than for some time, determined to break the faction working against him. On 19 May, Lord Lisle, the ineffectual deputy at Calais, was arrested on suspicion of dealings with Cardinal Pole, and on the 26th Cromwell (without Henry's previous knowledge) committed Bishop Sampson to the Tower in the hope of extracting details of conspiracies from one who had never been conspicuous for steadfast courage. Evidently he once more meant to use the weapons that had worked so well against the factions of Aragon and Courtenay—the charges of involvement with the enemy at Rome. It was too late. Allegedly he planned to lay hold of others among the men arrayed against him, but before he could get Henry's compliance Norfolk and Gardiner finally broke through. On

10 June he was himself arrested at the Council table, in the King's name, by the captain of the Guard, a member of Norfolk's reconstituted faction. Norfolk himself and his chief henchman, William Fitzwilliam, earl of Southampton, tore the garter from his neck, while Cromwell furiously cast his bonnet on the floor, denied that he had ever been a traitor, and asked only that they should make a swift end of him. Of this he could be sure. And so he passed into the Tower, whither he had sent so many men and women, never to leave it. His goods were seized at once, a fatally conclusive sign.

IV

Cromwell was condemned unheard, by act of attainder, without trial. It was alleged at the time (and has been said since) that he justly suffered by the bloody methods he himself had invented, but this is untrue: attainder without trial was used as early as 1459. Cromwell had countenanced the method only on the occasion when the overriding needs of policy seemed to him to call for the destruction of public enemies (the Nun of Kent and her accomplices) whose actions were not comprehended within the unreformed and inadequate treason law; its application to the countess of Salisbury owed nothing to him, and his own proceedings had in general been characterized by an almost painful devotion to the forms and rules of the common law. The act had passed both Houses by 29 June, but he was not brought to execution at once. Henry wanted his written testimony for the divorce proceedings against Anne of Cleves, and Cromwell duly obliged with all the sordid details. (Cranmer pronounced the marriage void on 10 July, and Henry married his second Catherine on 9 August. His second Anne retired prudently and contentedly upon the estates generously provided by her ex-husband.) The fallen minister used the delay to write letters pleading for mercy; he understood the King well enough to know that abject contrition might yet do the trick, though he also vigorously defended himself against the allegations of treason and heresy. He did succeed in briefly moving Henry who usually in such cases—as in Dudley's or Wolsey's—had shown an inclination to hedge his bets by keeping the disgraced man alive and, as it were, in reserve.

But the victorious faction could not afford a live Cromwell, even under sentence of death in the Tower, and on 28 July Henry's greatest servant, and the most remarkable statesman of the sixteenth century, went to execution. In his customary farewell address he prayed for the King and Prince Edward, repented of his sins and conceded that he stood condemned by the law, but also refused to renounce any of his doings or 'purge himself', as he knew had been expected of him. He ostentatiously refrained from commenting on the justice of his lawful end, and he baffled everyone by asserting that he died 'in the catholic faith of the Holy Church', a phrase which excludes sectarian heresies but does not necessarily imply denial of the moderately reformed faith which had so manifestly been his preferred choice since 1532 at least. His last prayer—to confuse the issue of allegiances further—was taken from Erasmus. Two days later, Barnes, Jerome and Garret were burned for heresy at Smithfield—without trial and without cause in law—while three long-term prisoners of the Aragonese faction (Edward Powell, Richard Fetherstone and Thomas Abel) suffered the death of traitors. It has been suggested that Henry knew little or nothing about these executions and that they should not, therefore, be interpreted, as used to be done, as a public demonstration of his impartiality among the parties: and this is indeed likely, as is the further suggestion that the killings (which in the case of the Protestants amounted to murder) were linked with the conspiracy that brought Cromwell down.[8] The three Protestants most probably died to justify the charge that the lord privy seal had protected heretics and to satisfy Gardiner's thirst for revenge; the Catholics probably suffered to announce the Henrician loyalties of the triumphant faction who were anxious to avoid any hint of links with the defunct treasons organized by Chapuys. If any of these sad victims were more directly implicated in what Norfolk and Gardiner had done, we know nothing about it.

For altogether Cromwell's fall, so exceptionally sudden, retains much mystery. The particular charges against him make it difficult rather than easy to understand why Henry should have thrown him over: the specified 'overt deeds' of his alleged treason are so absurd that the decision to avoid a trial becomes very comprehensible. It may, for instance, be doubted whether any witness could have been found capable of persuading a jury that Cromwell explicitly offered to take the field against Henry if the King refused to support the Reformation. Accusations of an abuse of power did not amount to treason, and the only specific example of his alleged heresy offered in the attainder was an assertion of the priesthood of all believers, which may well have been true but did not much offend Henry's own views. The difficulty is to know what it was that persuaded the King, and the likeliest interpretation must suppose that he allowed himself to believe that his vicegerent was indeed a sacramentarian

[8] J. J. Sacrisbrick, *Henry VIII*, pp. 380 ff.

heretic. Certainly there was some truth in the attainder's allegation that Cromwell had protected suspected traitors (that is, had refused to proceed against men falsely accused) and heretics (that is, had assisted reformers like Barnes and Jerome). Cromwell's fall was in general popular, though he had his friends who secretly lamented: once again Henry, in a cleft stick of policy at home and abroad, found that the offer of a scapegoat would best allow him to be free at one bound. We shall never know the full inwardness of the event, but I suggest that Norfolk's insinuations came handily to the King just when he saw himself tied in toils by international agreements he had certainly approved but now disliked, and just as he had grown extremely impatient with Cromwell's reluctance to help him out of the Cleves marriage. He had always been more readily managed than he ever admitted to himself: if Anne Boleyn could whisper in his ear, so could Catherine Howard. Told that he could have a new wife, a free hand in affairs, and religious peace in the realm if only he rid himself of Cromwell, he had no difficulty in believing—briefly but long enough for the purpose—that he had nurtured a sacramentarian viper in his innocently orthodox bosom. And Cromwell's reforming policy provided just enough truth to lend verisimilitude to the charge. By a final and devastating irony, Cromwell died because he had had a cause—because he was not the cynical time-server of tradition but a man possessed of an ideal that in the end he pursued with insufficient regard for his own safety.

Less than a year after the event Henry knew well enough that he had been tricked into killing 'the most faithful servant he had ever had'. By then it was much too late to rescue the realm from the consequences of that loss. More even than Cromwell's success in bringing down his adversaries, his death demonstrated the narrow limits and inherent weaknesses of Henry's famed 'control' over the events of his reign and the policies of his Council.

Thomas Cromwell had lived his political life in the shadow of the axe raised by himself when he undertook to rebuild the realm in the service of a shallow, capricious, self-righteous, immensely powerful egoist who would admit to no mistake and had developed to the highest degree a knack of grabbing the gold while casting the dirt upon others. Cromwell had taken his share in the bloody work, but the essence of his labours lay in the universal impact of a tenaciously constructive mind upon every problem affecting the body politic. Capable of cold-blooded ruthlessness in the service of cause and King, he took the blame for many decisions whose moral burden really rested upon Henry, and the evil reputation which attended him in life as well as after death is understandable and not without foundations. A man who pursued such drastic policies so unhesitatingly could not wonder at exciting the hatred that absolutely explodes in his attainder: bishops and dukes, priests and monks, the families of men eminent and unimportant whom his treason laws had killed, could all with good cause rejoice at the death of 'the foul churl'. If, because his personal share of atrocious deeds was deliberately augmented by that much larger part properly belonging to the King, his reputation sheered wildly from the truth, the nemesis that came to him yet stemmed from the political crimes he had thought it necessary to commit. Such balance sheets satisfy the moralistic ambitions of the uninvolved. Any great career deserves to be judged by its achievements rather than its enforced aberrations. Cromwell promoted a revolution in the kingdom from which the nation emerged transformed and altered in every aspect of its life. With singular tenacity he pursued his vision of a unitary realm reformed in body and soul, ordered better—and better pleasing to God—according to the best informed opinion of the day, under the protection of the law and ruled by the dynamic sovereignty of the King-in-Parliament. That vision cost him his life, but he laid foundations that did not crumble for centuries.

13 The Rule of King Henry

I

For two months after Cromwell's death the hottest summer of the century continued its course; the sun shone, the crops died, and the plague returned. King Henry, perfunctorily ordering prayers for rain, dived headlong into a second youth, celebrating his fifth marriage with a punishing regime of hunting, feasting and gallivanting. On the face of it, Cromwell's disappearance made little difference. None of his followers in court or Council suffered because of it, nor did the policies he had initiated come to an immediate end; even the supporters of the Reformation saw their worst fears falsified, though the Act of Six Articles claimed some victims in 1541 who would probably have escaped if Cromwell had lived. Exploiting the happy pretence that all service was unselfishly offered to the King, the administration adjusted itself easily to the disappearance of the minister who had engrossed all power, and in this it was helped by Cromwell's own bureaucratizing reforms which stood out more obviously now that he had gone. Above all, the reformed Privy Council took over the task for which Cromwell had designed it. On 10 August 1540, its nineteen members met to inaugurate a regular minute book and to appoint as their clerk William Paget, originally a client of Gardiner's who had later pursued his career and learned his business under Cromwell, and who was to take the lead in preserving the government created by Cromwell through the vicissitudes of the next eighteen years. From that time the Privy Council formed a corporate ruling committee, acting as a body to conduct the realm's affairs, though its members of course continued to discharge departmental duties and work for their own careers.

The earl of Southampton took the privy seal, but despite rumours that Bishop Tunstall would become vicegerent in spirituals that office lapsed for ever. In truth no one succeeded Cromwell, and Henry determined from now on to avoid reliance on single overpowerful ministers. From mid-1540 to mid-1546, he took sole responsibility for all that was attempted and done: those were the years of his truly personal rule. But if he supposed that he might thus free himself from the troubles of faction he was mistaken; behind the deceptive façade of a dominant kingship, the battles of ambition and policy continued as vigorous as ever. These oscillations have usually been read as events in the war of religions, and the struggles between reformers and conservatives did indeed form an important aspect of them. However, the real story involved political factions in court and Council, and possibly in the country too, though it is a story that has not yet been sufficiently elucidated and may for ever retain much obscurity. We shall tell it here so far as at present it can be discerned.

The King's fifth marriage and Norfolk's triumph over Cromwell ought to have put the Howards in the saddle, with Gardiner as the leading exponent of the ideology they espoused, but Henry did not mean to allow them an untrammelled ascendancy. In any case, the duke was growing old and his clan included only political light-weights; his faction really relied on established politicians like Southampton and Russell who could no more be trusted to back him in a difficult situation than Audley and Rich had backed Cromwell when the crunch came. The battles of 1536–8 had affec-tively removed the non-curial elements of the conservative factions. The main immediate beneficiary of the *coup* of 1540 was Thomas Wriothesley who had adroitly switched sides before Cromwell's fall and who now, as chief secretary, inherited his master's control of the executive. When Audley died in 1544, Wriothesley—rather surpris-ingly for one who was neither an eminent lawyer nor a churchman—took the great seal. His return to conservatism in religion proved enduring, and he displayed much administrative energy and competence; the new regime could not have operated without him, but he assuredly was no second Cromwell. Still, he added some political weight to the faction that won in 1540. Gardiner, on the other hand, did not. If he had hoped to destroy the reforming party in the Church he was at once disappointed; Henry continued to favour and protect Cranmer, and no change at all occurred on the bench of bishops. In November 1540, Gardiner was forced to accept an embassy to Charles V which, involving atten-dance at Regensburg where a last and vain attempt was made to end the religious schism, was intended to procure a rapprochement between Henry and the Emperor (and the Pope) but which in fact achieved no real relaxation of tension. Gardiner's contemporary and posthumous fame as a diplomat was exceeded only by his distaste for ambassadorships and his inevitable failure to bring negotiations to a successful conclusion. On this occasion he was away for nearly a year and in that time lost all he had gained in the fall of Cromwell. Henry respected the bishop's remarkable abilities but distrusted his ambition and arrogance, holding that he could be useful only when controlled by a powerful and experienced monarch. It was an accurate assessment, and it meant that while Henry lived Gardiner would never hold first place.

Thus nothing had really changed in July 1540, except that England now lacked the hand and mind of Thomas Cromwell—a large exception. Immediately this expressed itself in a rapid slowing down of the reforming movement in Church and state, especially noticeable in the work of Parliament. The remainder of Henry's reign witnessed the calling of two, the first of which sat for three sessions and the second for two; there were spring sessions of approximately two and a half months' duration in 1542, 1543, 1544 and 1547, and a pre-Christmas one month's session in 1545. On the face of it, therefore, the Cromwellian revival of Parliament continued vigorously, but its work-load changed; there were far fewer government bills, and supply now formed the chief reason for calling so many. Government bills concerned themselves in the main with working out the consequences of Cromwell's furious activity, either by completing initiatives begun in the 1530s or by amending earlier acts which proved to be deficient in detail. Thus Cromwell's administrative reforms dragged on into 1542 when the Court of General Surveyors completed his financial organization,[1] and his social reforms evoked echoes in such acts as those that reformed Quarter Sessions of the peace (1542), attempted to define the law of bankruptcy (1543), or protected natural timber resources (1544). In 1543 further acts mended some deficiencies in the enforcement clauses of the 1539 Proclamations Act and codified the long protracted settlement of Wales. The impetus was not dead but it slackened greatly; at best reform marked time, and new policies, inspired by the King, soon came to absorb attention and energy.

On the other hand, the novel standing of Parliament as the sovereign body of the realm was consolidated in those years as routine regularized the procedural and administrative transformations initiated under Cromwell. The point was made dramatically in 1542 when the burgess for Plymouth, George Ferrers, was arrested in a private suit for debt on his way to the chamber. The Commons, claiming (on good precedent) that their members were privileged against such action, sought to release him (unprecedentedly) by simply sending their serjeant-at-arms; when the jailer and the sheriffs of London roughly refused to obey the order of the House they were in turn imprisoned and forced to make their

[1] See above, p. 215.

humble apologies. The case established that the House could enforce its privileges by 'warrant of the mace', without the intervention of a writ out of Chancery (offered by Audley and refused by the House); and it moved Henry to make a public affirmation of his faith in Parliament, a faith of which he had shown no sign until he learned about it from Cromwell's administration. Calling together a meeting of judges and notables of both Houses, he expressed his approval of their action and declared that 'we be informed by our judges that we at no time stand so highly in our estate royal as in the time of Parliament, wherein we as head and you as members are conjoined and knit together as one body politic.' He added that according to his learned counsel the prerogative of Parliament overrode the acts and processes of all other courts. Thus the legal view of parliamentary sovereignty, upon which Cromwell's use and elevation of the institution had rested, received endorsement from the supreme head himself.

The greatest problems of reform continued to cluster around religion and the Church. Henry had no intention of surrendering any particle of the supremacy created in the 1530s, and those—the Pope among them—who had hoped for a reconciliation after Cromwell's fall were due for a disappointment. But his pretensions, now exercised without the mediation of vicegerent and vicar-general, necessarily involved Henry personally in the continuing struggles within the Church. The factions that destroyed Cromwell had certainly been moved by hatred and the thirst for power, but they had also wanted to change the King's policy and in the Act of Six Articles obtained a formidable instrument. Yet though there was some sporadic persecution, the expected conservative triumph did not materialize. Gardiner's long absence did not help, nor did the occurrence in 1541—quickly suppressed at the cost of some sixty executions—of yet another plot in Yorkshire which revived memories of the Pilgrimage of Grace. Cranmer meanwhile promoted reform in his diocese, as did other reformist bishops; even an outbreak of image-breaking in Kent did not interrupt the work of applying the 1538 Injunctions, still very much in force.

In November 1541 the conservatives suffered a severe setback when the Council learned that Queen Catherine had been involved in at least one adulterous relationship since her marriage. Henry, informed by Cranmer, at first refused to believe the truth; when he accepted it, it shattered him. In February–April 1542, acts of attainder and the axe disposed of the Queen, her confidante Lady Rochford (widow of Anne Boleyn's brother), and several accomplices. On this occasion the charges were true: Catherine, a highly sexed and reckless young woman, had seen no reason why marriage to a repulsively aging man of gross figure and habits, even if he was the King, should bar her from the pleasures to which she had been accustomed before her wedding. The duke of Norfolk hastened to safety by taking the lead against his niece, but the Howard influence was badly hit, and the conservative faction lost much ground in the vital centre of the Privy Chamber. Henry resolved to stay unmarried, a resolution which lasted some eighteen months; there was also now no mistaking his age and physical decline, aggravated by the continued agony of the ulcer in his leg. He grew extremely moody and ever more unpredictable, and although his mental powers seemed for the time unaffected it became clear that the collapse of his fifth marriage had greatly diminished his majestic control over affairs and factions.

This time, however, there was no Cromwell to exploit the disaster that had struck the enemies of reform, and the King, who more than ever resented his ungrateful subjects' unwillingness to accept their religion at his hands, went back to the search for uniformity. Early in 1543 the conservatives were allowed to go over to the attack. The spring of that year witnessed a massive heresy hunt, with some burnings and more humiliating recantations, as well as an attempt to bring Cranmer down through accusations manufactured by the clergy of his own cathedral. This so-called prebendaries' plot misfired because Cranmer had always been careful to distinguish between the lawful reform he practised and the heretical extremism of which he was accused, and because Henry continued to hold him surprisingly dear. Perhaps the King remembered how similar accusations had helped to deprive him of Cromwell. In the upshot Cranmer's accusers were remitted to his investigation and to punishment which was not vindictive. In other respects, however, the reaction scored some points. In the Convocation of 1542–3, the conservatives concentrated their attack on the Great Bible, charging it with tendentious and misleading renderings at important points and hinting that the vernacular scriptures should be withdrawn in the interests of religious peace. On this occasion the King supported Cranmer, but in 1543 he permitted the passage of an act which prohibited bible-reading to women and the lower orders, two groups thought to be too ill instructed and too volatile to be exposed to such heady stuff. Women and the lower orders continued to read the Bible. In May 1543 there appeared a revised formulary of the Christian religion, *A Necessary Doctrine and Erudition for any Christian Man*, popularly known as *The King's Book*. Henry had indeed contributed extensively to its composition: it represented the outcome of the debates he had been conducting with his theologians since he first expressed dissatisfaction with the *Bishops' Book* of 1537.

In the main, this now authoritative statement of the faith marked the arrest of further reform and a retreat from the position that Cromwell had favoured; it expressly endorsed the doctrinal conservatism of the Six Articles and placed all seven sacraments on an equal footing as necessary means of salvation.

Yet the victory of reaction remained very incomplete. Even the King would not return as far as the conservatives wanted: 'superstition' continued to be frowned upon, Erasmian reform (though not Lutheran) remained active, Cranmer continued his work on an English liturgy to replace the Latin mass, and Henry composed for himself an eclectic theology which varied his essential attachment to Catholic doctrine with some radical borrowings from the Protestants.[2] In July 1543 the cause of reform gained new hope when Henry married his sixth wife, Catherine Parr, thirty-one years old and sister to the rising courtier William earl of Essex. Sober and adroit, Catherine turned out to be a generally eirenic influence. She brought peace to Henry's declining years, so far as anyone could, and she gathered all his children into her household, thoroughly charming even the difficult Princess Mary. Above all, she provided a new focus for the reformers. Herself one of those noble ladies with a sentimental passion for spiritual regeneration who had been prominent at the courts of Europe for some thirty years, she leant towards Erasmus and the sort of cautious Reformation favoured by Cranmer. At the same time, the King's companions at court also began once more to move towards the more reformist wing: by mid-1543, Sir John Dudley, Viscount Lisle, who was making a name for himself in war, was of the Privy Chamber, while ascendancy in that inner centre of the court was passing to Sir Anthony Denny, distinctly a friend to reform. Though the battle was very far from over, by the end of that year it could be said that the radical party had definitely survived the fall of Cromwell. There is irony in the fact that after five years of often bitter turmoil and authoritarian pronouncements from above Henry could do no more in 1545, when addressing Parliament, than repeat the appeal for moderation and the middle way which Cromwell had delivered in the same forum in 1540.

While the party of reform manifestly still lacked a leader of political stature, the conservatives also failed to attract the services of outstanding political figures. Norfolk was old and ailing; Southampton died in 1542 and Suffolk in 1545; the younger generation were either third rate, like Sir Anthony Brown (master of the Horse) or quite untried, like Norfolk's son Henry, earl of Surrey. Few people trusted Wriothesley whose ambition was naked and

[2]J. J. Scarisbrick, *Henry VIII*, chapter 12.

background common. This was why the faction struggles of the time, centring upon religion, appeared to be so much a confrontation between Gardiner and Cranmer, as though the bishops and not the lay councillors dominated politics—a very misleading impression. The conservative factions never fully reconstituted themselves after the debacle of Catherine Howard, but the reformers were about to find their leader, thanks mainly to the King's new foreign policy and the war it produced. But first it is necessary to look at the one area of public affairs in which Cromwell's policy was fully reversed after his fall, namely Ireland.[3]

As we have seen, Cromwell had ended the medieval history of Ireland when he eliminated the Geraldine domination of the island and decided, in the interests of economy as well as the Reformation, to concentrate on controlling the foothold of the Pale from England. His policy was jeopardized by the crude rashness of Lord Leonard Grey, who kept stirring things up, by the tactless zeal of Archbishop Brown, and especially by the resentment of the active politicians of the Pale who wanted a share of rule and had their own ideas touching general reform. The threat of the Gaelic League, although in the end it collapsed, ruined Grey (executed in 1541 for an obscure treason) and persuaded Henry to try another policy. Its agent was the new deputy Sir Anthony St Leger, a client of Norfolk's but also a gentleman of the Privy Chamber, who had established good relations with the Irish reform party during his visit of inspection in 1537; his chief advisers were Edward Staples, bishop of Meath (author of an important reform treatise), and Thomas Cusack, a lawyer of the kind that in England managed the reforms of the Cromwellian regime. The new policy aimed to create a united national state for Ireland by bringing in all the lords, Irish as well as English, and thus ending the tripartite division of the island which had resulted from the collapse of the English lordship in the later middle ages. In this respect it looked like the policy advocated by Norfolk and espoused by Henry twenty years before, but there was a major difference: in place of force and guile, St Leger proposed to use genuine friendship and conciliation. To this task he brought a remarkable ability to convince the Gaelic lords, deeply suspicious and resentful after their experience of Grey, and for a time he was very successful.

St Leger operated at two levels. On the one hand, he endeavoured to come to firm agreements with the lords which would establish their loyalty to the Crown. This was the well known policy of surrender-and-regrant by which lords claiming rule under Gaelic arrangements were turned into feudal vassals of the Crown and

[3] For what follows see B. Bradshaw, 'The Irish Constitutional Revolution, 1515–1557', pp. 217ff.

agreed to introduce English law and customs in their lands. Such agreements were acceptable because they gave constitutional security of tenure to the Irish who themselves wished to end the danger of expropriation which threatened so long as English law regarded them as usurpers in their possessions; the policy was well received at the time, and only later bias came to see in it an attempt to destroy a valid Irish culture. The second plank of St Leger's proceedings consisted in giving a national superstructure to the whole island by turning Henry's lordship into a kingship—*rex Hiberniae*, not *dominus*. This, it was hoped, would end papal claims to overlordship and that search for another lord that had marked Irish politics for thirty years; but, as Henry realized, it would also commit him to direct rule in Ireland and a much more permanent and insistent involvement in its affairs than anything he had been accustomed to. As King of Ireland he would no longer be able to ignore his other dominion. Moreover, he correctly maintained that the revenues of the proposed kingdom fell a long way short of supporting the new status. In consequence it took time to persuade him to a step pressed hard by Staples and Cusak but at last, in June 1541, he allowed himself to be proclaimed King of Ireland. Meanwhile, St Leger's conciliation, backed at extreme need by a show of force followed by magnanimity, was really making peace. Desmond came to court, to be received with much honour, and the policy looked very good indeed when even O'Neill signed indentures of the sort that his great rival O'Donnell had entered into before, accepted the title of earl of Tyrone, and rendered fealty to the new King. The Parliament of 1541, attended for the first time by a sprinkling of Gaelic lords, symbolized the success of the new policy.

The result of all this was to lay the foundations of an Irish nation composed of both Anglo-Irish and Gaels, and separately governed from Dublin. Cromwell's plan to integrate Ireland into a single unitary state vanished, not to be revived until 1801. Whether Cromwell's or St Leger's programme was better conditioned to end the problems of Ireland may be a matter for debate; at the time, certainly, any hope of extending centralized rule beyond the Pale depended on a military conquest for which England had not the means and which Cromwell had deliberately postponed *sine die*. At least St Leger created an exceptional spirit of amity among the Irish which, for instance, kept them during the war years 1544-6 from reviving their customary disruptive politics. However, the essential component of St Leger's plans—the rendering constitutional of relations between King and lords by peaceful means—was not given the time it required. Only a few such agreements had been concluded when the policy was put into cold storage late in 1543. St

initiative was the war with France: that is where his heart lay. In all probability he simply wished to return to enterprises that had proved congenial before by once more asserting his greatness among the great of Europe; it seemed intolerable that he, the oldest and longest-reigning monarch in that generation, should be ignored. Quite possibly also the ambitions of the younger men who came to court in the 1540s played their part—the ambitions of a potential warrior caste deprived of their fun and games. In short, the King's reasons for re-entering Europe were most probably what they had been before, a conventional desire to display power and to gain glory in the proper sport of kings. In sixteenth-century terms, such motives need not be called frivolous; nevertheless, the consequences proved disastrous to the nation, and the wasteful folly of the reign's last years did very serious damage to the cause of necessary reform.

The chance offered because by the end of 1540 the artificial harmony between Charles V and Francis I was manifestly coming to an end. Like Cromwell, who had never believed that their amity would endure, Henry had been expecting this; unlike Cromwell with his anti-papal alliance, he meant to exploit the event in the fashion of Wolsey's day, despite the profound changes that had come over Europe in the previous fifteen years. The Habsburgs were no longer his natural allies, and yet the only ambitions of conquest that he could possibly entertain touched, as they had always done, France. In the complex diplomacy that followed he played a poorish hand with considerable skill, even though the result was unhappy.[4] In the first place he resolved to guard his backdoor by making sure of Scotland, a very ancient counsel of policy. That kingdom had by 1540 fully recovered from the effects of Flodden, and James V, still under thirty, had established a newly strong hold on his territories. He had raised the revenue of the Scottish crown to some £46,000 a year, about half as much again as his father had got, but his methods—severe at best, vindictive and ruthless at times—had made enemies among the temporarily cowed nobility of Scotland. The one thing the King absolutely refused to do was to receive the reform in his country; though Henry had several times explained to his nephew, in tones of superiority natural to himself but highly offensive to the recipient, how much kingly power could gain from expelling the pope and confiscating church lands, there had been no response. The dominant figure at James's court was David Beaton, cardinal-archbishop of St Andrews, a politician (of low morals) first,

---

[4] The only recent addition to the familiar literature on these events is D. L. Potter, 'Diplomacy in the mid-Sixteenth Century: England and France, 1536–1550' (unpublished dissertation, Cambridge, 1973), to which this account stands indebted.

but also a papist; and French influence, embodied in the Queen, Mary of Guise, also held Scotland to Rome.

Henry therefore resolved to force Scotland into acquiescence. In June 1541 he progressed as far north as York, in an endeavour to overawe that recently disturbed part of his realm; he wished to take the opportunity to meet James and overawe him too, but the Scots Council, afraid of a kidnapping, would not let their King come to England. The public waiting in vain constituted an insult which Henry meant to avenge. By the early months of 1542, his tortuous negotiations with France and the Emperor had resulted in an understanding with the latter which committed Henry to a joint invasion of France. However, when Charles opened hostilities in July Henry was in no way ready and in particular had still not settled the northern border. Characteristically he determined to bring matters to a head by various forms of provocation—with difficulty, because the Scots refused to be drawn. In October, finally, Henry sent Norfolk on a raid of destruction from Berwick; though the enterprise was thoroughly mismanaged and Norfolk cursed his old bones, it did the trick. A large Scots army crossed into the west march in November; but reluctance and disaffection weakened it, and when the warden, Thomas Wharton, with a greatly inferior force stood across its path at Solway Moss the Scottish contingents fled. There were few casualties, but a number of important men fell into English hands. James V died a fortnight later, allegedly from shame and despair. He left the crown of Scotland in the hands of his daughter Mary, just six days old, or rather in those of the warring factions.

Solway Moss freed Henry from threats in the north and should have enabled him to carry out his commitment to Charles, but it also opened up possibilities of ending the troubles with Scotland for good, and the King resolved to pursue these. He did conclude a firm, though still secret, alliance with the Emperor in February 1543 and sent a token force to assist Charles V in Flanders, but for the time he concentrated his efforts upon Scotland. Though his policy was at heart sound enough he managed to put every foot wrong. He proposed to unite the two kingdoms by marrying the infant Queen Mary to his heir, Edward, and to maintain English influence at Edinburgh by backing a subservient party of lords in the government of what was bound to be a long minority. But he ensured failure by two fatal mistakes: he hoped to achieve his ends without direct (and costly) involvement by using instead a group of Scots lords captured at Solway Moss who proved predictably unreliable, and he ignored the well informed reports of his envoy, Sir Ralph Sadler, who understood the crazy politics of the Scottish nobility much better than his King did. Instead of the 'English party', the earl of Arran, a Hamilton with a claim to the throne, took charge as regent. At first he seemed willing to play Henry's game, arresting Beaton, professing an inclination to religious reform, and coming to terms in July, in the treaties of Greenwich which made peace, betrothed the two children, envisaged a permanent alliance, but failed to commit the Scots explicitly to a renunciation of their French connection. The treaties were ill received in Scotland, and when Henry injudiciously brought pressure to bear his policy disintegrated. In September Arran deserted the English and allied with Beaton; in December the Scottish Parliament renounced the Greenwich treaties. For a time Henry continued to try devious diplomacy, but all hope of a peaceful settlement had gone; and in May 1544 he finally resorted to force. Edward Seymour, earl of Hertford, invaded Scotland by sea, took and burned Edinburgh, and retired, leaving the country wasted. As he had warned Henry, this sort of punitive expedition only stiffened Scottish resistance, and Henry now had on his hands exactly what he had been trying to avoid—a war with Scotland as well as a war with France. Hertford continued to do well, avenging the defeat of an English party at Ancrum Moor (February 1545) with yet another devastating invasion in September that year; but the Franco-popish party remained firmly in control in Scotland to the end of Henry's reign, even after Beaton was murdered in May 1546 by a group of Protestant lords.

Meanwhile, Henry attended to his first love. In June 1544, a great army of over 40,000 men crossed by stages to Calais, under the command of those ancient and rheumatic warhorses, the dukes of Suffolk and Norfolk. Henry, as a rule carried in a litter, followed soon after. But if the high command looked neither soldierly nor gallant, the force itself was impressive: the biggest expedition launched from England for over a century, well equipped and well organized, something of a triumph for the councillors (especially Gardiner and Wriothesley) who took charge of the preparations. Unfortunately little thought had been given to what it might actually do. Charles V expected his ally to join in a direct assault upon Paris which would finally put an end to the Valois threat on his imperial flank. This bold proposal, to which Henry had in effect agreed in the secret treaty of 1543, looked less enticing when the time came; all Henry's innate caution asserted itself, overcame his pose as the great warrior king, and left the concerted scheme in ruins. Instead the King decided to gain some French territory for himself by enlarging the Calais bridgehead. He began by dividing his impressive army. Norfolk, ordered to lay siege to Montreuil, made a mess of it; Suffolk marched upon Boulogne which surrendered on 18 September. The humiliation before Montreuil, from whence there issued little except wails and whines, in part nullified the apparent glory of Boulogne; and the capture of that city proved to be less a triumph than a burdensome complication since Henry clung to this supposed evidence of his martial greatness with a quite absurd tenacity, long after it was proved that the city had no value. On the very day that Boulogne fell to the English, Charles V, clear now that he had nothing to gain from his tiresome ally and intent only upon freeing his hands to deal with the German Protestants, made peace with France at Crépy. Henry was left alone, to face the might of France assisted by a feeble but truculent Scotland. His one consolation could be that thanks to St Leger Ireland provided not disaffected intrigues but eager recruits for his army in numbers large enough to embarrass a government which could not find the money to pay all who wanted to fight.

From the day that Boulogne fell the war deteriorated rapidly. Henry had returned to England, but the men on the spot regarded the conquest as untenable and despondently pleaded for withdrawal. The old dukes in fact left Boulogne for Calais, against orders and, strangely enough, without consequences to themselves. Hertford, temporarily withdrawn from the north, came to take over and reported the town unfit to defend (an opinion proved true by the easy English capture of it). Henry's only response was to order a comprehensive rebuilding programme which was begun, at astonishing cost. Rather surprisingly, Francis I made no immediate move to exploit his military superiority, though French forces dominated the countryside between Boulogne and Calais. Instead he opened negotiations which for the next two years turned upon the efforts of various parties to mediate between the Kings. Charles V offered to help, mainly in order that his imperial authority might be manifest; so did the princes of the Schmalkaldic League who wanted Francis freed from English problems so that he might protect them against the Emperor. Since their neutrality took the form of permitting both sides to recruit mercenaries in German territory, their mediation proved less than convincing. All efforts at peace shattered on the rock of Henry's determination to keep Boulogne. Thus in 1545 the French renewed military action and invested the poorly defended city whose English garrison through most of the year was commanded by a council of professionals from Calais. An attempt to raise the siege from the sea was unsuccessful; the English fleet, commanded by Lisle, failed to force an entry and retired to Portsmouth, to be followed by a French naval force which penetrated the Solent and descended upon various parts of the south coast. However, they in their turn withdrew, having failed of their chief purpose, the capture of the Isle of Wight. The rest of the year witnessed various coastal raids with some burning and destruction by both sides, but the expected major naval encounter between two very large fleets—the English had some 160 vessels and the French nearer 200—never materialized.

These desultory events underline a strange aspect of Henrician warfare. The King is usually regarded as one of the founders of the royal navy, even perhaps as the monarch who did more than anyone to bring it into existence. While there is not all that much evidence for his supposed personal initiatives, it remains true that during his reign much was done to improve the realm's naval defences. A heavy shipbuilding programme started in his early years, the pride of his fleet being the *Harry Grace à Dieu*, a vessel so large and so valuable that it was never allowed to see action. Thereafter the navy was maintained with care; ships were rebuilt and improved; the principle of equipping them with heavy guns was worked out in some detail, though Henrician ships did not have sufficient guns mounted for broadsides and naval tactics continued to rely on close fighting and boarding, rather than the long-range cannonade of the future; the royal dockyard at Plymouth received attention and new ones— capacious and well designed—were established at Woolwich (1515) and Deptford (1517). From 1524 the running of the navy rested in the capable hands of a professional clerk of the King's ships, William Gonson, and Cromwell had to find large sums of money to maintain England's wooden walls. By the end of the reign a company of professional sea captains had grown up which by stages replaced the traditional courtiers and gentlemen in the command of ships; and in 1545-6, after Gonson's death, Cromwellian principles of government came to affect the navy too, with the setting up of a permanent bureaucratic Navy Board, the foundation of all the future administration of the fleet. Yet the office of lord admiral, which normally involved far more activity in prize and mercantile jurisdiction than in fighting, remained reserved to non-professionals: even during the war of 1545, Lisle kept explaining his unfitness for the command, an assessment which his actions proved to be sound enough. What stands out is the lack of any positive warlike purposes behind all those reforms. There was more, though not more pointful, ship-to-ship fighting in the war of 1513 than in that of 1545 when the navy's one big loss had nothing to do with enemy action (big successes it had none): in June, the *Mary Rose* sank in Portsmouth harbour with the loss of 500 men as, with gun-ports opened, she turned too sharply and flooded. The navy escorted Henry's continental expeditions and conducted minor coastal raids; it failed to relieve Boulogne or to prevent the French invasion attempts which were beaten off by the land-based defences; when the chance of war at sea offered in 1545 it evaded conclusive action. The most successful use of the weapon was seen in Hertford's seaborne attack on Edinburgh. It is quite clear that neither Henry nor his seamen had any strategic concept for war at sea; the royal interest in promoting the fleet, though it may have served some purpose in domestic defence, would seem mainly to have arisen out of considerations of prestige. Certainly the biggest fuss was made over ships that were especially unhandy but looked most impressive.

Boulogne withstood the French siege, as much because that was pursued half-heartedly as because of its expensively rebuilt defences. In September Henry despatched the earl of Surrey, Norfolk's heir, to take charge of the town, but instead of seizing the chance of glory and favour the earl disobeyed orders consistently and failed to improve the position. Gradually Henry came to realize that some agreement was unavoidable: he could not finance any further serious action, the uselessness of his famed conquest was becoming painfully obvious, and it is also likely that by the middle of 1546 he was losing that single and ultimate control over English policy which he had exercised since Cromwell's fall. With Scotland still neither conquered nor pacified, the French adventure had to be brought to a close, and in June 1546 peace was made at Campe near Ardres. England was to retain Boulogne until 1554 when it was to be restored with the new fortifications (built with English money) intact, and the French were to renew the pension that had lapsed in 1535 (and which did not begin to cover the cost of running Boulogne).

The war had been a futile disaster. Henry had gained nothing of value, and his isolation in 1545 had revealed an unexpected vulnerability; in the very unsatisfactory settlement, which did not really end French hostility provoked by Henry's needless aggression, the King reaped a just reward for his perverse and pointless policy. Above all, he had succeeded in wrecking the Crown's finances and had plunged the country into a major economic crisis.

III

The war proved inordinately expensive. Fully accurate figures have not yet been worked out, but a good estimate of Edward VI's reign says that from the outbreak of the conflict with Scotland to the end of the reign the King spent over £2,000,000 on warlike purposes alone. However, some £203,000 of this went on the reformation of the defences begun in March 1539, a necessary expenditure even had there been no war. Nonetheless, the Boulogne campaign cost close to £600,000, and the fortifying and garrisoning of that city for a little more than two years swallowed up another £426,000. The actual cost of the 1544 campaign trebled Wriothesley's careful estimate of £260,000. Sums like these posed entirely new problems in government finance which faced an average annual extraordinary expenditure more than twice as large as the whole of the ordinary revenue, itself barely sufficient for the normal peace-time needs of the Crown—and that for years on end. In addition, Calais and Ireland regularly incurred deficits which had to be made up from the English Exchequer. No wonder that St Leger lost the battle for his reforms which for the forseeable future increased the Irish deficit incalculably. The Council's budgeting was regularly defeated by new increases in costs, aggravated by the general rise in price levels all over Europe. Among the particular contributors to the un-expected expensiveness of these wars must be reckoned the scale of the conflict once the attempt to eliminate Scotland had failed, the size of the armies produced, the exceptional reliance on very expen-sive foreign mercenaries (better troops than the levies raised by gentlemen and nobles, but unwilling to fight unless they were paid), and the great increase in the use of field and siege artillery. Especially the building of fortifications, lavishly engaged in at Boulogne, Calais, Berwick and the southern ports ran away with the money.

To cover this astonishing expenditure Henry resorted to a number of devices. In the first place, of course, he could and did call for parliamentary grants. Cromwell's last subsidy of 1540 covered a great part of the defence costs incurred in 1539–40, but new subsidies were granted in 1543 and 1545. Since their instalments were spread over the years, the Crown collected parliamentary taxation in every year after 1542 except in 1543; in 1546 instalments of two separate grants burdened the country with contributions amounting to over £150,000. The total yield of taxation in the years 1542–6 came to approximately £430,000, a truly unprecedented burden which seems to have been borne with amazing willingness, though the gap between the supposed net yield and the sums actually collected began to grow in 1546 from the habitual one per cent to something approaching six—a sign that taxpayers' resistance may have been increasing.

Legitimate exactions of this kind did not exhaust the King's call for aid. Twice, in 1542 and 1545, he resorted to forced loans yielding over £110,000 each, and the first of these was cancelled in 1543 by statute—that is, turned into a retrospective additional grant of supply. The second remained a debt charged against Henry's successors which also was never repaid. Even this total of over £650,000 extracted from the nation covered little more than a quarter of the expenses incurred, and loans taken up at interest—Henry's credit was never good enough to force the rate below thirteen per cent—in the Antwerp money market added at most another £100,000 (more likely less).[5] The vast gap left was more or less filled by two expedients disastrous to the Crown and the country respectively—the selling of assets, and the manipulation of the coinage. From 1542 onwards, the government began seriously to sell off crown lands, especially those acquired from the dissolved monasteries to which from 1545 new minor acquisitions (colleges and chantries) were being added. This operation has already been described. It did not lead to a collapse of the market value of land, and the Crown received a fair return for what it sold, but that does not alter the fact that the liquidation of some £40,000 of capital greatly reduced the income-producing fisc upon which future financial stability depended.

The debasement of the coinage did worse damage.[6] England's coins had traditionally been exceptionally sound—of a regular weight and fineness (proportion of precious metal to alloy)—with the result that they were usually overvalued against foreign coins and liable to hoarding; this aggravated the shortage of circulating medium, serious enough in any case. Wolsey's important monetary reforms of 1526 reduced the fineness of silver coins, established a new gold standard, based the English coinage on silver rather than gold, and by recoining made a small profit which unhappily was remembered. From 1536 onwards there are signs that Cromwell wished to repeat an experiment justified by the recurrent problem of keeping English coins circulating at home, though he first decided to experiment with the Irish coinage in 1540. In 1542, a new, slightly debased coinage was introduced in England under cover of the existing coins, and the success of this encouraged a really large-scale

    [5] In 1545–7, a total of about £270,000 was taken up at Antwerp (W. C. Richardson, *Stephen Vaughan, Financial Agent of Henry VIII*, 1953, p. 77). However, this sum contained considerable items of merchandise and non-negotiable materials forced upon Henry as a condition of lending at all; the figure also disguises the fact that new loans were constantly employed in paying off earlier short-term ones. No accurate calculation of net sums borrowed has yet proved possible. I am grateful to Dr R. B. Outhwaite for advice in this matter.

    [6] For the complicated problems of the debasement and the inflation see especially R. B. Outhwaite, *Inflation in Tudor and Stuart England* (1969); *The Price Revolution in Sixteenth Century England*, edited by P. H. Ramsey (1971); C. E. Challis, 'The Debasement of the Coinage', *Economic History Review* (1967), pp. 441 ff., and 'Currency and the Economy in mid-Tudor England', *Economic History Review* (1972), pp. 313 ff. I have also had the benefit, for which I am most grateful, of reading Dr Challis's forthcoming work on 'The Tudor Coinage' on which much of what follows is based. For prices I have relied on the tables in *Agrarian History of England and Wales* IV, edited by J. Thirsk, pp. 593 ff.

undertaking, begun in 1544 as the pressure of war expenditure came home to the Privy Council. In March, the whole system of the Mint was reorganized in order to cope with the expected increase of work, sixteenth-century coining being a slow and laborious manual industry. A second mint was set up in the Tower; that at Southwark was expanded; others appeared at Bristol, Durham House (London), Dublin and Waterford. The ecclesiastical mints at Canterbury, Durham and York were also brought into the operation, though long before the debasement was over they had altogether, and finally, gone out of business. The appointment of Sir Edmund Peckham, an experienced financial bureaucrat, as high treasurer over all the mints provided unification. Throughout, Tower One, Tower Two, Southwark and Bristol, in that order, played the largest part in the undertaking, and in the six years of debasement (1544–1551) these mints turned out coins to the face value of at least £4,300,000. Debased issues, mostly of silver, of ever decreasing fineness and some reduction in weight were made in 1544, 1545, 1546, 1548 and 1551; though from 1548 plans came to be promoted for reversing the process, until 1551 English coins deteriorated steadily and rapidly. The deterioration of their purchasing power, which lagged behind the reduction of bullion content, is difficult to estimate precisely, but what was happening is well illustrated by the fact that the exchange rate of the pound sterling against the pound Flemish was cut exactly in half between 1540 and 1551. The Crown made its profit from the difference between what it paid for the minting (which included not only the price of the metal bought in but also the costs of production) and the face value of the coins in which the expensive precious metals had been spread so much more thinly; it also benefited from the time-lag between the issue of a debased coinage and the inflationary effect this had on prices. Its total profit for the years 1542–51 has been calculated as amounting to close to £1,300,000. This approximately filled the gap between its income and the war expenditure, though right through complaints recur with convincing frequency that all the treasuries were empty; it filled the gap, moreover, at grievous cost to the national economy and thus also to the government itself, the largest employer of labour and the largest customer in the market.

The effects of the debasement were very mixed and continue to provide matter for debate among historians. The devaluation abroad of the pound has usually been supposed to have assisted the export trade, especially in cloth, and it seems likely that the leading exporters, the London Merchant Adventurers, did find conditions propitious in the later 1540s. Overall, however, the rate of expansion prevalent in the pre-war years 1539–44, when exports rose by fourteen per cent, was not thereafter maintained, despite the benefits of devaluation. Though it must be remembered that the market for unfinished cloth could not be indefinitely expanded, it is quite possible that the war, interrupting trade and enormously increasing the government's purchases of cloth for its armies, reduced the potential exports. The last debasement, in any case, coincided with a collapse of the critical Antwerp market, produced in part by over-stocking and in part by a financial crisis in the Habsburg empire; the cloth trade thereafter languished and despite partial recoveries never again reached the flourishing state of the 1530s and early 1540s. Debasement benefited the realm by increasing the amount of money in circulation: there had long not been enough of it, and all com-mercial life took advantage of the easier means of trading. Naturally, this depended upon people accepting the base money (preferably at face value) and on the whole it looks as though they did until the manipulations produced light coins with so low a silver content that resistance began to set in. This was particularly true of the notorious teston (one shilling) coined in 1546 which in size looked like a groat (fourpence) and in use soon showed a coppery sheen most in-appropriate for a silver coin. It was withdrawn two years later. The marginal advantages of debasement must, however, be set against the destruction of confidence in English coins at home and abroad, against problems caused in an economy which believed in an intrinsic value in money, and especially against the effect on prices. The debasement of the coinage must stand out as the biggest single contributor to the drastic inflation which began in 1544, even though the price rise never kept pace with the decline of the coinage and assuredly cannot be ascribed solely to it.

We have noted that Tudor England experienced a general inflation of prices from the 1490s, but what happened in the 1540s was some-thing special. By 1550 the price of agricultural products had nearly doubled in a decade, while industrial prices had increased by seventy per cent; and most of this upswing took place after 1544, producing a sudden concentrated leap which was exceptionally disconcerting. Wages, on the other hand, barely rose at all, and their purchasing power declined in the same period by something like fifty per cent. Even though it is dangerous to speak in terms of the pauperization of the lower orders—very few people lived exclusively on money wages, and most had some produce or goods to sell which made them tiny profiteers of the inflation—it nevertheless remains true that this sudden inflation caused very widespread hardship and also altered the economic balance of the nation fundamentally. It finally brought to an end a long period of peasant prosperity and put artificers at novel disadvantages; and from this time it became unwise to depend on any sort of fixed income, whether wages or salaries or rents. Survival even, let alone enrichment, demanded the energetic exploitation of marketable resources, a situation ready made for rural and urban entrepreneurship. Thus the inflation assisted the effects of the redistribution of landed wealth flowing from the Dissolution and the dispersal of crown lands. Those competent enough to seize the opportunities, whether gentry or yeomen or merchants or artisans, and lucky enough in their operations (and their family histories), built up wealth more rapidly than ever before, while those who could not raise rents, sell produce, mine minerals, or maintain a steady policy of expansion went to the wall. Economically speaking, the effects of the inflation in the long term almost certainly promoted the weal of the nation as a whole by increasing the general stock of wealth, but immediately they caused sudden hardship and consternation; above all, they always threatened to disturb that settled order of social stability which the sixteenth century, and Tudor governments in particular, regarded as essential. In retrospect we may discover and even admire the effects of social mobility and the stimulation of enterprise; at the time it was hard to see anything here except the collapse of security under the impact of those pressing forward too eagerly and those rebelling against the decline in their living standards. The search for a restoration of stability was to occupy government and thinkers for the rest of the century and beyond, but most earnestly in the years 1548–66 before it came to be realized that the major crisis was over and moreover had probably never been quite so serious as the myopia of contemporaries had supposed.

We shall later consider contemporary reactions to the inflation and the steps taken to deal with it;[7] here we are concerned with its causes. What happened in the later 1540s was a sudden upward kink in a generally rising graph, the superimposition of particular causes upon the underlying effects of population expansion, rising government expenditure resulting from increased responsibilities, and the influence of general European price movements. The upswing of 1544 grew directly from government policy and nothing else. It was the war that turned inflation from gentle to violent, directly by the vast increase in crown spending, indirectly by the means used to cover this—taxation, the sale of lands, and the debasement of the coinage. Between them these three enormously increased the circulation of money in the realm (itself an inflationary pressure) and at the same time drove up prices by undermining the trust in the money circulating. The crisis that ensued owed something to panic, but government policy had not been such as to make that panic

[7] See below, pp. 322–5, 343–5, 355–6.

14 The Crisis of Reform

Thomas Starkey died in 1538; Richard Morison fell silent after 1540 and abandoned reform and propaganda for a diplomatic career; Richard Taverner turned to the writing of music. Though Cranmer continued, privately, to move ever further towards Protestant doctrine, he had to surrender control of the Church (especially of Convocation) to Gardiner. Latimer stopped his preaching. The patchy enforcement of the Act of Six Articles drove some of the more determined Protestants to follow the example of the 1520s by fleeing abroad. John Hooper, William Turner and Thomas Becon, all men with a future, took refuge on the continent; but while Tyndale and Frith had settled at Antwerp and Barnes had gone to Wittenberg, this next generation of refugees sought the more radical climate of Strassburg and Zürich. In its adversity, English Protestantism was becoming dissatisfied with Luther and turned to look to Martin Bucer, to Henry Bullinger, and ultimately to John Calvin, barely a name at this time. However, while those refugees thus continued their education in the reform they could not for the moment exercise any influence upon events in their native country. At home, prudence or fears of an intrusive extremism caused some rethinking among men who had at first found Cromwellian reform attractive; as official policy turned, and as the disruptive tendencies of the drastic 1530s became apparent, men like Edmund Bonner (bishop of London), Thomas Thirlby (bishop of Westminster) and Nicholas Heath (bishop of Rochester) abandoned their earlier sympathies with reform and became authoritarian defenders of the established order. Disappointment of a different kind made its appearance among unrepentant radicals: thus Henry Brinkelow's *Complaint of Roderick Mors* (1543), reiterating at passionate length the protests against clerical corruption and lay oppression which had been the message of Barlow and Fish fifteen years earlier, testified to the fury of those who had thought that the new order would incontinently bring about the triumph of morality. Between them, those who expected too much of reform, those who had come to fear reform, and those who would not pursue reform at risk to themselves seemed to sound the death knell of a movement. It is noticeable that the occasional persecution of the 1540s once again, as in the days before Tyndale, tended to catch men from the lower orders of society whose offences must leave it doubtful whether they were new Lutherans or old Lollards. The Cromwellian impetus and its specific direction might well have seemed lost.

Nevertheless, the ground-swell of reform had not entirely ceased to roll, even if the drive of the 1530s had collapsed with the loss of the commanding leader who alone had given to different purposes and varied aspirations that positive force which makes a movement. Before long, new changes on the political scene and the outbreak of a major economic crisis under the impact of inflation were to restore the reformers to the public sight, but when this happened it also became plain that in the interval the Cromwellian cohesion had broken up. Those who advanced various radical policies in the later 1540s and early 1550s composed not a cooperative group of like-minded men but at least three quite distinguishable bodies and preoccupations.

Those historians who have discerned a continuity of Erasmian humanism into this later age have not been wholly mistaken. Erasmus continued to be read, and in some quarters to be heeded. Both the moderate personal piety and the dominant interest in education which had become the chief characteristics of his tradition still had their followers, especially in the circle of Catherine Parr both before and after her marriage to Henry VIII. The Queen herself wrote typical pieces of edification which yet are also stamped with her calm and devout personality. She even published them: *Prayers stirring the mind unto heavenly meditations* (1545), a rather derivative collection so popular as to be several times reprinted, and *Lamentation of a sinner* (1547), a pietistic outpouring of a very personal kind which nevertheless owed more than a little to Thomas à Kempis and Marguerite d'Angoulême. The Queen's concern for her stepchildren made the fortunes of several university humanists with a passion for education. Richard Coxe (1500–81), later Elizabeth's awkward bishop of Ely and at this time a man of eminence at Oxford, presided over Prince Edward's household, while Sir John Cheke (1514–57), a famed product of St John's College, Cambridge, acted as tutor-in-chief. Cheke brought in two more men from the same stable—Roger Ascham (1515–68), the best known English educational theorist of the century, and his short-lived pupil William Grindal (died 1548). With the help of other 'Erasmians', these men created for Edward and his sister Elizabeth a humanist school which put the pedagogic precepts of Erasmus and Vives into practice and attracted as pupils also the offspring of several court peers. It was this group of scholars that stood behind the drive for educational reform and investment which screwed the endowments for Christ Church, Oxford, and Trinity College, Cambridge, out of Henry's somewhat reluctant hands.[1] However, their real influence was on the future: they trained their charges successfully in the accomplishments of the humanist prince and, since all of them inclined in varying degree to the Reformation, laid in them foundations of a Protestant faith which was to help determine the fortunes of the Church of England. The fact that Henry allowed his heir to be raised in such an atmosphere has caused wonderment and especially some doubt whether he was really so conservative in his private religion as is usually supposed. However, it is not at all certain that he knew what advanced ideas were being slid into his offspring along with good letters and good manners; if they were to be brought up along truly modern lines—and with this Henry had no quarrel—their tutors really had to be found among men whose doctrinal orthodoxy was suspect, whether the King knew this or not.

A second group of potential radicals to emerge from the 1530s were the active clergy whose reforming zeal grew increasingly Protestant—really the only option to an ardent man dissatisfied with the Church of Rome. Under the temporarily ineffectual protection and guidance of Cranmer, and with Latimer waiting his chance in the wings, a younger generation of theologians and preachers grew up who were to dominate the Church of Edward VI—Nicholas Ridley (?1500–55), a Cambridge scholar making a high reputation in divinity, Thomas Lever (1521–77), a passionate lover of the pulpit and his own voice, Robert Crowley (?1518–88), printer and pamphleteer and a bitter enemy to moral delinquency which he discovered everywhere, John Ponet (?1514–56), later to succeed Gardiner at Winchester and later still to break ranks by proclaiming the validity of resistance to the ungodly prince. Together with the temporary exiles already mentioned, these and their like were carrying on, though for the moment mostly in private, the work of turning the Church away from both Roman and Henrician Catholicism which Cromwell had cautiously sponsored in the previous decade.

The most interesting group of intellectual radicals, however, were neither genuine Erasmians nor clerical Protestants, but laymen who had indeed come into contact with one or the other of both these movements but concentrated neither on education nor on Reformation. Instead, under the pressure of the economic crisis from about 1545 onwards, they continued to explore the important analysis of society and its ills which had been the backbone of the

[1]See above, p. 243.

Cromwellian reform movement. Among them we find John Hales of Coventry (died 1571), keeper of the hanaper in Chancery and an enthusiast for causes who was to take the lead in the fight against enclosures; the young William Cecil (1520–98), another Cambridge man of advanced views, pupil of Cheke, member of Gray's Inn, aspirant servant and within the decade effective master of the state—a man who exemplified the new type of layman whom Cromwell had hoped to call forth out of the marriage of reformed religion, reformed education, and a concern for the commonwealth; and especially Sir Thomas Smith (1513–77).

Smith's brilliant academic career reached its peak when in 1544 he became the first regius professor of civil law at Cambridge, on the strength of a visit to Padua which he had not in fact used for study.[2] Actually, he knew his Roman law and was far from ignorant of the common law; he knew much history, some science, some numismatics, but little divinity. He and Cheke were England's foremost Greek scholars of the day and remarkable by any standard, an accomplishment which in 1542 brought them into conflict with Gardiner when the bishop, Cromwell's successor as chancellor of the university, tried to suppress a 'new' (that is, more correct) pronunciation of Greek promoted by them under the influence of Erasmus's teaching. Gardiner won by imposing his authority—a characteristic piece of bullying; it throws light on his mind that while he never forgave the timorous Cheke, whom he was to pursue to the death, he seems to have been impressed by Smith's resolution as much as by his well timed surrender. Smith throughout his life displayed much moral courage, usually to the detriment of his public career; neither the Protector Somerset nor Queen Elizabeth, both of whom appointed him secretary of state, could stomach his outspoken criticism, so that he never quite made it to the top. He always remained the scholar in office, unlike Cecil who was always the politician with intellectual interests. Smith's writings on public matters are among the most interesting of the century, though since they were mostly evoked by immediate problems they never became a coherent body of political doctrine.

Erasmian educators, clerical radicals, lay students of the body politic: though one must not draw the lines too rigorously between them, and though several of them shared interests and opinions across the divides, the existence of three distinct modes of thinking is manifest. It will not do to comprehend them all under the title of 'commonwealth men', a description really invented for them by

---

[2] See Mary Dewar, *Sir Thomas Smith: a Tudor Intellectual in Office* (1964), which has settled the range of his interests and productions. His best known book, *De Republica Anglorum*, was not written until 1565.

modern historians who have treated them as a single body of thinkers and as a powerful and effective pressure group for the promotion of social reform.[3] Certainly they all favoured some aspect of reform and all leant (at varying angles) to the Protestant Reformation, but the only conviction which they all shared was dislike of popular resistance, subversion and sedition. The rebellions of 1549 provoked Cheke's *Hurt of Sedition*,[4] Cranmer's fierce denunciation article by article of the Cornish rebels' demands, Becon's advice that the poor must not think of helping themselves against their oppressors, and Smith's uncompromising support for the repressive measures of the government. But for the rest one sees little common ground or intersecting argument. The 'Erasmians' concentrated on personal piety and a humanist education: they wished to produce godly rulers but offered no advice on action in rule. Ascham's lively treatise on archery, *Toxophilus* (1545), continues a tradition of English patriotism vigorously initiated by Richard Morison but, apart from its main interest (instruction in the use of the bow), attends only to the decline of military training, not the ills of the commonweal. The preachers—once they came into the open after 1547—certainly spent an inordinate amount of time denouncing the evil practices of those whom they identified as the enemies of the commonweal, but since they had no remedy to offer beyond moral exhortation they really went back to the type of futile lamentation which had been heard for centuries. There is not one word in the famous sermons of Latimer and Lever, with all their impassioned oratory against enclosers of commons, engrossers of merchandise, exploiters of the coinage, which suggests that they either understood the problems of the economy or thought it necessary to find answers beyond urging their hearers to be good. Becon, who drafted prayers for all the orders in the commonwealth, would tell the poor only that their prayer must be for contentment with that station into which it had pleased God to place them. By the side of a priest like Starkey, these men dwindle into purveyors of moral commonplaces, redeemed (if that is the word) only by the splendour and ferocity of their homiletic language.

As it happens, they got their answer from Smith: 'Can we devise that all covetousness may be taken from men? No, no more than we can make men be without ire, without gladness, without fear, and

---

[3] The idea of a 'commonwealth party', put about (misleadingly) in 1549, has been too readily extended to cover the reform thinkers of the earlier and following decades; this is not justified by the facts. In contrast to the Cromwellian legislation, that of Edward VI includes none with true 'commonwealth' preambles, the keyword itself occuring only nine times in five sessions and 118 acts.

[4] 'To have no gentlemen because ye be none is to bring down an estate and to mend none'— a comprehensive answer to all unthinking egalitarianism.

without all affections.' Talk of changing human nature, or demanding that men act nobly beyond their capacity, was so much vapour. What Smith called for instead were measures to render those economic activities which he diagnosed as dangerous less profitable than enterprises more beneficial to the commonweal. He looked not for regeneration but for a sensitive manipulation of the economy which would, for instance, offer better returns from arable husbandry than from sheepfarming. The true Cromwellian tradition found its heirs in the very small group of men who really wished to solve practical problems practically.

Even allowing for a few anonymous treatises, the number of people who are known to have written about the real troubles of society in an age of drastic inflation is not large. They all had their own diagnosis and their own remedies. The still unidentified author of 'Politics to reduce this realm of England unto a prosperous wealth and estate' (1549), who claimed to have been studying the problem for four or five years, discerned two causes of inflation—the devaluation of sterling on the international money market (which made all imports very dear) and the engrossing (hoarding) of commodities by selfish interests intent upon pushing up prices. The second was a commonplace (and sometimes true); the first mistook an effect for a cause. He hoped to cure the second by a vigorous programme of supporting food production and especially fishing: apparently he thought that an abundance of fish would drive down meat prices because people would be able to refuse to buy at the inflated price. As to the first—and in his opinion fundamental—trouble, he suggested ways of improving England's balance of trade which involved very heavy import duties (up to twenty-five per cent *ad valorem*), in the belief that this would attract bullion into the country as well as reduce purchases overseas. On this heart of his discourse he is anything but clear—far less clear than in his opinion that managing food prices was pointless (one lesson learned from Cromwell's failure) or his proposal that sheepfarming be controlled by the imposition of a tax per head of sheep to keep flocks small (this was tried).

On the other hand, William Forrest, who did not improve his economic analysis by putting it into unmelodious verse, had no doubt that unemployment was caused by the export of wool and unfinished cloth, while he ascribed the inflation of food prices to the raising of rents by landlords. He called for an embargo on the trade in wool (another writer who failed to realize that his proposals would ruin the commerce dependent on the continental demand for English raw materials and semi-finished products only) and for the restoration of rents to the level of some twenty years before. His attention to rents has recently received some support. At one time we all discounted this element because the evidence seemed to show that the upward movement of rents always followed in the wake of price inflation, but we now have reason to think that a reverse relationship occurred.[5] Nevertheless, though there was some inflationary manipulation of rents, Forrest's concentration on this one 'cause' was mistaken; in many places rents rose after prices, and a large part of England's primary producers were protected by the customary law against any, or any marked, increase in rents and entry fines. On balance (and subject to what further research may discover) rising rents should still be regarded as landlords' necessary reaction to the inflation of their costs and as generally, though not invariably, supportable by a peasantry who were selling their produce on a rising market.

The most conventional and least convincing explanation of all was offered by John Hales who readopted the ancient complaints against enclosing and sheepfarming which he saw as the sole cause of shortages and rising prices—even at a time (1546–8) when abundant harvests made nonsense of the argument that conversion to pasture had condemned the realm to a permanent deficiency in food production. Unfortunately, for reasons of his own, the Protector Somerset accepted Hales's view and permitted the initiation of the one active social reform campaign of the age upon a false diagnosis, by inadequate means, and with tragic consequences.[6] He would have done better to heed the advice of Thomas Smith, his secretary, written in 1549 during several months of leisure enforced upon the scholar by a temporary disfavour.

Smith's *Discourse of the Commonweal of this Realm of England* remains beyond question the century's outstanding contribution to social and economic analysis.[7] The work should really be considered in the context of his study of the Roman coinage, the problems of international exchange,[8] and even the art of war (with its emphasis on a healthy population available for military service), but it needs particular attention with respect to the reform programme of the 1540s. Presented as a dialogue between a knight (gentleman landowner), husbandman, merchant (exporter), capper (who stands for all artificers troubled by foreign competition), and doctor (of the civil law), it allows each representative to put his sectional grievances and

---

[5] E. Kerridge, 'The Movement of Rent, 1540–1640', *Economic History Review*, 2nd series, VI (1953), pp. 16 ff.

[6] See below, pp. 343–5.

[7] Smith's authorship has been conclusively proved by Mrs Dewar: see her edition of the work in Folger Documents of Tudor and Stuart Civilization (1969).

[8] The treatise on the exchange usually ascribed to Thomas Gresham (R. de Roover, *Gresham on Foreign Exchange*, 1949) was almost certainly also written by Smith.

point of view very fairly. Smith must be identified with the doctor who had the widest vision and whose answers clearly represent the author's own views. Smith understood and lucidly analysed the symptoms of inflation, nor did he entirely disallow any of them as part causes: he admits that enclosing, sheepfarming, enhancing of rents, problems of international trade, the import of rival manufactures and especially of luxuries can all contribute to the economic problems of the nation. Among the writers on the subject he stands out by refusing to seek a single cause. At the same time he shows that none of these issues can be charged with being the ultimate or dominant stimulant to inflation, and that many sectional complaints cancel one another out or fall down because they fail to take account of the difficulties encountered by the other sectors. Above all, he explicitly refuses to seek either cause or remedy in economic self-interest and its repression: he recognizes self-interest as legitimate, understands the principle of social improvement by economic activism, and wants to solve problems not by penal legislation but by intelligent management which will induce people to seek their own interest in such a way that it profits rather than harms the common interest. This is an enormous advance over the legalistic and moralizing stance which had still been at the heart of the measures promoted by Cromwell's thinkers and in part had also animated Cromwell's own handling of the economy, though Smith may well have noted the many steps Cromwell had taken on the advice of practical experience and in the cause of general harmony. Smith's highly 'modern' beliefs—there are times when his first name might seem to have been Adam[9]—made no overt converts; control by law and in the service of a moral concept of society remained the avowed policy of the century. In practice, however, his views may be seen reflected in Cecil's later inclination to guided innovation and enterprise which often allowed supervised self-interest more play than the words of statutes and proclamations might lead one to suspect.

In the end Smith identified as the primary (not sole) cause of the particular inflation since 1544 the debasement of the coinage. He denied the common argument that money was but a token and might as well be made of paper or leather as of silver; those who held this view could not see why prices should rise since they were measured in an instrument itself without worth which merely defined a relative value between the goods exchanged. Instead he quite rightly recognized that money had an intrinsic value represented by the price agreed to be ascribable to its content of precious metal;

[9]Smith was no naked profit-maximizing capitalist: to the knight's question, 'If they find more profit thereby than otherwise, why should they not?', he has the doctor reply, 'they may not purchase themselves profit by that that may be hurtful to others.'

from this, and a competent analysis of both domestic and international exchange, he deduced that debasement would force up prices especially of imports whose role in determining price levels he understood. Smith is particularly impressive when explaining England's role as part of an international nexus of trade: the ignorant and disastrous policies advocated by those who thought in terms of a self-sufficiency and independence that simply could not exist had no attraction for him. In the upshot he called for the restoration of the coinage as the basis of a stable economy; and in the conditions of his day he was perfectly correct.

Unfortunately, he was also ignored, at least for the time being. The mythical commonwealth movement of 1547–51 not only did not consist of a concerted effort made by various groups and people towards a common end; in addition it lacked the crucial element of guidance and participation from above. The noise made by reformers was louder this time than in the 1530s, in step with the much more difficult situation encountered; there was economic crisis in the later 1540s, while there had just been problems in Cromwell's day. But their impact on government was incomparably weaker. Smith and Cecil as yet carried little weight. The powerful group of conservatives in Council and at court (led by Gardiner and Wriothesley) would have nothing to do with reformers who, one way and another, leant to Protestantism, and who therefore could not even speak out before the end of Henry VIII's reign. Among the men of power only one had contacts with them—William Paget, a man in the Cromwell mould though of markedly lesser stature. Also born the son of a clothworker (in 1505 or 1506), he had risen in the bureaucracy of the 1530s, befriended at first by Gardiner but then by Cromwell and Wriothesley. Unlike Cromwell he had a Cambridge education; his college was Trinity Hall, the home of civil lawyers, but unlike its master, Gardiner, he had no need to enter the Church as his seniors, intent upon the public service, had always done. Secretarial and diplomatic employments had prospered a middling sort of career until in April 1543 he became principal secretary of state and inherited a part of the Cromwell mantle. Leaving the routine of the office to his colleague William Petre (another of Cromwell's young men), he continued active on important embassies and by about 1545 had become the indispensable man in government. Unlike Cromwell, Paget was the true bureaucrat in office to whom the work itself always came first. In a time of spiritual turmoil he saw no difficulty in adapting himself to whatever the official order required. Certainly opposed to the papacy, he also eschewed serious attachment to the reformed religion and probably through his life preferred the Henrician compromise which he had

seen created in his formative years. At the same time, he held to
some firm principles. He reserved his passion for efficiency and
effectiveness: his voice rises notably higher when he has to admonish
others for endangering the stability of government by acts of policy,
and he was happiest devising good orders for Privy Council and
secretariats. However, unlike Petre (a similar type), he shared something of Cromwell's larger vision of the well ordered and prosperous
commonwealth, and he fully understood the claims of politics. Paget
wanted power, both for himself and for the cause he served—the
cause, essentially, of preserving the Cromwellian revolution through
the vicissitudes that beset it after Cromwell's death; though his
understanding of that revolution did not necessarily include a
Protestant Reformation he was willing to accept one if he could not
get the rest without it. And in 1545–6 Paget recognized where the
road to power lay: he made himself the guiding spirit of the most
promising faction of the day which was building around the
Seymour interest.

However, even Paget's, and ultimately Somerset's, interest in
reform agitation did not turn these protesters into the sort of
movement which had made the 1530s into an age of reform. By
contrast with Cromwell's day we find no general attack on the
problems of the commonwealth, hardly any government bills in
Parliament and certainly no government programme there, no
drafting and redrafting of proposals, no proposals (significantly) in
the form of acts of Parliament. The political leaders accepted by this
inchoate movement were no Cromwells. Either, like Somerset, they
were men of muddled sympathies willing to do this or that provided
nothing interfered with the primary personal concerns; or like Paget
they wished to maintain the Cromwellian achievements in the
reconstruction of the state rather than follow the Cromwellian
purpose of using the reconstructed state for social betterment.
Nevertheless, the hopes of reform inexorably turned towards the
Seymour circle which, almost by accident, provided the one connection that united the disparate reform groups of the 1540s.

The Seymours had links with Catherine Parr's coterie: Edward
Seymour, earl of Hertford, was Prince Edward's uncle, and after the
death of her second husband (the aged Lord Latimer) Catherine had
meant to marry Hertford's brother Thomas, a sexually attractive
personage with a dangerously unstable temperament, until Henry
VIII imperiously, and somewhat inexplicably, entered his claims.
Both Hertford and his entourage inclined to the reformed religion: in
power, the earl appointed Hooper, Becon and Turner his chaplains;
the Seymours, like the Queen, also stood well with Cramner. As for
the social analysts, both Smith and Cecil became Hertford's secre-

taries. The links existed between Seymour and reform, though they were not overwhelmingly strong except perhaps in religion; the hopes of reformers pointed, somewhat unsteadily, to the Seymour faction, especially once Paget had joined it; the political events of the decisive year 1546 made certain that power should go to the Seymours, and reform needed power if it was to become active again. In measure, the alliance between government and reform was reforged at this time: but it was an alliance between a government which had neither a positive programme nor a consistent purpose, and a reform which lacked cohesion and agreed ideas. From the first there were signs that recklessness and incomprehension might take the place of Cromwellian determination, cautious planning and thorough execution. The prospects were not improved by the multiple crisis in the Church, the economy, and foreign relations which Henry VIII's late policies had done so much to bring into threatening existence.

15 The Seymour Ascendancy

I

By early 1546, the realm and the politicians had to face the like-lihood that Henry VIII's long reign was drawing to a close. Though he remained intermittently active and never lost his powers alto-gether, the King was now rarely free of a complex of illnesses which would have destroyed a man less given to excess, and which could not possibly leave his mind as sovereign and unclouded as the traditional interpretation has always supposed.[1] His approaching end compelled the men of power—the leaders of Privy Council and Privy Chamber—to prepare themselves for a struggle over the succession, for since the heir to the throne was not yet ten years old the next reign was bound to start with a minority during which rule would fall to him who jockeyed himself into the saddle before King Henry died. Thus factions coalesced until two parties stood face to face and battled for control. Each side fought for power, the more determinedly so because defeat was likely to equal destruction, but each side also fought for a cause. Ever since the break with Rome, court factions had represented not only personal ambitions but also ideological conflicts; in 1546, the line between them more clearly than ever divided friends to reform and Reformation from those who wished to stand upon the ancient ways.

In this struggle the reformers held quite marked advantages. The conservatives still lacked adequate leadership. Suffolk died in 1545 and Norfolk, nearly twenty years older than Henry, was a spent force. His son, Surrey, impressed all observers as unstable, irrespon-sible and foolishly arrogant—not a man to command loyalty or trust. Gardiner, politically the most notable among them, always made enemies more readily than friends, while Wriothesley, despite

[1]For the established view see J. J. Scarisbrick, *Henry VIII*, chapter 14. L. B. Smith, *Henry VIII: the Mask of Royalty* (1971), offers some interesting speculations on the King's personality and treats Henry to the end as the ruler of all around him, but the interpretation rests on some rather bold use of dubious evidence. The King's deterioration seems patent to me, as do the machinations of the factions over whom his power was at best occasional.

the chancellorship, never quite lost the air of a second-rank politician. In consequence the outlines of this faction remained uncertain and its policies disarrayed. The other side not only contained abler (and younger) men but also knew its mind much better. It looked to several prominent men as leaders. Edward Seymour, earl of Hertford, a man of consuming ambition, could hope to exploit his relationship to Prince Edward. John Dudley, Viscount Lisle, shared Hertford's inclination to Protestantism, his military reputation, and also his self-confident ambition, but at this time thought to advance his cause best by allying with the Seymour interest. Sir Anthony Denny and Sir William Herbert, Henry's close companions in the Privy Chamber and the second also Catherine Parr's brother-in-law, both favoured reform. They could control the court, while Paget, as has already been said, not only dominated the administration but added to the faction the best political talent of the day. Cranmer willy-nilly lent such support as was within his power. By late 1545 this alliance had evidently been cemented. The Parliament of November–December that year contained a sizable Seymour-Herbert group, to testify to the faction's willingness to put out its strength in every centre of government. But the real struggle was necessarily fought out at court, around the monstrous hulk of the man who had dominated his world for so long. Since statute empowered Henry to make all arrangements for what was to happen after his death, it was necessary to capture his support during life; and he remained sufficiently alert and dangerous to make the contestants proceed with circumspection.

The growing ascendancy of the reforming party provoked the conservatives into firing the first shots. They relied on well tried methods, hoping to exploit Henry's horror of heresy and thinking their enemies vulnerable on that score. What had brought Cromwell down would surely do for Seymour. Thus in the spring of 1546 the persecution of Protestants resumed in a concerted effort which penetrated into the court itself. Material lay readily to hand. When familiar suspects like Latimer and Crome came under attack, the latter implicated members of the Parr circle, and Gardiner thought he had the key to success in the person of Anne Askew, a Lincolnshire gentlewoman who had been dangerously frank about her very heretical views of the sacraments. The investigators tried hard to get her to denounce five ladies of the court, including the wives of Hertford and Denny; they used torture, with two prominent conservative councillors, Wriothesley and Rich, themselves working the rack; but all in vain. Though the unhappy woman, truly a martyr, was burned with three others on 16 July, the main assault failed. Thus the further attempt to persuade Henry that his last

Queen was also tainted with heresy lacked persuasiveness, and Catherine, by the sort of careful submission that usually worked wonders with Henry, easily extricated herself from the toils. Indeed, this attempt to destroy the radical faction backfired. Henry was so pleased with Catherine's elegant surrender to his supremacy that Gardiner, not for the first time, fell right out of favour.

This left the road clear for the Seymour faction, and from the middle of the year they rapidly occupied every point of importance. In August they regularized their hold upon the King's mind by institutionalizing a piece of machinery which they had managed to keep under their hands from the first.[2] This was the instrument known as the King's dry stamp which from September 1545 in effect replaced the royal signature on all warrants and papers of state, at first because Henry wished to avoid the tedium of signing but before long because it suited the winning party. The stamp was used to impress a blind replica of the sign manual which was then traced in ink by a person authorized to do so. Denny had all along controlled it: his associate John Gates had custody of it, and his servant William Clerc had sole authority to employ it. Thus Denny, who in October replaced a conservative as head of the Privy Chamber, not only commanded the route of access to the King, a vital enough asset in the battle, but also superintended the use of the royal signature in all matters of patronage and politics.

With the court, and the King, thus firmly in their hands, the faction turned to securing the Privy Council which for a crucial month (8 December 1546 to 4 January 1547) met not at court but in Hertford's town house. Gardiner, already suspect after the affair of the Queen, got further into trouble with the King by allegedly refusing to agree to an exchange of lands; he denied his supposed obstinacy, and the story is indeed so improbable that we may well suspect successful and misleading whispers in Henry's receptive ear. At any rate, Gardiner ceased to attend the Privy Council in mid-November. Wriothesley and Rich were ready meat for pretended friendliness and promises of a share in the benefits expected at Henry's death. The Howards, however, who had come to hate Hertford especially and who alone could seriously dispute the rule of a minority with him, had to be destroyed, and Surrey's folly created a convenient opportunity. The earl, a poet of some power who naturalized the Italian sonnet in English, had always overplayed his hand, and ever since he mismanaged the defence of Boulogne Henry had disliked and distrusted him. Thus when his enemies, producing slender proof, charged him with treasonable ambition for the throne, the King at once withdrew his protecting hand. On 12 December

[2]D. R. Starkey, 'The King's Privy Chamber, 1485–1547', pp. 342 ff.

both father and son were arrested; by 19 January Surrey had died by the axe; on the 28th the old duke, the biter of so many better men at last himself bit, would have followed him if Henry had not opportunely died in the night. Norfolk remained in the Tower throughout the next reign.

Thus by the end of 1546 Hertford and his allies were in full control; it remained so to arrange matters that their takeover at Henry's death (which could not now be long delayed) would be smooth. For this they employed Henry's secret weapon, his last will and testament, and the handling of this tricky business was Paget's masterpiece.[3] Henry's will had become a major political instrument when the Second and Third Acts of Succession empowered him to settle the succession by means of it (subject to certain limitations) and to nominate his successor's Council. It was therefore important to the Seymour faction to—shall we say—influence its terms. They could not hope to dictate them, for this was one piece of policy which even in his last decline the King would not let go out of his hands; and they certainly did not mean to practise wholesale forgery—too dangerous, quite unthinkable for men who remained in awe of Henry VIII, and in any case not necessary. These were all good servants of the Tudor monarchy, intent, to be sure, upon power, intent upon their policies, men of ambition, but also devoted to the loyalties and legalisms which ruled the political community. As it was, their control of the dry stamp enabled them to get what they wanted with just a little doctoring.

On 26 December 1546 Henry called for his will because he wanted to make some changes in it; especially he determined to put Gardiner out of the regency Council and did so even though those attending—all members of Hertford's party—tried (as they later claimed) to dissuade him. Perhaps they did: they could safely calculate that their representations would make no difference. On the 30th the revised will was approved by the King but, despite statements to the contrary, it was not then signed, either by hand or stamp. Henry's health improved a little, and throughout January (unwilling to contemplate his own death) he refused all solicitations to append his signature. Thus when by about the 26th the end was manifestly near there was still no valid will in existence. Henry may at the last have authorized the application of the stamp—he never signed the will by hand—or this may have been done after he ceased

---

[3] The truth about Henry's will remains much disputed. For a full statement of the most widely held traditional view see Scarisbrick, *Henry VIII*, pp. 488 ff. Smith (*Henry VIII*, pp. 267 ff.) idiosyncratically thinks that Henry used his will as a weapon 'with which to cudgel his servants' after his death. There are serious weaknesses in all the usual interpretations, and I follow in the main an unpublished analysis by Dr D. R. Starkey; I am most grateful to him for letting me see and use his account.

to be able to speak, or even after his death. What matters is that the document stamped had been altered from that approved a month earlier. There had been further convenient changes in the composition of the successor Council, and a (probably) new clause authorized that body to bestow unspecified gifts, honours and estates which, it was alleged, the King had meant to distribute among his faithful councillors. In its final form, therefore, the will left the crown to Edward, Mary and Elizabeth in that order (if each in turn failed to produce heirs), excluded the Stuart descendants of Henry's elder sister Margaret, but allowed in the Grey heirs of his younger sister Mary, nominated a Privy Council of sixteen executors who were left free to come to whatever arrangements they pleased, and made general promises of advancement and profit to those whom this Council might favour. No one can tell how much of this Henry still understood. There need be no doubt that the descent of the crown was in accord with his desires; only he, in his hatred of his Scottish relatives, would have cut out the Stuarts. But the arrangements which enabled the Seymour faction to grasp the reins and to enrich themselves in effect frustrated the King's supposed determination to extend his dominance beyond the grave: they may well have been inserted without his perfect knowledge.

Henry VIII died in the early hours of 28 January 1547, his hand in Cranmer's and his speech gone. At the last he turned to the one man among his spiritual advisers whom he had always respected. His death was easy enough, and he seems to have felt sure of his destination. The faction which had conspired to take power from him needed a little time to complete its arrangements: Hertford wanted to secure the person of the new King, and the Council remained undecided whether to execute Norfolk. Then, after three days of secrecy, Lord Chancellor Wriothesley, in tears, announced the demise of the crown in the House of Lords. Paget read out the will, and King Henry's last Parliament went home. The father of his people, the great cloud hanging over them, was gone. In thirty-eight years of rule he had done and witnessed great things; the England from which he departed was an altogether different realm from that which he had inherited. Of all the kings of England he stands forth as the most monarchical; no one had ever entirely ruled his mind or his purposes, no one had ever fully penetrated the stupendous egotism of his inner core, no one had ever been really safe with him. Yet neither had he ruled his destiny and his country's in that sovereign fashion that he persuaded himself and posterity had been his personal contribution. His reign owed its successes and virtues to better and greater men about him; most of its horrors and failures sprang more directly from himself.

II

The victorious faction went smoothly into action; the efficiency of the takeover, in marked contrast to its leader's usual incompetence in politics, betrays the mind and hand of Paget.[4] Everyone, of course, remembered the precedents for royal minorities. First one had to secure the person of the boy King, preferably before his predecessor's death was known. Hertford at once collected Edward and brought him to London where on 31 January he presented him at the Tower to the Council of executors nominated in Henry's will. At the same meeting he also got his fellow councillors to name him Protector of the realm—another conventional measure in minorities, taken for instance in 1422 and 1483. Although it is usually alleged that Henry had meant to prevent just this elevation of a single person, the terms of his will in fact left this obvious possibility open. As on the earlier occasions, the office went to the King's uncle. All this, therefore, followed precedent quite painfully. At this point, however, the preparations were nearly upset by an intervention from Hertford's turbulent brother Thomas whom (it appears) Lisle (John Dudley) stirred into seeking the governorship of the King's person. The Protector had no intention of dividing one office from another, but he had to buy his brother off with immediate admission to the Council (from which Henry had excluded him)[5] and a promise of a share in the forthcoming distribution of benefits. This itself was initiated at once. On 6 February, Paget and Herbert delivered a long statement to the Council in which they explained Henry's alleged intention to raise certain of his councillors to a higher rank in the peerage and endow them with lands sufficient to maintain their new state. Quite possibly Henry did intend some such generosity, and the fact that Paget himself went at this time empty-handed may support the truth of his statement. However, it is also apparent that the vague promise in the will was inserted by the management of the beneficiaries, and the lavish scale of the hand-out does not in the least correspond to Henry's usual practice. Lord Chancellor Wriothesley was among those promoted, but he was only temporarily bought off and began to build a party in the Council against the Seymour domination. Political ambition rather than religious

[4] Much of the traditional story of Edward VI's reign and Somerset's protectorate, as told by A. F. Pollard (*England under Protector Somerset*, 1900, and *Political History of England* v, 1910) and by W. K. Jordan (*Edward VI*, 2 volumes, 1968, 1970) has been demolished by two recent studies: M. L. Bush, *The Government Policy of Protector Somerset* (1975) and D. E. Hoak, *The King's Council in the Reign of Edward VI* (1976).

[5] Seymour was admitted to the Privy Council on 23 January, but Henry was later reported to have refused to keep him in the Council of executors. In the will he appears among the 'assistants' only. His treatment proves that the will was still being revised in the last week of Henry's life.

differences most likely lay behind his opposition. By early March, the Protector, now duke of Somerset, felt strong enough to destroy the chancellor; using a possibly inspired common lawyers' protest against Wriothesley's use of his court as well as two doubtfully valid commissions by means of which he had delegated his authority there to substitutes so as to be freer for politics, Somerset forced him on the 5th to resign from office and Council.

So far everything had been done by authority of Henry's will which vested power corporately in the executors, so that Somerset in manner still remained their creature. Determined to set up a free personal rule, the duke on 12 March obtained letters patent (in the new King's name) which empowered him to appoint the King's Council, and from that moment his autocratic system was complete. He at once reorganized the Privy Council, bringing in some of Henry's old councillors whom the will had relegated to an inferior position, but (probably thanks to Paget's advice) he firmly adhered to the Cromwellian principle of keeping the body small and professional—round about the twenty or so officeholders that had been its members since 1536. Actually, membership of the Privy Council mattered little at this time because Somerset proceeded to rule without its participation. For something like two years, the Council lost much of its authority and even reality, becoming little more than a body whom Somerset occasionally called in to rubber-stamp his decisions.[6] Had he been a more political man he might have been more careful of the feelings of his fellow magnates among whom Lisle (now earl of Warwick) lay deceptively low after the failure of his brief attempt to disrupt the creation of a substitute monarchy. As it was, he neglected the Council far more than Henry VIII, Cromwell or even Wolsey had done. Another possibly ominous event occurred when Thomas Seymour, baulked of the governorship, in April married Henry's widow—his own intended since 1543—and thus maintained dangerously close contacts with the royal family.

The new Protector was in some ways singularly ill suited for the post. Rude, harsh and arrogant in manner and speech, he made enemies at every turn, their number being further augmented by his intolerable wife. Though unquestionably an able enough soldier, he had so far given no sign of political or administrative competence, and his rule was to demonstrate that he possessed none. The notion that he was a generous and visionary idealist, 'ahead of his time', in the end defeated by wicked and selfish opposition from fellow nobles to wise measures of reform will not stand up to investigation.[7] True,

---

[6] Hoak, *King's Council*, pp. 22 ff., 103 ff.
[7] The case is argued by Dr Bush in the book cited above.

he had links with various reforming groups and especially—of this there can be no doubt—favoured moves in the direction of a Protestant Reformation, but his policy was dictated by convention, self-interest and irresolution in the face of difficulties. He simply lacked both the intelligence and the skill to carry out the concerted improvement for which the state of the nation was calling. Despite a sternly authoritarian temper which mistook rigidity for firmness and self-will for rational conviction, he was not inclined to cruelty and wanted a reputation for good virtue: hence those intermittent displays of mildness and those frequent expressions of lofty senti-ments. In consequence he was always liable to do the wrong thing—to persist with disastrous policies long after their effects had become manifest, and to indulge in loosely liberal attitudes at the very moments when his normal rigour would have been more approp-riate. He was soon to drive his supporters to despair. Paget, who always wrote frankly, did his best to teach him the error of his ways, but in the end had to admit to himself that he had picked the wrong man for leader. Tall, gloomy, withdrawn, given to suffering looks, Somerset lacked even the presence to support his pretended king-ship. But perhaps his worst failing was a ruthless acquisitiveness of which he gave plentiful evidence during the years that he struggled upward,[8] and which had free rein now that he commanded power. His building up of a great territorial complex in Wiltshire and Somerset, at the expense of the Crown and of the bishopric of Bath and Wells whose possessions he decimated, offers no support for the illusion which speaks of idealism and care for the poor.[9] Somerset wanted great wealth and got it; he wanted great power, and having got it did not know what to do with it.

Not that he stood alone in his greed, though he satisfied it better than the rest could hope to do while he ruled. In the two years of Somerset's ascendancy, about £20,000 of the Crown's annual landed income was transferred to private hands, some forty per cent of it in gifts; this total was doubled by a further distribution made after his fall. Free gifts predominated predictably in the two years, 1547 and 1550, in which two victorious faction leaders bought the loyalty of their followers.[10] Much of this property was the remainder of the

[8] M. L. Bush, 'The Rise to Power of Edward Seymour, Protector Somerset, 1500–1547' (un-published dissertation, Cambridge, 1965), tells a sad tale of grasping greed for land, calculated switches of friendship, and notable success in war.

[9] The act of 1549 (2 & 3 Ed. VI c. 12) which is often cited to prove his generosity to his tenants actually establishes rights of his own doubtful at law and confirms the lawfulness of his demands for rents etc.

[10] See the discussion in Jordan, *Edward VI* I, pp. 103 ff., and especially the table on p. 118. Jordan deals in what he calls capital values and does not explain how he arrived at them; they appear to be the sales prices (vouched for or conjectured?). Since so much was given away and sales terms differed, I prefer to use annual yields. However, my figures, derived as they are from Jordan's confusing totals, must be regarded as very approximate.

monastic estates; some came from earlier crown lands; in addition
the properties of chantries and guilds dissolved progressively from
1545 onwards moved rapidly into private hands. The dissolution
of the chantries, consolidated by statute in 1547,[11] completed
the attack on the Church's corporate property; but we should not
forget the further inroads made by private assaults on bishops'
lands (acquired by extorted sales and exchanges) of which
Somerset's dealings with William Barlow of Bath and Wells were
only the outstanding case. The reign of Edward VI marked the
triumph of those ambitions to secularize the possessions of the
Church which had so usefully supported the jurisdictional revolution
of the 1530s; they also marked the end of the endeavour to give
permanent solidity to the King's finances. Though less land left
crown hands than in Henry VIII's sales, far more yielded no profit
at all to the Exchequer, and the crown lands now permanently
surrendered their place of primacy in the royal financial administration. Instead, landed wealth was distributed widely across the
nation. Little enough of it contributed to the purposes of reform
which had been loudly proclaimed in the 1530s. We no longer
suppose that the dissolution of the chantries destroyed a working
school system: there had been no such thing, though some chantry
priests provided some instruction in the rudiments of learning.
Neither do we believe that the secularization of land led to the
endowment of a whole new system of King Edward VI grammar
schools, though a start was indeed made. By assisting in the foundation and refoundation of schools, several men of property proved
their attachment to the cause of educational reform designed to
create a godly nation and commonweal,[12] but most of the new
owners made it plain that they acquired their wealth for themselves
and their families.

Who were the new owners? It has already been emphasized that
the great redistribution of land enlarged and fortified the existing lay
social structure: the gentry and nobility took the bulk. Between 1547
and 1553 they took about seventy per cent of what was going.
However, the events of Edward's reign created a certain bias within
that general body of traditional landowners. More than half the
property transferred went to men in government service, from privy
councillors downwards. They had naturally always been in the best
position to enrich themselves, but where Henry VIII's sales had
indifferently profited purchasers of all kinds, the 'country' gentry
well to the fore, his son's assisted mainly the men of power. To speak,

[11] The act of 1545 lapsed before it took effect. The 1547 bill led to opposition from some
burgesses anxious to save local religious guilds, but chantries—foundations linked with the
religious observances of a Catholic past—found no defender.

[12] J. Simon, *Education and Society in Tudor England*, chapter 9.

as Jordan does,[13] of 'old' and 'new' nobility is somewhat misleading. His analysis demonstrates the success of faction, and the successful factions consisted of men who had come to the fore in the age of Cromwell, many of them at Cromwell's promotion. The rain of honours in February 1547 made a duke of Edward Seymour (Somerset), a marquess of William Parr (Northampton), earls of Thomas Wriothesley (Southampton) and John Dudley (Warwick), barons of Thomas Seymour, Richard Rich, William Willoughby and Edward Sheffield. Advancement came later to William Paget (a baron in September 1549), William Paulet (earl of Wiltshire 1550, marquess of Winchester 1551), John Russell (earl of Bedford 1550), and William Herbert (earl of Pembroke 1551). Anthony Denny, that useful and influential man, died too soon (September 1549) to reap his full reward. But all these, and others of slightly inferior standing, entered public life (sometimes from earlier court service) in the 1530s. Of the twenty-two members of Somerset's first Privy Council, only two—the earl of Arundel and Bishop Tunstall—belonged to an earlier political generation. It was not a question of religion: that Council readily accommodated both Cranmer and Tunstall, both Russell and Rich, both Anthony Denny and Anthony Brown, men who did not agree on the nature of the sacraments or the doctrine of justification by faith. They all, however, quite firmly believed in the new order—the royal supremacy, the reformed unitary commonwealth, the predominance of the laity in the affairs of the Church. In age they ranged quite widely, and none was young; several had been well into middle age before they experienced the drastic transformation of the realm and its politics. But that transformation made them into a post-revolutionary generation who had taken over from contemporaries driven by it out of public life. The 1530s can in retrospect be seen as a watershed also in their effect upon individuals: so many careers then came to an end while others started. The age of Cromwell marked all the ruling caste of Edward's reign, their feuds and enmities notwithstanding.

Despite the prevalence of faction, the caste's coherence in attitudes, purposes and ethos, which overrode political and religious disagreements, accounts in part for the stability of a potentially unstable situation. It is true that, unlike the royal minorities of 1422 and 1483, that of 1547 had been foreseeable for some time; the ease of the takeover owed something to the fact that the victors had been able to prepare it for several months. It also owed a good deal to Cromwell's administrative reforms which made possible a continuity in government that the older system had lacked, with its dependence on the personal activity of the king and his chosen helpers in the

[13] Jordan, *Edward VI* 1, pp. 89 ff.

Household. No such hesitations, backtrackings and delays as marked the years 1485–7 and 1509–12 appeared in 1547; the administration ran on without a break or even a hiccough. In one respect, the new reign further advanced Cromwell's principles of government: the Privy Chamber, that last fling of the medieval Household system, abdicated from participation in public administration, mainly because a child's personal attendants were in no position to exercise the sort of influence that had been available to Henry's friends. On the other hand, Somerset's efforts to turn the protectorship into a form of personal monarchy threatened for a time to undermine the bureaucratic foundations of the reformed administration. He ignored the Council, ruled by proclamation (issuing far more than any of his predecessors or successors), and tried to dominate even the law courts through his private household. His secretaries, Thomas Smith and William Cecil, temporarily rivalled the influence of the King's principal secretaries, Paget and Petre, in the channelling of patronage and protection.[14] But the effort soon weakened. By mid-1548 the Council was reasserting itself; the courts of law and equity refused to become the Protector's instruments; in April 1548 Smith's position was regularized when he inherited Paget's secretaryship on that minister's promotion to the sinecure office (with cabinet rank) of comptroller of the Household. The national bureaucracy resumed control. Perhaps, if Somerset had been a man of ability and clear-headed purpose he could have undone Cromwell's achievement in giving centralized and stable government to the realm. As it was, his incompetence and arrogance produced a crisis which destroyed him but left the state secure.

III

What would Somerset do with his power, now that he had got it? Not without reason his faction had been regarded as the Protestant party, and the friends of the new religion expected early moves towards a Reformation. The self-exiled preachers rushed home, and the English correspondents of Zürich wrote letters full of joy and hope. Before long, England in her turn became a refuge for foreign reformers. When Charles V destroyed the Schmalkaldic League in

[14] Hoak, *King's Council*, p. 115. The story that Somerset set up a Court of Requests in his own house is untrue and part of the legend that makes him a friend of the poor. Cecil, as his master of Requests, processed the many petitions for relief which naturally reached the Protector, mainly by forwarding them to the established Court of Requests at Westminster (D. A. Knox, 'The Court of Requests in the Reign of Edward VI'.

April 1547, Strassburg ceased to be the Protestant haven it had been for a quarter century; and elsewhere too the Counter-Reformation was making life unpleasant for committed men who found in Cranmer a welcoming host. Martin Bucer exchanged Strassburg for Cambridge; John à Lasco arrived from Poland; Peter Martyr Vermigli and Bernardino Ochino, wandering exiles from Italy, settled for a time in London and Oxford. Some people began to take the law into their own hands. Subversive preaching, suppressed in the 1540s, started up again; here and there the mass ceased to be celebrated; there were outbreaks of iconoclasm.

Yet the government proved slow in offering any sort of lead. On 31 July 1547, a full six months after Henry's death, Cranmer reissued Cromwell's Injunctions, with additions. These last were neither extensive nor revolutionary, but they listed Erasmus's *Paraphrases* (disliked by traditionalists) as the authoritative guide to Bible-reading and ordered the use of a set of prepared sermons, the *Homilies appointed by the King's Majesty to be declared and read ... every Sunday*, which contain strong elements of Protestant doctrine. Gardiner, who had watched the collapse of Henrician uniformity with fear and anger, saw his chance here: he could argue that these additions contravened the Act of Six Articles, the *King's Book*, and the act of 1543 which controlled the reading of the Bible. His vigorous protests to Somerset adopted a self-righteously constitutional stance: he wished to obey the law, and—since nothing could abrogate an act of Parliament except another such act—what right had anyone to issue orders contrary to statute? He soon found himself in the Fleet (September 1547 to January 1548), but as the Edwardian Reformation progressed he would be neither silent nor obedient. From June 1548 he was in the Tower, without trial or formal deprivation which came only in January 1551. Through most of the reign, this most powerful opponent of innovation was rendered helpless—helpless but not, be it noted, permanently disposed of. Gardiner's enemies never found an opportunity to shut his mouth for ever; his law, and their scruples, saved him throughout his stormy career.

Of the bishops, only Edmund Bonner of London joined Winchester's protest: he was in fact deprived first (October 1549). In 1551 further advance towards reform proved too much for the ancient John Vesey of Exeter, who resigned, and for George Day (Chichester) and Nicholas Heath (Worcester), both one-time reformers, who were removed from their sees. These vacancies, augmented by three deaths, enabled Edward's ministers to promote ardent Protestants like Nicolas Ridley (London, 1550), John Ponet (Winchester, 1551), Miles Coverdale (Exeter, 1551), John Scory

(Chichester, 1552) and John Hooper (Worcester, 1552); but most sees remained in hands that had been safely and conscientiously Henrician. The erastianism hidden in Cranmer's Protestant obedience to the divinely appointed ruler extended also to the more Catholic consciences of men like Richard Sampson. Latimer, who had found his episcopal office at Worcester rather limiting in the 1530s, refused to be again distracted from the preaching which he regarded as his first duty.

However, as Gardiner had acutely pointed out, any real change in England's official religion required a Parliament to alter the law, and Somerset was slow in calling one. His first concern lay with affairs outside England, and it was to be November before he could give time to matters domestic. As so often, the European scene was transformed by a few sudden events—Charles V's victory over the German Protestants (April 1547) and the death of Francis I (March). Where Henry VIII had been succeeded by a child, Francis's heir, Henry II, was a young man who, like his father before, wished to cut a dash on the public stage and (unlike his father) plotted long and deep plans of aggressive expansion. He meant to secure Boulogne at once and ultimately to throw the English altogether out of France by capturing Calais, and he knew how to exploit the still unfinished state of war subsisting between England and Scotland. French help enabled the regent Arran to overcome the last resistance of the English (and Protestant) party; in July, the castle of St Andrews surrendered, some of its inmates (including John Knox, already prominent as a preacher of reform) being taken off to French galleys, and French ascendancy in Scotland seemed assured. Yet Somerset's one clear and determined policy, his obsession throughout his years of power, aimed to realize Henry VIII's design for Scotland by bringing about the personal union of the two royal houses agreed in the treaties in 1543. With France rampant once more he needed at least neutrality from the triumphant Emperor, a fact which by itself compelled him to go slow on Reformation. Everything was to be subordinated to the settlement of Scotland.

Thus in August Somerset prepared for the renewal of war in the north. In September he invaded Scotland with a powerful army containing an exceptionally large contingent of mercenaries, and on the 10th he destroyed the Scots, much more numerous but ill equipped and poorly led, at Pinkie. It was Flodden all over again: the Scots lost thousands. Yet real victory remained as far off as ever. Somerset tried to subdue the country by establishing permanent garrisons in strongpoints along the border and up the east coast as far as Dundee; he built a formidable fort at Haddington, eighteen miles from Edinburgh, and occupied Inchkeith in the Forth. The policy did not, as has been supposed, rely on persuasion and some kind of Great British ideal: he had conquest in mind, and the garrisons were instructed to use systematic destruction as a means of gaining Scottish compliance. What Somerset did hope from them was a financial saving: the garrisons were to make expensive expeditions unnecessary.

Instead, their presence and activities stiffened Scottish resistance, in any case still supported by France, as English attempts had always done; and they ran away with money. In his two years, Somerset spent £351,000 on the war—half as much again as Henry had needed in five years.[15] In his purblind endeavour to make his policy work he swallowed repeated French insults and provocations, to no purpose. His policy really collapsed in July 1548 when 10,000 French troops arrived in Scotland, occupied Edinburgh and protected the removal of the young Queen of Scots to France, out of her intended English husband's reach. Yet even though he had lost all chance of enforcing the 1543 treaty, Somerset persisted, pouring more and more money into this lost cause. Finally Henry II had enough. He declared war in August 1549, invested and half overran Boulogne, and stepped up the attacks on the English strongholds in Scotland. In September Somerset had to accept defeat and to authorize the evacuation of Haddington. The long effort to make Scotland English had only made her totally French and had put a powerful French army on England's northern border.

Moreover, Somerset's obstinate concentration on this one end had meanwhile produced neglect, error and disaster at home. In the immediate aftermath of Pinkie, when he was riding high, he at last called a Parliament. It met on 4 November 1547 and in just over five years held altogether four sessions. Thus the sovereign body continued to sit pretty much as frequently as in the previous twenty years, but the decline of legislative activity, so marked in Henry VIII's last Parliaments, also continued into his son's reign.

The session of 1547 did nothing significant to promote reform either spiritual or secular, and what was attempted owed almost nothing to official initiative. At least two bills that might have resulted in serious law reform failed to pass; it is unlikely that they were promoted by the government. The only important social act of the session also cannot safely be ascribed to the crown. This was the notorious poor law which repealed all existing legislation and condemned the persistent vagrant to slavery for a first refusal to work and death for a second. The frequent expression of surprise that the 'mild duke' should have obtained so savage an act misses

[15] Bush, *Government Policy*, p. 33.

two points: Somerset was no more inclined to mildness towards
vagabonds than any other member of his order, and the act looks
much more like the product of a privately promoted bill. Its curiously inapposite savagery—slavery being by this time unknown in
English law—very possibly reflects the views of academic critics and
the influence of the Roman law;[16] so far as we know, it was never put
into effect, and it was certainly repealed in the next session of
Parliament.

It comes, however, as a surprise to find that the most important
act of the session also was not simply a government measure. This is
the act which abolished all the treasons and felonies created under
Henry VIII, did away with the existing heresy legislation, repealed
the two Acts of Proclamations, demolished benefit of clergy (in most
crimes) for members of the Church but created it for members of the
peerage, and subjected remaining treasons to proof by two witnesses.
It is mainly on the strength of this statute that Somerset's regime has
persistently been called liberal, and indeed the act claimed as much,
declaring in its government-inspired preamble that the happier
climate of the new reign did not require the severe restraints of more
tempestuous times. The act followed precedent by opening a new
reign with the assuaging of resentments and oppressions which was
the more desirable to a regime badly in need of popularity; but it did
so with an unusual thoroughness, though it was not Somerset's doing
when some of its more liberal provisions were added by the
Parliament.[17] In any case, despite the removal of Henrician treasons
the act brought back treason by words (with safeguards) and the
offence of concealment of treasons, one of Cromwell's most severe
weapons. While unquestionably both government and Parliament
wished to remove the excessive harshness which the problem of
enforcing the break with Rome had brought into the law, the act's
chief effects were to free Somerset for his preferred policy of government by proclamation and to remove the obstacles to a Protestant
Reformation which Gardiner had rightly discerned in the Henrician
statutes. The Act of Six Articles went, as did the Lancastrian heresy
laws. An attempt was made to balance the dangers of excessive
liberalism—which worried Paget and other more practical members
of the administration—by an act punishing irreverent speaking
against the sacrament, a feeble enough measure. As for treasons and
felonies, some of them crept back soon enough and more returned in
the next two reigns. The statute, liberalized by Parliament, proclaimed a generosity which was not without obvious calculation; it

---

[16]C. S. L. Davies, 'Slavery and Protector Somerset: the Vagrancy Act of 1547', *Economic
History Review*, 2nd series XIX (1966), pp. 533 ff.

[17]Bush, *Government Policy*, pp. 145 ff.

deserves some commendation, but it also weakened the ability of government to govern at a difficult time.

In any case, Somerset still did not mean the reformers to have their way, and Cranmer, as usual, believed in caution. The end of the Six Articles and all the rest certainly produced ever more vigorous propaganda by pen and word from the more ardent Protestants as well as here and there unauthorized reforms of the order of service and of ceremonies. The government responded with proclamations against disputes over the eucharist (December 1547) and against all private innovation (February 1548); finally it for a time prohibited all preaching, a desperate measure provoked by the flood of public debate (September 1548). Nevertheless, sheer pressure from the reformers compelled more positive steps; the unresolved confusion created by the demolition of Henrician uniformity was tearing the realm to pieces and could not be allowed to continue much longer. The proclamation of September 1548 announced the Protector's intention to produce a general reform. However, before Parliament could reassemble to attend to this necessity another disruptive crisis occurred in the body politic.

By the spring of 1548 it was clear that something would have to be done about the price inflation which was troubling the rich and ruining the poor. Thomas Smith, as we have seen, had the right answer when he advised the restoration of the coinage, but to follow his counsel would have meant cutting off the supply of money for the Scottish war, and this Somerset would not contemplate. Thus he turned to John Hales, that notable example of the confident economic expert who gets it all wrong. In times of crisis the man with a panacea to offer usually receives a grateful hearing. In 1548, the Protector and his Council eagerly agreed that indeed the only cause of the trouble was selfish greed (did they not have support for this view from Latimer and Lever?) and that the solution lay in destroying illegal enclosures and in making and enforcing further laws against antisocial practices. For something like a year the government's economic policy was in effect handed over to Hales; the Protector continued to wrestle with his Scottish troubles but gave ever-ready support to his single-minded adviser.[18]

The campaign opened on 1 June 1548 with a proclamation announcing the appointment of commissions to enforce the existing legislation against enclosures. Their instructions were drawn up by Hales who explained that he was looking only for damaging

---

[18] Hales later denied the charge that the attack on enclosures and its consequences originated solely with him, but his memorials make it plain that he produced the various programmes of action and then sought and got support from leading councillors (*Discourse of the Common Weal*, edited by E. Lamont, pp. xlii ff., lii ff.). His views were, of course, shared by others, but what actually happened sprang entirely from his energetic agitation.

enclosures—of commons, of engrossed farms, and of parks—but used highly coloured language here and in his addresses to such commissioners as he could reach. Actually, the only commission to get going was that of which he was himself a member and which covered the important open-field regions of the southern Midlands. They turned up a quantity of unlawful activity and tactlessly ploughed a furrow across a park of the earl of Warwick's, but no serious results followed from their activities and nothing at all happened anywhere else. Disappointed, Hales decided to attack through Parliament of which he was a member. The session that opened on 24 November 1548 and lasted exceptionally long, to 14 March, witnessed the only attempt of the reign to put through a prepared programme; but while the programme had official support (to the point that Somerset prolonged the session in order to get several bills through) it originated with Hales.[19] The reformer particularly resented the loss of three of his bills for which evidently he did not have Council support; they would have extended the illegality of enclosing well beyond the current cut-off date of 1489, prevented graziers from making quick profits on the rapid resale of cattle, and promoted dairy farming. All offended powerful interests represented in the Commons. What did get through was a set of measures designed to bribe landlords into better behaviour by remitting certain charges on their lands and to assist the urban poor by temporarily assigning to poor relief certain duties payable to the Crown. In return the government received a novel tax much favoured by the social reformers: a surcharge of $1d$ per sheep owned over 150, and $8d$ in the pound on every cloth in store—attempts to make sheep and wool less profitable. Even though Somerset thus got supply which could be represented as sound social engineering and enabled him to go without a subsidy, Hales's parliamentary assault was a failure. The frustration of both reformer and Protector appeared in the reissue of the enclosure commission in May 1549 when the exhortatory and conciliatory tone of the year before gave way to urgent instructions to do something.

It is usually said that the worthy purpose of the 'commonwealth party' suffered defeat at the hands of selfish interests in Parliament, and that is certainly what Hales himself believed. No doubt it is in part what happened, but it may be questioned whether historians have been wise in so generally accepting a partisan view of the day. Hales's diagnosis and remedies were at best inadequate, and

[19] Bush, *Government Policy*, pp. 48 ff. I do not always agree with Dr Bush on the official or private origins of bills (some of the economic bills of the session seem to me private and no part of any programme), and I think the evidence shows not so much 'government' action as action by Hales receiving support from Somerset, but those are minor differences of opinion.

Somerset's concern was less with help for the suffering poor than that such help should be given without diminishing his ability to carry on his Scottish folly. So far as we can reconstruct Hales's lost bills from his own brief remarks, they look either dangerous or pointless. His undertaking to improve the supply of milk, butter and cheese depended on supposing that every sheepfarmer possessed of over 120 sheep disposed of additional grazing land suitable for cows, and on assuming that the production of calves was mathematically assured. He was right to emphasize that most of the decay of tillage by enclosure had occurred before the reign of Henry VII, but if he really meant (as he hinted he did) to restore the population distribution of Edward I's day he was an ass. His remedies for inflation not only offended entrepreneurial interests but would have been either futile or positively harmful to those they aimed to protect. The real remedy lay ready to hand, and it was Somerset's fault that it was not tried.

Though most of this session's business touched matters economic, the most important act dealt with religion. The promised attempt to settle the faith of the Church of England produced the first Act of Uniformity which imposed the first Edwardian prayer book (1549). The act had major constitutional significance: where hitherto definitions of the faith had come from the supreme head, with Parliament at best, as in 1539, providing penalties to ensure obedience, the new prayer book was a schedule to a statute so that doctrine and ceremonies now rested upon statutory authority. The implication always present in the supremacy—that despite its origin in God's grant to the King it was really vested in the King-in-Parliament—finally came into the open; Cromwell's concept triumphed over Henry VIII's.[20] The prayer book was Cranmer's work, but in its passage through Parliament it underwent important changes: where the original version had plainly denied transubstantiation and abolished the mass, compromises introduced to conciliate conservative opinion in the Lords produced so much ambiguity that both Protestants and Catholics could suppose themselves reasonably satisfied. However, the Zwinglians were furious, Bucer disapproved, and convinced English Protestants like Ridley and Hooper soon called for changes; and Gardiner in effect destroyed the book when he agreed that it did no harm. The government's willingness to accept so unclear a settlement owed much, once again, to the international situation: despite his own positive views, Somerset was anxious not to offend Charles V to whom he urgently represented the reform as entirely conservative. Nevertheless, the new liturgy marked a clear step towards the reformed religion, especially in that

[20] See above, p. 197.

it replaced the Latin service by an English one. The penalties of the act applied mainly to the clergy ordered to use this form of service; laymen procuring a priest's disobedience could be fined. By sixteenth-century standards the act was mild enough, though persistent offenders would lose their benefices and could suffer life imprisonment.

Even while Parliament was still sitting, Somerset's nemesis—the reward of his insensitive arrogance and mistaken policies—was beginning to take a hand. He had never been sure of his insufferable brother who had not given up his ambition to control the King's person and was altogether dissatisfied with his low rank in the peerage and his office of admiral. It seems probable that Warwick, always fearful of too solid a Seymour ascendancy which threatened to thwart his ambitions, did his best to undermine the Protector's regard for his brother,[21] but Seymour's own deeds spoke at least as loudly as any insinuations. When Catherine Parr died in childbirth in September 1548, he plotted to marry the Princess Elizabeth who, aged fifteen, had fallen for his notorious charm. He also obscurely plotted against the Protector's rule and person, and more plainly got involved in various corrupt practices. His unstable temper made many enemies, and in the last months of 1548 he seems to have been losing all control over himself. His wild talk, and the discovery that he had shared in a fraud by which the profits of the Bristol mint found their way into private pockets, provided material for a charge of treason. The Council, to which Warwick's influence at the crucial moment restored the earl of Southampton, investigated, considerately (they said) wishing to relieve the Protector of the burden. They had Seymour arrested (January 1549) and proceeded against him by bill of attainder. He was never tried; like Cromwell, he would have been hard to convict. Somerset refused to extend the expected protection, from high-mindedness rather than resentment, and his brother went to execution in late March. He was no loss, and in some unclear way he does seem to have been guilty of treasonable plotting. However, in reality he died because he was a thoroughly incompetent politician of overweening ambition and absurd recklessness; he died because his behaviour offered a chance to get at the Seymour ascendancy; and his death damaged most the person most innocent of it—the Protector himself whose failure to save a brother, however much it stemmed from a lofty refusal to allow personal considerations to weigh, was made to look like inhumanity.

Somerset would have been wise to take note of the Council's zeal in going after the younger Seymour, but he learned no lessons; he continued to walk his solitary and superior way. And soon enough he

[21] Hoak, *King's Council*, pp. 239 ff.

the occasion of the outbreak was the continued enforcement of the
1547 Injunctions with their attack on familiar saints, images and holy
days, together with the introduction on Whitsunday (9 June) of the
new English prayer book which the Cornish rebels said they found
incomprehensible. Cranmer, who felt called upon to deal at length
with their protest, asked pertinently whether they understood the old
Latin any better. However, what they abominated was the break
with tradition, though they asked for no more than a return to the
Church of Henry VIII's last days. Lord Russell, despatched to
restore peace, found himself facing much superior forces that intended to march upon London and compel the Council to abandon
the Reformation. But they would not move while Exeter held out
against them, and the siege of the city gave time for the government
to gather an army. On 6 August, Russell, now joined by William
Herbert and in command of a professional force, easily raised the
siege; on the 17th he met the rebel host and scattered it with heavy
losses. Energetic repression followed; the gallows were once more
busy. No one has yet worked out any reliable figures, but the general
impression must be that the government's vengeance was both
extreme and cruel, well matched to the fright they had had.
Contrary to reports at the time, Somerset, so far from trying to arrest
it, thought that not all the guilty men had been brought to book.

On 10 July, exactly a month after the outbreak in Cornwall,
trouble started at the other end of the country, in Norfolk. Here
hostility between lords and commons had a long history mainly
derived from the conflict of interests between a tenantry primarily
occupied in arable husbandry and a body of landlords engaged in
profitable sheep and cattle rearing who for a generation had been
enclosing and engrossing village commons, the only open grazing
available in that well populated shire. Even in 1537, some conspirators who hoped to repeat the northern rebellion had, unlike
their exemplar, gone for the throats of the gentry. The Norfolk rising
became so very serious because the shire was very poorly controlled
and because the rebels found an exceptionally able leader. The
destruction of the Howard power in early 1547 had removed the one
family that could command obedience, while the numerous gentry of
the shire were much too busy with their own ambitions and feuds to
attend in time to signs of discontent. And in Robert Ket, a middling
tradesman from Wymondham who had personal reasons for war
against exploiters of the commonalty, the rebels found a man in the
Aske mould. From 12 July to 26 August, he commanded an armed
camp on Mousehold Heath, just outside Norwich, where rebellious
peasantry from northwest and central Norfolk as well as northeast Suffolk gathered to assert their power and grievances. The

demands were mainly for agrarian reform—against the use of commons for private pasture, for lower rents, and so forth. This typical radical programme for the small man also contained some rather old-fashioned anticlericalism and points borrowed from German rebels; Ket was a Protestant, as were his followers. The Norfolk men did not regard themselves as rebels and never intended to march upon London; on the contrary, they believed that they had the government's (that is, Somerset's) support against their local enemies. In this they were sadly mistaken: two days before they rose, Somerset had come round to the views of his fellow councillors and had issued stringent instructions across the country for the relentless suppression of all disturbers of the peace. As usual, he acted incompetently: having called forth hopes for concessions that he did not know how to fulfil, he then revoked them at the wrong moment.

Ket presented even more of a military problem than did the western rebels. He organized his host well for civil and warlike purposes, and he had artillery. Twice he captured Norwich and the second time he occupied it. His self-confidence showed clearly in his refusal of four offered pardons, on the grounds that men not guilty of any offence required no pardoning. He needed little more than a show of force to drive away the first magnate sent against him, the marquess of Northampton who ignominiously turned tail. There could nevertheless be but one end to the rising, especially once Russell had disposed of the threat to the southwest. On 17 August, the earl of Warwick took command of the action against Ket. With a large force containing a sizable contingent of mercenaries, he easily drove the rebels from Norwich, forced them out of their defensible camp, and on the 27th cut them to pieces at Dussindale. Some 3,000 were allegedly killed on the day; the aftermath of trials and executions killed about another fifty, Ket naturally among them, though there was also some pardoning. The gentry's vengeance here remained within bounds: that agricultural shire needed men to till the ground. So far as we know, peace came back swiftly and lastingly, a strange ending to the violence of the summer.

The risings, and the despair behind them, merit the understanding that historians have traditionally given them. Times were hard, and there had been much abuse of wealth and power. Somerset's advertised willingness to enforce the protective laws encouraged hopes of better things, even as his failure to achieve anything drove men to active protest. Yet it must also be recognized that the disturbances undermined that very order which the rebels, especially in Norfolk, claimed to be defending. Until we know much more than at present we do about the real state of rural England at this time, and especially about the particular causes—often highly local, even personal—which transformed discontent into rioting and rioting into rebellion, we cannot fully assess the nature of the crisis. One thing, however, stands out clearly: the events of the summer demonstrated a failure of government. Not only Northampton but Somerset himself had shown signs of a loss of nerve, especially when he stood down from the command against Ket in favour of Warwick. In so far as it was any man's, it was his doing that the situation had got out of control; his embittered dedication to the Scottish business combined with his feckless support for mistaken social measures to bring the realm to the brink of ruin. As peace returned to the countryside, the Privy Council gathered itself together to remove this disastrous Protector and provide for better government. Though in the process they created for him the legend of his liberalism, they really had a very good case for wishing to be rid of him. Unfortunately, in the absence of constitutional machinery the only available method was a conspiracy.

The *coup d'état* which overthrew Somerset looks straightforward enough on the face of it, but it is only very recently that its true complexity (which tells a great deal about Tudor faction politics) has been convincingly unravelled.[25] By 1 October, Somerset knew his danger and issued a proclamation calling upon everyone to come to his aid at Hampton Court. No one stirred. For greater safety he removed himself and the King to Windsor. Meanwhile the Council in London published accusations of misgovernment and secured the cooperation of the city. Everybody, even Paget, deserted Somerset who after all had never tried to make friends. For several days negotiations continued between Windsor and London, as well as an outpouring of rival propaganda. Somerset held on in hopes of Russell and Herbert who were returning with their army from Devon, but on the 8th he learned that they had thrown in with the Council. On the 11th he was arrested and on the 14th removed to the Tower, while the King was brought to Richmond, nearer the Council's authority: the *coup* was over.

But who had guided it and who now ruled? Ultimately, in February 1550, the earl of Warwick emerged as Somerset's virtual successor, and we may be sure that he had always meant to get there. However, it had been a far from straight road for him. The *coup* had, with good reason, at first been read as a reactionary blow to the Reformation, before Warwick somehow turned round and presented himself as an even more radical Protestant than Somerset. For several weeks the reformers looked forward to a variety of disasters ranging from exile to death, while the conservatives rode high and the Emperor's ambassador cheered them on. Possibly, of

[25] Hoak, *King's Council*, pp. 241 ff.

course, Warwick simply played a deep game throughout, rather like Cromwell's in 1536 when also a conservative faction was used to destroy an unwanted radical faction and then in turn defeated so that a more radical faction still could take charge. But in fact Warwick had not plotted events from the first: he was driven into complicated action almost day by day.

Two things determined the course of events: Warwick's firm ambition, and the coexistence on the Council of two factions whom only opposition to Somerset united. Warwick, a Protestant who wanted to rule through King Edward (a devout Protestant), commanded the safe support of only seven councillors, including the prestigious but rather useless Cranmer; at least fourteen in various degrees favoured an arrest to the Reformation and an understanding with Charles V, and they had their leaders in the earls of Arundel and Southampton. The second especially, that Lord Chancellor Wriothesley who owed Somerset and the Reformation no thanks, emerged as an able intriguer, only not quite so able as the earl of Warwick. Arundel and Southampton looked to the Princess Mary whom they intended to appoint regent for her brother, so as to avoid any more overambitious subjects in positions of rule. Warned by her experiences in 1536, Mary took care to remain uncommitted. But the threat of such a development sufficed to drive Warwick into the pretence that Edward was now capable of ruling in person and also into extreme forms of Protestantism which probably he had not wanted: he needed the Reformation to keep Edward on top and the princess out. First he strengthened his weak hand in the Council, though he did not manage to gain a majority; next he made sure of the King (in any case hostile to his half-sister) by surrounding him with friends of his own. The conservatives suffered a decisive setback when Charles V refused to intercede with France to save Boulogne for England. This persuaded Paget that there was nothing to be got from an Imperial and Marian policy; he made his peace with Warwick and got his peerage.

Beaten at this turn of the game, Southampton tried a new tack. The Council still had the fallen Somerset on their hands whose fate remained in the balance, and Southampton reckoned that it should be possible to involve Warwick—loyal enough to Somerset until August 1549—in the destruction of the duke. So he energetically promoted the execution of Somerset and got useful statements from him: whatever he had done, the duke maintained, had been done with Warwick's advice and consent. Before this intrigue could mature Warwick got warning of it: and he was thus compelled in self-defence to save Somerset from Southampton. This he did by getting his fallen rival to submit himself to the judgement of

Parliament (reconvened on 4 November) and by persuading Parliament to accept the duke's humble surrender (14 January). This ended the struggle. Southampton and Arundel were put off the Council, and their faction dissolved in wholesale desertions to Warwick. In the last resort, the majority of councillors wanted stable government, so that, led by St John, the lord treasurer (rewarded with the earldom of Wiltshire), and Paget, the supreme factotum, they joined the side that looked like winning. Southampton died soon after, allegedly of the broken heart that always seems to afflict the losers in the history books, and on 2 February Warwick became lord president of the Council and ruler of England, committed far more than he had intended to a policy of furthering the Reformation and keeping out the Princess Mary.

16 The Protestant Reformation

The earl of Warwick[1] was the eldest son of that Edmund Dudley who, having served Henry VII too well, was judicially murdered by Henry VIII. He was barely six when his father died in 1510; restored in blood by the Parliament of 1512, he seems never to have felt anything about the first disaster that struck his family during its steady march from the obscurity of the lesser gentry to political and social eminence. His career under Henry VIII paralleled that of Somerset, in a lower key because no sister of his married the King. As a courtier he gathered favour and lands; as a soldier he acquired a respected reputation; and as a politician he came to prominence in the aftermath of Somerset's seizure of power which, so far as the evidence goes, he did not help to engineer. As has been seen, he refused to become Somerset's humble adherent, but until he took charge of the *coup* against the Protector he served him faithfully enough and reaped sufficient rewards in property and honours. For himself, he remains a figure of some mystery. Traditionally he has been regarded as one of the bad men of Tudor history, in part at least because he toppled that idealized hero, the Protector Somerset; the soberer view of Somerset may yet lead to a revised view of Warwick. Certainly it is not easy to reconcile the picture of a wicked, amoral, wildly ambitious intriguer with the evidence of many of his actions and most of his surviving letters which show him often hesitant, compliant, apprehensive and even tearful. The work is yet to do; but while for the present any deviation from the traditional norm must be speculative it is also no longer possible simply to adhere to that tradition.

One thing is clear about Warwick's policy: he deliberately reversed his predecessor's practices and attempted to undo what were regarded as the evil effects of Somerset's regime. He refused to continue the office of protector, contenting himself with the pre-

[1] John Dudley, earl of Warwick, became duke of Northumberland in October 1551; I shall use the title by which he was known at any given time.

sidency of the Privy Council. The King now came to attend quite regularly at the Council's meetings; he was encouraged to give thought to its business and draft agendas; action taken cited his authority. His role remained to a large extent pretence—or should be seen as part of his education in the business of kingship—but he was no longer a child and began to have a genuine though very occasional influence on affairs. In particular Warwick had to take account of his sovereign's iron devotion to the Protestant religion, an uncompromising bigotry very characteristic of the newly converted adolescent.

In fact Warwick tried to organize a genuine committee government, and his ascendancy witnessed the temporary elevation of the Privy Council to corporate rule. The affairs of the kingdom were now generally under the guidance of the whole body which remained efficient and effective even though it grew in size. Nor was it ever subdivided into the committees once supposed to have existed. As reconstituted in February 1550, the Council consisted of twenty-five members the majority of whom inclined to reform and Reformation. Guided by Paget, it thoroughly revised its procedure and equipped itself with the machinery it needed if it was to be more than the body of advisers or even onlookers that it had become under Somerset. Thus it was Paget, encouraged by Warwick, who rescued Cromwell's Council reform and preserved the institution for its Elizabethan heyday. Warwick never hesitated to add members: he preferred to have all men of weight openly on it, so long as at moments of crisis he could be sure of majority support. Even the fallen Somerset rejoined the board in early April 1550, playing a role most unusual in the sixteenth century—that of elder statesman retired from the primacy of power. Later additions and subtractions expanded the Council to a maximum size of thirty-three (October 1551), but the threat to efficiency implicit in this was much reduced by the fact that the working membership ran at around twenty. The new members came from Warwick's personal faction in court and bureaucracy and especially from the new nobility. These changes increased the political character of the body at the expense of its administrative complexion, not a surprising thing to find when the Council was being forced to play a political role.

The regime did something, too, to reform administration. In September 1550, William Cecil joined the entrenched Sir William Petre in the secretaryship, and it was Cecil who, working in the closest possible contact with the lord president, revived the Cromwellian use of the office.[2] In June 1553 it was thought neces-

---

[2] Sir Thomas Smith had lost the office at the time of Somerset's fall, the place being filled for nearly a year by an ineffectual diplomat, Sir Nicholas Wotton.

sary to add a third secretary, a post conferred upon Edward's old tutor Sir John Cheke. This short-lived reform owed something to Petre's calculated withdrawal from affairs as the crisis of Edward's death was approaching, but something also to the need to alleviate the burdens resting upon the secretaryship under conciliar rule. With the threads of intelligence and information once again running firmly to a competent central officer, it proved easier to bring the localities back into the control which the events of 1549 had shown to be seriously deficient. Warwick also began to maintain permanent representatives of the Crown in the counties when he kept in being the lords lieutenant appointed at the time of the disturbances. The office was given statutory backing in the session of November 1549, and from early 1550 annual commissions provided each shire with a nobleman or leading gentleman responsible ostensibly for managing its military forces but in fact for the general political oversight of the region. Naturally the men picked (some of whom controlled several shires) were those upon whose political allegiance the earl thought he could rely, but this does not detract from the importance of a reform which linked centre and regions through the good services of men powerful both in Council and in their home county.

The most notable administrative reforms undertaken touched the Crown's finances, ruined by war, debasement, extravagance and corruption. The new regime had to deal with the consequences of ten years of mismanagement and did not, in the less than four years at its disposal, succeed in remedying them all, but it made an impressive start. Though the earl himself clearly understood little of the complex issues involved, other members of the administration did, especially Smith, Cecil and Lord Treasurer Winchester (who held office from 1550 to 1572); they had the excellent expert advice of Sir Walter Mildmay, whose forty years of service were to contribute greatly to Elizabethan stability, and of Sir Thomas Gresham, the skilled international financier who handled English relations with the Antwerp money market. The problems before them resolved themselves into two—the restoration of the coinage, and the reorganization of the financial machinery.

By 1550 Smith's opinion that inflation must be cured by reversing the disastrous experiment in debasement had become common property, and in April 1551 the Council resolved to embark upon the necessary measures. Unfortunately, the attraction of quick profits triumphed one last time, with a final drastic debasement in May that year which totally destroyed public confidence in the coinage and blew the crisis up to even vaster proportions. Money, good and bad, vanished from circulation, and the government, despite large nominal gains, found itself unable to meet either current expenditure or the servicing of its enormous debts.[3] The disaster at last gave a free hand to the men of sense, and in the course of 1552 a variety of measures began to restore stability. A new coin issue adopted respectable standards of fineness and related bullion content fairly to face value; severe retrenchment made possible interim repayments on some foreign loans; Gresham began his operations to restore the exchange with Flanders; and for the first time in living memory prices fell. It was not until well into Elizabeth's reign that the inflation settled to a gentle increase and that soundness fully returned to the basis of financial dealings, but the credit for initiating the action, in the face of much resentment and greed, must go to the Council of Edward VI's later years.

The same is true of the other problem tackled, the repair of the Crown's financial agencies. The restoration of the coinage brought back rational conditions for business, but in itself it reduced the government's opportunity to stave off bankruptcy by manipulation and therefore demanded an urgent effort to improve the ordinary revenue and its administration. Cromwell's reforms had unquestionably burdened the state with too many departments, desirable for the better (because closer) management of diverse sources of income, but expensive in salaries and likely to escape proper supervision unless given the sort of control of which only a Cromwell was capable. The fact had been recognized in 1546 when the declining revenues in the crown lands departments (Augmentations and General Surveyors), occasioned by the massive sales, induced the government to amalgamate the two into the second Court of Augmentations, a sensible piece of rationalization. However, this still left too many offices. In Somerset's day the officers of the departments succeeded in cushioning themselves against inflation by unauthorized increases in fees and allowances; in 1552 it was discovered that these costs of administration had very nearly doubled since 1547 and now ran, in the financial departments alone, at about £17,500 a year, or something like eight per cent of the total revenue. The new regime also discovered several spectacular scandals (embezzlement and theft) in the Exchequer, the Court of Wards, and the Mint.

This situation was met with the kind of thorough care which betrays the minds of Warwick's competent fellow councillors. They undertook three types of remedy. Cash liquidity was improved by recreating the office of keeper of the Privy Purse, Peter Osborn (a client of Cheke's and Cecil's) being appointed in January 1552; the

[3]As late as October 1552, when things were looking up, Cecil calculated that the Crown's debt stood at approximately £200,000, about equally divided between domestic and foreign obligations.

transfer of reserves from the departments into his honest hands ended the opportunities for embezzlement. Secondly the Council instituted a major drive, by means of investigating commissions, for the recovery of negligently uncollected revenues; this, pursued throughout 1552, appears to have had considerable success in restoring the actual yield of the revenue to its nominal level. And lastly, the government tackled the problem of administrative reorganization which alone could hope to prevent the frequent recurrence of these troubles.

The Royal Commission for the Courts of Revenue was one of the more remarkable achievements of Tudor administration.[4] It was appointed by letters patent of 23 March 1552 and reported on 10 December. During its existence it investigated every department in the most minute detail, obtained a mass of written evidence and conducted long verbal enquiries. It consisted of six active members of whom only three were councillors—and these men of modest social weight who enjoyed Northumberland's confidence as administrators and politicians. The non-Council members were experienced bureaucrats, including the commission's real driving force, Sir Walter Mildmay. Their report was divided into three parts. First they gave a complete and very detailed survey of the royal revenues for the financial year 1550–1; next they analysed the inadequacies and faults of every one of the five departments; lastly they proposed three possible ways of achieving economies. By better management the Crown could save money without administrative rearrangements; it could reduce the departments to two, an office for crown lands (including the duchy of Lancaster) and the Exchequer for the rest; lastly, and this was the commission's preferred solution, it could merge all the departments in the Exchequer.

Unfortunately the report came out rather too late in the reign to lead to immediate action. The Council did not ignore it: in the Parliament of 1553 it took statutory powers to amalgamate the revenue courts. But the last months of Edward's life offered no leisure for such tricky tasks. The recommendations of the commission were not carried into effect until the next reign, early in 1554, and what was done deviated somewhat from what the commissioners had recommended. Under Mary, favour and friendship once again played a large part in the running of affairs, and those who would have suffered from the abolition of the duchy and the Court of Wards included some of her devoted followers. Thus the letters patent of January 1554, which gave effect to the reform, preserved these two departments but transferred the business of the Courts of Augmentations and First Fruits to the Exchequer. For all

[4] *The Report of the Royal Commission of 1552*, edited by W. C. Richardson (1974).

practical purposes, this, the most ancient department, now became the real ministry of finance, an event which gave a spuriously 'medieval' air to the Elizabethan administration of the finances. Some historians have therefore read this reconstruction as marking the end of 'Household' experiments going back to the 1470s and a return to the bureaucratic order settled by the fourteenth century. Actually, however, the reforms of 1554 derived from Cromwell's attacks on Household methods. The reconstituted Exchequer shared little except a name with its medieval predecessor; internal re-organization as well as the preservation of the new accounting methods practised in the abolished courts altered its routines, its records and its effective personnel so drastically that those expert in its earlier history flounder badly when confronted with the modern department. The work of 1552–4 completed rather than superseded that of Cromwell when it brought the novel institutions devised in the 1530s under one roof and rebuilt the house itself.

This major administrative reform was planned by Edward's ministers and carried out by them in the next reign. Credit is usually given to Lord Treasurer Winchester and Sir Walter Mildmay, and this may well be correct even though Winchester has left behind remarkably little evidence for his long tenure of office. It is at least possible that the guiding hand was that of Sir William Cecil who in due course succeeded to the lord treasureship; at any rate, the important steps to bring the reorganization into operation were not taken until the later 1560s, by which time Cecil had effectively superseded the ancient though still living Winchester.[5] However that may have been, it is manifest that this was a genuine reform administration, the first since Cromwell's fall and the first to follow up the initiatives started by Cromwell. It really took hold of England's government and tackled the crying needs of the day, and it did so with a thoroughness and competence that approached (at a distance) those customary in the 1530s. This judgement is also borne out by the larger policies of the day and by the gradual reappearance of government-sponsored reform legislation in Parliament.

II

Although the Parliament did not reassemble until 4 November 1549, well after the arrest of Somerset, the power struggle in the Council

[5] I owe this information to Mr C. H. D. Coleman who is at present investigating the history of the Elizabethan Exchequer.

was, as we have seen, far from over; at the start one therefore cannot expect to find evidence of a government policy. Social and economic issues attracted only private attention. The first bills likely to have originated with the Council dealt with public order, attempting to stamp out seditious talk and to tighten up the law against rioters; both started in the Lords and became law, after much revision. On such matters, as also on the repeal of the 1549 'slavery' act, differences of opinion lacked ideological content, but the intrusion of religion soon enough showed up existing differences. The conservatives made the first moves. On the 9th they introduced a bill to repeal parts of the 1549 Act of Uniformity, and on the 14th the bishops presented a petition complaining of their inability to enforce their jurisdiction as they ought to. The bill ran for a while but then disappeared; as for the petition, although the news distressed the Lords, nothing happened because the bishops failed to introduce the measure they were encouraged to prepare. The hierarchy, in fact, were in two minds about their jurisdiction. Yet another act setting up a commission to reform the canon law passed against the opposition of all the bishops present except one; Cranmer, already well engaged on law reform, voted against it, presumably because he shared the reluctance to admit the laity to any consideration of the spiritual courts. The reformers' moves proved altogether more effective. On Christmas Day the Council by proclamation ordered the destruction of all old service books rendered redundant by the Book of Common Prayer; this was followed by a bill against missals and false images produced in the Commons and passed in the Lords by a majority of eight in a House of thirty, six bishops and five lay peers voting against. The divisions on the episcopal bench also failed to stop the bill appointing a commission to revise the ordination of priests, an official measure against which five out of fourteen bishops voted on the last division.

The Council sent the Parliament home (by prorogation) on 1 February 1550 to free itself for the final power struggle from which Warwick at once emerged total victor. Determined to reverse Somerset's disastrous policies, he first had to find a way out of the hopeless and ruinous war which had frustrated all endeavours to restore prosperity. Peace was made with France without delay and at the cost of what can only be called surrender: by the treaty of Boulogne (29 March 1550) England returned that town at once instead of in 1554 as had been agreed at Campe (1546) and received only half the compensation stipulated on the earlier occasion. Although the settlement with Scotland took longer, Warwick immediately terminated active involvement there and withdrew the English forces from their remaining strongholds; on 19 July 1551, the treaty of Angers did away with the last of Henry VIII's so-called triumphs by abandoning Edward's claims to the hand of Mary Queen of Scots. Instead, to proclaim the new and ardent amity with France, he was betrothed to a French princess. From Henry II's point of view, all these moves went to the shaping of the anti-Habsburg alliance which in 1552 was to destroy the Emperor's ascendancy in Germany, but though Warwick deliberately decided for a drift to France, who now treated Scotland like a province and England like a client, he managed to avoid binding commitments. The earl has been much blamed for so feeble a policy, but he had no choice. The realm could not support any more wars—there was no money, the navy had had to be decimated, coastal defence lay in ruins—and the Council's desire to proceed with the Reformation in the Church made accommodation with Charles V impossible. There was nothing for it but to kow-tow to France, in the hope that renewal of the Habsburg-Valois wars would leave England free to recover her strength.

This reversal of Somerset's programme was accomplished in the face of Somerset's disapproving presence in the Council, and from June 1550 the superficial peace between him and Warwick showed frequent signs of strain. In his desire to recover power the duke engaged in intrigues against his rival and even solicited men (such as Gardiner and Arundel) who had earlier suffered at his own hands. The summer of 1550 witnessed ominous recurrences of public disorder: after all, the inflation was still rampant, the coinage unreformed, and the harvest once again bad. Here, too, Warwick adopted measures to contrast with Somerset's: initial firmness suppressed discontent without necessitating the holocausts of the previous year, and the opportunity was taken to expand the shire lieutenancies. But the regime had no reason to feel secure.

It was in the midst of these uncertainties that Warwick encouraged (or permitted—no one can tell which) the transformation of the Church of England into an unmistakably Protestant body. In May 1550, the new Ordinal, produced by the statutory commission set up in the last session of Parliament, demolished the essence of traditional beliefs when it turned the Catholic priest into the Protestant minister. The Ordinal did not look revolutionary—Cranmer saw to that—but at the crucial point the ordinand was now given authority to preach the gospel and administer the sacraments instead of being charged 'to offer sacrifice and celebrate mass both for the living and the dead'. In the same month, Ridley issued his order which turned all altars in the diocese of London into communion tables (stood lengthways in the chancel, to symbolize the removal of barriers between officiating priest and participating laity), and other bishops followed by degrees. The enforcement of the first Act of Uniformity and the replacement of traditional services by the prayer book thus received further assistance in disturbing the people.

Very soon also the government found themselves forced to recognize the existence of passionate extremists likely to prove hard to contain. John Hooper, who in July 1550 accepted nomination to the see of Gloucester, refused to wear the episcopal vestments which were still the law of the Church, and it took some ten months of argument and strife (in which Warwick supported the recalcitrant bishop-elect against the law-abiding archbishop) to arrive at a compromise: Hooper gave way in practice while saving his principle. Men of his type were to become the bane of moderate reform and possibly of all improvement in the Church—men of rock-hard convictions standing on principle who would rather lose all in the cause of what they believed to be God's will than allow peace and spiritual hope to grow out of accommodation. In his battle against the doctrine of 'things indifferent'—the doctrine that Cranmer had embraced in the 1530s and continued to propagate—Hooper had allies, especially John Knox. Knox got back from France in March 1549 and by late 1550 was carrying out a fiery ministry at Newcastle where his uncompromising attacks on corruption and popery attracted much attention. On the whole he enjoyed Warwick's favour, to the point of being able to use violently offensive language to his patron which elicited only lachrymose whines in self-defence. Warwick's behaviour towards these firebrands—sometimes petulant and resentful, but always submissive in the end—must seriously call in doubt the general opinion that his attachment to the Reformation owed nothing to faith and everything to policy—that at best he just followed the King's desires and at worst thought only to gain at the expense of bishops' lands. He certainly profited from the enforced changes on the bench, and his attempt in May 1553 to reconstitute the bishopric of Durham under two salaried bishops not only followed up long advised radical reforms but also put property in his pocket;[6] no one wants to exonerate him of the greed common to his order and kind. But the signs are strong that at this time he really favoured the more apocalyptic preachers, perhaps from inner fears that their dire prophecies might be right—just one of the so far unresolved mysteries about this strange man.

From early in 1551 Cranmer once more turned his attention to the true faith. The first prayer book had found no real favour anywhere, and Cranmer himself was persuaded by Bucer's criticisms

---

[6] In planning to reabsorb what remained of Durham's palatine jurisdiction, Warwick also meant to complete the reform initiated by Cromwell's Act against Franchises (1536).

that it did not embody the truth of the Scriptures. Discussions and distractions went on for nearly two years, during which time Bucer died (February 1551) and the influence of less peaceful continental reformers grew. The relative freedom of Edwardian England, which attracted persecuted Protestants from abroad, had from the first threatened to give more opportunity for sectarian extremism than anyone in government circles or among the bishops liked to see, and the protest in Parliament about the general contempt for episcopal correction drew substance from the spread of Anabaptist and similar ideas. Two extremists were burned in May 1550—Joan Bocher, the English wife of a German tradesman settled in London, for denying the humanity of Christ, and George van Paris, a Dutch surgeon, for denying his divinity. Cranmer took his share in these proceedings, contrary to his usual repugnance for extreme measures of intolerance, though it must be remembered that the heresies involved were those that the Church had always regarded as ultimate and singularly unforgivable since the ancient days when Arianism had nearly destroyed the Catholic Church. Sectarianism of another but equally disquieting kind made its appearance in London where strangers' churches—self-administering congregations of Zwinglians and Calvinists, under their own ministers and permitted to opt out of the religion ordained by Parliament—weakened the bishop's control. Ridley might be seeking a further reform, but he did not wish to see uniformity infringed.

It was not, however, sects and extremists that held up the further settlement sought by Cranmer: first he needed more unity among bishops and councillors. This was in fact brought about in the course of 1551. That year witnessed the worst visitation ever of the so-called sweating sickness, a virus disease which has never been identified and which killed very quickly indeed, often within a few hours of the first onset. In 1551, encouraged by a mild spring, it raged throughout the land and may have killed tens of thousands. It helped to accentuate the general social depression (though by making men flee their neighbours the sweat hindered rather than promoted riotous disturbances), but it also brought a growing fear of the scourge of God. God, it seemed, had visited his wrath upon the backsliding faithful: and the Council stepped up the campaign of reform. Nicholas Heath of Worcester, the most consistent opponent of reform in the last parliamentary session, was in prison from about May 1550 and deprived in October 1551. In February that year, Gardiner (long since in the Tower) lost his see. George Day of Chichester, another hard-core conservative, was deprived at the same time as Heath. Against Tunstall Warwick worked up some dubious charges of treasonable conspiracy (1550) but contented himself with getting the bishop removed, after much resistance from Cranmer, in October 1552. Vacancies were filled, often after much delay, with sound or even eager reformers, and by late 1551 the episcopate stood squarely behind the further progress of the Reformation.

About this time, too, Warwick (now duke of Northumberland) at last freed himself of the looming presence of Somerset who was arrested on 16 October on a charge of treason, tried on 1 December, convicted not of treason but of the lesser crime of felony, and executed on 22 January. At his death the people groaned and indeed caused a disturbance which, it was thought, nearly enabled him to escape: the legend of the 'good duke' really began with the fall of his head on the scaffold. Since his first arrest he had not in men's minds been associated with the Council's rule, and by late 1551 the opinion that three years earlier he had tried to help 'the poor' had no doubt gained conviction from distance of time. Northumberland, it is usually said, in this murder of a greater and nobler man simply displayed his evil nature. But the story, as so often, is less simple than than that.[7] Somerset had never accepted defeat and from the moment that he returned to the Council had looked for ways to destroy his rival. At least that is what the French ambassador reported who owed his information to Northumberland and had reasons for believing a politician so anxious to please France. Yet there is enough independent evidence to support the view that Northumberland had behaved with patience and tolerance, qualities not common in these faction struggles, when he left the defeated man not only alive but even still at the centre of affairs. In view of Somerset's proud and vengeful temperament, he thus set up an impossible situation; the wonder must be that it lasted so long.

However, in the end Northumberland (as he admitted at his own execution) undoubtedly contrived Somerset's death. He repeated his successful nobbling of the Council by offering promotions in the peerage to wavering adherents, increased the size of that body so as to strengthen his hand on it, and stage-managed the arrest and trial. He took no care to make the specific charges remotely credible, and the jury's refusal to convict of treason, a real rebuff, demonstrates the rushed inefficiency of his conspiring. It looks, in fact, as though he managed to strike just ahead of Somerset who in the summer of 1551 was with some success building up a faction designed to restore him to power and arrest the Reformation. Both men were victims of personal ambition operating in the savage climate of faction warfare and religious disputes; Northumberland deserves to have it remembered that he held off from the final confrontation for so long, while Somerset unquestionably died through accusations as purely

[7] For the best account see D. E. Hoak, *The King's Council in the Reign of Edward VI*, pp. 74 ff.

fudged up as those that destroyed Edmund Dudley and Thomas Cromwell. With Somerset fell Paget, arrested in November 1551 but never tried; released in June 1552 he kept out of affairs for the rest of the reign. He was suspected of support for Somerset, but it is also relevant that he, a man who carried much weight as a respected statesman and administrator, despite his approval of reform never favoured the Protestant Reformation. These Council battles not only freed Northumberland from rivals but also cleared the road for the introduction of the reformed religion.

Thus Cranmer presided over the great transformation, as he had presided with equal sincerity over every change since 1533—equal sincerity, for it would be wrong to regard him as a time-serving hypocrite. The road followed by the Church of England was signposted by the continuous intellectual and spiritual development of its primate who always lacked the rigour that comes from inner convictions of righteousness and throughout his life believed in the need to learn more and better. Parliament reassembled on 23 January 1552, and this time it considered a number of officially inspired reform bills. Two left unfinished in the previous session now passed: one restricted the number of holy days and the other limited the traffic in public offices. The milder climate of 1547 being long since gone, a government bill revived the Treason Act of 1534. A very important regulating act comprehensively reviewed the manufacture of woollens; it summed up a generation of piecemeal reform and became the foundation for all future attention to this vital industry. A Council proclamation of July 1551 was transformed into yet another act against the speculation in foodstuffs known as engrossing and forestalling, as well intentioned and as fruitless a commonwealth measure as any. On the other hand, two important acts of the session do not look to have originated with the Council—the act against usury which prohibited the taking of all interest upon loans, and the famous act for the control of ale houses by justices of the peace from which the whole history of licensing in the liquor trade has descended. Both exemplify moral views among reformers but they were at least let through by Northumberland and his government. Even in this session of the main body of socio-economic legislation derived from private initiatives, and without the sort of programmatic planning which Cromwell had thought desirable, and several such bills got nowhere, among them yet another attack on the increasingly monopolistic behaviour of the London Merchant Adventurers, anxious to keep the declining export trade in cloth to themselves.[8]

[8] Attacks on the London merchants were probably supported by private interests, for the government favoured the Adventurers. In 1551 these provoked a quarrel with the Hanseatic League which came to a head during this session of Parliament when the Council revoked the privileges of the Hanse.

The main business of the session touched the settlement of religion, an issue which, while apparently it caused no stir in the Commons, still led to divisions among the Lords. Abortive bills displayed a variety of inspirations. Official concerns sought an act to compel attendance at the divine services of the established Church; clericalists advanced a bill to save any spiritual person from being charged with praemunire unless he expressly ignored a writ of prohibition out of the King's courts; radical anticlericalism wanted an act against simony; conservatives tried to prevent men from putting away their wives without a formal sentence of divorce, and to save the realm from heresies spread by foreigners. The bill that mattered, and which became law, was the second Act of Uniformity, not introduced in the Lords until 9 March and passed there against the dissent of three persistent peers and two bishops. The act used more stringent language and penalties than that of 1549: the bill for attendance at services was incorporated in it, a step which opened the long history of enforcing Sunday conformity upon all Englishmen, and the sole use of the new prayer book was protected by severe penalties upon clergy and congregation alike.

The second Book of Common Prayer marked a really revolutionary departure from the first which had evolved from medieval orders of service. Though its liturgy retained Cranmer's poetic splendour, the book now tried to institute only forms of worship which could be derived from Scripture. A good many inherited practices and formulae vanished, and the central point of dispute—the sacrament of the altar—lost every vestige of the mass. As usual the theologians have debated whether the new communion service embodied a Zwinglian, Calvinist or possibly Anglican-traditional view of the real presence; to the less involved historian it looks like an essentially Zwinglian rite (commemorative of Christ's sacrifice) carefully hedged by phrases which allow for belief in a spiritual real presence activated by the faith of the communicant. Predictably it caused trouble with real radicals, especially because it enjoined kneeling at the communion which to rigorous opinion recalled the popish ceremony of the adoration of the transubstantiated elements. In September 1552, in a sermon at court which moved the King, Knox drew attention to these dregs of popery. Cranmer would not yield to pressure to remove the rule, but the Council by-passed him and inserted a gloss in the already printed book (the so-called Black Rubric) that kneeling signified only respect, not adoration.

The prayer book of 1552—which after modifications in 1559, reenactment in 1662, verbal changes in 1928, and new liturgical attacks in recent years still remains the foundation of the Church of England's divine service—marked the full arrival of the Protestant Reformation and set the crown on Cranmer's work. Characteristically, it left much still open to debate. The same inconclusiveness (or perhaps comprehension of varying opinions) hangs about the archbishop's further attempt to give his Church an authorized definition of the faith. A document listing forty-two such articles was produced after the usual protracted discussions but did not receive the supreme head's consent until June 1553, too late to have become known, let alone properly imposed, anywhere in the realm; however, the Elizabethan Thirty-Nine Articles derived directly from Cranmer's attempt. The articles made the Church's Protestantism even plainer than did the prayer book. On test questions like justification by faith alone or the nature of predestination, their formulation was Calvinist rather than Lutheran. But the articles were shaped by the desire to refute radical, especially Anabaptist, doctrines (on such things as free will, the nature of the Church, consciousness of election) rather than Catholic tenets which at the time were still being hammered out by the Council of Trent; and this helped to keep them sufficiently imprecise on some of the issues which later arose between the post-Tridentine Church of Rome and post-Calvinist Protestant Churches to allow the retention of an eirenic adiaphorism[9] in the Church of England. In this busy year of 1552 Cranmer also produced a full-scale revision of the canon law—*Reformatio Legum Ecclesiasticarum*—based on the labours of lawyers and commissions dating back to 1535, but this never received authorization from either King or Parliament. Edward was taught that the supervision of spiritual discipline should be taken away from the bishops' courts where popery and immorality allegedly still found a refuge, an attitude which well reflected the general distrust of the church courts even though that distrust never grew strong enough to seek their abolition. Thus they continued to exist and to operate, on the basis of a muddle of old law and new opinions which made them both cautious and unpredictable; they became most effective in the least satisfactory area of their competence, the enforcement of clerical property rights (especially tithe), and least where the moral convictions of the age called on them for better performance, as in matters matrimonial and in the spiritual improvement of the nation.

[9] See above, p. 166.

III

Officially, therefore, England was now a Protestant country, observing a much changed faith, constrained to uniformity of a revolutionary kind, though still served by a Church whose political and administrative structure remained unaltered from pre-Reformation days. In this contrast lay seeds of violent disagreement which came to flowering in the various protest movements of Elizabeth's reign and which from the first struck roots in the dissatisfactions of men like Knox to whom Zürich and Geneva remained the true pattern of Christ's Church. But in the last years of Edward's reign these major debates among Protestants mattered less than the first question whether the official Protestantism of the Church could be established in the hearts and minds of a people many of whose traditional beliefs had barely yet been accommodated to Christianity itself. The attack on superstition, which runs through all the reforming activity of that age, aimed to replace not only popery but belief in witchcraft, divination and magic by what was held to be the truth of the gospel.[10] How effective were these reformers in changing not the law but the reality of England's religion?

The usual answer is that no one really knows or is ever likely to know, at least not with assurance. It is partly a problem of the evidence. Those who have used the lamentations of contemporary reformers to prove that the innovations did not penetrate the hearts of the people ought to have remembered that transformations of this sort do not ever come at the speed desired by zealots, and also that zealots will use the language of moral despair at every opportunity.[11] Most accounts of the Edwardian Reformation have concentrated on the official measures—injunctions, proclamations, statutes, episcopal decrees, the promotion of preaching—and have not been able to demonstrate the effect, if any, that all this may have had on the attitudes and beliefs of those subjected to the barrage.[12] Two regions for which the question has been studied with the actuality of reform rather than the government's intentions in mind are Yorkshire and Lancashire, neither sufficiently typical of the country as a whole to justify general conclusions being drawn; in any case, each investigator arrived at very different answers for his particular

[10] K. V. Thomas, *Religion and the Decline of Magic* (1971).

[11] Philip Hughes, *The Reformation in England* II, pp. 138 ff., well exemplifies this sort of Roman Catholic sneer.

[12] J. E. Oxley, in his *The Reformation in Essex to the Death of Mary* (1965), set out to discover how Protestant the shire became but had to rest content with showing how hard the authorities worked at making it Protestant; and Essex offers better evidence of the progress of the Reformation than most other shires.

county.[13] As a rule, therefore, comments retire to the cautious position of supposing that the actual effects of the Reformation were minimal, often adding that association with much hated regimes made the path of reform thornier than it might have been. Yet there are grounds for doubting this sceptical view, though a deviant opinion must obviously be treated as provisional and speculative.

Some things are certain. The framework of a fully reformed and Protestant Church was built without reservations: by early 1552 official policy had created all the conditions necessary for the transformation. Furthermore, from 1548 onwards the new order was applied, in a crescendo of pressure, in many parts of the country. A great deal depended on the bishops who acted with varying degrees of zeal; but some of them certainly proved to be very energetic. No one could doubt Ridley's earnestness in the diocese of London, and Hooper, notwithstanding his disputes with the authorities, turned out to be a very authoritarian shepherd at Gloucester (and later at Worcester) who with some success set about turning an ignorant and idle body of clergy into one capable of transmitting the faith to their congregations. At York, Robert Holgate, in general a cautious and somewhat bureaucratic reformer, paid special attention to education and used his own money to found several reformist schools. Freed from involvement in Council politics and royal administration, the new episcopate in most parts of the realm did devote itself to its pastoral duties.

Whether in all this they had the support—the very necessary support—of the lay rulers of the localities is a much more difficult matter to establish. Conservative peers like Derby in Lancashire, Arundel in Sussex, or Shrewsbury in the northern Midlands resorted to obstruction; the influence of Pembroke or Northumberland or Dorset, powerful across much of the south and expanding territorially into the north, worked strongly for reform. In Lancashire, resistance to innovation had the support of the local magistracy, but so far nothing of the kind has been discovered anywhere else. If the behaviour of the gentry in the reign of Mary offers any guidance, it looks as though a large number of the upper sort were withdrawing from the old ways, though naturally conservatism also retained notable strength. Especially among the generation that grew up after 1535, traditional anticlericalism was acquiring a newly positive Protestant tinge not visible in the reign of Henry VIII. Much the same is true of many town oligarchies, especially but not solely in

[13] A. G. Dickens, *Lollards and Protestants in the Diocese of York*, pp. 168 ff.; C. A. Haigh, *Reformation and Resistance in Tudor Lancashire* (1975), pp. 139 ff. Professor Dickens concedes that the rise of popular Protestantism cannot be assessed in real statistical terms, while Dr Haigh, whose methods are the best yet used to study these problems, has to admit that Lancashire's entrenched conservatism looks to have been untypical.

London. There was no wild enthusiastic wave of regeneration but also very little significant resistance to the new order of things. Reactions varied from the grudgingly accommodating to the willing, with real zeal much more common among the acceptors than the resisters; and the hindering effects of the Council's alleged unpopularity do not appear outside historians' speculations. By and large, the bishops' efforts seem to have been backed by the lay authorities.

Reactions among the parish clergy naturally also varied enormously, from place to place and man to man. The one measure of the new regime which met with enthusiasm was the abolition of clerical celibacy: priests married in their hundreds. And while it has been remarked that this proves little for their inclination to the Protestant faith, it must also be admitted that it proves less for their attachment to the ways of tradition. By definition, no married priest was a good Catholic—as many were to discover in the reign of Mary. However, beyond this there are sufficient signs that the official campaign exacted obedience. Everywhere altars made way for communion tables, though often the old altars were preserved in safe-keeping, just in case. Everywhere parishes acquired the new service books, though the order that the old one must be surrendered for destruction proved harder to enforce. The chantries, those symbols of the outlawed belief in prayers for the dead, vanished with remarkable ease and speed: we hear of no protests at a measure which ought to have created much evidence of appalled reactions from those who adhered to the old techniques for seeking eternal bliss. The commissioners who in 1552 and 1553 went about confiscating church plate and vestments encountered some obstruction and more evasion, but far less of either than would justify the view that the reform made no real progress. So far as the outward transformation of the Church was concerned, it established itself in the reality of religious services and parish life.

However, religious services and changes in the lives of clergy and parishioners still do not amount to making people into believing Protestants, and here of necessity we meet something like a blank wall. How does one discover what 'the people' believed over 400 years ago? The only Englishmen and women whose beliefs can be known are those who suffered persecution; we therefore know about Protestants in the 1540s and after 1553 but not during the years when Protestantism ruled. The reign of Edward practised something so like tolerance that the only believers of whose faith we can be quite sure were the few extremists—Anabaptists and other sectaries whom even Cranmer's patience would not suffer. Thanks to the Marian persecution and John Foxe's historical labours we know of a good many more who had turned reformed by 1553 at the latest, but that still gives us barely 700 names in a population approaching three millions. The question should really be not whether the Edwardian Reformation made England Protestant (an achievement for which it hardly had time), but whether Englishmen on the whole accepted or resisted the pressures to receive the Protestant faith. Acceptance, for whatever reasons, creates an opportunity for real conversion; and the signs are that acceptance, varying from patient to eager, was the commonest reaction.

After all, by 1553 the realm had been exposed to some twenty years of exhortation, most of it reformist, mostly encouraged from above, and even when (as in Henry's last years) frowned upon by the authorities never seriously interrupted. Ever since the break with Rome the active voices had carried Protestant resonances; tradition had found defenders in action but few in speech. During Edward's reign the preaching campaign reached a new intensity. It was less well organized than in Cromwell's day, but it commanded the services of far more volunteers. Most of the learned clergy now being bred at the universities were men of the reform. Even conservative Lancashire saw some of its younger scholars embrace Protestantism; though none of them returned to livings in that poverty-stricken part of the Church, several—including the zealous John Bradford—came back to preach.[14] The generation which grew up in the 1530s and after lived in an atmosphere of constant and ever vaster change, and while those whom change strikes when their ways are settled will resent and resist it, those who experience it as the natural setting of their lives normally welcome it. It would have been utterly peculiar if those twenty years had not brought about really noticeable alterations in the matters most talked about in pulpits and tracts—in the religion of the nation. We should concentrate not on the continued complaints about immorality, indifference and ribaldry—the commonplaces of Christian lament about the manners of the multitude—but on the virtual absence of any reports touching resistance, even the sort of individual resistance which pulls the minister out of the pulpit or tears up the prayer book. Of course, some people and some places did offer resistance, but even in relatively conservative regions the new order found solid footing. Halifax already acquired that reputation for advanced thinking which in the second half of the century made it a centre of puritan nonconformity, while the Catholic main parts of Lancashire had to suffer the sight of a thoroughly Protestant Manchester deanery in the southeast of the county.

In short, the Edwardian Reformation, exploiting the preparatory

[14] Haigh, *Reformation and Resistance*, pp. 163 ff.

work of preachers, teachers and lay rulers that extended in manner back even before the break with Rome, was within limits a real Reformation. Those who in the next reign held that a powerful heresy needed tearing from the hearts and minds of the nation saw more correctly than historians have seen since who have denied the effect of measures which, though often haphazard, poorly coordinated and at times oppressive, yet amounted altogether to a serious and strenuous effort to move from theological debate and administrative rearrangement to a real transformation among the people. Lack of time, much dragging of feet, a frequent preoccupation with spoiling the Church rather than renewing it hindered the work, and at best the compliance obtained was bound to include much indifference and obedience for the sake of peace. Fortunately, perhaps, neither the Edwardian reformers nor their Elizabethan successors ever fully succeeded in their efforts to create a zealous nation; happily cakes and ale were for ever to confine even an uncloistered virtue to its proper sphere. But the fact is that by 1553 England was almost certainly nearer to being a Protestant country than to anything else; unless that fact is recognized, what followed becomes incomprehensible.

IV

At the same time, it is true that the Protestant Church was not in the reign of Edward VI remotely so entrenched that it could well survive reaction: everything still depended on the policy of the ruler. It is not now possible to tell how much the Edwardian Reformation owed to King Edward's religion. Despite the King's occasional interventions, it remains hard to believe that he pursued genuinely personal policies or exercised a dominant influence at any time during his short life; rather he was always used by the succession of powerful politicians who ruled during his reign. But Edward was unquestionably an ardent Protestant—possibly the most determined lay Protestant in the realm—and his preferences presumably influenced the rush towards Protestantism under Northumberland's regime. It was Edward who so hated popery that he came deeply to hate his sister Mary, and it was Edward who insisted that she must not be allowed even the private exercise of her religion. Since the King combined his rigid beliefs with a powerful dose of Tudor arrogance he promised to become a more dangerous man than his father. Of Henry's three children two were bigots; fortunately for the realm they were also the two who died soonest.

Edward's character remains in many ways unclear, no wonder since he lived so short a time. On the other hand, more writings survive from his hand than from that of any other Tudor, and these have led to much speculation, especially in the notion of a highly intelligent young ruler who in his mid-teens was composing pro- found state papers. In such memorials Edward demonstrably was copying other people's drafts, though no doubt he contributed this or that point himself; more purely personal is the diary he kept from early in the reign to the days of his last illness. Again, over-ingenious inferences have been drawn from the tone of what by its nature was bound to be the merest record of event: thus it is a mistake to judge Edward's feelings about his uncles from his notes about their deaths. On the other hand, the King's 'majesty' comes through strongly in his frequent assertion of personal authority: Edward was a boy tyrant.

Whoever, therefore, really devised policy, no one could afford to ignore the King's religion, and no one could ignore the religion of the natural heir. If Edward died, the throne would fall to a pas- sionate papist, and it was rightly taken for granted that this would mean the overthrow of English Protestantism. Furthermore Northumberland had climbed to power by treading Mary down; the duke knew well that his ascendancy depended on the King's life. By late 1552 this had become problematical; as Edward emerged from what would seem to have been quite a healthy childhood he became increasingly subject to chest troubles. The duke did his best to free himself from sole dependence on the King by enlarging his support among the aristocracy and in Council. In December 1551 Rich was driven to resign the chancellorship, on the grounds of ill health; since he lived on quite contentedly until 1567, conservative dislike of the regime's religious reforms probably had more to do with his retire- ment. The great seal went to Bishop Goodrich of Ely, a safe refor- mer. Throughout 1551, Northumberland supporters of lowly rank achieved membership of the Privy Council, and his intimate adviser Sir John Gates became in effect the ruler of the court and something like King Edward's jailer. The peerage was wooed with new titles and more gifts of crown lands. Yet the appearance of a universal Dudley interest was somewhat misleading: none of the duke's sons appeared in the Council, and until the last crisis he could not even find impressive marriage alliances for them. Moreover, his own health was clearly breaking down; in 1552 he was repeatedly incapacitated by illness and losing a dominance which had stemmed from determined ambition rather than great abilities or bold policies.

By February 1553, Edward's health gave rise to grave apprehensions: winter colds turned into the onset of tuberculosis, and the King was doomed. In January Northumberland had demanded the calling of a new Parliament because the government needed money, but Parliament offered him no opportunity to prepare for a future without a Protestant ruler. In this first general election since 1549, the Council made some efforts to influence the localities, but its rather off-handedly crude methods roused only resentment. The Houses that assembled on 1 March and sat to the end of the month—the shortest Tudor Parliament on record—did not reflect any particular political position and were not called upon to carry out any government programme. The few economic measures of the session once again came from private interests, and the Crown concentrated on getting supply—the first ordinary taxation of the reign. The laity granted a subsidy and two fifteenths and tenths; the clergy, as usual, did worse, being made to pay 6s in the pound spread over two years. As was customary, the Parliament in return obtained a general pardon. An air of unreality hangs about this Parliament: it was somehow irrelevant to the political problems of the succession which occupied the men of power.

As the summer progressed, everybody who mattered came to realize that Edward was dying, and out of this disaster grew a desperate attempt to subvert the succession. Keeping Mary off the throne meant disregarding the Succession Act of 1543 as well as Henry VIII's will which both gave the crown to her if Edward should die without issue. The facts of the conspiracy are perfectly clear. On 21 May, Northumberland tied his family to the throne when his eldest son Guildford married Lady Jane Grey, eldest daughter to the marquess of Dorset and after the end of the direct Tudor line residuary successor under Henry's will.[15] Jane's sister Catherine was linked to the son of the earl of Pembroke, Northumberland's ally, and the duke's daughter Catherine married the young Lord Hastings, heir to the recently created earldom of Huntingdon, who also had a distant claim to the throne. Thus, one way and another, Dudleys entered where the crown of England might come to rest. Next a 'device' was drawn up (drafted and amended in Edward's own hand) by which the King disinherited his sisters and left the crown to the Lady Jane and her heirs.[16] On 11 June, the judges were summoned and ordered to prepare a formal

[15] Lady Jane inherited from her mother, a daughter to Henry VIII's sister Mary whom his will had preferred to the exclusion of the Stuart claimants descended from his sister Margaret. See above, p. 332.

[16] The exclusion of Elizabeth, whom Edward liked well, does not disprove his initiative: if Mary was to be deprived for illegitimacy the younger sister would of necessity suffer the same fate.

document based on this draft, and though for a while they resisted what they regarded as an illegal demand, all in the end gave way. So did the privy councillors, allegedly—according to their own later confessions—constrained by violent bullying from the duke. In the last week of June, a new imperial ambassador, Simon Renard, arrived with instructions to protect Mary's claims; Charles V, at this point determined to reverse his defeats in the war with France and anxious to keep England friendly, was prepared to have his cousin rule a Protestant realm provided she could herself follow her own religion, but this odd scheme stood no chance either with Mary or against the conspirators. On 3 July, Mary, then living at Hunsdon in Hertfordshire, was warned by several Protestant politicians who could not stomach the proposed violence to the law and to the rights of dynastic legitimism that the King was about to die; she immediately fled to Framlingham Castle in Suffolk—Howard country where she was surrounded by loyally Catholic gentry. On the 6th Edward finally died, and after keeping the news secret for some days the Council on the 10th proclaimed the accession of Queen Jane.

Until recently nobody ever doubted that the whole plot was Northumberland's own device intended to rescue him from the consequences of Edward's death. Now, however, it has been strongly urged that the move originated with the King himself who drove a reluctant duke into compliance.[17] Can we decide who started the plot? Certainly the duke's interest was best served by it. He had made an enemy of Mary in early 1550 and by his Reformation; he had secured the benefits of the *putsch* to his own family; masterminded the attempt to bring the conspiracy to a successful conclusion. Unlike Edward he was bound to remember how the Seymour faction had used Henry's will to achieve their triumph. On the other hand, the King's writing and not the duke's appears in the documents; the judges obeyed his personal and very imperious order; the preservation of the Protestant Church of England is much more likely to have been the passionate concern of the dying Edward than of the struggling duke. At the crucial time Northumberland was mostly ill in bed, and in the outcome he mishandled essential parts of the plot. Also he tried to keep on terms with Mary whom he courteously informed of the progress of Edward's illness throughout June. Afterwards, of course, everybody put the blame on him alone, as did Jane Grey who reckoned that his ambition had ruined her and her family, but that proves nothing. The likeliest answer must allow for cooperation between King and duke: neither forced the other into steps which increasingly left reality behind. It may well be that the first impetus came from Edward, desperate to prevent a

[17] W. K. Jordan, *Edward VI* II, pp. 517 ff.

popish succession and certainly persuaded that by his royal authority he stood above the law which bound lesser mortals; psychologically, the overriding of statute and of Henry's will is more likely to have been possible to Henry's own heir with his very high view of monarchy. But it is hard to believe that Northumberland, driving on the plot and so clearly its first beneficiary, played a purely passive role.

Perhaps the strongest grounds for blaming Edward lie in the incompetent way in which the plot was carried out. Northumberland had before this proved his skill as a plotter; on this occasion everything went wrong, even though there had been plenty of time to prepare. The duke's extraordinary failure to secure Mary's person, so conveniently at hand until a few days before the final crisis, sealed his fate. Queen Jane might be proclaimed in London, but at Framlingham Mary proclaimed herself and gathered forces to conquer the throne rightfully hers. Thus Northumberland was forced into a war for the crown which he had no hope of winning. Compelled by his fellow councillors to take command in person, he got as far as Cambridge before it became plain to him that no one supported the substitute queen. At Cambridge he gave up, himself shouting for Queen Mary on 20 July. The day before, the councillors left in London, increasingly scared of what they had done, had already accepted the facts of the case; Dorset himself declared his daughter deposed. Mary swept on to London, casually arresting the duke *en route*; she entered the capital on 3 August, amid scenes of loyal rejoicing. Lady Jane, her husband and her family disappeared into the Tower, joined there by all the Dudley clan.

The new Queen's easy triumph in what could possibly have become a re-enactment of the dynastic struggles laid to rest by Henry VII owed most to her descent from Henry VIII, something to the general dislike of Northumberland and the incompetence of his faction, and virtually nothing to her religion. The events of July–August 1553 did not constitute a vote against the Reformation but a victory for legitimism and for fear of civil war, feelings which even overcame apprehensions at seeing the realm ruled, for the first time, by a woman. Nevertheless, by destroying Northumberland and bearing up Henry's daughter, the realm—Council, nobility, gentry and commonalty—brought back Rome and the mass. This they must have known, however little it was the motive of their action; all the indications are that they did not understand what it would mean.

17 Counter-Reformation and Reform

I

It has become something of a commonplace to assert that Mary Tudor was the most attractive member of her family—kind, long-suffering, gentle, considerate. The evidence of her recorded words and actions hardly bears this out; it shows her rather to have been arrogant, assertive, bigoted, stubborn, suspicious, and (not to put too fine a point upon it) rather stupid. Her portraits show a bitter and narrow-minded woman, curiously unlike her father, brother and sister. Certainly, she had led a truly unhappy life ever since, a girl of eleven, she had seen her father throw her mother out of bed and home. For twenty years before her accession she had lived in the shadows, though never (it might be remembered) in the shadow of death by execution which she was to cast over so many; her experience would very probably have soured a sweeter and more tolerant temper. The fact remains that she was ill prepared to be England's first woman sovereign. She had ever been her mother's daughter rather than her father's; devoid of political skill, unable to compromise, set only on the wholesale reversal of a generation's history, she was a manifest portent of strife. Her persistent attachment to the papal Church and religion made her exceptional even among those who had watched the Reformation with misgivings and reluctance. Humanism had passed her by as much as had Protestantism. If it is not clear whether she leant towards the new rigour of the rising Counter-Reformation or a pre-Lutheran conventional piety, this is mainly because she never gave any sign of a genuinely intelligent interest in the issues that confronted her; she depended on the mass because it gave her emotional satisfaction. Thirty-seven years old, she seized a power rightfully hers for the exercise of which she was utterly unsuited.

At the start, as at the start of every reign, peace and popularity were the watchwords. Mary arrived in London on 3 August; writs for a Parliament went out on the 14th. On the 22nd the inevitable victims of Northumberland's plot died on the scaffold for their treasons, but the government restrained its vengeance. Apart from the duke, who went to pieces and scored a great propaganda triumph for Mary when at the end he abjured his Protestantism and confessed his heresy, only Sir Thomas Palmer and Sir John Gates were executed, two close associates of his who preserved their contemptuous integrity to the death. The next day Gardiner, released at once from the Tower and restored to his see of Winchester, received the great seal and with it at long last the position of political command which had eluded him for so long. It was a fateful step, for Gardiner had grudges to pay off and a cause to defend; and he soon showed that in both respects he would be ruthless and unscrupulous. But no other office changed hands, and about half of Northumberland's Council were at once sworn of Mary's. Two of these lords, Arundel and Paget, had been mainly responsible for organizing Mary's triumph; in return, they secured continued employment not only for themselves but also for the bulk of the active councillors.

In any case, the Queen could not have ruled without the assistance of such experienced officials as Lord Treasurer Winchester or Mr Secretary Petre; she could not help ignoring the treasons which Edward's councillors and judges had committed when forced to support Jane Grey. However, this necessity combined with other pressures to produce at once an over-large Council of about fifty members. Apart from retaining seventeen Edwardians, Mary dug out a number of Henrician survivals: not only Gardiner but Norfolk, too, left the Tower for the Council chamber, and several elderly bishops came back. And since Mary always obeyed the calls of friendship and loyalty, the Council came to include a large group of her personal followers who had gathered to acclaim her at Framlingham. The danger to conciliar efficiency was lessened in actual practice. The Framlingham group played very little part in central government, hardly any of them ever attending meetings, though its members served to uphold Mary's rule in their various localities. Of the Henricians some were old and frequently ill; Norfolk (at last) leading in August 1554, they gradually went the way of all flesh (Bishop Tunstall excepted). In practice the Council operated at the reformed size of about twenty members. It was never, however, a very united body. That there were regular conciliar factions led by Gardiner and Paget is probably a *canard* derived from the ambassadorial reports whose interested misrepresentations have been relied upon a little too trustingly by historians. It would seem to be nearer the truth to say that the chancellor, arrogant and irascible, often found himself out of step on policy and dubbed all disagreement faction. While everybody knew that the mass would come back, not everybody agreed that the church lands would have to stay where they had wandered, and different people viewed the political consequences of the Queen's religion differently. There was a real rift between those (the majority) who had no thought of altering the reformed state bequeathed by Henry VIII in which the Church submitted to the rule of the laity, and the bishops (old and new) who desired a return to the Church's lost liberties and properties. Now that at last he had his chance, Gardiner very much wanted to undo Cromwell's work; Paget, Petre, Bedford and even such conservative peers as Derby and Arundel for their own reasons meant to preserve it. This major division apart, there were plenty of personal and policy disagreements in this Council, and the Queen never succeeded in imposing her authority upon it.[1]

These uncertainties at the centre of government were aggravated by the fact that the Queen early decided to rely to a dangerous extent on advisers outside the Council, especially the Emperor's ambassador, Simon Renard, whom Council leaders had to use rather deviously if they wished their advice to reach the royal ear. Immediately two demands of policy rose up before everybody. Mary meant to abolish the Reformation both of her brother and her father; and she needed to look for a husband. At thirty-seven she could not wait if she was to produce the heir who would ensure the future stability of a Catholic England. The second problem, as it turned out, seriously delayed the solution of the first. Mary herself, of course, took the line that the royal supremacy was an offence against God and his Church, and therefore plainly void, but she soon discovered that without a repeal in Parliament she could not rid herself of what statute had bestowed on her. Thus the loyal servant of the papacy was compelled for the time being to remain supreme head of the Church of England, a fact thinly disguised by the use of an 'etcetera' in her title to avoid at least the explicit use of the unpalatable words. The resettlement of religion had to await prolonged political debate and especially the obtaining of assurances touching the secularized lands. Immediately the Queen contented herself with a moratorium on all public argument and preaching (18 August 1553), while waiting for the arrival of the papal legate appointed at Rome as soon as her accession was known there. That legate was Cardinal Pole, despatched in early August with a com-

---

[1]For all this see G. A. Lemasters, 'The Privy Council in the Reign of Queen Mary I' (unpublished dissertation, Cambridge, 1971). This revises the political history of the reign and especially modifies the story as derived from ambassadorial reports and expounded in E. H. Harbison's *Rival Ambassadors at the Court of Queen Mary* (1940).

mission to reconcile England to the papacy and to absolve it from the sin of schism. However, Charles V had no intention of letting loose such potentially disturbing events until the needs of his policy were served, and Pole was kept in the Netherlands until November 1554. Whatever Mary's conscience might demand, the end of the Henrician schism could not be brought about at a stroke.

Some first steps proved possible. In August and September Gardiner got going on his revenge when he had the leaders of Edwardian Protestantism—Cranmer, Ridley, Latimer and Hooper—arrested on charges of treason (since the laws against heresy had not yet been revived) and secured the resignations of several bishops. The first Parliament of the reign met on 5 October: though it was planned to clear the ground of all the recent innovations, nothing had been achieved a fortnight later except the repeal of new treasons, a familiar device for gaining popularity which backed up the gracious remission, by proclamation on 1 September, of taxes hanging over unpaid from the previous reign. On 21 October the Parliament was prorogued, to free Queen and Council for the negotiations over her marriage. From the first, the leading candidate was the Emperor's son Philip (eleven years Mary's junior) whose cause was pressingly promoted by Renard and who attracted Mary because of her deep feelings for her mother's family. Two different interests tried to work against the Habsburg alliance. There were those, led by Gardiner, who wished to avoid a foreign king and tried to find a candidate among the native aristocracy, a search so much doomed to disappointment that some even talked of marrying Mary to Reginald Pole, still in deacon's orders and therefore not yet committed to celibacy. Secondly, Henry II of France, whose ambassador François de Noailles rivalled Renard in ability and lack of scruple, sought to prevent the incorporation of England in the Habsburg empire. But Gardiner's candidate, Edward Courtenay, survivor of the 1538 holocaust and taken from the Tower in September 1553 to be restored to the earldom of Devon, had no attraction for Mary and little for anybody else: weak, inexperienced, apparently pretty stupid, and far from reliable in religion, he was too obviously the chancellor's puppet. In any case, Mary almost at once set her heart on the yet unseen Philip, and she repeatedly made it plain that she would suffer nobody's interference in so private an affair. Others could not regard the fate of the realm as a matter private to the Queen, but when the reconvened Parliament (25 October to 5 December) begged her not to marry abroad it received a really savage answer. This second session got through a lot of solid business, legitimizing Mary, attainting the Dudleys (Northumberland, his sons and Lady Jane) as well as

Cranmer, confirming the cancellation of Edward's subsidy, granting tunnage and poundage for life, and passing a few privately promoted acts for the commonweal. Above all, it repealed the 1552 Act of Uniformity and concomitant legislation: by December the realm stood in religion where it had been at Henry VIII's death. But though Reformation vanished, schism remained: Charles V was quite clear that he wanted to see his cousin safely married to his son before contention could arise over the Roman obedience and the fate of abbey lands.

Before, however, the proposed alliance could be concluded, its prospect provoked a sudden and dangerous rebellion which justified the Emperor's caution. It would have been more dangerous still if the original scheme—which involved Courtenay support in Devon, Grey support in the Midlands and the raising of the Welsh marches—had proved practicable. The French ambassador had his fingers in the pie to the knuckle and further, and the conspirators planned to substitute the Princess Elizabeth for her sister, though it is not certain that that cautious young woman had given them unequivocal encouragement. The plot—a political rather than a religious protest—meant to exploit general apprehensions about Spanish influence and Spanish arrogance, and the rebuff adminis-tered to Parliament persuaded many that the dangers to English freedoms were real. In the event, Gardiner's vigilance and his close relations with Courtenay threatened to expose the plot, so that the conspirators were forced to act before they were ready; only one part of them, the Kentish gentry raised by Sir Thomas Wyatt, son of the poet, went into action. Kent rose on 25 January 1554, hardly the best time of year for armed rebellion, and Wyatt seems never to have had more than 3,000 men with him. Even so, a rising within striking distance of the capital, itself full of disturbing rumours and dubious loyalties, posed a formidable threat to the regime. It survived because Wyatt very incompetently failed to exploit his initial success, because Mary overcame the fears of some of her councillors and stayed in London to rally resistance, and because Wyatt's miscon-ceived flanking march up the Thames to Kingston gave Pembroke time to organize a counter-force.

By the end of February it was all over. Some one hundred rebels died for treason, Wyatt naturally among them, and the Queen's vengeance took the lives of Lady Jane Grey and her husband, under suspended sentence of death, even though neither of these unhappy innocents had ever figured in Wyatt's plans. In reality they were sacrificed because the government could not agree who among those implicated should suffer. Gardiner protected Courtenay whom Paget was ready to throw to the hangman; Paget guarded Elizabeth whom

Gardiner wished to see removed. Renard first advocated general severity; later, instructed by Charles V who was anxious to see peace rapidly restored, he favoured clemency, though he continued to distrust Elizabeth, as indeed did Mary. Elizabeth, who spent a couple of months in the Tower, remained for years unsure of her fate; never again at ease with her sister, she began that careful practice of survival which in the end paid off but marked her character for life. Mary usually receives praise for withholding her hand, but her recorded behaviour to Elizabeth strongly suggests that she would have liked to kill her if she had not been restrained by the scruples of others; the actual victims of 1554, relatively far more numerous than those of Henry VIII in 1537, show well enough that the gentle kindness ascribed to the Queen had its limits.

However, Wyatt's failure definitely settled the issue of the marriage. The second Parliament of the reign met on 2 April 1554 and in the five weeks of its duration was mainly preoccupied with the arrangements for Philip's kingship. There was now no hope of avoiding a Spanish king, but the Queen's desire to lay herself and her realm unconditionally at his feet met opposition in both Council and Parliament. Gardiner had come to accept the inevitable: about this time he began to write a curious treatise on English history which was to instruct the new King in the task of securing his rule and which surprisingly demonstrated that the chancellor had made a very thorough study of Machiavelli's writings.[2] For once he and Paget were agreed: they looked for safeguards. The act which ratified the marriage treaties carefully limited Philip to a crown matrimonial (which would not survive his wife) and provided against the intrusion of Spaniards into English public life, offices and patronage. Gardiner had meant to use this Parliament to initiate the fight for the faith: he promoted a bill for the persecution of heresy which was thrown out in the Lords at Paget's urging. In this endeavour to prevent trouble in the realm Paget was still in league with Renard and Charles V, but his cautious policy disgraced him with the Queen, and it was only Philip's arrival that restored him to favour. These public disagreements on fundamental points of policy, fought out in Parliament between the leading councillors, again did not augur well for the success of Mary's government.

The marriage was celebrated on 25 July 1554. Charles V could rest satisfied: at last he had extended Habsburg power across the Channel, one ambition of family policy entertained ever since Catherine of Aragon arrived in England and now achieved by the preferred Austrian method of marriage alliances. Philip dutifully

[2] *A Machiavellian Treatise by Stephen Gardiner*, edited by P. S. Donaldson (1975). The work did not reach Philip until after Gardiner's death, in the form of an Italian translation.

professed himself pleased, though he never developed any sort of affection for his elderly and unattractive bride. Mary, on the other hand, at once persuaded herself into passionate love: if in general it will not do to make a tragic heroine out of her, she deserves sympathy and compassion for this final disaster of her private life. The Spaniards in Philip's entourage soon justified everybody's worst fears, partly because they were as arrogant as pictured and partly because they found the strange and hostile country bewildering. Clashes between them and London's turbulent apprentices punctuated the history of the reign, as did rumours and the occasional reality of conspiracy and rebellion. Superficially the realm looked almost as disturbed as in the days of Lancastrian collapse: Wyatt's rebellion and the Spanish match left everybody in a jittery condition well reflected in the conduct of the Council, sniffing trouble at the slightest sign or none, and of Renard who came to regard the English as utterly fickle and ungovernable. In actual fact, public order was never again seriously threatened because the political classes, content to use ordinary political means to fulfil their ambitions, had lost the taste for revolution. Nevertheless, the Queen's marriage, which gave her so much short-lived joy, was the first and fatal mistake of her reign from which she and it could not recover. Since it also left her free to attend to the cause of true religion, it set the stage for the second disaster.

II

As soon as the new reign opened, the more committed Protestants began to take the now familiar step of fleeing abroad. The exodus grew so sizable that it has led to some vogue in mistaken ideas of an organized emigration designed to create a platform for a future resumption of the Reformation.[3] Between late 1553 and the middle of 1555, close to 800 English Protestants (some of them not as Protestant as all that), both laymen and clergy, found a refuge on the continent. Eirenic Strassburg being no longer very open, most of them gathered at Frankfurt and Zürich; some went to Geneva and imbibed Calvinism. Factions soon developed, as is the habit among dedicated fanatics living in the unreal atmosphere of exile, but the 'troubles at Frankfurt' later described by William Whittingham did not prevent the preservation of a Protestant party able to exploit the

[3] C. H. Garrett, *The Marian Exiles, 1553–1558* (1938) provides a valuable and fairly reliable catalogue of emigrés, but her enthusiastic speculations about an alleged Protestant travel agency run by Cecil and some London merchants will not stand up.

better times that were to come in 1558. On the whole Mary's government put no obstacles in the way of emigration; Gardiner in particular thought the realm well rid of trouble-makers. Here, too, the regime betrayed its incompetence: the exiles easily remained in touch with sympathizers at home, and their very active propaganda flooded the country with subversive literature which official censorship was powerless to suppress, while hardly any efforts were made to produce effective counterattacks in print.[4] Now and again exasperation prevailed and agents went over to catch the enemy, but the government scored their only success when they kidnapped Sir John Cheke in the Netherlands in 1556, after he had been released from prison for exile the previous year. He was forced to recant his Protestantism and died, back in prison, a year later.

While the English Reformation thus preserved itself by flight, the problems of adjusting to the sudden reversal of the official faith multiplied at home. As has been said, Mary's desire to do away at once with the abominations of heresy and schism had to bow before the legal and political difficulties involved in undoing a revolution twenty years old. From the first there was some unofficial resumption of the old ways; cases are known of Catholics being encouraged to break what was still the law of the land. Nevertheless, the abrogation of the Reformation proceeded by legal stages and for a year and a half really by means available to Mary only in her capacity as supreme head, the office she regarded as blasphemous and sinful. While the realm awaited the much delayed arrival of the papal legate who would put the clock back to 1529, the government prepared for the reaction in a piecemeal fashion. Baulked by Parliament in the spring of 1554 of his desire to revive the heresy-hunting powers abolished in Edward's reign, Gardiner encouraged episcopal action against probable nonconformists. Throughout 1554 reaction concentrated upon married priests, compelled to put away their wives, do penance, and abandon their livings. The campaign sprang directly from the Queen's personal wishes: like her father she abominated broken vows of celibacy. Most of the approximately 800 affected appear to have been found cures of souls elsewhere; anything else would have left the realm unclergied. After May 1554, the Edwardian prayer book was illegal, but even so the official religion of the realm remained very uncertain. Gardiner, anxious to restore

[4]D. M. Loades, 'The Press under the Early Tudors', *Transactions of the Cambridge Bibliographical Society* IV (1964), pp. 29 ff. The exiles did much to make available the writings of Protestant prisoners in England; the most considerable pamphlets produced abroad were John Ponet's *Short Treatise of Politique Power* (1556) which justified resistance to ungodly rulers and advocated tyrannicide, and John Knox's *First Blast of the Trumpet against the Monstrous Regiment of Women* (1558), directed against Mary but so unfortunate in its timing that it appeared to be an attack on her successor.

the clerical liberties which to him were the chief victims of Cromwell's lay revolution, concentrated on reconstructing the episcopate. In the autumn of 1553, a few resignations and arrests had made possible the return of good Catholics at Bath, Chichester, Exeter, London, Winchester and Worcester; a wave of deprivations (by commissions appointed by the supreme head!) in the spring of 1554 provided suitable men at Gloucester, Hereford, Lincoln, Rochester and York. By the end of the reign a very solid front had been built up; when in 1558 the Marian bishops almost to a man refused, to Elizabeth's patent astonishment, to turn once more, they testified to the one real success of this Counter-Reformation.

At last, on 24 November 1554, Pole landed in England and, six days later, in a moving ceremony, absolved the realm from sin and restored it to the papal obedience. The Parliament that sat from 12 November to 16 January submitted to the legate and revived the old heresy laws, but it did so only after full assurance had been obtained that there would be no tampering with the lands secularized since 1536. Pole, who had accepted this concession to necessity with the greatest reluctance, now stood ready to reintroduce all the old order. He combined qualities which made him in theory very suitable and in practice quite unfit for his intended duties. A man of integrity and pastoral concern, usually unwilling to use extremes of force and inclined to treat true repentance generously, he nevertheless believed firmly that heresy and schism needed stern measures to root them out. Like More before him, he accepted the need and justice of persecution: heretics tainted the people they infected and had to be destroyed. Like Mary, he had bitter memories of the Cromwellian era which, together with a retiring temperament and a taciturn manner, made him appear austere and remote. He lacked administrative experience and, as the event proved, ability; and yet he tried to reimpose Rome largely by administrative and legal action. Though of royal descent, he knew little of his native country which he had not seen since 1532, adding his own alienated incomprehension to that of the hispanicized Queen. An additional complication arose from his own relations with Rome. Appointed by popes who had shared his concern for reform and his management of the Council of Trent, he failed to negotiate the cataracts when his enemy Carafa became Pope Paul IV in 1556. Carafa distrusted Pole's orthodoxy, not without reason,[5] and hated the Spanish Habsburgs. In April 1557 he withdrew Pole's legatine commission and summoned him to Rome; though Pole refused to go and as archbishop of Canterbury (from December 1555) still held auth-

[5] For Pole's leaning towards Lutheran tenets see D. Fenlon, *Heresy and Obedience in Tridentine Italy: Cardinal Pole and the Counter-Reformation* (1972).

ority, his highly equivocal position in the last year of his life did nothing to assist the campaign against the Reformation.

Contrary to an older opinion, it is now clear that Pole tried hard and that he pursued a considered and consistent policy.[6] Confronted by utter confusion, he determined to produce order by bringing back the old traditional system in full, without conceding anything to what had happened since the break with Rome, a purpose which marched well with Gardiner's clericalist ambitions. However, since he was not allowed to take back the expropriated lands, the restoration always lacked an essential ingredient. Pole also meant to purify tradition by the removal of unspiritual accretions. The synod he convened in the winter of 1555 issued a series of decrees which not only restored the mass, all orthodox ceremonies and the Roman canon law, but also attempted to impose the sort of reforms in liturgy, clerical manners and education, and episcopal supervision which Pole had advocated at Rome as long ago as 1536. The Romanism of Pole's Counter-Reformation was distinctly humanist, even Erasmian (and in this once again agreeable enough to Gardiner and the memories of Thomas More, rediscovered in this reign); he avoided more recent developments and refused aid from the Jesuits whom after his experience of them at Trent he thought unduly enthusiastic and anti-intellectual. As a result, all he did turned out to be formal, legalistic and administrative; no move was made in the direction of spiritual zeal and regeneration, the trump cards of the Protestants. It was not that Pole could not have provided spiritual guidance: on the contrary, his real gifts lay there. But since he felt convinced that the uncertainties created by two decades of upheaval needed sorting out before the nation could be usefully introduced to a better understanding of the Christian faith, and also that only bewilderment kept the English from recognizing the superior truth of Roman Catholicism, he first had to create order: and this preliminary task simply took a very long time. Thus, for instance, Pole rightly regarded it as necessary to repair the battered finances of the Church, an objective in which he had help from the Queen who returned the clerical tenths and first fruits to the legate so that he might employ them in improving stipends. Before, however, he could do so he needed to discover what money was available and where it would do most good, and the consequent investigations (which occupied Exchequer officials for three years) outlasted his chance to use the money.[7] This experience summed up

[6]R. H. Pogson, 'Cardinal Pole—Legate to England in Mary Tudor's Reign' (unpublished dissertation, Cambridge, 1972).
[7]R. H. Pogson, 'Revival and Reform in Mary Tudor's Church: a Question of Money', *Journal of Ecclesiastical History* xxv (1974), pp. 249 ff.

the whole cause and fact of failure: determined to proceed by accepted means, determined to create a firm and unambiguous basis for the backward-looking renovation which he regarded as essential in the fight against Protestantism, he used up the time allowed him without ever getting near to real restoration or real reform. That he had only three years to do the work was not his fault; but that span of time was rendered even more insufficient by the order of priorities he adopted.

Thus the positive efforts at a Counter-Reformation made no significant impact, with the result that what men came to recall of the Marian Church was the active persecution of heresy initiated in January 1555, as soon as the law again supported such attacks. The burnings of Mary's reign remain the thing best remembered about it; and they would have done so even without the enormous effect created by John Foxe's great historical study of them. Foxe's *Acts and Monuments* (his *Book of Martyrs*), first published in 1563, did not (as apologists would have it) create a legend; it commemorated a truth. Of course, he meant to make a case, to celebrate witnesses to the true faith, and to prove the workings of God's will in the triumph of English Protestantism, but he did not have to invent the fires of Smithfield and elsewhere that burned men and women in Queen Mary's reign. The persecution began with the execution of John Rogers in February 1555 and went on into 1558, until a minimum of 274 had died in the flames lit by religious passion. The south-east supplied most of the victims—112 in the diocese of London, 31 in Norwich, 49 in Canterbury, 41 (rather surprisingly) in Chichester. Elsewhere the numbers were small: only one man died in Yorkshire, for instance, and one only in the southwest. This distribution no doubt reflects the varying incidence of Protestant and sectarian heresy, but also varying degrees of energy on the part of ecclesiastical and secular authorities.[8]

A good number of the victims were people of little standing— artisans and their wives, some of them manifestly extremists disliked by all the major denominations, though hardly any Anabaptists have been found among them. Virtually no laymen of superior status suffered. But of the clergy burned many were eminent, well known and well loved preachers and pastors like Rowland Taylor of Suffolk or John Bradford of London and Lancashire. Above all, the per-secution caught some of the real leaders of the English Reformation, imprisoned from the beginning of the reign and always intended for

---

[8]For the best recent account see D. M. Loades, *The Oxford Martyrs* (1970). There is a remarkably subtle, and remarkably unconvincing, attempt to demolish inherited views without actually approving of the burning of heretics in Philip Hughes, *The Reformation in England* II, part III, chapter 2.

destruction because of the part they had played in the decline of the clerisy. Hooper (burned at Gloucester in 1555), Ridley and Latimer (burned at Oxford on 16 October 1555), and especially Cranmer (burned there on 21 March 1556) fell victims not only to the general persecution but also to Gardiner's particular hatred. Unlike his own enemies, the bishop of Winchester had always well understood that stone-dead has no fellow. After their success with the duke of Northumberland, the government entertained some hopes of getting these founding fathers of the Protestant Church of England to renounce their faith in terror of death, and with Cranmer they looked likely to succeed. The old archbishop had ever been a man who met crises with perplexity; neither coward nor time-server, he always saw too many sides to every question to enjoy the single-minded confidence that inspired a hard man like Ridley, a fanatic like Hooper, or a simple soul like Latimer. Cleverly handled at his trial and after, he soon felt doubts about resisting the Queen's authority and (without Ridley's strengthening presence) about his developed views on popes and sacraments. In fact he drew up several recantations and may have hoped for a pardon. But even before he learned that the Queen's vengeance would never let off the man who had declared her mother an adulteress and herself a bastard, he somehow recovered his serenity. Taken out to be burned, he announced his steadfastness and denied his uncertainties to those come to hear his abjuration, so that the effect of his death was the very opposite of what Mary and Pole (Gardiner had died before his enemy) had hoped for.

Altogether, the persecution, quite apart from its horror,[9] turned out to be a monumentally disastrous mistake. Gardiner had initiated it in the confident belief that a few burnings would strike sufficient terror to put an end to heresy; when he discovered how much exalted fanaticism there was that made so many face a horrible death with joy he tried too late to arrest the proceedings. Mary and Pole, on the other hand, seem never to have developed any doubt about what was going on. So far from wishing to mitigate severity the Queen demanded it, insisting only that it should always follow the correct processes of the law and appear to all to have been meted out to deserving cases. Driven on by Queen and legate, the bishops could not help themselves, but in any case they too acted from conviction. Edmund Bonner of London, Foxe's particular villain,

---

[9] Even by contemporary standards the Marian heresy-hunt was exceptionally bloody. To take the worst case for comparison: the notorious *chambre ardente* of Henry II in a comparable three-year period (1547–50) burned notably fewer people; and in the sixteenth century the French normally used more habitual savagery in enforcing religious conformity than did the English.

was certainly not the monster of tradition,[10] but since his diocese harboured more heretics than anyone else's he was necessarily exceptionally active, nor did he ever regret his obedience to higher authority. Queen, bishops, inquisitors, lawyers—they all thought they were doing God's work, cleansing the realm and teaching it a necessary and effective lesson. It was an appalling misjudgement. The people of Tudor England ordinarily looked upon public executions with equanimity and rejoiced in the deaths of traitors, murderers and thieves, convinced that such men had died for their crimes. But death at the stake had been quite rare in England, and the behaviour of the victims soon persuaded onlookers that they were witnessing the unjust fate of true believers. As the burnings went on, reluctance to assist spread among those involved—the sheriffs who had to superintend them, and the justices of the peace and mayors urged to present suspects—while the populace at large made their anguished disapproval ever plainer. Latimer's famous words, as he staggered on ancient legs to the death awaiting him, spoke a plain truth: they did that day light a candle which was not so soon to go out.

Thus the persecution set the seal on Mary's failure to restore the Church of Rome in England, but that failure was pretty much guaranteed also by Pole's policies and by the fact that, as we have seen, the earlier Reformation had taken a much firmer hold than has often been supposed. The signs are everywhere. The steadfastness of those executed proved so effective because they were setting their example to men and women more than half persuaded. The new owners' determination to retain the secularized lands not only demonstrated an understandable attachment to property, but also testified to the continued absence of any scruple about sacrilege. The Queen wished to reintroduce the monastic orders, and Westminster briefly became an abbey again, but there was no enthusiasm. Despite herself, Mary throughout acted as the ruler of a Church which yet she believed was ruled solely by the pope, a point underlined when Philip and Paul IV came to blows and Pole lost the special papal authority which had lent some credibility to the notion that everything was done by and for Rome. The laity—in the persons of councillors, noblemen and gentry—easily frustrated the clericalist ambitions that animated Gardiner and his chosen bishops. The fact was that Cromwell's revolution had employed some dominant attitudes and desires which had grown only more solid during twenty years of success. The majority of the political nation might still not be Protestant in any meaningful sense, though more of them turned out to be so than Queen and legate and chancellor had

[10]Gina Alexander, 'Bonner and the Marian persecutions', *History* LX (1975), pp. 374 ff.

suspected, but they remained attached to the political revolution out of which Protestantism had grown and which Protestantism protected. Perhaps, if he had accepted the Cromwellian state (as in 1535 he had done),[11] Gardiner might have governed with success: he could have aimed to restore the Henrician Church (supposing the Queen would have let him) or he could have aspired to the form of federalism in the universal Church represented by the Gallicanism of France. But between them, the rulers of this English Church insisted on a return to a past that was wholly lost; and because they staked everything on religion they lost everything also in politics. Even as persecutors they proved incompetent: their victims, before and during execution,[12] won the battle for men's minds, and their inability to touch the lay leadership at home or abroad left the future in the hands of the Reformation. If Mary had lived, we are often told, there is no knowing what might have happened. True, we cannot be sure, but if we may judge from what happened while she lived we must doubt very much whether she, her agents and her policies could ever really have done more than put off the consequences of the 1530s by a few years.

III

In some respects, in any case, Mary's agents wished to give force to the consequences of the 1530s. The spectacular events of the reconciliation with Rome and the drive against heresy have so much taken the eye that other activities have been overlooked. The professionals in Mary's Council, though troubled by the faction disputes and policy disagreements so well played up by the foreign ambassadors anxious to use England for their own purposes, did more than not neglect good government: they worked hard at improving it. In quite a number of ways, this otherwise so disastrous reign witnessed the successful culmination of policies first seriously promoted by Cromwell whose initiatives continued to dominate the state into the 1560s—and did so even while his revolutionary measures were being reversed in the Church.

Despite the attempts at recovery begun under Northumberland,

---

[11]The Protestant exiles greatly embarrassed Gardiner by publishing in 1553 an English translation of his *De Vera Obedientia*, and the suspects he interrogated often twitted him with his earlier views.

[12]The 'Oxford martyrs' in particular throughout their imprisonment remained in touch with their followers and produced a stream of exhortatory writings which reached those for whom they were intended.

the years 1540–52 had left much trouble behind, but Mary's enforced retention of so many of her brother's councillors maintained the
momentum of reform. Winchester and Mildmay, as we have seen,
carried out the reorganization of the revenue courts which gave
stability to the Cromwellian system, though we still need to learn
much more about all they did in and with the Exchequer. The drive
against corruption initiated in 1551 carried on, with the result that
revenue rose, especially that from crown lands which had been much
concealed during the bad years. Winchester also looked to the even
more important customs revenue which Cromwell had not found
time to reform, as he well knew it needed to be. In 1558, a new book
of the rates chargeable on exports and imports took account of
inflation and changes in trade, so that a source of revenue which had
yielded barely £30,000 a year before 1553 rose to about £80,000 from
Elizabeth's first year onwards.[13] Expenditure dropped as economies
and control replaced the extravagant and irresponsible carelessness
of the war years and the age of debasement. Gresham continued his
manipulation of the foreign exchange rates and foreign loans as
though there had been no change of government at all. The problem
of the cloth trade, confronted with the collapse of the Antwerp
market, inspired the search for new outlets to which Hugh
Willoughby's and Richard Chancellor's Russia voyage of 1553
(planned by Northumberland) was a promising beginning; in 1555
the Muscovy Company, prototype of a new trading organization,
was founded with Council assistance. And when the crown obtained
a subsidy in the last Parliament of the reign (20 January to 7 March
1558), it offered striking evidence of its continued adherence to a
new order. Although that taxation was needed for war, the bill made
no attempt to justify it on grounds that had traditionally been used
until 1534; instead the preamble very briefly alleged the costs of
ordinary government and thus confirmed the Cromwellian principle
of peace-time taxation. The finances were still, of course, far from
satisfactory; such restoration takes time, and when war came again it
proved necessary to raise funds by means of a forced loan. But the
continued drive of administrative reform is plain.

It was equally plain in the treatment of the Privy Council after its
efficiency became threatened by its politically motivated enlargement. If Winchester guarded the Cromwell tradition in the finances,
Paget did the same for the Council. At first he experimented with
dividing it into standing committees for various purposes, but
these—which could have undermined the authority of the Council
as a body—soon lapsed. Then in 1555, when Philip's departure

---

[13]These approximate figures are derived from the work of F. C. Dietz: they cry out for re-
examination. But the general increase need not be doubted.

made it necessary so to organize business that the King could keep in touch with what went on, Paget secured the setting up of a steering committee, called the Select Council, which left administration in the hands of the Privy Council as a whole but rendered policy-making more effective. In the face of the Queen's preference for an over-large Council Paget therefore preserved the essence of Cromwell's concept in a flexible manner, so that the principle survived to be reapplied by Elizabeth on her accession. In this reign as in the last, and despite an occasional political eclipse, Paget devoted himself to preserving the reformed government of the realm which he had helped create under Henry VIII and was to hand on to William Cecil.[14]

Wherever, in fact, one looks one sees a generation of administrators quietly continuing the elaboration of reforms begun in the days of their youth. It was Mary's government that rebuilt the navy and, guided by the officers of Cromwell's reform, improved its administrative organization. The rebuilding of the country's defences, begun in 1539, culminated in the great works at Berwick, completed in 1557; the reform of the militia, initiated by Cromwell's muster survey of 1539, led to the important statute of 1558 which was to form the foundation for national levies under Elizabeth and the early Stuarts. We find 'commonwealth' echoes in officially inspired bills. Enclosure legislation reached its apogee in the act of 1555 which vested great powers in commissioners appointed under it; another act carried out a plan which Cromwell had thought unwise by restricting retail trade to townspeople (fortunately it was much weakened by exceptions); a revision of sumptuary legislation followed up Cromwell's innovating act of 1532. Officially promoted statutes provided also for some important law reforms which in effect codified practices developed in the 1530s (and occasionally under Wolsey). An act against riotous assemblies and similar offences (1553) actually constituted a powerful peace-keeping code that organized and legitimated much summary and Star Chamber practice. The treason statute of 1554 finally accepted that Cromwell had seen more clearly than those who used the treason law to hunt popularity: it in effect revived the act of 1534, with the addition of the important provision first enacted in 1551 (and first found in Cromwell's memoranda) that a conviction for treason required two witnesses. Two acts of 1554 and 1555 transferred to justices of the peace the duty of preparing criminal cases for prosecution at the assizes and extended their powers to grant bail: these adapted to the law the enforcement practices developed by Cromwell for his work in suppressing treason, sedition and general crime.

[14]Lemasters, 'Privy Council', especially pp. 289 ff.

All this activity needs much more study: so far we know too little about its effects or indeed about the inspiration behind it. But the indications are that the kind of reform administration first set up in the 1530s and then tentatively revived under Northumberland carried over into Mary's reign, probably without any participation by the Queen, her cardinal, and even her chancellor. Its labours achieved some very positive results behind all the turmoil of the battle for the faith. In her treatment of Church, clergy and religion, Mary attempted a counter-revolution which failed; meanwhile her better councillors ensured a truer continuity which helps in great part to explain the ease of her sister's succession. Cromwell's reform of the state, which had helped on the untroubled accession of a minor and of a Queen who in vain tried to undo his work, was still to assist in the accession of a second Queen whose rein was to ensure the endurance of what he had created. All those public tempests notwithstanding, the society and the government of England during the so-called 'mid-Tudor crisis' never really strayed from the path on which they were set in the 1530s.

There was, however, one problem of government in which Mary's Council departed from the policies of the 1530s and 1540s: and it was a pity that it did so. In Ireland aggression took over from conciliation. Actually, the trouble had started in the previous reign when the policies of Cromwell and Henry VIII, which demanded genuine control from England, gave way to uncontrolled actions by the council in Dublin, dominated by 'new English', mostly men of Cromwell's appointing who escaped supervision after his death and turned to seek power and wealth at the expense of Anglo-Irish and Gaels alike. Together with the attempt to import the Edwardian Reformation wholesale, the ruthlessness of these new men had put an end to hopes of peaceful accommodation. Though St Leger returned repeatedly to his old charge until finally replaced by the earl of Sussex in 1556, he was suspected of popery by the Edwardian Councils and distrusted as too gentle by those of Mary; he never had a free hand again. Unrest, stirred up by the selfish policies of Dublin, offered an opportunity for intervention in the Irish lands near the Pale, and in 1557 Leix and Offaly, converted into King's County and Queen's County, were occupied by English settlers. This first 'plantation' backed by force ended all chances of mutual concession and agreement; it set the stage for the Elizabethan policy which in the end led to constant unrest, major rebellion and military reconquest. The unhappy modern history of troubles in Ireland began not with the Reformation in the reign of Henry VIII, but with Somerset's neglect and Mary's interventionism upon which the Elizabethan Reformation superimposed the great religious divide.

IV

Queen Mary had three happy days in her reign—the day she was crowned, the day she was wed, and the day she saw the realm brought back to the holy father at Rome, when at last it seemed as though the twenty years' nightmare were ended. Thereafter nothing every really went right for her again. By the end of 1554 she believed herself to be pregnant, a terrible illusion probably induced by the symptoms of the illness which in the end killed her, but an illusion to which she clung long after anyone else was able to believe in it. As the persecution mounted, her early popularity vanished; and Elizabeth, as she was to recall later, had the dangerous experience of being treated as the rising sun at a time when the setting sun still had the power to extinguish her. Plots recurred, though only one, raised by Sir Henry Dudley (not one of *the* Dudleys) with French support, produced an actual rising, in March 1556. It was put down without difficulty, but the Queen discovered her standing in the realm when a jury unhesitatingly acquitted Sir Nicholas Throckmorton, one of those allegedly implicated. Natural disasters added their contribution to a tally which makes one understand, even if it cannot make one accept, historians' friendly sympathy for the unfortunate Queen. The harvests of 1556 and 1557 were very bad, after a run of reasonable yields, and (as so often) a sudden revival of bubonic plague accompanied famine; in 1558 a devastating epidemic of influenza swept the country, killing tens of thousands. It seems quite likely that in those three years a possible fifth of England's population died, a brutal reversal of the steady expansion of the previous half century. One result was that the next reign began with the endemic problems of unemployment and pauperization much reduced, but that was no consolation to those who lived through the deaths of relatives and friends and who, in the sixteenth-century manner, saw God's disapproval manifested in the disasters that struck them. From late in 1555, policy came to augment the growing climate of depression as the consequences of the Spanish match at last proved the gloomiest prognostications correct.

Philip left England in September 1555 to take charge of his territories after his father's abdication. He took Renard with him, so that Mary at one blow stood deprived of those she loved and trusted best. In November Gardiner died, the only one of her councillors in whom she still had some confidence. In his years of power, the bishop of Winchester had borne out King Henry's assessment of him as a man who must not hold sway unless controlled by a strong hand. Highly intelligent, often shrewd, something of a patriot, and full of energy and experience, he spoilt his abilities by ruthless arrogance, unvarying deviousness, and a relentless hatred for men who disagreed with him. It is absolutely characteristic of the man that he could simply not understand why others should venture to dispute his rulings on the faith, and that he regarded such incomprehensible resistance to his authority as proof of devilish inspiration to be punished by the fire of the stake. Modern attempts to redeem his character from Foxe's vilification do not really convince. Among the power-hungry politicians of the age he stood out as the one man who played the game invariably for keeps: none of his opponents escaped a violent death. His positive contributions were minimal because in an age of rapid change and novel ideas he set his mind to maintaining the claims of an unjustifiably privileged estate. It is hard to know how sincere he ever was in his Catholic phases—Roman or Henrician or Roman again—but it is apparent that his lawyer's mind adhered throughout to the conviction that the spiritual realm belonged to princely prelates like himself. From first to last, his powerful influence had worked against the political, social and ultimately religious interests of the nation, and if the hatred bestowed on him was exaggerated he did much to earn it.

But his death, and Renard's going, meant that the Council lost control over the Queen's policy which came to be made at the Habsburg courts, in Madrid and Brussels. General dissatisfaction as well as the lack of positive conciliar leadership caused a lot of trouble in the next Parliament (21 October to 9 December 1555) where what looks like an organized opposition group gave voice to dislike of Spain and reluctance to allow Philip any real power. The debates emphasized the weakness of the government, but they also testified to the enduring effects of Cromwell's careful nurturing of parliamentary activity; naturally, they made no difference to the course of events. This was dictated by the continuing war between France and the Habsburgs in which the latter demanded active English participation. The discovery of the Dudley conspiracy, in which the French ambassador had been very deeply involved, nearly led to the outbreak of hostilities, and when yet another hare-brained adventurer, Thomas Stafford, with French support launched a ridiculous invasion upon Scarborough Castle the Council were forced to abandon their opposition to a war which the Queen demanded at her husband's behest (June 1557). In the summer of this year Philip had briefly returned to England in order to exact the pound of flesh for which he had entered his distasteful marriage; his behaviour on this occasion really finished the Queen as a person.

Queen Mary's war was the most disastrous of the century. Though some English troops did well at the Spanish victory of St Quentin in

1557, the country demonstrated its feelings against this pointless involvement. The forced loan led to something very like the taxpayers' strike of 1526, and people even voted against the war by staying away from mass. The French had hoped to avoid English intervention, but having got it they made the most of it. On 7 January 1558, after a week's investment, Calais surrendered to the duke de Guise: after two centuries, the last English possession on the continent, the last token of past greatness and for practical purposes at this time a town much more English than French, fell to the enemy virtually without resistance. Perhaps Calais was nothing but a liability, though its commercial and political usefulness should not be underrated. However, the historian's cool assessment at this distance of time ill expresses the feelings of the day. Queen Mary shared her nation's fury at this dishonourable loss, but that did not prevent the nation from blaming it on the Queen. From that day her regime was doomed; even if she had lived she had forfeited the loyalties which, less than five years before, had so easily brought her to the throne.

The last months of the reign, as the Queen grew increasingly ill and helpless, offered consolation only to the enemies of Spain and Rome: the exiles in their Protestant fastnesses were preparing for their return and concerting things with the secret friends who had stayed at home. Mary died on 17 November 1558; a few hours later, by a fateful coincidence, Cardinal Pole followed her to the grave. Because her rule had really died before her there was no crisis of a succession; Elizabeth, at Hatfield, held court before her sister had drawn her last breath. The ruin of Mary's reign owed something to her religion: her attempt to bring back Rome had been finally wrecked by the stupidity which created influential martyrs. But it owed most to the fact that she had consistently broken the rules of the political game. She had made no effort to retain the support of that aristocratic layer of society—nobility and gentry—on whose voluntary and conscientious cooperation Tudor government depended, so that by late 1557 the Council could no longer be sure that any of its orders would be carried out. Contact was being lost with the rulers of the localities. Mary had subordinated the interests—as they saw them—of Englishmen to the service of Spain and of her religion, and the loss of Calais symbolized the worth of such doings. She had put her trust in advisers as ill instructed in the country she governed as she herself was. A proud and stubborn bigotry had directed her steps when flexible good sense was needed, and in the one place where she should have fully asserted herself, in the marriage chamber, she had practised her only servility. She, who by her accession proved the hold of the Tudor myth upon her

Bibliography

The mass of writings on the period makes anything resembling an exhaustive list impossible; the existence of good bibliographies makes it unnecessary. This essay will concentrate on the more recent contributions to knowledge. Footnotes have already been used to give guidance some of which will be repeated here, sometimes (to save space) by reference to the note in question.

Abbreviations

BIHR	*Bulletin of the Institute of Historical Research*
EcHR	*Economic History Review*
EHR	*English Historical Review*
HJ	*Historical Journal*
JEH	*Journal of Ecclesiastical History*
PP	*Past and Present*
TRHS	*Transactions of the Royal Historical Society.*

1. Guides

Conyers Read, *Bibliography of British History: The Tudor Period, 1485–1603* (2nd edition, Oxford, 1959) provides a very full list down to publications of 1956. The slightly more selective list in M. Levine, *Bibliographical Handbooks: Tudor England, 1485–1603* (Cambridge, 1968) extends coverage to 1966; the concise relevant sections of G. R. Elton, *Modern Historians on British History, 1485–1945* (London, 1970) go down to 1969. Recent literature on the history of religion is covered in D. Baker, editor, *The Bibliography of the Reform 1450–1648 relating to the United Kingdom and Ireland for the years 1955–70* (Oxford, 1975), which includes unpublished dissertations; for dissertations on all subjects produced in the United Kingdom see P. M. Jacobs, editor, *History Theses, 1901–70* (London, 1976). The most important aid to the archives is *Guide to the Contents of the Public Record Office* (2 vols, London, 1963); more detailed information is provided by *Public Record Office: Lists and Indexes* (55 vols, London, 1892–1936); some 140 more such lists have so far been published by the List and Index Society (London, 1965–). The important collection at the House of Lords Record Office is described in M. F. Bond, editor, *Guide to the Records of Parliament* (London, 1971); those scattered around the country in *Reports and Calendars issued by the Royal Commission on Historical Manuscripts* (London, 1847–) and *The Bulletins of the National Register of Archives* (London, 1948–). For the best introduction to the ecclesiastical archives see D. M. Owen, *The Records of the Established Church in England, excluding Parochial Records* (London, 1970).

2. Sources

A vast amount of original material for the period is in print; down to 1956 this is well enough listed in Read's *Bibliography*. Of editions published since then the following are especially important: A. G. Dickens, editor, *Tudor Treatises* (Yorkshire Archaeological Society, 1959); P. L. Hughes and J. F. Larkin, editors, *Tudor Royal Proclamations* I, *The Early Tudors* (New Haven, 1964; with additions in vol. III, published in 1969); E. F. Rogers, editor, *The Letters of Sir John Hackett, 1526–1534* (Morgantown, W. Va., 1971); C. J. Harrison, 'The Petition of Edmund Dudley', *EHR* LXXXVII (1972), pp. 82 ff.; B. L. Beer and S. M. Jack, editors, *The Letters of William Lord Paget of Beaudesert, 1547–1563*, Camden Miscellany XXV (London, 1974); T. F. T. Plucknett and J. L. Barton, editors, *St German's Doctor and Student* (Selden Society, London, 1974); W. C. Richardson, editor, *The Report of the Royal Commission of 1552* (Morgantown, W. Va., 1974).

3. General

Of the many surveys which deal with this period four, offering in part differing and contrasting analyses, may be mentioned: G. R. Elton, *England under the Tudors* (2nd edition, London, 1974); D. M. Loades, *Politics and the Nation, 1450–1660* (London, 1974); A. J. Slavin, *The Precarious Balance: English Government and Society, 1450–1640* (New York, 1973); C. S. L. Davies, *Peace, Print and Protestantism, 1450–1558* (London, 1976). The papers collected in G. R. Elton, *Studies in Tudor and Stuart Politics and Government* (2 vols, Cambridge, 1974) contain various relevant discussions some of which will be noted in the appropriate places. W. R. D. Jones, *The Mid-Tudor Crisis, 1539–1563* (London, 1973) provides a somewhat conventional survey. R. B. Wernham, *Before the Armada: the Growth of English Foreign Policy, 1485–1588* (London, 1966) is thin on this period but raises a few interesting points concerning Wolsey's policy.

4. Social structure and population

Virtually no reliable work has yet been done on counting heads, but J. Cornwall, 'English Population in the Early Sixteenth Century', *EcHR*, 2nd series XXIII (1970), pp. 32 ff., bravely grasps the nettle, while I. Blanchard, 'Population Change, Enclosure and the Early Tudor Economy', *ibid.*, pp. 470 ff., attempts to link observed economic change to postulated changes in population figures. R. S. Schofield (above, p. 31, n. 11) usefully criticizes the evidence of tax returns upon which census makers in the main rely.

Work on social groupings naturally covers longer periods but little of it has really looked at this one. The age, so to speak, sits between McFarlane and Stone—between the study of the late medieval aristocracy and gentry on the one hand, and on the other the interest shown in alleged trans-formations worked by the secularization of lands after 1540. Only two studies cover expressly the main part of the century's first half: J. Cornwall, 'The Early Tudor Gentry', *EcHR*, 2nd series XVII (1965), pp. 456 ff., and J. M. W. Bean, *The Estates of the Percy Family, 1416–1537* (Oxford, 1958). An ambitious and not very convincing paper—L. Stone and A. M. Everitt, 'Social Mobility in England, 1500–1700', *PP* 33 (1966), pp. 16 ff.—does extend back behind the magic date, but the more detailed work barely touches our concerns. This is particularly true of the famous controversy over the supposed rise of the gentry, well summarized and killed by J. H. Hexter, 'Storm over the Gentry', *Reappraisals in History* (London, 1961), pp. 117 ff. (which usefully lists the various earlier contributions). Hexter's earlier demolition job ('The Myth of the Middle Class in Tudor England', *Reappraisals*, pp. 71 ff.) disposed of yet another misleading concept in the social analysis of the age. Of the more particular studies only one, L. Stone's *The Crisis of the Aristocracy, 1558–1641* (Oxford, 1965), professes to find support for theory in fact. This book, relevant here because it really extends the search for antecedents into the mid-Tudor period, contains much important social history; for doubts touching its statistics, upon which its major argument depends, see *EcHR*, 2nd series xxv (1972), pp. 124 ff. Some specific analyses of gentle and noble fortunes, none of which lends substance to convenient generalizations, have things to say before 1558: M. Finch, *The Wealth of Five Northamptonshire Families, 1540–1640* (Oxford, 1956); A. Simpson, *The Wealth of the Gentry, 1540–1640: East Anglian Studies* (Chicago, 1961); J. T. Cliffe, *The Yorkshire Gentry from the Reformation to the Civil War* (London, 1969). R. B. Smith's study of the West Riding (below, p. 407) is relevant here, too.

Urban history has attracted hardly anyone so far, and London especially returns a blank. But see W. G. Hoskins, 'English Provincial Towns in the Early Sixteenth Century', *TRHS* (1956), pp. 1 ff., and W. T. MacCaffrey, *Exeter, 1540–1640* (Cambridge, Mass., 1958).

Two works investigate the ethos of the ruling classes, for which also Sir Thomas Elyot, *The Boke named the Governour* (edited by H. H. S. Croft, London, 1883) remains illuminating: R. Kelso, *The Doctrine of the English Gentleman in the Sixteenth Century* (Urbana, Ill., 1929), and A. B. Ferguson, *The Indian Summer of English Chivalry* (Durham, N.C., 1960).

There are no studies of the silent majority or of women.

5. Social policy

Social policy is commonly the product of private thinking and public action. A. B. Ferguson, *The Articulate Citizen and the English Renaissance* (Durham, N.C., 1965) analyses the growth of socio-economic programmes in the minds of English humanists; W. G. Zeeveld, *Foundations of Tudor Policy* (Cambridge, Mass., 1948) discusses the ideas of a group of humanists who offered their services to Cromwell's administration; W. R. D. Jones, *The Tudor Commonwealth, 1529–1559* (London, 1970) assembles much information about social problems and the remedies proffered. The effect of this in government action is investigated in G. R. Elton, *Reform and Renewal: Thomas Cromwell and the Common Weal* (Cambridge, 1973). Light on two social thinkers is provided by S. E. Lehmberg, *Sir Thomas Elyot, Tudor Humanist* (Austin, Texas, 1960), and G. R. Elton, 'Thomas Starkey's *Dialogue* and Thomas Cromwell's Policy', in *Studies* ii, pp. 236 ff.

There has been some debate on whether one can in fact speak of government policy at all. The doubts expressed by G. R. Elton, 'State Planning in Early-Tudor England', *Studies* i, pp. 285 ff., are partially set at rest by L. A. Clarkson, 'English Economic Policy in the Sixteenth and Seventeenth Centuries: the Case of the Leather Industry', *BIHR* xxxviii (1965), pp. 149 ff. Heinze's work on proclamations (below, p. 402) makes a valuable contribution to this question.

Private rather than public action is the theme of W. K. Jordan, *Philan-*

thropy in England, 1480–1660 (New York, 1959: with several regional studies in support) which argues, from the evidence of wills, that the Reformation not only redirected philanthropy into secular channels but also produced a great increase in charitable giving. The first is dubious: it depends on definitions of 'secular'. The second falls down because Jordan's figures take no account of the great inflation: W. G. Bittle and R. T. Lane, 'Inflation and Philanthropy in England; a Reassessment of W. K. Jordan's Data', *EcHR*, 2nd series XXIX (1976), pp. 203 ff., firmly documents long-held doubts. Charitable giving declined in the wake of the early Reformation. However, the theoretical interest in education did produce some redirection of resources. K. Charlton, *Education in Renaissance England* (London, 1965), and J. Simon, *Education and Society in Tudor England* (Cambridge, 1966) between them provide a fairly full picture of the scene—universities, schools, private tuition.

6. Economic affairs

A useful introduction can be got from P. H. Ramsey, *Tudor Economic Problems* (London, 1963) and L. Clarkson, *The Preindustrial Economy in England* (New York, 1972); S. M. Jack, *Trade and Industry in Tudor and Stuart England* (forthcoming, London, ?1977), resting on a more sophisticated use of economic theory, cuts deeper than either.

Agriculture is well served by two large and detailed books. J. Thirsk, editor, *The Agrarian History of England and Wales* IV, *1500–1640* (Cambridge, 1967), a cooperative work, deals with all aspects, including landownership and wool production; it has an excellent bibliography. E. Kerridge, *The Agrarian Revolution* (London, 1967) displays the variety of land-use and emphasizes innovation (mostly after 1560). Though R. H. Tawney's classic attack on 'capitalist' agriculture, *The Agrarian Problem of the Sixteenth Century* (London, 1912), still merits mention, it is really superseded by E. Kerridge, *The Agrarian Problems of the Sixteenth Century and After* (London, 1969) which deploys a better grasp of both agriculture and the law. J. Thirsk, *English Peasant Farming: the Agrarian History of Lincolnshire from Tudor to Recent Times* (London, 1957) and W. G. Hoskins, *The Midland Peasant: the Economic and Social History of a Leicestershire Village* (London, 1957), illumine rural society at ground level. Of the vast literature on enclosing and depopulation (well summarized in the cooperative *Agrarian History*) two works should be specially mentioned: M. W. Beresford, *The Lost Villages of England* (London, 1954) shows that most enclosure predated the Tudors, and E. Kerridge, 'The Returns of the Inquisition of Depopulation', *EHR* LXX (1955), pp. 212 ff. opens the serious study of countermeasures.

G. D. Ramsay, *English Trade in the Centuries of Emergence* (London, 1957) provides a modest introduction and a guide to the older literature. Despite its age, G. Schanz, *Englische Handelspolitik gegen Ende des Mittelalters* (2 vols, Leipzig, 1881) retains great value, but fuller and better figures can now be got from E. M. Carus-Wilson and O. Coleman, *England's Export Trade, 1275–1547* (Oxford, 1963). In the absence of any history of the London Merchant Adventurers, O. de Smedt's look at their activities in the Netherlands—*De Engelske natie te Antwerpen in de 16e eeuw* (2 vols, Antwerp, 1950, 1954)—tells something about their trade; W. C. Richardson, *Stephen Vaughan, Financial Agent of Henry VIII* (Baton Rouge, 1953) adds some detail. A declining trade is discussed in A. Ruddock, *Italian Merchants and Shipping in Southampton, 1270–1600* (Southampton, 1951); one that was rapidly increasing (though doomed to collapse by war) in G. Connell-Smith's *Forerunners of Drake: a Study of English Trade with Spain in the Early Tudor Period* (London, 1954). D. Burwash, *English Merchant Shipping, 1460–1540* (Toronto, 1947) makes a start on its subject. The beginnings of a new wider-ranging enterprise in trading are studied in T. S. Willan, *The Early History of the Russia Company* (Manchester, 1956). Transatlantic expansion was not really a feature of the age, but some activity there was, especially at Bristol; the classic account by J. A. Williamson, *The Voyages of the Cabots and the English Discovery of North America under Henry VII and Henry VIII* (London, 1929) is partly superseded and partly expanded in the collected papers of D. B. Quinn, *England and the Discovery of America, 1481–1620* (London, 1974).

The assessment of England's export trade has for long depended on F. J. Fisher's 'Commercial Trends and Policy in Sixteenth-Century England', *EcHR* x (1940), pp. 95 ff.; however, Gould (*Great Debasement*, see below) shows that this article relied on insufficient figures derived from concentration upon London and insufficient theory derived from too simple a view of the effect of inflation on foreign exchange rates. Trade in cloth (it seems) boomed before the inflation and ceased to expand with it.

For the inflation and associated problems the best introduction is R. B. Outhwaite, *Inflation in Tudor and Stuart England* (London, 1969); several important contributions to the active debate on the theme are collected in P. H. Ramsey, editor, *The Price Revolution in Sixteenth-Century England* (London, 1971). See also C. E. Challis, 'The Debasement of the Coinage, 1542–1551', *EcHR*, 2nd series xx (1967), pp. 441 ff. J. D. Gould, *The Great Debasement: Currency and the Economy in Mid-Tudor England* (Oxford, 1970) is more trustworthy on the history of exports than on that of the Mint; for this C. A. Challis, *The Tudor Coinage* (forthcoming, Manchester, ?1977) supersedes all other studies. The mysteries of foreign exchange are mysteriously explained in R. de Roover, *Gresham on Foreign Exchange* (Cambridge, Mass., 1949), though the author of the treatise there printed was probably Thomas Smith, not Thomas Gresham.

7. Government and law

G. R. Elton, *The Tudor Constitution: Documents and Commentary* (Cambridge, 1960) gives a succinct account of institutions, with a full bibliography down to 1959. The general description in W. S. Holdsworth, *History of English Law* iv (3rd edition, London, 1945) cannot be relied on. A debate concerning the Henrician constitution and changes within it, between G. L. Harriss, P. H. Williams, G. R. Elton and J. P. Cooper, is found in *PP* 25 (1963), pp. 3 ff.; 26 (1963), pp. 110 ff.; 29 (1964), pp. 26 ff.; 32 (1965), pp. 103 ff.

The Crown F. L. Baumer, *The Early Tudor Theory of Kingship* (New Haven, 1940), though marred by error and anachronism, is still useful; see also G. R. Elton, 'The Divine Right of Kings', *Studies* ii, pp. 193 ff. There has been some debate about the relationship of kingship and law: W. H. Dunham, 'Regal Power and the Rule of Law: a Tudor Paradox', *Journal of British Studies* iii (1964), pp. 24 ff.; J. Hurstfield, 'Was there a Tudor Depotism after all?', *TRHS* (1967), pp. 83 ff.; G. R. Elton, 'The Rule of

Law in Sixteenth-Century England', *Studies* I, pp. 260 ff. R. Koebner, '"The Imperial Crown of the Realm": Henry VIII, Constantine the Great, and Polydore Vergil', *BIHR* xxvi (1953), pp. 29 ff., has often been praised but leads to a dead end. For the royal prerogative of issuing proclamations see R. W. Heinze, *The Proclamations of the Tudor Kings* (Cambridge, 1976) which also reviews (with references) the long debate over the 1539 Act of Proclamations. The reign of Mary is covered in F. A. Youngs, *The Proclamations of the Tudor Queens* (Cambridge, 1976). The political and constitutional consequences of the royal family's history are well drawn out in M. Levine, *Tudor Dynastic Problems, 1460–1571* (London, 1973).

The Council •For the problems see G. R. Elton, 'Why the History of the Early-Tudor Council Remains Unwritten', *Studies* I, pp. 308 ff., and 'Tudor Government: the Points of Contact II: The Council', *TRHS* (1975), pp. 195 ff. Wolsey's treatment of the Council is discussed, with errors, by W. H. Dunham: see especially 'Henry VIII's Whole Council and its Parts', *Huntington Library Quarterly* vii (1943), pp. 7 ff., and 'Wolsey's Rule of the King's Whole Council', *American Historical Review* il (1944), pp. 644 ff. Important corrections are supplied by Guy's work on Star Chamber (below). For Cromwell's reform see Elton, *Tudor Revolution* (below). Between them, D. E. Hoak, *The King's Council in the Reign of Edward VI* (Cambridge, 1976) and G. A. Lemasters, 'The Privy Council in the Reign of Queen Mary I' (unpublished dissertation, Cambridge, 1971) have made the history of the institution between 1547 and 1558 one of the best known aspects of Tudor government; both also offer important new insights into the politics of the age.

Parliament   The general perspectives are discussed in G. R. Elton, '"The Body of the Whole Realm": Parliament and Representation in Medieval and Tudor England', *Studies* ii, pp. 19 ff., and 'Tudor Government: the Points of Contact I: Parliament', *TRHS* (1974), pp. 183 ff. We now have a full narrative history of nearly twenty years of parliamentary meetings: S. E. Lehmberg, *The Reformation Parliament, 1529–1536* (Cambridge, 1970) and *The Later Parliaments of Henry VIII, 1536–1547* (Cambridge, 1977). Problems of law-making are especially discussed in Elton's *Reform and Renewal* (above, p. 399), and the authority of statute is probed in S. E. Thorne's introduction to his edition of *A Discourse upon the Exposicion & Understandinge of Statutes* (San Marino, Calif., 1942). For important technical problems in the work of Parliament see S. E. Lehmberg, 'Parliamentary Attainder under Henry VIII', *HJ* xviii (1975), pp. 675 ff.; G. R. Elton, 'The Early Journals of the House of Lords', *EHR* lxxxix (1974), pp. 481 ff.; H. Miller, 'London and Parliament in the Reign of Henry VIII', *BIHR* xxxv (1962), pp. 128 ff., and 'Attendance in the House of Lords during the Reign of Henry VIII', *HJ* x (1967), pp. 325 ff.

Finance   The only comprehensive treatment—F. C. Dietz, *English Government Finance, 1485–1558* (Urbana, Ill., 1920)—is notoriously and incomprehensibly shot through with error. For parliamentary taxation R. S. Schofield's unpublished dissertation (Cambridge, 1963), 'Parliamentary Lay Taxation, 1485–1547', is indispensable. Clerical contributions receive attention in J. J. Scarisbrick, 'Clerical Taxation in England, 1485–1547', *JEH* xi (1960), pp. 41 ff., and F. M. Heal, 'Clerical Tax Collection under the

Tudors', *Continuity and Change* (below, p. 405), pp. 92 ff. The landed revenue down to the great additions is well discussed by B. P. Wolffe, *The Crown Lands, 1461–1536* (London, 1970); for its later history see Richardson's *Augmentations* (below), Challis's book on the coinage (above, p. 401) is important for finance, and there are relevant contributions in the works listed below under 'Administration'.

Administration G. R. Elton, *The Tudor Revolution in Government: Administrative Changes in the Reign of Henry VIII* (Cambridge, 1953), still the foundation of the interpretation offered in this volume, deals with the agencies of finance, the secretariats and the Household. The only serious dent in its thesis has been made by D. R. Starkey's very important unpublished dissertation (Cambridge, 1973), 'The King's Privy Chamber, 1485–1547', which describes a revival of Household methods previously unsuspected (and also contributes weightily to the history of politics). No one has studied the Exchequer, but all other financial institutions have received treatment: W. C. Richardson, *Tudor Chamber Administration, 1485–1547* (Baton Rouge, 1952: general thesis misleading and some detail erroneous, but still has useful things to say) and *The History of the Court of Augmentations* (Baton Rouge, 1962); R. Somerville, *History of the Duchy of Lancaster, 1265–1603* (London, 1953); H. E. Bell, *An Introduction to the History and Records of the Court of Wards and Liveries* (Cambridge, 1953). This last is augmented by J. Hurstfield, 'The Profits of Fiscal Feudalism, 1541–1602', *EcHR*, 2nd series VIII (1955), pp. 53 ff. For the secretaryship, F. M. G. Evans, *The Principal Secretary of State: a Survey of the Office from 1558 to 1640* (Manchester, 1923) needs to be supplemented by Elton's *Tudor Revolution* and the work on Sadler, Paulet and Petre listed below (p. 407). All three regional councils have been well described. Nothing has yet superseded the institutional analysis in R. R. Reid, *The King's Council in the North* (London, 1921); P. H. Williams, *The Council in the Marches of Wales under Elizabeth I* (Cardiff, 1958) contains a good account of the early Tudor prehistory; J. Youings, 'The Council of the West', *TRHS* (1960), pp. 19 ff., disposes of legends. H. M. Colvin, D. R. Ransome and J. Summerson, *The History of the King's Works* III, *1465–1660*, part I (London, 1975) confirms for its own theme the general evidence of administrative practices and reform; it also contributes to the history of charitable giving (Henry VII's Savoy Hospital), religion (chapels at Westminster and Cambridge), and war (castles and fortifications).

Law Little is so far known about the history of the law itself, for reasons made plain by J. H. Baker's essay on 'The Dark Age of English Legal History', in *Legal History Studies 1972*, edited by D. Jenkins (Cardiff, 1975), pp. 1 ff. The account given in Holdsworth, *History of English Law* IV and V, based as it is on printed materials only, often cannot be relied on. Some studies of particular problems, covering long periods, have useful things to say about the early sixteenth century: A. W. B. Simpson, *An Introduction to the History of the Land Law* (London, 1961); G. Jones, *History of the Law of Charity, 1532–1827* (Cambridge, 1969); J. P. Dawson, *A History of Lay Judges* (Cambridge, Mass., 1960: useful on the growth and place of equity). On the land law see also E. W. Ives, 'The Genesis of the Statute of Uses', *EHR* LXXXII (1967), pp. 673 ff., which convinces better than do the remarks on the same subject in J. M. W. Bean, *The Decline of English Feudalism* (Manchester, 1968). For the law of treason see Elton, *Policy and Police* (below, p. 405), chapter 6. Ives has provided a valuable analysis of the legal profession: 'Promotion in the Legal Profession of Yorkist and Early Tudor England', *Law Quarterly Review* LXXV (1959), pp. 348 ff.; 'The Reputation of the Common Lawyers in English Society, 1450–1550', *University of Birmingham Historical Journal* VII (1960), pp. 130 ff.; 'The Common Lawyers in Pre-Reformation England', *TRHS* (1968), pp. 145 ff. Lawyers' books are discussed in L. C. Abbott, *Law Reporting in England, 1485–1585* (London, 1973), and E. W. Ives, 'The Purpose and Making of the Later Year Books', *Law Quarterly Review* LXXXIX (1973), pp. 64 ff. R. M. Fisher, 'The Inns of Court and the Reformation, 1530–1580' (unpublished dissertation, Cambridge, 1974) covers even more ground than the title indicates.

Law courts   These are worse served still, especially as older treatments of the new courts should be forgotten, and Richardson's *Augmentations* is weak on law. On Star Chamber, only J. A. Guy's work, so far unpublished, is worth consideration: 'The Court of Star Chamber during Wolsey's Ascendancy' (Cambridge, 1973); see also his articles (above, p. 59, n. 18). Requests must be studied in another Cambridge dissertation (1974): D. A. Knox, 'The Court of Requests in the Reign of Edward VI' (which says important things also about the reign of Henry VIII); see also M. L. Bush, 'Protector Somerset and Requests', *HJ* XVII (1974), pp. 451 ff.

8. Church and religion

A. G. Dickens, *The English Reformation* (London, 1964) provides the best introduction and survey, though P. Hughes, *The Reformation in England* (3 vols, London, 1951–4), with an obvious Roman Catholic bias, contains some useful discussions of doctrinal and organizational details. The pre-Reformation clergy are rescued from obloquy by Heath and Bowker (above, p. 10, n. 5); for late medieval heresy reaching into the reign of Henry VIII see Thompson (above, p. 11, n. 6); also M. Aston, 'Lollardy and the Reformation: Survival or Revival?', *History* IL (1964), pp. 149 ff., and A. G. Dickens, 'Heresy and the Origins of English Protestantism', *Britain and the Netherlands*, edited by J. S. Bromley and E. H. Kassman, II (Groningen, 1964), pp. 47 ff. Another approach is covered in J. Fines, 'Heresy Trials in the Diocese of Coventry and Lichfield', *JEH* XIV (1963), pp. 160 ff. The best analysis of the unreformed Church as an institution is M. J. Kelly, 'Canterbury Jurisdiction and Influence during the Episcopate of William Warham, 1503–1532', (unpublished dissertation, Cambridge, 1963). W. Clebsch, *England's Earliest Protestants, 1520–1535* (New haven, 1964) introduces Tyndale & Co. but too much ignores all influence except Luther's; E. G. Rupp, *Studies in the Making of the English Protestant Tradition* (Cambridge, 1947), while less systematic has better insight. J. F. Mozley, *William Tyndale* (London, 1937) gives the facts but leaves the proto-reformer still in need of a good study; the best account of Barnes is by J. Lusardi in *The Complete Works of St. Thomas More*, 8/III (New Haven, 1973), pp. 1365 ff. Other biographies which contain much on the progress of the Reformation are J. Ridley, *Nicholas Ridley* (London, 1951) and *Thomas Cranmer* (Oxford, 1962; somewhat unsympathetic to C.); A. G. Chester, *Hugh Latimer: Apostle to the English* (Philadelphia, 1954); C. Hopf, *Martin Bucer and the English Reformation* (Oxford, 1946).

The history of religious change can be studied in some regions. A. G. Dickens, *Lollards and Protestants in the Diocese of York, 1509–1558* (Oxford, 1959) finds more progress than was suspected. J. Oxley, *The Reformation in Essex to the Death of Mary* (Manchester, 1965) does little more than enlarge on Foxe. C. Haigh, *Reformation and Resistance in Tudor Lancashire* (Cambridge, 1975) best describes the real problems of converting a reluctant people. For what was involved in bringing the Reformation to the nation see G. R. Elton, *Policy and Police: the Enforcement of the Reformation in the Age of Thomas Cromwell* (Cambridge, 1972).

Next, the problems of the episcopate, as a body and in particular dioceses. L. B. Smith, *Tudor Prelates and Politics* (Princeton, 1953) is both inaccurate and too schematic (and ignores Bishop Fisher) but contains useful details about the Henrician hierarchy; J. J. Scarisbrick, 'The Conservative Episcopate in England, 1529–1535' (unpublished dissertation, Cambridge, 1955) defends the bishops against charges of over-ready collapse. C. Sturge, *Cuthbert Tunstall* (London, 1938) straightforwardly recounts the career of one bishop who lasted through all the changes. Diocesan studies of value, showing the impact of the Reformation and generally toning down conventional notions of unreformed corruption are: S. J. Lander, 'The Diocese of Chichester, 1508–58' (unpublished dissertation, Cambridge, 1974); F. M. Heal, 'The Bishops of Ely in their Diocese during the Reformation Period' (unpublished dissertation, Cambridge, 1972; and see her 'The Tudors and Church Lands: Economic Problems of the Bishops of Ely in the Sixteenth Century', *EcHR*, 2nd series XXVI (1973), pp. 198 ff.); P. M. Hembry, *The Bishops of Bath and Wells, 1540–1640* (London, 1967). Quite useful essays on particular diocesan problems are collected in R. O'Day and F. M. Heal, editors, *Continuity and Change: Personnel and Administration of the Church of England, 1500–1642* (Leicester, 1976).

For the best history of the Marian persecution see D. M. Loades, *The Oxford Martyrs* (London, 1967). The only useful account of the attempt to reintroduce Rome is R. H. Pogson's unpublished dissertation (Cambridge, 1972), 'Cardinal Pole—Legate to England in Mary Tudor's Reign'; for an indication of his major conclusions see his 'Reginald Pole and the Priorities of Government in Mary Tudor's Church', *HJ* XVIII (1975), pp. 3 ff. A. G. Dickens, *The Marian Reaction in the Diocese of York* (2 parts, York, 1957) analyses the effects upon both clergy and laity; and G. Alexander, 'Bonner and the Marian Persecutions', *History* LX (1975), pp. 374 ff., does something to rescue her man from John Foxe.

Particular episodes. The Hunne case is well described and placed in context in A. Ogle, *The Tragedy of the Lollards Tower* (Oxford, 1949). For the controversy surrounding the Commons' Supplication of 1532 see above, p. 150, n. 27. Henry VIII's hot-and-cold attitudes to the General Council of the Church have been elucidated by P. Sawada, especially in 'Das Imperium Heinrichs VIII. und die erste Phase seiner Konzilspolitik', *Reformata Reformanda* [*Festschrift Hubert Jedin, Münster, 1965*] *1, pp. 476 ff.* The story of the vernacular Scripture is most clearly summarized in S. Greenslade, 'English Versions of the Bible, 1525–1611', *Cambridge History of the Bible: the West from the Reformation to the Present Day* (Cambridge, 1963), pp. 141 ff.

For the Dissolution of the Monasteries see especially the works by D. Knowles, *The Religious Orders in England* III, *The Tudor Age* (Cambridge, 1959), and J. Youings, *The Dissolution of the Monasteries* (London, 1971); the first includes an exhaustive bibliography which is most usefully supplemented by a list of later publications in the second. Attention is drawn to C. Haigh, _The Last Days of the Lancashire Monasteries and the Pilgrimage of Grace_ (Manchester, 1969), and G. A. J. Hodgett, _The State of the Ex-Religious and former Chantry Priests in the Diocese of Lincoln, 1547–1574_ (Lincoln, 1959).

9. Politics and personalities

J. J. Scarisbrick. _Henry VIII_ (London, 1968) is not only the best biography of the King but also the fullest political history of the reign. For the reasons which lead me to differ somewhat in interpretation see G. R. Elton, _Henry VIII: an Essay in Revision_ (London, 1962) and _Studies_ I, pp. 100 ff. L. B. Smith, _Henry VIII: the Mask of Royalty_ (London, 1971), a highly personal but interesting essay, would be more convincing if the evidence behind it were more trustworthy. The reign of Edward VI is very fully described in W. K. Jordan, _Edward VI: the Young King_ (London, 1968) and _Edward VI: the Threshold of Power_ (London, 1970), but this work is so very full of error and unacceptable interpretations that its use is problematic. Sounder knowledge is provided by Hoak on the Council (above, p. 402); M. L. Bush, _The Government Policy of Protector Somerset_ (London, 1975: a severe attack on Somerset's policy and reputation); and B. L. Beer, _Northumberland: the Political Career of John Dudley, Earl of Warwick and Duke of Northumberland_ (Kent State University Press, 1973). For Somerset's earlier career see M. L. Bush, 'The Rise to Power of Edward Seymour, Protector Somerset, 1500–1547' (unpublished dissertation, Cambridge, 1965). Two books on mother and daughter, though heavily biased and rather sentimental, tell the tale well and supply much careful detail: G. Mattingly, _Catherine of Aragon_ (London, 1942) and H. F. M. Prescott, _Mary Tudor_ (London, 1952). For the political history of Mary's reign three books are fundamental: Lemasters, 'The Privy Council' (above, p. 402); E. H. Harbison, _Rival Ambassadors at the Court of Queen Mary_ (Princeton, 1940); D. M. Loades, _Two Tudor Conspiracies_ (Cambridge, 1965: i.e. Wyatt and Dudley).

We lack a good recent study of Wolsey; A. F. Pollard's _Wolsey_ (London, 1929), a collection of analytical essays rather than a biography, remains valuable. See also G. R. Elton's reconsideration in _Studies_ I, pp. 109 ff., and D. S. Chambers, 'Cardinal Wolsey and the Papal Tiara', _BIHR_ xxxviii (1965), pp. 20 ff. A. G. Dickens, _Thomas Cromwell and the English Reformation_ (London, 1959) provides a good introduction; various aspects of Cromwell's work are discussed in Elton's _Tudor Revolution, Policy and Police_, and _Reform and Renewal_, and in _Studies_ ii, pp. 215 ff. ('The Political Creed of Thomas Cromwell'). R. W. Chambers, _Thomas More_ (London, 1935), though often praised, is a hagiographical biography much in need of replacement, especially as work on More has been active. Above all, there is the Yale University Press edition of _The Complete Works of St. Thomas More_ (general editor R. S. Sylvester, New Haven, 1963–) of which the following volumes (some in several parts) have so far appeared: 2 _The History of King Richard III_, edited by R. S. Silvester (1963); 3 _Translations of Lucian_, edited by C. R. Thompson (1974); 4 _Utopia_, edited by E. Surtz and J. H. Hexter (1965); 5 _Responsio ad Lutherum_, edited by J. M. Headley (1969); 8 _The Confutation of Tyndale's Answer_, edited by L. A. Schuster, R. Marius, J. P. Lusardi and R. J. Schoeck (1973). Two of the valuable editorial contributions call for special mention: R. Marius, 'Thomas More's View of the Church', *Confutation*, pp. 1269 ff., and J. H. Hexter's share in the introduction to *Utopia* which complements his *More's 'Utopia': the Biography of an Idea* (Princeton, 1952). G. R. Elton has taken a sterner look at the saint's political activities: 'Thomas More, Councillor,' and 'Sir Thomas More and the Opposition to Henry VIII,' in *Studies* I, pp. 129 ff., 155 ff. R. Pineas, *Thomas More and Tudor Polemics* (Bloomington, Ind., 1968) analyses a less agreeable side of More's, and L. Miles, 'Persecution and the Charges against Thomas More,' *Journal of British Studies* v (1965), pp. 19 ff., establishes the case against the apologists. For Gardiner we have only the rather simple book by J. A. Muller, *Stephen Gardiner and the Tudor Reaction* (London, 1926); a new look, long overdue, is rendered the more urgent by the discovery of his 'Machiavellian treatise' (above, p. 381, n. 2). A. J. Slavin has studied both Cromwell's secretaries, throwing light on personalities, politics and the machinery of government: *Politics and Profit: a study of Sir Ralph Sadler, 1507–1547* (Cambridge, 1966), and 'Lord Chancellor Wriothesley and Reform of Augmentations', in *Tudor Men and Institutions*, edited by A. J. Slavin (Baton Rouge, 1972) pp. 49 ff. S. E. Lehmberg, 'Sir Thomas Audley: a Soul.as Black as Marble?', *ibid.*, pp. 70 ff., does justice to Cromwell's chief assistant; his *Sir Walter Mildmay and Tudor Government* (Austin, Texas, 1964), though mainly concerned with the years after 1558, relates to the financial administration of the little Tudors' reigns. The labours and influence of principal secretaries are variously treated in three biographies: S. R. Gammon, *Statesman and Schemer: William first Lord Paget, Tudor Minister* (Newton Abbot, 1973: but see Hoak and Lemasters on the Council (above, p. 402) for a more subtle interpretation); F. G. Emmison, *Tudor Secretary: Sir William Petre* (London, 1961); M. Dewar, *Sir Thomas Smith: a Tudor Intellectual in Office* (London, 1964: important also for intellectual history).

The important theme of the politics of faction—adumbrated in G. R. Elton, 'Tudor Government: the Points of Contact; III: the Court', *TRHS* (1976), pp. 211 ff., and several times illumined in Starkey's 'Privy Chamber' and Hoak's *King's Council* (above, pp. 402–3)—has been particularly studied for five episodes: M. Levine, 'The Fall of Edward, Duke of Buckingham', in *Tudor Men and Institutions*, edited by A. J. Slavin (Baton Rouge, 1972), pp. 32 ff. (see also B. Harris, 'The Trial of the Third Duke of Buckingham: a Revisionist View', *American Journal of Legal History* xx (1976), pp. 15 ff.); E. W. Ives, 'Faction at the Court of Henry VIII: the Fall of Anne Boleyn', *History* LVII (1972), pp. 169 ff.; M. L. Bush, 'The Lisle-Seymour Land Disputes: a Study of Power and Influence in the 1530s', *HJ* IX (1966), pp. 255 ff.; G. R. Elton, 'Thomas Cromwell's Decline and Fall', *Studies* I, pp. 189 ff.; A. J. Slavin, 'The Fall of Lord Chancellor Wriothesley: a Study in the Politics of Conspiracy', *Albion* VII (1975), pp. 265 ff.

Regional studies, when not strictly agrarian, have concentrated on areas that witnessed major rebellion (see especially Reid's *Council of the North* (above, p. 403) for its analysis of northern society). Two of them nevertheless extend well beyond that particular aspect: M. E. James, *Family, Lineage and Civil Society: a Study of Society, Politics and Mentality in the Durham Region, 1500–1640* (Oxford, 1974), and R. B. Smith, *Land and Politics in the England of Henry VIII: the West Riding of Yorkshire, 1530–46* (Oxford, 1970). M. E. James, *Change and Continuity in the Tudor North: the Rise of Thomas first Lord Wharton* (York, 1965) uses the troubles to explore larger sociopolitical issues. For the northern risings themselves M. E. and R. Dodds, *The Pilgrimage of Grace, 1536–37, and the Exeter Conspiracy* (2 vols, Cambridge, 1915) remains the fullest and basic account, but much recent work has attempted to take a new interpretative look. See especially A. G. Dickens, 'Secular and Religious Motivation in the Pilgrimage of Grace', in *Studies in Church History* IV, edited by G. J. Cuming (London, 1967), pp. 39 ff.; C. S. L. Davies, 'The Pilgrimage of Grace Reconsidered', *PP* 41 (1968), pp. 338 ff.; M. E. James, 'Obedience and Dissent in Henrician England: the Lincolnshire Rebellion of 1536', *PP* 48 (1970), pp. 3 ff. These and other contributions are reviewed in G. R. Elton, 'Politics and the Pilgrimage of Grace' (forthcoming, ?1977), which finds the origins of the troubles in Court politics. For later northern difficulties see A. G. Dickens, 'Sedition and Conspiracy in Yorkshire during the later years of Henry VIII', *Yorkshire Archaeological Journal* XXXIV (1939), pp. 379 ff. (on 1541), and 'Some Popular Reactions to the Edwardian Reformation in Yorkshire', *ibid.*, pp. 151 ff. (on 1549). S. T. Bindoff, *Ket's Rebellion* (London, 1949) despite its brevity says all that at present is known about that event; F. Rose-Troup, *The Western Rebellion of 1549* (London, 1913)—helped out by A. L. Rowse, *Tudor Cornwall* (London, 1941)—at great length does the same for its theme.

Not much has lately been done on foreign policy but important revisions concerning English relations with the papacy are found in D. S. Chambers, *Cardinal Bainbridge in the Court of Rome* (Oxford, 1965) and W. E. Wilkie, *The Cardinal Protectors of England: Rome and the Tudors before the Reformation* (Cambridge, 1974). N. S. Tiernagel, *Henry VIII and the Lutherans: a Study in Anglo-Lutheran Relations from 1521 to 1547* (St Louis, Mo., 1965) mingles useful points of foreign policy with an inadequate understanding of English politics. D. L. Potter's Cambridge dissertation (above, p. 305, no. 4) newly investigates relations with France in mid-century, for which see also Bush, *Protector Somerset* (above, p. 406). For the navy we still really have to rely on M. Oppenheim's ancient *History of the Administration of the Royal Navy* (London, 1896), but the army and the wars themselves have attracted new work. C. G. Cruickshank, *Army Royal: Henry VIII's Invasion of France, 1513* (Oxford, 1969) and *The English Occupation of Tournai, 1513–1519* (Oxford, 1971) between them analyse both military organization and action; C. S. L. Davies, 'Provision for Armies, 1509–1560: a Study of the Effectiveness of Early Tudor Government', *EcHR*, 2nd series XVII (1964–5), pp. 234 ff., adds the administrative dimension; J. J. Goring, 'Social Change and Military Decline in Mid-Tudor England', *History* LX (1975), pp. 185 ff., looks at military problems through the eyes of the social critics.

Rather on its own stands S. Anglo, *Spectacle, Pageantry and Early Tudor Policy* (Oxford, 1969) which uses public displays to investigate political purposes, but despite interesting points on the first two parts of its trinity does not really come to grips with the third.

10. Wales

All earlier accounts of the reorganization 1536–43 are superseded by P. R. Roberts, 'The "Acts of Union" and the Tudor Settlement of Wales' unpublished dissertation, Cambridge, 1966); Roberts has also given a new interpretation of that event's consequences in 'The Union with England and the Identity of "Anglican" Wales', *TRHS* (1972), pp. 49 ff. The social and political structure of the upper classes is investigated in T. B. Pugh, editor, *The Marcher Lordships of South Wales, 1415–1536* (Cardiff, 1963), and H. A. Lloyd,

The Gentry of Southwest Wales (Cardiff 1968). G. Williams, *The Welsh Church from the Conquest to the Reformation* (Cardiff, 1962) barely reaches our period; while we await the next volume, his *Welsh Reformation Essays* (Cardiff, 1967) help to fill the gap.

11. Ireland

While quite recently it seemed as though D. B. Quinn, 'Henry VIII and Ireland, 1509–1534', *Irish Historical Studies* XII (1961), pp. 318 ff., had fully explained Anglo-Irish relations before the Cromwellian revolution, two un-published dissertations have now altered the picture considerably: B. Brad-shaw, 'The Irish Constitutional Revolution, 1515–1557' (Cambridge, 1975), and S. G. Ellis, 'The Kildare Rebellion of 1534' (Manchester, 1974). The for-mer indeed amounts to a major revision, with its better analysis of the situation and its emphasis on an indigenous reform movement in the Pale. See also, B. Bradshaw, 'Cromwellian Reform and the Origins of the Kildare Rebellion, 1533–4', *TRHS* (forthcoming, 1977), and D. G. White, 'The Reign of Edward VI in Ireland: Some Political, Social and Economic Aspects', *Irish Historical Studies* XIV (1964–5), pp. 197 ff. R. D. Edwards, 'The Irish Reformation Parliament of Henry VIII, 1536–7', *Historical Studies* VI (1968), pp. 59 ff., reconstructs the achievements of that Parliament, but B. Bradshaw, 'The Opposition to the Ecclesiastical Legislation in the Irish Reformation Parliament', *Irish Historical Studies* XVI (1969), pp. 285 ff., demonstrates that opposition did not arise from reluctance to accept the schism. Bradshaw has also given an account of the first real impact of religious reform—'George Brown, First Reformation Archbishop of Dublin, 1536–1554', *JEH* XXI (1970), pp. 301 ff.—and provided the definitive work on *The Dissolution of the Religious Orders in Ireland under Henry VIII* (Cam-bridge, 1974).

12. Scotland

Since the terms of reference given to this author specifically excluded the domestic history of Scotland, it may suffice here to draw attention to the two volumes in the 'Edinburgh History of Scotland' which cover the period: R. Nicholson, *Scotland: the Later Middle Ages* (Edinburgh, 1974), and G. Donaldson, *Scotland: James V to James VII* (Edinburgh, 1965).

Additional note: very recent work

The Annual Bibliography of British and Irish History, edited by G. R. Elton for the Royal Historical Society (Hassocks, 1976 onwards) should be added to the Guides listed on p. 397; and Claire Cross, *Church and People, 1450–1660: Triumph of the Laity in the English Church* (London, 1976) to the general accounts listed on p. 398. J. A. Guy has now published a book derived from his dissertation (see above, p. 59, n. 18): *The Cardinal's Court: the Impact of Thomas Wolsey in Star Chamber* (Hassocks, 1977); in this he takes a more fav-ourable view of Wolsey's achievement. This revision is also supported by F. Metzger in his study of Wolsey as chancellor, 'Das englische Kanzlei-gericht unter Kardinal Wolsey' (unpublished dissertation, Erlangen, 1976); he distinguishes the late-medieval system of equitable arbitration from the modern system of equitable jurisdiction and regards Wolsey as a consistent and distinguished practitioner of the earlier manner. G. D. Nicholson's dissertation (forecast above, p. 103, n. 1) is completed: 'The Nature and Function of Historical Argument in the Henrician Reformation' (Cambridge, 1977). H. A. Kelly, *The Matrimonial Trials of Henry VIII* (Stanford, 1976) reviews the canon law of Henry's divorces (see above, pp. 106–7); he credits the King with developing a doctrine of consanguinity superior to that of the Church. While the book resolves some of the difficulties left unsettled by J. J. Scarisbrick, it too much ignores the political issues and personal desires involved. F. Heal and R. O'Day, editors, *Church and Society in England: Henry VIII to James I* (London, 1977) contains useful essays especially on the impact of the Reformation on the people at large. G. R. Elton, 'Reform and the "Commonwealth-Men" of Edward VI's Reign' (in a forthcoming volume dedicated to J. Hurstfield) documents the dismissal of the so-called commonwealth party of 1549 (see above, p. 325). D. A. Cressy, 'Educational Opportunity in Tudor and Stuart England,' *History of Education Quarterly* (1976), pp 301–20, questions over-optimistic views of the effects of educational reform; and K. V. Thomas, 'Age and Authority in Early Modern England,' Raleigh Lecture on History (London, British Academy, 1976) modifies some conventional notions of social attitudes in that hierarchic society.

Index

Constantly recurring titles are indexed selectively though extensively. To assist those who would wish to pursue certain main themes which recur at intervals in the narrative, general entries have been provided for Administration and government, Diplomacy and war, Ecclesiastical history, Economic and social problems, Intellectual history, Ireland.